*Immigration and Integration
in Urban Communities*

Immigration and Integration in Urban Communities

Renegotiating the City

Edited by Lisa M. Hanley, Blair A. Ruble, and Allison M. Garland

WITHDRAWN
UTSA Libraries

Woodrow Wilson Center Press
Washington, D.C.

The Johns Hopkins University Press
Baltimore

EDITORIAL OFFICES

Woodrow Wilson Center Press
Woodrow Wilson International Center for Scholars
One Woodrow Wilson Plaza
1300 Pennsylvania Avenue, N.W.
Washington, D.C. 20004-3027
Telephone: 202-691-4010
www.wilsoncenter.org

ORDER FROM

The Johns Hopkins University Press
Hampden Station
P.O. Box 50370
Baltimore, Maryland 21211
Telephone: 1-800-537-5487
www.press.jhu.edu/books/

2 4 6 8 9 7 5 3 1

Library of Congress Cataloging-in-Publication Data

Immigration and integration in urban communities : renegotiating the city / edited by Lisa M.
Hanley, Blair A. Ruble, and Allison M. Garland
   p. cm.
   Includes index.
   ISBN 978-0-8018-8841-0 (cloth : alk paper)
   1. Emigration and immigration—Social aspects. 2. Social integration. 3. Immigrants—
Cultural assimilation. I. Hanley, Lisa M. II. Ruble, Blair A., 1949– III. Garland, Allison M.,
1965–
   JV6225.I47   2008
   304. 809173'2—dc22

                                                                                    2008003942

**Woodrow Wilson
International
Center
for Scholars**

The Woodrow Wilson International Center for Scholars, established by Congress in 1968 and headquartered in Washington, D.C., is the living, national memorial to President Wilson.

The Center is a nonpartisan institution of advanced research, supported by public and private funds, engaged in the study of national and world affairs. The Center establishes and maintains a neutral forum for free, open, and informed dialogue.

The Center's mission is to commemorate the ideals and concerns of Woodrow Wilson by providing a link between the world of ideas and the world of policy, by bringing a broad spectrum of individuals together to discuss important public policy issues, by serving to bridge cultures and viewpoints, and by seeking to find common ground.

Conclusions or opinions expressed in Center publications and programs are those of the authors and speakers and do not necessarily reflect the views of the Center staff, fellows, trustees, advisory groups, or any individuals or organizations that provide financial support to the Center.

The Center is the publisher of *The Wilson Quarterly* and home of Woodrow Wilson Center Press, *dialogue* radio and television, and the monthly newsletter "Centerpoint." For more information about the Center's activities and publications, please visit us on the web at www.wilsoncenter.org.

Contents

Tables and Figures ix

Acknowledgments xi

Introduction: Renegotiating the City 1
Blair A. Ruble, Lisa M. Hanley, and Allison M. Garland

Part I. The Renegotiation of Urban Space

1 Immigrant Incorporation in Suburbia: Spatial Sorting,
   Ethnic Mobilization, and Receiving Institutions 19
   Michael Jones-Correa

2 The Placelessness of Migrant Filipina Domestic Workers 49
   Rhacel Salazar Parreñas

3 "It's Just That People Mix Better Here": Household
   Narratives of Belonging and Displacement in Seattle 73
   Serin D. Houston and Richard Wright

4 Spatial and Symbolic Patterns of Migrant Settlement:
   The Case of Muslim Diasporas in Europe 97
   Chantal Saint-Blancat

5 Moving toward Uncertainty: Migration and the Turbulence
   of African Urban Life 123
   AbdouMaliq Simone

Part II. The Renegotiation of Urban Citizenship

6 Immigrants in a Sunbelt Metropolis: The Transformation
   of an Urban Place and the Construction of Community   143
   Caroline B. Brettell

7 Postmulticulturalism?   177
   David Ley

8 "Community" Health and Transnational Communities:
   Undocumented Andean Migrants and Tuberculosis Control
   in a New Immigrant Gateway   197
   Jason Pribilsky

9 Local Authority Responses to Immigrants: The German Case   237
   Barbara Schmitter Heisler

10 Urban Migrants and the Claims of Citizenship in
   Postcolonial Africa   269
   Dickson Eyoh

Contributors   297

Index   303

Tables and Figures

Tables

1.1 U.S. Population by Area of Residence, 1999   22

1.2 Population by Race and Ethnicity, Washington Metropolitan Area, 1990 and 2000   29

1.3 Montgomery County, Maryland, Racial/Ethnic Origin Composition, 1980, 1990, and 2000   29

1.4 Fairfax County, Virginia, Racial/Ethnic Origin Composition, 1980, 1990, and 2000   30

6.1 Population of the Dallas–Fort Worth Area, 1900–30   148

6.2 Race/Ethnicity and Foreign Born as Percentage of Total Population, Dallas Primary Metropolitan Statistical Area, Central City, and Suburbs, 1980, 1990, and 2000   151

6.3 Ranking of Attractiveness to Immigrants and Proportion of Foreign Born, Four Emerging Gateways, 1990 and 2000   153

6.4 Year of Entry of Foreign-Born Population, Dallas–Fort Worth Primary Metroplex, Various Time Periods   154

6.5 Changes in Foreign-Born Population, Dallas–Fort Worth Metroplex, 1990–2000   156

6.6 Household Income and Housing by County, Dallas–Fort Worth Metroplex, 1999   157

6.7 Place of Birth and Citizenship of Asian and Hispanic Residents, Dallas–Fort Worth Metroplex, 1999   158

6.8   Foreign-Born Population, Dallas–Fort Worth Metroplex,
      1990 and 2000   160

6.9   Selected Foreign-Born Population Groups, Selected
      Suburban Cities, Dallas–Fort Worth Metroplex, 1999   162

Figures

1.1   Residential Distribution of African Immigrants in the
      Washington Metropolitan Region by Census Tract, 2000   32

1.2   Percentage of Foreign Born by Census Tract, Washington
      Metropolitan Region, 2000   33

1.3   Residential Distribution of Latin American Immigrants in
      the Washington Metropolitan Region by Census Tract, 2000   34

1.4   Residential Distribution of Asian Immigrants in the
      Washington Metropolitan Region by Census Tract, 2000   35

6.1   Map of the Dallas–Fort Worth Metroplex   155

Acknowledgments

Despite attempts by industrial countries to control the inflow of migrants, millions of people make their way to these regions every year. Historically, immigrants have settled in urban areas, seeking to capitalize on the economic opportunities cities offer. Current trends appear to be no different, although immigrants may be seeking smaller cities or moving away from the "classical" immigrant magnet cities. Either way, adjusting to a new city is no easy task. Immigrants are often faced with language barriers, racial discrimination, unfamiliar cultures, and hostile labor markets that make integration a great challenge.

In April 2004 and in January and May 2005, the Comparative Urban Studies Project of the Woodrow Wilson International Center for Scholars convened academics and practitioners to participate in a series of seminars titled "Concepts of Immigration and Integration in Urban Areas." These meetings examined the urban policies, spatial patterns, and attitudes that influence and shape the role migrants play in cities. This book is the product of the collective work and insight of the following individuals: Kengo Akizuki, Caroline Brettell, Dickson Eyoh, Barbara Schmitter Heisler, Michael Jones-Correa, David Ley, Tonatiuh Guillén López, Rhacel Salazar Parreñas, Jason Pribilsky, Brian Ray, Chantal Saint-Blancat, AbdouMaliq Simone, Erin Trouth, and Richard Wright. We would also like to especially thank the former program assistant for the Comparative Urban Studies Project, Karen Towers, for organizing the seminar series.

Immigration and Integration
in Urban Communities

Introduction:
Renegotiating the City

Blair A. Ruble, Lisa M. Hanley, and Allison M. Garland

One of the greatest challenges facing many world cities today is to facilitate the expression of ethnic and cultural diversity that enriches city life while at the same time working against the physical and psychological barriers, hostility, and violence that can paralyze and impoverish it.

—Scott A. Bollens, 1999[1]

As 2006 drew to a close, the prestigious Migration Policy Institute in Washington posted a list of the year's leading migration stories on its Migration Information Source Web site. The number one development of the year, according to the "Source Team," had proved to be the turn away in many countries from strategies of multiculturalism toward assimilationism.[2] In many societies, efforts to create a middle ground—allowing migrants to adapt to the host country's norms and values while maintaining their culture and traditions—have been losing out to an increasingly dominant mentality of "play the game by our rules or leave."

1

The chapters that follow challenge the wisdom of such a shift in either academic analysis or policy formation. In doing so, the authors do not deny the veracity of the Migration Information Source story in the sense that the trend away from accommodation and toward assimilation is evident in the politics of migration—and in the migration policies—of many states around the world. Rather, their contributions highlight the various ways such tendencies—undeniable though they may be—fail to capture the reality of the migration experience on the ground.

More specifically, this book argues that host communities are not as static and migrants are not as passive as the counterpositioning of "multiculturalism" and "assimilationism" might suggest. Societies, as described in the pages that follow, constantly respond to any number of forces buffeting them, of which migration is but one. They have no essentialist elements that form a permanent core of values, norms, customs, traditions, and habits into which migrants might assimilate. Societies are dynamic and mutable.

Migrants, whether from elsewhere in a country or outside the nation, are themselves actors rather than objects on which the host communities impose their will. By their presence and behavior, migrants make demands on their hosts that promote change. As numerous examples in the following chapters reveal, individual migrants and migrant communities force societies to alter how they function in both large and small ways.

In other words, the multiculturalists are wrong, in that migrants do not merely adapt as they sustain their own traditions; nor do migrants fully integrate into an objectified host society, as the assimilationists might wish. Migrants continually negotiate and renegotiate the terms of their presence with society at large. As a result, migrants and communities are constantly evolving and changing. When viewed from this perspective, the very real debate between "multiculturalists" and "assimilationists," as identified by the Migration Information Web site as heating up, is misplaced. Accordingly, the contributors to this volume challenge policymakers and academic analysts alike to reformulate their presuppositions for framing discussions of migrants in society.

The chapters that follow highlight the reality that much of this renegotiation between migrants and society takes place within the physical environment of the "city." Urban communities have become home to a majority of humanity and serve as a primary site for migrant-host interaction. The term "city"—as used in this context—refers to large, densely populated metropolitan regions that are becoming omnipresent around the globe. Scholarly research on the migrant experience in the United States draws useful contrasts between those central municipalities known as "cities" and the increasingly dominant surrounding jurisdictions known as "suburbs." Nonetheless, for much of the world outside the United States, areas that might be considered by Americans as "suburban" are integral parts of broad metropolitan regions that have become sufficiently urbanized to also be considered "the city." As this volume reveals, such conurbations powerfully determine how migrants and societies interact and negotiate with one another.

Thus, the contributors to this volume seek to recalibrate academic and policy discussions of migration by viewing societies as more variable, migrants as more proactive, and cities as more meaningful than current public debates swirling around such concepts as "multiculturalism" and "assimilationism" might suggest. They do so with the hope of enhancing the understanding of one of the most defining phenomena of the present era: the increasingly rapid movement and change of residence from place to place by human beings around the world.

Migrants and Contemporary Urbanity

Although contemporary migration is taking place at an unprecedented rate, the ties and links that migrants maintain with their home communities are still strong. These connections can interfere with local policies of incorporation, as migrants strive to maintain and pass down both cultural and linguistic traditions.

Migrants remain connected to their home country through communication, new information technologies, and financial ties, creating the dual characteristic of migrants: a tentative residence in a host city and multi-threaded ties to a community of origin. Moreover, various migrant communities have differing levels of residential commitment to their new host communities.[3] Many will settle for a number of generations; others view their host communities as temporary.

These technology-enhanced flows of transnational and domestic migrants have become a significant presence in metropolitan communities. A new global hierarchy of urban migrant destinations has taken shape in every region around the world.[4] Though many leading migrant cities—such as New York, Toronto, Dubai, Los Angeles, London, Sydney, Miami, Melbourne, Amsterdam, and Vancouver—immediately come to mind, many other migrant magnet cities are unexpected, revealing how widely and deeply migration flows are reaching into the global urban system. For example, Kyiv, Dusseldorf, Houston, Bonn, Minneapolis–Saint Paul, Tbilisi, and Oslo have become major recipients of international migrants, largely for the first time in their histories.

Marie Price and Lisa Benton-Short have identified twenty cities with immigrant populations exceeding 1 million, representing the destinations for one in five of migrants worldwide.[5] Cities in the United States (nine), Europe (three), the Middle East (three), Australia/Oceania (two), and Asia (two) are represented, revealing how immigrant gateways can be found in every global region. More generally, UN Habitat reported in 2005 that the world was home to some 175 million international migrants worldwide, not including undocumented immigrants.[6]

These data demonstrate the extent to which migration is no longer a "singular" event tied in some manner to a "crisis." Rather, migration is simply part and parcel of human existence.[7] The great migrations of the past are being reexamined and reinterpreted in light of new perspectives that view even mass migration as more or less a normal state of being.[8] However, the complexities of contemporary migration and migrant incorporation in a rapidly globalizing world require further attention.

Any effort to consider the challenges confronting cities within this new global migration context must seek to integrate the experiences of cities on all continents—rich cities and poor cities, large cities and small cities. Similarly, observers must begin to look beyond residential communities and neighborhoods and also consider workplaces, schools, and public space as venues for negotiation between migrants and urban society. The migrant city emerges as a much more dynamic form of social organization when viewed from the perspective of transnational migration.

Understanding Migration

How one thinks about the contemporary metropolitan-scale city must be informed by how one thinks about migrants. At times, various theoretical approaches to the initiation and sustenance of international migration have obscured the reality of migration on the ground.[9] Each approach—such as those derived from neoclassical macroeconomics, neoclassical microeconomics, segmented labor market theory, world systems theory, and social capital theory—has failed in different ways to deal adequately with the complexities of present migratory patterns. For example, researchers examining dissimilar variables have often explained the behavior of the very

r. Caroline Brettell concisely summarizes a quarter century of
discourse by noting that "the concept, 'the city as context,' was
ed within anthropology when the sub-field of urban anthropology
in its infancy and was part of the challenge to distinguish between
logy *in* cities and the anthropology *of* cities, or, as Ulf Hannerz
it, the city as the locus rather than the focus of anthropology."[18]
ll continues on to suggest that this notion of "city as context" fell
ogue before being resurrected in the 1990s.[19] She argues that cities
r metropolitan regions should become a fundamental "unit of analy-
nmigration research" because the city is a primary destination for
: newcomers.[20] She is intent on demonstrating how the impact of loan culture, tradition, economic vitality, and spatial patterns on mi-
eveals the influence that migrants exert over urban communities in
In so doing, she amplifies a dynamic interrelationship—a process of
t renegotiation—that the contributors to this volume explore.[21]

Renegotiating the Meaning of Urban Citizenship

successful in a time of rapid global population movement such as the
wenty-first century, a city must simultaneously accept both different
ared points of reference. Local legends, memories, and histories must
ond exclusionary understandings of society to embrace an inclusive
ism. In other words, civic identity must somehow embrace a variety
an groups and individuals, breaking down the barriers that have fre-
y divided groups from different racial, ethnic, and socioeconomic
rounds. Even if they have been divided in the past, cities must some-
reate a shared sense of responsibility and identity for a common fund the continued manifestation of social and economic disparity must
olved.
r an inclusive civic identity to develop, city residents need to relate to
nother in a shared public manner that transcends individual needs and
ptions. Cities are inevitably diverse, the center of changing patterns of
connections. Therefore, cities must strive to provide protected public
ing places where diverse people can come and go and interact with
other, incorporating their multiple histories of space, place, and iden-
To do so, public space and the public domain (both literal and figura-
must be both shared and protected. The city must be subject to con-
: renegotiation among all residents and businesses to reestablish the
daries—both physical and metaphysical—of the local social, eco-

same migrants from such different perspectives
explanations of their actions.[10] Analysts all too (
of diverse background as similar in "taste and
sufficient room for population movements that
ture. These various theories are not necessarily n
as they operate at very different levels of analys
national, and international).

Often, such differences increasingly reflect
proaches. Anthropologists, for example, focus c
context of migrant behavior, while demographers
efforts on population dynamics. Economists expl
of migration; historians, the migrant experience;
gration law and policy. Political scientists analyze
ogists seek to identify sources of social capital an
plinary perspectives lean toward macro-level ques
from other disciplines engage in micro-level analy
migration research and theorizing become possib
from the study of the American experience to a mo

There is thus a distinct need for concepts, questi
proaches that integrate a variety of perspectives on
migration is a dynamic process that takes place arc
spective at the heart of this volume—enables just s
vating analysis beyond specific countries of origin a

Cities as More Than Context

The growing trend in migration research to focus on a
exploration of the two-way relationship between interr
host societies.[14] Urban life transforms migrant groups
nities with shared memories and perceptions, because
that migrants discover their own similarities in oppc
around them.[15] Cities become the locus of migration c
networks in which brokers move easily between minori
societies at large.[16] These brokers—ranging from stree
international bankers—integrate migrant communities i
They most often are concentrated in just a few cities.[17]

The role of the city as the venue of exchange between
societies has been the subject of scholarly debate among

nomic, political, cultural, and linguistic landscape. At present, this renegotiation process—in which urban citizens create physical and political space
and voice in attempting to become full members of the city's social and political fabric—is rarely studied and poorly understood. The chapters in this
volume explore the renegotiation of citizenship as it is reflected through the
cultural, political, and economic dimensions of the urban experience.

In an equitable society, individuals have choices that are governed by attitudes, traditions, and culture. However, no city is equitable; and, choices
and opportunities are frequently limited by race, national origin, or class.
The increasingly multicultural composition of cities brings to the forefront
the need to consider traditionally exclusionary policies and the renegotiation of such opportunities and choices in a more equitable and inclusive
manner. As migrants attempt to exercise rights in the changing nature of the
increasingly globalized world, urbanites are forced to rethink notions of citizenship and membership in society. As borders diminish and cities are
resurging as important global actors, full membership in society, once conceived as national citizenship, is changing.

Most modern analyses of citizenship follow T. H. Marshall's framework
of citizenship rights as encompassing civil, political, and social rights.[22]
This framework, however, is not unproblematic—particularly because it
links the notion of citizenship in a sovereign state to clearly defined geographic boundaries. In addition, various kinds of citizenship rights may be
distributed unevenly, resulting in an expansion or contraction of rights in
different areas.[23] The concept of citizenship stands at the center of the renegotiation of place.

The contributors to this volume argue that democracy and citizenship
must be conceived as inherently connected; both must be extended beyond
the political to also include civil and socioeconomic aspects. In other words,
both democracy and citizenship must be studied in context, with consideration given to the particular cultural, historical, and economic situation of
each country.[24] Students of the city must study the "full experience of democratic citizenship" if they are to comprehend the forces that form the contemporary city; likewise, students of democracy must pay attention to the
city because so much of the negotiation that shapes citizenship transpires in
the city.[25]

The contributors do not judge whether minorities and migrants evade
civic duties in negotiating their presence in the urban community. More
simply, they suggest that migrants constantly raise their voices and assert
their political and economic presence. This process of advancing demands
by migrants and minorities is forcing new definitions of contemporary cit-

izenship in cities and suburbs across the globe. As migrants leverage their rights as members of the social network, they challenge what it means to be a member and bring the notion of inclusive urban citizenship to the fore-front of local politics. This renegotiation of citizenship stands at the center of the processes highlighted in the chapters that follow.

Lessons from the Street

The processes by which migrant communities are incorporated into a par-ticular urban region vary from city to city. The history of place, community identities, and public policy all have an impact on this process. Further un-derstanding of the challenges faced by cities and migrants alike requires theories that embrace the empirical richness of everyday urban life. Case studies can be especially powerful research tools because they clarify the complexity of the reality on the ground in many urban communities around the world.[26] Therefore, this volume explores how globalization in some cases has brought agency to marginalized sectors of society and the role lo-cal government can play in setting the stage for more inclusive governance. The book is organized around the examination of specific moments in time in particular urban places that are meaningfully different from one another.

As members of migrant communities seek to become incorporated into the life of their new city, they face language barriers, racial discrimination, unfamiliar cultures, and hostile labor markets that make integration a great challenge. Thus, these migrants must find an appropriate balance between maintaining their cultural and ethnic integrity while simultaneously ac-cessing their new city's social, political, and economic opportunities. As the forces of globalization create ever-widening income disparities in urban areas and opportunities for employment, education, and basic services re-main limited, it becomes more and more important to address the issues of process and integration.

The development of mobile populations, often related to the globaliza-tion of economic and communication flows, constitutes a new urban real-ity—particularly because "the flow of space is globally integrated, the place space is locally fragmented."[27] Cities around the world have become ag-glomerations of neighborhoods defined by ethnicity, religion, or national-ity. To create inclusive, socially sustainable cities, urban policies need to pay close attention to how neighborhoods and local government interact to engender community, foster economic and educational opportunities, and provide services. And it is essential to develop local and national policies that will encourage viable urban governance structures and strong, democratic civic cultures.

The twinned global trends of decentralization and the growth of civil society have contributed to the ever-growing voice of migrants worldwide. The "new social movements" of the past decades have demonstrated a new trend in organization and negotiation with the state. The searches for culture and identity are at the forefront of these movements and embody widening sociopolitical citizenship.

Urbanization on the scale of the large metropolitan city accelerates the search for space of expression as it politicizes people and makes the political incorporation of the general public unavoidable.[28] Social demands have exceeded the infrastructure of the state, and the search for autonomy has resulted in a growing tension between an aging state and a society that wants to grow. The state is faced with significant societal breakdown and fragmentation. The creation of urban policies that will ameliorate instead of alienate urban migrants is critical.

The city can be viewed as historical layers, some that have disappeared and others that are still shaping space and identity. New migrant populations continue to add to these layers, altering the historical and physical form of the city and transforming the city into a space of hybridity. The city's spatial multiplicity and hybridity contributes to its heterogeneity but also reinforces unequal development and power relations. Thus urban citizenship constantly reflects these multiplicities and renegotiations of history and space, which both subordinate and coordinate other identities such as religion, family, gender, and ethnicity.[29]

Some have argued that globalization has rendered space irrelevant. The chapters that follow demonstrate the opposite. Although borders are eroding, the notions of space and place and their links to citizenship are growing stronger. Cities are the spaces of both conflict and negotiation. Space has become an increasing point of tension, because the use of space for one reason or by one group generally violates others' claim to space.

The Plan of the Book: Urban Migration and Urban Citizenship

The ten chapters in this volume offer case studies that cover a range of nations, issues, and policies. More important, these chapters cut across disciplines, bringing in perspectives from geography, political science, anthropology, and law so that the reader may begin to comprehensively understand the obstacles faced by migrant populations, as well as the challenges that lie ahead in making cities both socially sustainable and equitable places for all. They do so by focusing on two different arenas for the renegotiation of the city. In part I, Michael Jones-Correa, Rhacel Salazar Parreñas, Serin Houston, Richard Wright, Chantal Saint-Blancat, and AbdouMaliq Simone examine how the presence of new migrant communities forces *the renegotiation of urban space*. In part II, Caroline Brettell, David Ley, Jason Pribilsky, Barbara Schmitter Heisler, and Dickson Eyoh explore how migrant communities have compelled *the renegotiation of urban citizenship* by examining a series of case studies in urban planning, health care, education, and changing official attitudes toward migrants.

In chapter 1, Michael Jones-Correa analyzes the demographic dispersion of migrants to suburban locations of gateway cities. More specifically, he explores issues of residential sorting in suburbia, the effects on networks, and how local government responds to the demographic shift in suburbs. The chapter is based on a case study of the Washington metropolitan area. Although inner cities have typically been receiving points for the nation's migrants, a recent shift has witnessed a large number of migrants moving directly into suburban neighborhoods. The chapter examines the implications for both the migrants and local governments to better explain the spatial reality of migrants and ethnic minorities living in the United States today.

In chapter 2, Rhacel Salazar Parreñas introduces the worlds of Filipina domestic workers in Rome and Los Angeles. Drawing on Saskia Sassen's work, which reflects the growing wage inequalities in global cities and the devaluation of personal service workers, Parreñas examines the peripheralization and placelessness of Filipina domestic migrants. She argues that Filipina migrants are excluded in their host society, in both social and physical spaces, with mixing limited to a few public spheres such as buses. She brings to the forefront the need to consider race and class when examining women migrants, which she argues are frequently left out of the women's studies literature.

In chapter 3, Serin Houston and Richard Wright shed new insights on the mixing of people in urban spaces. Through the lens of performativity, they challenge notions of migration and examine new spaces of racial and ethnic integration at a micro scale. Their focus on workplace, household, leisure activities, and the Internet, along with everyday spaces, provides a new, fine-grained way to see how people of different backgrounds, ethnicity, and birthplace interact on a daily basis, particularly in migrant gateways. Houston and Wright point out the obvious segregation in space that exists in the United States, but they cleverly examine the mixed household's interaction to demonstrate the everyday renegotiations of urban space. Through performativity, they spell out how mixed households navigate urban spaces where they are accepted and integrated, as well as contested and disputed. Houston and Wright open up the discussion of ethnic mixing to broaden the debate and more fully illustrate the renegotiation of migrant cities.

In chapter 4, Chantal Saint-Blancat builds on concepts introduced by Houston and Wright by examining the contentious public spaces created through efforts to build mosques in Europe as well as the new visibility of young Muslims born and socialized in Europe. Like other transnational migrants, Muslims were considered temporary workers when they first arrived. But today, rather than hosting male guest workers who will return home, European cities need to accommodate Muslim families who have settled down for good. The construction of mosques in the European landscape has brought a certain legitimacy, symbolism, and controversy to the religious pluralism emerging in Europe. The mosque symbolizes social formation and cultural solidity in public space. Religious tolerance does not concede the accession of public space—demand for Muslim public space denotes a new culture of consumption and new modes of everyday interaction in public space.

In chapter 5, AbdouMaliq Simone takes us from Europe to the dynamic urban communities of Africa. He demonstrates how the African urban experience becomes more comprehensible when long-standing, primarily Western assumptions about urban analysis are left behind. For him, life in Africa revolves around constant movement and mobility. Migration—rather than a disruptive factor—becomes the platform on which a semblance of stability and coherent social existence can be built. He explores how migrants have engaged the city and, in the process, redefined urban space and relationships. His chapter draws upon the experience of the Congolese diaspora in Johannesburg to detail this dynamic relationship between urbanization and migration.

In chapter 6, Caroline Brettel begins part II of the volume with a discussion of multiculturalism and community construction centering on an emerging gateway city, the Dallas–Fort Worth metroplex. Although major U.S. cities such as Los Angeles and New York have traditionally been migrant receiving points, cities in the Sunbelt and Midwest are now also being transformed into migrant gateways. Brettell's framework focuses on the city as a unit of analysis. Returning to the issues raised at the book's outset by Jones-Correa, she stresses the relationship between the city and suburb in terms of migrant incorporation. She does so by discussing the construction of space as well as the implications of the rapid transformation of new migrant gateway cities.

In chapter 7, David Ley explores the current trend toward multicultural policies through a discussion of the monster house controversy in Vancouver, which exemplifies the potential for multicultural planning and how migrants can renegotiate political space by exercising their political rights in the planning process. He touches on skepticisms from both the left and the right with regard to multiculturalism. Is it a veil that hides gross economic and political inequalities, or is it a tool used to fragment national identity? Of particular importance, he notes how ethnicity is used to renegotiate urban citizenship.

In chapter 8, Jason Pribilsky examines the implications of culture and agency for migrant health. He focuses on how concepts of community are related to spatial assumptions about public health and, more important, to temporal ones. Having noted that many public health practitioners operate under an assumption of acculturation that is no longer valid in this transnational world, he goes on to explain why they instead need to understand that migrants live in a world spanning both their new host country and country of origin. He examines the health challenges faced by transnational migrants through an intricate case study of tuberculosis among Ecuadorian migrants living in Rockland County, New York.

In chapter 9, Barbara Schmitter Heisler outlines how Stuttgart and Munich, which are typically perceived as conservative and antimigrant cities, have made significant efforts to integrate and accommodate their foreign-born populations. She challenges stereotypes of German cities and the German state as unwelcoming to migrants, noting both the relatively few serious incidents of ethnic clashes and the progressive efforts of a number of local governments, which are responsible for creating socially sustainable cities. Although there are flaws in the German integration system, as she notes, particularly in education, the overall ability of German cities to adapt migrant-friendly policies and programs does not fit the typical image of the unwelcoming German city.

In chapter 10, Dickson Eyoh concludes the volume by placing the issues of urban citizenship raised by the other contributors within the context of Africa. He draws on issues posed by transnational migration to examine continuities and shifts in official attitudes toward immigrants, which he sees as having have been conditioned by the changing dynamic patterns of cross-border migrations for states whose histories are quite diverse. He takes the reader through three periods of history—the colonial era; the postcolonial era until the 1980s; and the post-1980 period, which has been characterized by the legitimacy of the postcolonial state. The exclusions of Africans from citizenship were characteristic of colonial governance—colonial cities were spaces where both internal and transnational migrants had to construct new identities and forms of social interaction. The concept of migrants as the "Other" made them vulnerable to the denial of basic citizenship rights and marked the difference between migrant and citizen.

The emergence of nations and international boundaries reinforced the concept of legal and illegal, or who belonged and who did not, prolonging the colonial relations of subjects and rulers. Finally, Eyoh notes that the predominant concept of citizenship, which has been fostered by perceptions of nationalist belonging, leaves migrants with limited access to basic rights, including economic and political resources. Migrants have transformed—and are changing—cities everywhere, renegotiating city space through their daily interactions.

Seeking Middle Ground

The contributors to this volume do not provide a comprehensive overview of the vast global transformation of the urban experience in an age of mass migration. Rather, they set out an album of verbal snapshots that are intended to alert the reader to today's profound recalibration of urban life, which is seldom seen in its entirety. Migrants are remaking relatively homogenous cities and recasting historical divisions in previously divided urban communities everywhere. Power relationships are shifting and cracking as once-homogenous communities and long-entrenched, divided cities reconstitute themselves under the constant and unrelenting pressure of newly arriving migrants who are demanding their own place in town. Every aspect of urban life is being renegotiated every day.

Heightened anxiety over international terrorism has cast suspicion on the city as a social form and on migration as a social phenomenon. As noted above, host countries are more and more assuming a "play the game by our rules or leave" mentality instead of allowing migrants to adapt to the country's norms and values but maintain their culture and traditions.[30] The national impulse to retreat into a cocoon of homogeneity increasingly undermines the celebration of difference.

The authors of the pages that follow explicitly highlight an alternative reality. They forcefully argue that cities have come to represent lively alternatives to a twenty-first-century future where everyone seeks protection from others unlike themselves. Despite all their obvious imperfections, the robust intercultural vitality of cities suggests successful strategies for a twenty-first century in which people moving around the world remain a normal aspect of human existence. The message of this volume is that twenty-first-century academics, politicians, and citizens must turn toward rather than away from the metropolitan-scale city to understand how societies can harness the dynamism and mutability of a world where there are no essentialist elements that can form a permanent core of values, norms, customs, traditions, or habits for any society.

Notes

1. Scott A. Bollens, *Urban Peace-Building in Divided Societies:. Belfast and Johannesburg* (Boulder, Colo.: Westview Press, 1999), 10.

2. Migration Policy Institute, "Top 10 Migration Issues of 2006," December 1, 2006, available at http://www.migrationpolicy.org.

3. Jonathan Friedman, *The Prospect of Cities* (Minneapolis: University of Minnesota Press, 2002), 42.

4. Lisa Benton-Short, Marie D. Price, and Samantha Friedman, "Globalization from Below: The Ranking of Global Immigrant Cities," *International Journal of Urban and Regional Research* 29, no. 4 (2005): 945–59.

5. Marie Price and Lisa Benton-Short, "Counting Migrants in Cities across the Globe," January 2007, available at http://www.mpi.org.

6. Douglas S. Massey, Joaquin Arango, Graeme Hugo, Ali Kouauci, Adela Pellegrino, and J. Edward Taylor, eds., *Worlds in Motion: Understanding International Migration at the End of the Millennium* (Oxford: Clarendon Press, 1998), 1–8.

7. This is a point explored by Jan Lucassen and Leo Lucassen, "Migration, Migration History, History: Old Paradigms and New Perspectives," in *Migration, Migration History, History: Old Paradigms and New Perspectives,* ed. Jan Lucassen and Leo Lucassen (Amsterdam: International Institute of Social History; and Berlin: Peter Lang, 1997), 9–38.

8. See, e.g., Timothy J. Hatton and Jeffrey G. Williamson, *The Age of Mass Migration: Causes and Economic Impact* (New York: Oxford University Press, 1998).

9. Massey et al., *Worlds in Motion,* 1–59.

10. This is an observation emphasized by John O'Loughlin, "Foreign Minorities in Continental European Cities," in *Foreign Minorities in Continental European Cities,* ed. Gunthar Glebe and John O'Loughlin (Stuttgart: Franz Steiner, 1987), 9–29; the citation here is on 11.

11. Massey et al., *Worlds in Motion,* 8.

12. Caroline B. Brettell and James F. Hollifield, "Introduction to Migration Theory: Talking across Disciplines," in *Worlds in Motion,* ed. Massey et al., 1–26.

13. The intellectual and analytic shift away from approaching migration as a one-way process rather than as a dynamic interactive and multidirectional phenomenon has taken place during the past quarter century as researchers have begun to examine migration systems outside the context of the classic transatlantic migration paradigm. For a discussion of this transformation within migration studies, see Dirk Hoerder's 1993 lecture for the German Historical Institute in Washington: Dirk Hoerder, *People on the Move: Migration, Acculturation, and Ethnic Interaction in Europe and North America* (Providence: Gerb, 1993).

14. Nancy Foner, ed., *New Immigrants in New York* (New York: Columbia University Press, 1987), 17–29; and Nancy Foner, *From Ellis Island to JFK: New York's Two Great Waves of Immigration* (New Haven and New York: Yale University Press and Russell Sage Foundation, 2000).

15. Alejandro Portes, "Children of Immigrants: Segmented Assimilation and its Determinants," in *The Economic Sociology of Immigration: Essays on Networks, Ethnicity and Entrepreneurship,* ed. Alejandro Portes (New York: Russell Sage Foundation, 1995), 248–62; the citation here is on 257.

16. Larry S. Bourne, "Designing a Metropolitan Region: The Lessons and Lost Opportunities of the Toronto Experience," in *The Challenge of Urban Government: Policies and Practices,* ed. Mila Freire and Richard Stren (Washington, D.C.: World Bank, 2001), 27–46.

17. Thomas Sowell, *Migrations and Cultures: A World View* (New York: Basic Books, 1996), 25–32.

18. Caroline B. Brettell, "Bringing the City Back In: Cities as Contexts for Immigrant Incorporation," paper prepared for advanced seminar on "Anthropology and Contemporary Immigration," School of American Research, Santa Fe, October 7–11, 2001, 4; an earlier version of this paper is Caroline B. Brettell, "The City as Context: Approaches to Immigrants and Cities," in *Metropolis International Workshop Proceedings,* ed. Luso-American Development Foundation (Lisbon: Fundação Luso-Americana para o Desenvolvimento, 1998), 141–54. In particular, Bretell cities Jack Rollwagen, "Introduction: The City as Context: A Symposium," *Urban Anthropology* 4 (1975): 1–4; John Gulick, "The City as Microcosm of Society," *Urban Anthropology* 4 (1975): 5–15; and Louise Lamphere, ed., *Structuring Diversity: Ethnographic Perspectives on the New Immigration* (Chicago: University of Chicago Press, 1992). Also see Ulf Hannerz, *Exploring the City* (New York: Columbia University Press, 1980).

19. Brettell,, "Bringing the City Back In," 5.

20. Brettell makes the case for the city as an appropriate unit of analysis for migration studies by recounting recent research on the migrant experience in New York, Dallas, Washington, Montreal, Philadelphia, Atlanta, Los Angeles, Las Vegas, Providence, and a number of other North American communities; ibid., 30.

21. This analysis, therefore, seeks to build on the insights and path-breaking migration scholarship of Myron Weiner; see, e.g., Myron Weiner, *The Global Migration Crisis: Challenge to States and to Human Rights* (New York: HarperCollins, 1995).

22. T. H. Marshall, *Citizenship and Social Class, and Other Essays* (Cambridge: Cambridge University Press), 1950.

23. James Holston and Teresa P. R. Caldeira, "Democracy, Law, and Violence: Disjunctures of Brazilian Citizenship," in *Fault Lines of Democracy in Post-Transition Latin America,* ed. Felipe Aguero and Jeffrey Stark (Boulder, Colo.: Lynne Rienner, 1998), 263–98.

24. Along these lines, Aihwa Ong presents a more "flexible" notion of citizenship and negotiation of rights. She begins her analysis with reference to Western democracies, in which, she argues, hierarchies of racial and cultural differences intersect in complex and contingent ways. To function, nonwhites and migrants from poorer countries must daily negotiate their own space to cross over lines and boundaries established by public agencies and the general civil society. She considers citizenship a cultural process of "self-making" and "being made" by power relations that are negotiated and contested with the state and civil society. She defines "flexible citizenship" as one where individuals seek as many rights as possible while minimizing responsibilities. Aihwa Ong, "Cultural Citizenship as Subject Making," *Current Anthropology* 37, no. 5 (1996): 737–62; and Aihwa Ong, *Flexible Citizenship: The Cultural Logistics of Transnationality* (Durham, N.C.: Duke University Press, 1999). As Sharon Zukin writes, "Culture has also become a more explicit site of conflicts over social difference and urban fears. Large numbers of new migrants and ethnic minorities have put pressure on public institutions, from schools to political parties to deal with their individual demands"; Sharon Zukin, *The Culture of Cities* (Cambridge: Blackwell,1995).

25. Holston and Caldeira, "Democracy, Law, and Violence," 288.

26. This point is powerfully argued by A. C. Hepburn, *Ethnicity and Power in Contested Cities: The Historical Experience,* Woodrow Wilson Center Comparative Urban Studies Project Urban Update 7 (Washington, D.C.: Woodrow Wilson International Center for Scholars, 2006).

27. Jordi Borja and Manuel Castells, *Local and Global: Management of Cities in the Information Age* (London: Earthscan, 1997), 44.

28. Elizabeth Jelin has defined social action as the process through which structure and agency interact in manifold ways and actors produce meanings, negotiate, and make decisions. Social movements become engaged through political struggle to gain access to mechanisms of power, and through cultural struggle in the search for identity. Elizabeth Jelin, *Women and Social Change in Latin America* (New York: UNRISD and Zed Books, 1990).

29. James Holston and A. Appadurai, "Introduction," in *Cities and Citizenship* (Durham, N.C.: Duke University Press, 1999).

30. Migration Policy Institute, "Top 10 Migration Issues of 2006."

Part I

The Renegotiation of Urban Space

1

Immigrant Incorporation in Suburbia: Spatial Sorting, Ethnic Mobilization, and Receiving Institutions

Michael Jones-Correa

More than half of all Americans—as well as almost half of all ethnic and racial minorities—now live in "suburbia," those urban areas outside of what the U.S. Census defines as "central cities." As immigrants and ethnic minorities in the United States move to suburbs in unprecedented numbers, remarkably little is known about how and why they make their residential decisions, or how they are changing, and changed by, their suburban context. The starting point for this chapter is that these suburban contexts are, in fact, generally quite different from those of central cities, and that we cannot simply assume that our understanding of the processes of spatial sorting, ethnic identity and mobilization, and institutional policy response that guided much of our earlier understandings of racial/ethnic incorporation in central cities can be unquestioningly transferred to make sense of the changes under way in suburbia. In practice, immigrant settlement, mobilization, and incorporation in suburbia are the result of complex interactions between migrants and communities jointly configuring these metropolitan areas. This chapter is a preliminary exploration of questions regarding the mechanisms shaping the demographic transformation of suburbia in the United States, the effects of suburbanization on ethnic and racial organization and mobilization, and the role of local governmental actors attempting to respond to the demographic changes brought about by immigration.

As such, this chapter poses three interrelated sets of questions. First, although there is a considerable literature on racial/ethnic sorting in urban areas, these findings have not kept pace with the demographic changes that have taken place across many metropolitan areas in the United States. The mechanisms and differential effects of racial/ethnic spatial sorting in suburbia remain underexplored. If racial/ethnic groups in suburbia are experiencing residential sorting, how much of this sorting is shaped, among other factors, by housing policies, zoning restrictions, and tax policies? And are groups sorting in similar ways or are there variations across racial/ethnic groups?

Second, assuming that some form of spatial sorting occurs, how does this affect the formation and maintenance of ethnic networks and organization? Do ethnic/racial identity and organization take different forms in suburbia than they do in the very distinct geography of central cities?

Third, once ethnic/racial diversity is present in suburban areas, how do local jurisdictions adapt their public policies and services in response to these demographic changes? And what drives these adaptive responses? Do these responses reflect ethnic/racial sorting, the mobilization of new racial/ethnic actors, or the differential responsiveness of administrative agencies, or some combination of these?

On the basis of the evidence from fieldwork conducted in the Washington metropolitan area, I argue that it is likely that immigrants will experience residential sorting in suburbia differently from blacks, and that the differential residential sorting of ethnic/racial groups in suburbia will have an effect on ethnic identity and mobilization. Second, residential dispersal in suburbia will have important implications for ethnic organization and mobilization, with ethnic networks drawing widely from across the region. Finally, policymakers in local suburban jurisdictions will respond differently to diversity depending on the characteristics of local bureaucracies. The complex processes of immigrant choice of residential location, and the creation and mobilization of, and the response of local jurisdictions to, their presence are jointly shaping suburban spaces across metropolitan areas in the United States.

Changes in Context

Over the last generation, America's metropolitan areas have been transformed. More than half of all Americans now live in "suburbia," urban areas outside what the U.S. Census defines as "central cities." The stereotypical view of suburbs is that they are overwhelmingly white and middle class. These generalizations, however, are faulty. Even during the postwar suburban boom, commentators were already noting the growing incidence of minority (mostly black) suburbanization.[1] The increase in the numbers of the black middle class has only accelerated African American migration to the suburbs.[2] As immigration increased through the 1980s and 1990s, it became apparent that suburbia is becoming even more multiethnic.[3] Post-1965 immigrants, having become economically and socially established, have been moving, like previous waves of immigrants before them, out of central city areas and settling in outlying suburban areas. One of the more interesting and understudied phenomena of the recent immigration is that a substantial portion has been skipping settlement in cities entirely, moving directly into suburban neighborhoods.[4] Despite this, much of the recent literature on immigrants and ethnic minorities still maintains a traditional focus on the urban core.[5] Immigrants and other ethnic minorities in suburbia remain, in many respects, an unknown quantity.

In 1990, 94 percent of the foreign born had settled in metropolitan areas, with over 40 percent living in the New York and Los Angeles metropolitan areas alone. Forty-eight percent of immigrants resided in suburbs.[6] Thanks in large part to the suburbanization of immigrants, the proportions of minorities in suburbs increased dramatically as well: in 1999, 31 percent of blacks, 44 percent of Latinos, and 51 percent of Asian Americans lived in suburbs.[7] These figures, confirmed by the 2000 census, indicate that the suburbanization of immigrants and minorities is approaching, and in some cases has surpassed, that of the population as a whole (table 1.1).

Debates

There are three areas in which the suburbanization of immigrants and racial and ethnic minorities should lead us to reexamine some of the assumptions social scientists and policymakers have held about immigrant social and political incorporation. First, the suburbanization of ethnic and racial minori-

Table 1.1. U.S. Population by Area of Residence, 1999 (percent)

Type of Population	Urban	Suburban	Rural
Immigrants	47	48	5
Native-born	28	51	21
Non-Hispanic white	22	53	22
Black	55	31	14
Hispanic	48	44	8
Asian American	45	51	4

Source: U.S. Census, 1999 Current Population Survey.

ties, and that of immigrants in particular, is likely to have an impact on the spatial sorting of racial and ethnic minorities in suburbia, in ways distinct from prior patterns. Second, the suburbanization of racial/ethnic groups should lead us to reopen the question of the intersection between spatial contexts and ethnic identity and mobilization. And third, the suburbanization of these new groups should lead us to reexamine assumptions about the nature of suburbia itself, and particularly of suburban institutions and politics.

Spatial Sorting in Suburbia

The connections between spatial location and race/ethnicity have long interested researchers across a range of disciplines. In the 1920s, researchers at the University of Chicago led by Ernest Burgess connected race and ethnicity with space via class position; to the extent that racial and ethnic minorities earn lower incomes than native-born whites, they argued, these minorities will sort out in space according to their class position.[8] Later research qualified Burgess's contentions,[9] but his observation that people sort out spatially according to race and class has generally been reinforced over time. For example, Alonso, Muth, and Mills have used economic theory to show why, particularly in the United States, upper-income people tend to live far from central business districts and lower-income people closer in.[10] With multiple central business districts in a single metropolitan region, the Alonso-Mills-Muth model becomes more complicated, but its principles are still regarded as holding roughly true.[11] Tiebout provided a theoretical model to describe the mechanism of spatial sorting by expanding on what economists call the "exit option."[12] Tiebout's sorting model assumes that residents have varying desires (or utility) for public services and varying tolerance for tax payments. Given varying revenue and expenditure patterns across urban areas, Tiebout writes, "the consumer-voter moves to that community whose local government best satisfies his set of preferences. The greater the number of communities and the greater the variance among them, the closer the consumer will come to fully realizing his preference position."[13] Given this insight, the application of Tiebout's model to suburban settings, with their multiple, competing jurisdictions, seems a natural extension of the theory. Schneider, for example, finds support for Tiebout's sorting hypothesis in suburbia, in which the "buyers" are both the residents and businesses that choose to locate within a given jurisdiction and the "sellers" are the corresponding local governments.[14] Competition among multiple suburban governments, coupled with the diversity in the goods and services provided by local governments, creates a "market" for local public goods in suburbia. Schneider points to individual preference revelation attributes and to the reduction in the variance of demands for publicly provided goods and services in some communities as empirical evidence supporting the Tiebout hypothesis.[15]

However, as critics have pointed out, the Tiebout model depends on citizens making decisions based on information they have about levels of taxation and services across jurisdictions, whereas in actuality "citizen consumers" know little about levels of public services, much less how these might compare across jurisdictions. Lowery and Lyons and Padon argue that sorting models require unrealistically high levels of information on the part of individual citizen consumers.[16] They argue that the class and racial sorting that plays out in suburbia occurs as the result of an explicit bias in favor of upper-income groups who are those most able, and most likely, to move to take advantage of lower taxes and higher levels of services in favorable jurisdictions. Others have noted that this biased sorting is significantly aided by exclusionary zoning mechanisms that reinforce residential class stratification.[17] But these deliberate biases only exacerbate underlying tendencies; the "exit" options exercised by these groups need not rely on explicit bias—those with greater access to information, and the resources to act this information, are more likely to move (or at least to move in a manner maximizing their interests), whereas those with less information are less likely to move. In short, because income/information is highly correlated with race and ethnicity, Tiebout's "exit option" is less viable for lower-income groups who, not coincidentally, are disproportionately immigrant and racial/ethnic minority populations.

These assumptions—that low-income households, racial minorities, and immigrants would tend to live in or near the central city; that people who lived in suburbs would tend to sort out according to shared preferences for public services; and that middle- and upper-class whites in suburbs would generally use local land use and housing prerogatives to exclude racial minorities—have shaped thinking about suburbs and suburban politics for at least fifty years. However, these arguments for suburban homogeneity are complicated, if not contradicted, by trends over the last thirty years toward increasing ethnic and racial diversity both across suburbs and within suburbs. Though commentators have noted incidences of minority (mostly black) suburbanization during the postwar boom,[18] this diversification of suburbia has accelerated in the past decade. By 2000, 58 percent of Asians lived in suburbs, up from 53 percent in 1990. Hispanic suburbanization grew 3 percentage points, from 46 percent in 1990 to 49 percent in 2000, while African American suburbanization increased by 5 percentage points, from 34 percent in 1990 to 39 percent in 2000.

It could be that earlier theories of racial sorting—with their emphasis on a high correlation between class and race, and the uses of exclusionary zoning to enforce distinctions of class and race—are simply out of date in many contemporary suburban settings. In these settings, racial and ethnic minorities may have "cleared the bar," so to speak, of income, allowing them wide leeway in their selection of residence in these areas. If so, then class trumps individuals' racial or ethnic background. Many studies have echoed and supported the contention by Massey that spatial assimilation mirrors social assimilation.[19] If this is the case, then, as Logan and his colleagues conclude, "as minorities become assimilated into mainstream society, participating in American culture and advancing in education and class status, they are expected to move out of traditional enclaves and ghettos," to suburbia.[20]

However, though the proportion of blacks living in suburbs has significantly increased, it remains significantly lower than both Asian and Hispanic suburbanization and trails white suburbanization at 71percent by 32 percentage points.[21] Thus, spatial assimilation theories seems a poor fit for the African American experience in the United States; unlike white ethnics, who suburbanized in the postwar period, blacks have been subject to widespread and interlocking systems of discrimination that many have argued has resulted in dual housing markets for whites and blacks.[22] Even the most affluent, well-educated African Americans have not assimilated spatially to the extent that lower-income racial and ethnic minorities have done.[23] These results have given rise to place-stratification theory, which argues that spatial assimilation still varies considerably according to race and ethnicity, and that racial sorting still takes place, but across suburbs, rather than simply between suburbs and central cities, as earlier sorting theories had argued. In addition, there is still significant uncertainly whether Asian and Hispanic immigrants to the United States will follow the spatial assimilation or place-stratification models. For example, whereas Asian and Hispanic Americans are rapidly suburbanizing, some argue that their residential segregation, particularly in larger metropolitan areas, is increasing.[24]

Given the debates outlined above, several questions remain: With increasing numbers of racial and ethnic minorities living in suburbia, is residence still sorted by class and/or race? If the answer to this question is "yes," by what mechanism are people being sorted out? Is the Tiebout model of individual choice the principal factor in sorting, or are there institutionalized barriers, like exclusionary zoning, that drive residential sorting by race, ethnicity, and class? If there is residential sorting going on, is it playing itself out similarly across racial and ethnic groups, particularly blacks, Latinos, and Asian Americans?

Racial/Ethnic Identity and Mobilization in Suburbia

The mobilization of racial/ethnic minorities is one of the central themes of the urban literature in the social sciences. Much of this literature on urban ethnic organization and mobilization focuses on place-based neighborhood organizations in central cities, built around a sense of compact geographic "community."[25] Thus, the incorporation of minorities is seen as having both a spatial and temporal dimension, moving from tight-knit ethnic urban neighborhoods to assimilated suburbs, and from ethnic organization to electoral incorporation. In Dahl's classic *Who Governs?* for instance, he argues that political incorporation occurs only as newcomers shift from their corporate ethnic loyalties to partisan mobilization, in which ethnicity plays at most a symbolic role.[26] This shift, taking place over generations, is paralleled by a demographic dispersal into the suburbs.[27]

For this reason, immigrants' social and political organization is seen as an essentially urban phenomenon, and one located only in central cities at that. Thus, despite the fact that almost half of all racial and ethnic minorities now live in suburbia, the focus of much of the recent literature on ethnic political mobilization continues to be on the roles these groups play in central cities.[28] The relatively small literature on racial and ethnic minorities in suburbia, for its part, does not pay particular attention to the distinctive spatial setting of suburbia itself.[29] In these cases, where ethnic mobilization is observed in suburbia, it is because ethnic residential patterns take on the characteristics of older urban configurations, with high concentrations of tight-knit ethnic groups. Very little is made of these studies' suburban locations, the implication being that the results would have been much the same if the studies had been conducted in central cities.

The urban literature assumes that ethnic organization and mobilization go hand-in-hand with place stratification, and that as racial/ethnic groups assimilate spatially, their mobilization efforts become less distinguishable from those of the population as a whole. Zelinsky and Lee suggest that neither of these assumptions necessarily holds true.[30] They argue that one of the distinctive features of contemporary ethnic/racial migration to suburbia is that much of it is the result of direct migration to suburbia from abroad, so that new ethnic/racial minorities are bypassing the model of spatial and social assimilation into suburbia. Second, Zelinsky and Lee posit that the existence of ethnic communities may not be bounded by a resident's immediate geographic surroundings. Instead, these communities might be situated around places of worship, organizations, and the like that are physically distant from one another. This implies that ethnic organization may adapt itself to the spatial distinctiveness of suburbia, and that these adaptations might take quite different forms from previous forms of ethnic/racial organization in urban areas.

The implication of the argument posited by Zelinsky and Lee is that neither the spatial assimilation nor place-stratification models may entirely explain ethnic identity and mobilization. Ethnic and racial minorities, whether living in relative concentrations or living diffused throughout what may seem to be featureless suburban landscapes, may still effectively construct and maintain ethnic social networks, and these networks may not be limited to bounded geographic areas like traditional ethnic neighborhoods. The social and organizational networks ethnic and racial minorities construct may be separate from the residential choices they make.[31] Among the questions still to be resolved are these: If there is variance in the spatial sorting of ethnic and racial groups in suburbia, is this reflected in corresponding forms of ethnic organization and mobilization (as suggested by Cohen and Dawson)?[32] If not, are forms of ethnic organization and mobilization shaped less by the residential decisions of ethnic and racial minorities and more by the characteristic diffuseness of the suburban landscape itself, with ethnic networks and organization potentially sprawling across entire metropolitan areas rather than being organized from the immediate residential area, as in older models of ethnic organization? And if the latter is the case, is there variation in forms of social organization and mobilization depending on the physical characteristics of the suburban landscape? (i.e., differing densities and age of housing; proximity to transportation networks, and so on, as suggested by Huckfeldt and Sprague).[33]

Receiving Institutions in Suburbia

Suburbs have long been stereotyped as homogeneously white and middle class; correspondingly, the politics of suburbs are generally assumed to be more conservative than those of urban areas and to deal largely with allocative issues rather than distributive ones (i.e., providing basic "housekeeping" services, rather than shifting resources from the most well off to the least well off).[34] The arguments for the homogeneity of suburbs and their fiscally conservative policies go hand in hand. As a result of their similarities in race and class, the argument goes, suburbanites become inward looking and defensive of their perquisites, and increasingly dissatisfied with federal programs and the national tax policies that sustain those programs, which as far as they see do little to benefit suburban residents.[35] However, as ethnic and racial minorities become more numerous in suburbia, local governments may, perforce, be confronted with issues raised by heterogeneity. Administrators in local jurisdictions must often decide, for example, whether to provide specialized social services, perhaps in other languages, or to address issues of adequate political representation, among other things.[36] The range of adaptations undertaken by local governments and planning agencies in response to demographic change have been documented by scholars working on several fronts.[37]

In general, the analysis of adaptive change by governmental institutions assumes that these adaptations are driven by changes in the electoral equation; that is, change occurs once new actors—the racial and ethnic minorities moving to suburbia—have the resources and the inclination to challenge local political regimes in the electoral arena.[38] Until this happens, established political actors may engage in "backlash" politics, attempting to protect perceived prerogatives from the effects of the demographic changes taking place. However, some research suggests that the assumption that institutions adapt only in response to electoral pressure may well miss aspects of adaptive policymaking driven by actors outside the electoral arena. For example, scholars of bureaucracy have noted that employees in administrative agencies often act independently to set and implement policy,[39] and that these decisions are often set in motion by a sense of bureaucratic mission that may be at odds with the priorities and agendas of elected officials. Furthermore, there may be differences not only between elected officials and bureaucratic administrators but also across bureaucracies. Following Derthick's discussion of bureaucracies with "client-serving ethics,"[40] Jones-Correa distinguishes between "service bureaucracies," which build relationships with the individuals to whom they provide a service, and "administrative bureaucracies," which see their role primarily as the fair and impartial enforcement of rules.[41] In this view, different bureaucratic missions lead to different outcomes for the incorporation of ethnic and racial minorities.

Once again, given the debates outlined above, some questions remain: Do public policies in suburban jurisdictions adapt their public policies and services in response to changes in the racial/ethnic makeup of their populations? If local jurisdictions are adapting to demographic change, what drives these adaptive responses? Does it reflect ethnic/racial spatial sorting, the incorporation of new ethnic/racial minorities driven by the responsiveness of the electoral arena to ethnic/racial actors, the responsiveness of administrative agencies, or some combination of these? And how do administrative agencies differ from one another in their responsiveness to ethnic/racial minorities?

The Case

The primary case I draw on to explore some of these issues is the metropolitan Washington area. Metropolitan Washington has experienced rapid demographic shifts over the last twenty years, increasing rapidly in both population and ethnic/racial diversity (see table 1.2). During the past ten years, the area has seen relative stagnation or decline in its non-Hispanic white population while experiencing rapid increases in its Asian, Latino, and black populations.

The diversification of the Washington metropolitan area has taken place largely, though not solely, as the result of immigration. The Washington area's population currently ranks seventh among the ten largest metropolitan areas in the United States receiving immigration. Metropolitan Washington's foreign-born population grew by 70 percent in the 1990s, to nearly 350,000 immigrants in 2000 (and up from only 127,579 in 1970).[42] Sixty-one percent of the Washington area's population is racial/ethnic minorities,

Table 1.2. Population by Race and Ethnicity, Washington Metropolitan Area, 1990 and 2000

Component of Population	1990	2000	Change, 1990s Absolute	Change, 1990s Percent	Percentage of Total 1990	Percentage of Total 2000
Total	4,223,485	4,923,153	699,668	16.6	100.0	100.0
Non-Hispanic white	2,722,555	2,762,241	39,686	1.5	64.5	56.1
Non-Hispanic black	1,057,330	1,266,672	209,342	19.8	25.0	25.7
Non-Hispanic Asian/Pacific	199,863	330,813	130,950	65.5	4.7	6.7
Hispanic	228,199	432,003	203,804	89.3	5.4	8.8

Sources: U.S. Census Bureau, Census of Population, 1990 and 2000.

while 41 percent of its suburban population is racial/ethnic minorities.[43] These demographic patterns are particularly pronounced in the two most populous counties in the Washington suburban area: Montgomery County, Maryland, and Fairfax County, Virginia. Table 1.3 presents the racial and ethnic origin composition in Montgomery County since 1980. It indicates that while the proportion of the county's non-Hispanic white population decreased from 86 percent in 1980 to 64 percent in 2002, both the Asian and Hispanic populations in the county increased dramatically, from 4 percent in 1980 to 11 percent and 12 percent in 2002, respectively. The African American population in Montgomery County increased, though to a lesser degree, from 9 percent in 1980 to 15 percent in 2002.

A similar demographic shift has took place in northern Virginia's Fairfax County. Table 1.4 shows that while the county's non-Hispanic white population decreased from 86 percent in 1980 to 62 percent in 2002, its

Table 1.3. Montgomery County, Maryland, Racial/Ethnic Origin Composition, 1980, 1990, and 2000 (percent)

Racial/Ethnic Origin	1980	1990	2002
Non-Hispanic white	85.6	76.7	64.8
Non-Hispanic black	8.8	12.2	15.1
Hispanic	3.9	7.4	11.5
Non-Hispanic Asian	3.9	8.2	11.1
Other	0.5	2.7	5.0

Sources: U.S. Census Bureau, 1980 and 1990 censuses and 2002 American Community Survey.

*Table 1.4. Fairfax County, Virginia, Racial/
Ethnic Origin Composition, 1980, 1990, and
2000 (percent)*

Racial/Ethnic Origin	1980	1990	2002
Non-Hispanic white	86.2	77.5	62.2
Non-Hispanic black	5.8	7.6	7.8
Hispanic	3.3	6.3	12.3
Non-Hispanic Asian	3.8	8.3	15.0
Other	1.0	0.3	2.6

Sources: U.S. Census Bureau, 1980 and 1990 censuses and 2002
American Community Survey.

Asian and Hispanic populations soared, from 4 and 3 percent, respectively, in 1980 to 15 and 12 percent in 2002. However, note that the African American population in Fairfax County increased only marginally, from 6 to 8 percent, over that same period.

Apart from these demographic changes, the Washington area is an attractive candidate for study for two reasons. First, it has a relatively simple set of governing structures. County governments together with a scattering of independent municipalities dominate the suburban area. The Metropolitan Washington Council of Governments, the umbrella organization of the region's governments, has only nineteen members, including the governments of Washington itself and its surrounding counties. School district boundaries in metropolitan Washington coincide with the boundaries of counties (counties and cities in Virginia). This relatively uncomplicated governing structure facilitates comparisons among the counties and cities in the area. Second, an additional comparative advantage of studying the Washington metro area is that it extends into two quite different states: Maryland, which allows considerable leeway to its local jurisdictions, and Virginia, in which the state retains strict oversight on its delegation of powers to local municipalities. Comparisons among the political arenas in the metropolitan area were designed to highlight state-level differences.

Some Evidence

The evidence presented in the chapter is based on fieldwork carried out in the Washington metropolitan area in 2003–4.[44] As part of this research, I conducted three clusters of interviews—with immigrant organizations, elected representatives, and local bureaucrats—for 113 interviews in all.[45] I draw on this field research, as well as that of other scholars working on demographic changes and their implications for the Washington area, to illustrate the arguments I make here.

Spatial Sorting

The evidence on spatial sorting in the Washington area is mixed. African Americans are clearly more residentially segregated than any other group, particularly when accounting for their socioeconomic backgrounds. Prince George's County, which in the 1980s was still predominantly white, now has a largely African American population. Black residential choices in Fairfax and Montgomery are concentrated within relatively narrow portions of these counties. This is still somewhat the case even for black immigrants who have arrived to the Washington area from Somalia, Ethiopia, Haiti, and areas of West Africa and the Caribbean (figure 1.1). However, black immigrants are more likely to live in suburbs, and occupy residential areas in the "buffer zones" between native-born African Americans and other immigrant or native-born residents. Previous research on residential patterns in the Washington metro area indicates that most immigrants are dispersed throughout the suburbs rather than remaining in ethnic enclaves.[46] Although immigrants sometimes cluster in particular residential neighborhoods, these are not dominated by any single ethnic group (see figure 1.2).

Singer and her colleagues found that while more than half of all zip codes in the Washington area were places of residence for recent foreign-born arrivals, the zip code areas that attracted the highest percentage of immigrants were also some of the most ethnically diverse, with none having a majority of any single national-origin group, and often having representation from over 100 different nationalities.[47] And while there is some concentration in immigrant neighborhoods (as opposed to ethnic enclaves), there is a countervailing pattern of dispersal. Asian and Latino immigrants, in particular, are widely dispersed throughout the metropolitan region, even as there are signs of some emerging concentrations in parts of the suburban counties (see figures 1.3 and 1.4).

The patterns of immigrant settlement evident from these census data suggest some residential concentration, but together with considerable resi-

Figure 1.1. Residential Distribution of African Immigrants in the Washington
Metropolitan Region by Census Tract, 2000

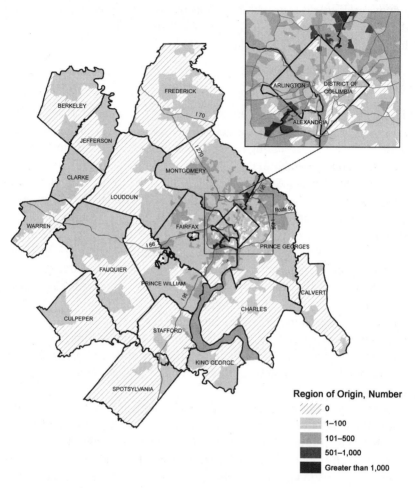

Region of Origin, Number

- 0
- 1–100
- 101–500
- 501–1,000
- Greater than 1,000

Sources: U.S. Census; map from Audrey Singer, Brookings Institution.

dential dispersal. The evidence from the Washington case runs counter to
the emphasis in the earlier literature on immigration, which saw immigrant
neighborhoods as easily delimited (the classic examples being case studies
of immigrant neighborhoods in Chicago, Boston, or New York: the Lower
East Side in Manhattan, the North End in Boston, etc.), and counter to the
emphasis on strict racial sorting implied in much of the urban literature.

Figure 1.2. Percentage of Foreign Born by Census Tract, Washington Metropolitan Region, 2000

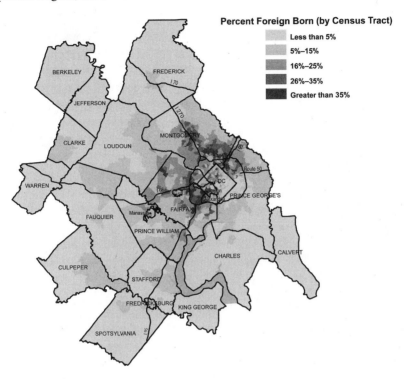

Sources: U.S. Census; map from Audrey Singer, "At Home in the Nation's Capital: Immigrant Trends in Metropolitan Washington," Brookings Institution, June 2003.

Ethnic Organization

So what are the implications of suburbanization and residential dispersion for immigrants and other new arrivals? What does it imply for the formation of ethnic communities and ethnic mobilization? One set of questions here is about the role of spatial contexts and ethnic mobilization. Much of the social science literature on urban ethnic organization focuses on place-based neighborhood organizations in central cities, built around a sense of compact geographic "community." But "community" in suburbia may not refer at all to a resident's immediate geographic surroundings. As posited above, "community" might instead be situated around places of worship miles away from an individual's place of residence, and miles more from

Figure 1.3. Residential Distribution of Latin American Immigrants in the Washington Metropolitan Region by Census Tract, 2000

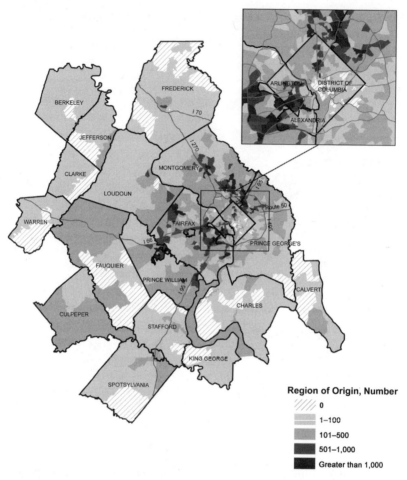

Region of Origin, Number

- 0
- 1–100
- 101–500
- 501–1,000
- Greater than 1,000

Sources: U.S. Census; map from Audrey Singer, Brookings Institution.

the ethnic grocery store or restaurant that serves as a gathering place, or the place of work owned by co-ethnics.

Does ethnic organization in suburbs still follow neighborhood lines, or does it draw its members across a region along functional lines? In suburbs, for instance, where an ethnic group might be widely scattered, an organization might attract members from far beyond its immediate vicinity. What

Figure 1.4. Residential Distribution of Asian Immigrants in the Washington Metropolitan Region by Census Tract, 2000

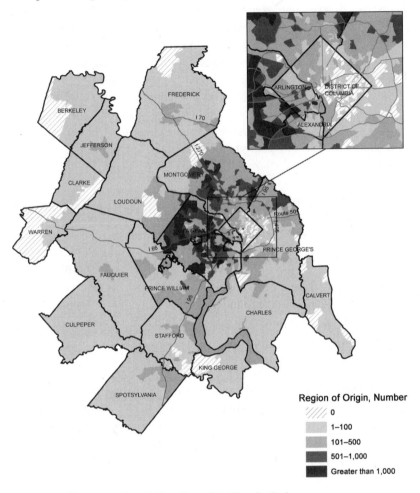

Region of Origin, Number
- 0
- 1–100
- 101–500
- 501–1,000
- Greater than 1,000

Sources: U.S. Census; map from Audrey Singer, Brookings Institution.

implications does this have for ethnic mobilization and politics? It may be that the spatial organization of ethnic groups does not intersect with the geography of political jurisdictions. What happens then? How do ethnic organizations adapt to suburban settings?

To illustrate both the persistence and adaptation of organizational forms, I present some excerpts below from interviews with members of one of four national-origin groups I researched in the Washington area.[48] Like the immigrant community as a whole, the Chinese in the Washington area are themselves diverse, with some being native born, and others new arrivals as immigrants; among new arrivals, some have arrived either directly or indirectly from Hong Kong, Taiwan, and mainland China, with the mainland Chinese divided between Cantonese and Mandarin speakers. This internal diversity likely led to difficulties in ethnic organization.

So how do these immigrants find and connect with networks of co-ethnics in suburban Washington? And what organizational forms do these networks take? Mary Au, a longtime organizer in the Chinese American community in Maryland, points to the importance of Chinese provincial and kinship ties:

> Each of [these immigrants] are usually from different provinces. . . . So every time [immigrants] leave, they are given a list of contacts. In Chinatown, there's a, it's quite a network; in Chinatown each of the person registers at like a post-office box in this grocery store. . . . [Take, for example] the Lee Association, that's from a certain area. The Wong Association, that's from a certain area. So they know [to look you up]. . . . That's how [Chinese] credit unions, started actually . . . helping [immigrants] set up credit unions so that you could borrow money, get started, and pay it back.

These initial contacts are based on kinship and provincial ties. Like the social ties built around college alumni networks and occupation, they are important for social connectedness but are not the basis for ethnic mobilization.

Once Chinese immigrants settle, they seek out more formal organizations. Churches, for example, are central organizations in the Chinese community. Montgomery County Parent-Teacher Association president Michelle Yu notes the important role of the church for Chinese in Maryland:

> I know Korean and Chinese [immigrants], a lot of them really . . . rely on the church, the support system. And so if you want to . . . convey any information, if you can be a part of the church-goers, you can definitely make an influence, okay, because they go there regularly. [The] local cultural school, and church, are the two, you know, regular places that you'll see people.

Note that Yu points to Chinese-language schools, which, like churches, function to bring a wide range of Chinese families together:

The Chinese schools, it's like a marketplace—you know, people come there, and leave their kids in the classroom, and parents just chat in the cafeteria, and then somebody will . . . sell something [they've made themselves, like] fish, and, you know, seafood, and they chat.

Unlike in the public schools, where Asian parents are often reluctant to become involved in the local Parent-Teacher Associations because of language and other issues, Chinese parents are much more likely to be involved with Chinese schools, because such schools are essentially run by the parents. Yu indicates, for example, that

[parent-run Chinese-language] schools play . . . a very important role [in the Chinese community]. So, I say, okay, I'm going to form my own Chinese school. After working so long . . . with my previous Chinese [school, maybe] I wanted one for my own, because I can bring in this resource, that resource. So I just get a license, get a location, you know. I can have it in any [public] high school, and then I start to [place] advertisement[s], and people come and enroll, and you . . . ask this parent here and there, hey, why don't you teach first grade, hey, you come teach second grade, and we are a Chinese school! And that's why everybody's involved, because it's kind of self-governed, community based.

These schools rely on the intensive voluntary efforts of the parents involved.

These Chinese-language schools also provide a place for parents to retain a sense of status and rebuild social ties they had before immigration.[49] In the Taiwanese schools, for instance,

of course it's [about individual] interest, it's about power, but a lot of times it's about the— . . . how do I describe it? . . . You see, we are foreign, we are immigrant, and . . . we need this sense of belonging. Where do you find this sense of belonging? . . . Sometimes, you really feel lonely, especially we intellectuals. A lot of us have PhD degrees, and went through college in Taiwan. . . . Here, finally, [we] settled down with a stable job, with our kids, and everything—all set. [But] I want someplace where I can contribute. . . . Many times, a lot of [this effort goes into] Chinese schools. Just put yourself in my shoes. I want to do something. I want to do *something*. . . . The reasons to start a Chinese school may be varied, but the level of involvement can be attributed to that need, the need to really do something for my kid, and eventually for my social circle. And . . . we get together, and we have a group. Prior to that, I am just an employee . . . and you know, it's very lonely. . . . So, . . . you get a sense of belonging in those cultural schools.

Note that these schools are not only Chinese but also more specifically Taiwanese, mainland Chinese (teaching in Mandarin and Cantonese), and Hong Kong Chinese. As Yu points out:

> So there is a Taiwanese school here . . . every Saturday they meet; . . . because I am also Taiwanese, my parents [were Taiwanese], you know we all spoke Chinese. So the Taiwanese community, . . . they . . . said, "Come and be our principal, come and be the principal at our Taiwanese school," and [I] was the director of the Chinese school. In Chinese school, you speak Mandarin; in Taiwanese school, you speak Taiwanese. And, all those Taiwanese school's parents are almost 100 percent [pro]-Taiwan independence thinking.

Schools and churches both bridge and replicate the social, cultural, and political differences in the community.

In many ways the interviews reinforce findings in earlier research: that immigrants first seek out informal networks before tapping into or building more formal organizations, that these organizations fill a need immigrants feel for social connectedness and social status, and that the universe of organizations reflects the range of differences in the immigrant community. However, the key point here is that nascent immigrant organizations succeed in suburbia by appealing to immigrants' need for social connectedness, not along neighborhood lines, but instead by building social networks that cast a wide net across the entire metropolitan area. In the automobile-driven culture of the Washington suburbs, churches and schools draw Chinese immigrants from miles away. What brings immigrants together are key organizational nodes, such as churches and language schools, from which individuals' social networks radiate outwards like spokes on a wheel. This is a very different portrait of immigrant organization from those captured by urban ethnographies of past generations of immigrants, portrayed as living in distinct ethnic neighborhoods each with its own dense fabric of ethnic organization.

Receiving Institutions

Once immigrants settle in these suburban areas, how do localities respond, and is there variation across localities? My initial assumption, in choosing the Washington metropolitan area as a case study, was that the major differences would be across state jurisdictions, because Maryland and Virginia, the two states that divide metropolitan Washington are a contrast in their political leanings (liberal vs. conservative), as well (and perhaps relatedly) as in their approach to the delegation of powers to their localities. Virginia is a Dillon's rule state, regarding municipalities largely as creatures of the state, whereas Maryland delegates many powers to its localities.

However, the primary variation observed in local responses to immigration was not across states (although some certainly exists) but across public agencies; similar public agencies in both Montgomery County, Maryland, and Fairfax County, Virginia, reacted to immigration and demographic change in similar ways.[50] For instance, take libraries. Public libraries in the two counties adapted to demographic change by keeping track of demographic changes (librarians in these counties put together fat binders on neighborhood demographic characteristics compiled from census and county data), polling their users on a regular basis, actively seeking foreign-language speaking staff, and increasing their holdings in foreign-language books and media.

Between 2000 and 2003, many counties in the United States were going through severe budgetary crises, in many cases the most severe suffered since the depression of the 1930s. Fairfax and Montgomery counties were no exception. In Fairfax County, for instance, libraries had 30 percent of their purchasing budgets cut. Foreign-language books were expensive and were used by only a small portion of their readership—and a politically inactive one at that. Yet the county library system protected its foreign-language acquisitions from budget cuts. These areas had no cuts, even though, for Spanish-language books, for instance, circulation per volume was a tenth that of English-language volumes (librarians keep track of how often each book circulates in any year: Spanish-language volumes in the Fairfax library system, for example, circulated about 1.2 times in a year, versus 11 times a year for their English-language counterparts). The librarians interviewed protected these areas from budget cutbacks because they saw them as critical to the mission of public libraries: to provide materials to their clientele, and the people who walked through their doors were all clients, regardless of national origin or legal status.

Zoning inspectors, conversely, also acted similarly across the two counties, but their primary similarity was in the *absence* of an institutional response to the demographic changes taking place. These inspectors have a number of tasks, but among them they enforce zoning codes in residential areas in the county. They spend much of their day driving through neighborhoods, responding to complaints. These complaints are often immigration related, for example, overcrowding of housing (unrelated families living in the same house) or private businesses being run out of homes. Interactions with actual people are quite limited; inspectors may try to determine, for instance, if persons living in the same house are related (under county codes, there are no limits on the numbers of related individuals who may live in a single-family home, but quite strict limitations on the numbers of unrelated people inhabiting the same home). To determine who lives in a home, inspectors will knock on the door, asking their questions in English. None of the field staff in Fairfax County speaks any language other than English. The interviewees in the county mentioned no intention to hire such staff, even though many of the complaints zoning inspectors receive are immigrant related. Translation services are uneven and ad hoc. One zoning inspector interviewed mentioned that a secretary at the county's zoning office spoke Spanish, and if the language barrier proved insurmountable, he might call her and ask her act as an intermediary. Of course, if she was not there, or if the interactions were in any of the other several dozen languages spoken in homes in the county, then the possibilities for misunderstandings between the inspector and residents were high. If these limited interactions did not resolve the issue, then the complaint would move onward to an administrative or civil court. In short, unlike librarians, zoning inspectors work with no demographic data, have not hired any new staff to interact with recent arrivals, and have no sustained contact with county residents in the course of their jobs. As a result, despite the kinds of complaints received, the Zoning Department in Fairfax County continues to act, essentially, as if the county had undergone no demographic changes at all.

Different bureaucratic cultures lead to different outcomes for immigrant incorporation. Regulatory agencies like the Zoning Department see their tasks as the even-handed administration and enforcement of rules, have minimal relationships with the objects of their responsibility, and respond minimally to demographic changes. Service bureaucracies such as libraries, for their part, may incorporate immigrants; that is, they treat immigrants, whatever their legal status, as clients, and seek to build relationships with them. To effectively communicate with immigrant communities, they tend, unlike their regulatory counterparts, to hire staff from among the immigrant population. The differential response to demographic change has very different outcomes for immigrant incorporation.

Conclusion

This chapter has explored three sets of questions dealing with racial and ethnic diversity in suburbia, regarding racial sorting, ethnic organization, and the responses of local government actors. I started out by hypothesizing that the suburbanization of immigration would lend itself to different dynamics for each of these three questions than what many analysts have assumed from past experience.

From the metropolitan Washington case material sketched out above, it appears a reconsideration of these questions is indeed overdue. First, racial sorting in suburban Washington appears to play out differently across racial and ethnic groups. Immigrants sort out spatially differently from the native born, and Latinos and Asian Americans sort out spatially differently from blacks. Second, variance in racial sorting shapes the opportunity for organization among both native-born and immigrant racial and ethnic minorities. Forms of organization are correlated to the density of residential patterns (or spatial sorting), and more generally are likely to reflect the density of housing, transportation, and other infrastructure. It's also the case that ethnic organization in suburbia will likely reflect, in part, differences in racial sorting. For instance, given greater racial sorting for native-born blacks, blacks will pursue organizational strategies that maximize the advantages of that sorting. However, ethnic organization in suburbia will occur even in the absence of racial sorting. For instance, if Latinos and Asian Americans sort out differently from native-born blacks, their organizational strategies will correspond to their spatial diffusion in suburban areas and differ from that of native-born blacks. Last, it appears ethnic organization reflects physical and spatial differences between suburban and central city contexts. Suburban ethnic organizations manifest adaptations to the more spatially dispersed context of suburbs.

Third, local policies change in response to ethnic and racial diversity propelled by advocacy and anticipatory responses. On the advocacy side, for example, new residents may ask a school board to develop new after-school programs to teach English as a second language; or as an example of negative feedback, established residents may lobby or elect officials to place a moratorium on permits for additional multifamily or denser housing in a jurisdiction. Examples of anticipatory response might include cases, as we saw in the Washington area, of individuals working in government agencies—teachers, principals, city planners, affordable housing program managers—

who may respond directly to the needs of their clientele by initiating new policies even before any demand for these policies is transmitted through the electoral political system. As outlined above, suburban adaptations are likely to vary systematically across types of administrative agencies in suburban jurisdictions. "Service bureaucracies" will be more likely to adopt diversity-friendly policy changes than will "administrative bureaucracies."

Each of these findings runs against the grain of much of the literature on the incorporation of racial/ethnic minorities and immigrants in the United States. At least some of this, I suspect, is due to the persistence in thinking of these groups as residing in residentially compact neighborhoods with dense social networks, an assumption that is less likely to be true now that half of all immigrants and almost that percentage of those of Latino or Asian descent are living in suburbs, where for the most part they are more dispersed and their social networks are more far-flung as well. These changes in residential patterns, ethnic mobilization, and community response in suburbia require a reconsideration of the ways migrants and communities mutually negotiate the processes of immigrant incorporation. In many metropolitan areas in the United States, the daily negotiations between migrants and local receiving communities are shaped by their suburban setting, and shape them in turn. In short, this chapter is a plea for the consideration of context when developing analyses of the processes of immigrant incorporation, and it is a call to pay greater attention to the places where many immigrants now call home: suburbia.

Notes

1. Reynolds Farley, "The Changing Distribution of Negroes within Metropolitan Areas: The Emergence of Black Suburbs," *American Journal of Sociology* 75 (January 1970): 512–29; Harold Rose, *Black Suburbanization* (Cambridge, Mass.: Ballinger, 1976).

2. Mark Schneider and Thomas Phelan, "Black Suburbanization in the 1980s," *Demography* 30, no. 2 (May 1993): 269–79; John M. Stahura, "Changing Patterns of Suburban Racial Composition, 1970–1980," *Urban Affairs Quarterly* 23, no. 3 March 1988: 448–60; John Logan and Mark Schneider, "Racial Segregation and Racial Change in American Suburbs, 1970–1980," *American Journal of Sociology* 89, no. 4 (1984): 874–88.

3. William Frey and Douglas Geverdt, "Changing Suburban Demographics: Beyond the 'Black-White, City-Suburb' Typology," paper presented at Suburban Racial Change Conference, Harvard University, Cambridge, Mass., March 28, 1998; Nancy Denton and Richard Alba, "Suburban Racial and Ethnic Change at the Neighborhood Level: The Declining Number of All-White Neighborhoods," paper presented at Sub-

urban Racial Change Conference, Harvard University, Cambridge, Mass., March 28, 1998.

4. Doug Massey and Nancy Denton, "Suburbanization and Segregation in U.S. Metropolitan Areas," *American Journal of Sociology* 94 (1988): 592–626.

5. Some important recent scholarship on racial and ethnic issues draws on field-work in suburbia but makes little of the fact. See, e.g., Leland Saito, *Race and Politics: Asian Americans, Latinos, and Whites in a Los Angeles Suburb* (Urbana: University of Illinois Press, 1998); Timothy Fong, *The First Suburban Chinatown: The Remaking of Monterey Park* (Philadelphia: Temple University Press, 1994); John Horton, *The Politics of Diversity: Immigration, Resistance and Change in Monterey Park, California* (Philadelphia: Temple University Press, 1995); and Sarah Mahler, *American Dreaming: Immigrant Life on the Margins* (Princeton, N.J.: Princeton University Press, 1995). Though all these books describe immigration and ethnic relations in suburbia, there is little analysis of what might make ethnic politics in suburbia different from the experience described in the traditional urban case study.

6. A. Dianne Schmidley and Campbell Gibson, *Profile of the Foreign Born Population in the United States,* Current Population Reports, U.S. Census Bureau (Washington, D.C.: U.S. Government Printing Office, 1999).

7. Jesse McKinnon and Karen Humes, *Black Population in the United States, March 1999,* Current Population Reports, U.S. Census Bureau (Washington, D.C.: U.S. Government Printing Office, 2000); Karen Humes and Jesse McKinnon, *Asian and Pacific Islander Population in the United States: March 1999,* Current Population Reports, U.S. Census Bureau (Washington, D.C.: U.S. Government Printing Office, 2000); http://www.census.gov/populationsocdemo/hispanic/cps99/tab16-1.txt.

8. Ernest W. Burgess, "The Growth of the City: An Introduction to a Research Program," in *The City,* ed. Ernest W. Burgess and Roderick D. McKenzie (Chicago: University of Chicago Press, 1967; orig. pub. 1925), 47–62; reprinted from *Publications of the American Sociological Society, Annual* 18 (1924): 85–97.

9. Milla Alihan, *Social Ecology: A Critical Analysis* (New York: Columbia University Press, 1938); Homer Hoyt, *The Structure and Growth of Residential Neighborhoods in American Cities* (Washington, D.C.: Federal Housing Administration, 1939); Homer Hoyt, *Where the Rich and the Poor People Live* (Washington, D.C.: Urban Land Institute Press, 1966).

10. See William Alonso, *Location and Land Use: Toward a General Theory of Land Rent* (Cambridge, Mass.: Harvard University Press, 1964); Richard F. Muth, *Cities and Housing: The Spatial Pattern of Residential Land Use* (Chicago: University of Chicago Press, 1969); and Edwin S. Mills, *Studies in the Structure of the Urban Economy* (Baltimore: Johns Hopkins University Press, 1972). Also see Arthur C. Nelson and Thomas W. Sanchez, "Debunking the Exurban Myth: A Comparison of Suburban Households," *Housing Policy Debate* 10, no. 3 (1999): 689–709.

11. E. Heikkila, D. Dale-Johnson, P. Gordon, J. I. Kim, R. B. Peiser, and H. W. Richardson, "What Happened to the CBD-Distance Gradient? Land Values in a Polycentric City," *Environment and Planning A* 21 (1989): 221–32; Daniel P. McMillen and John F. McDonald, "Employment Subcenters and Land Values in a Polycentric Urban Area: The Case of Chicago," *Environment and Planning A* 22 (1990): 1561–74.

12. Charles Tiebout, "A Pure Theory of Local Expenditures," *Journal of Political Economy* 64, no. 5 (1956): 416–24.

13. Ibid., 418.

14. Mark Schneider, "Intermunicipal Competition, Budget-Maximizing Bureaucrats, and the Level of Suburban Competition," *American Journal of Political Science* 33, no. 3 (1989): 612–28.

15. Ibid.; Mark Schneider, *The Competitive City: The Political Economy of Suburbia* (Pittsburgh: University of Pittsburgh Press, 1989).

16. David Lowery and William E. Lyons, "The Impact of Jurisdictional Boundaries: An Individual Level Test of the Tiebout Model," *Journal of Politics* 48, no. 1 (1989): 73–97; Andrew Padon, "Pseudo-Public Goods and Urban Development: A Game Theoretical Model of Local Public Goods," *Journal of Urban Affairs* 21, no. 2 (1999): 213–35.

17. Anthony Downs, *Opening Up the Suburbs: An Urban Strategy for America* (New Haven, Conn.: Yale University Press, 1973); Michael N. Danielson, *The Politics of Exclusion* (New York: Columbia University Press, 1976); Peter Dreier, John Mollenkopf, and Todd Swanstrom, *Place Matters: Metropolitics for the Twenty-First Century* (Lawrence: University Press of Kansas, 2001); Paul Lewis, *Shaping Suburbia: How Political Institutions Organize Urban Development* (Pittsburgh: University of Pittsburgh Press, 1996).

18. Reynolds Farley, "The Changing Distribution of Negroes within Metropolitan Areas: The Emergence of Black Suburbs," *American Journal of Sociology* 75 (1970): 512–29; Harold Rose, *Black Suburbanization* (Cambridge, Mass.: Ballinger, 1976).

19. Douglas Massey, "Ethnic Residential Segregation: A Theoretical Synthesis and Empirical Review," *Sociology and Social Research* 69 (1985): 315–50.

20. John R. Logan, Richard D. Alba, and Shu-Yin Leung, "Minority Access to White Suburbs: A Multiregional Comparison," *Social Forces* 74, no. 3 (1996): 851–81. Also see Richard Alba and Victor Nee, *Remaking the American Mainstream: Assimilation and Contemporary Immigration* (Cambridge, Mass.: Harvard University Press, 2003) and James Gimpel, *Separate Destinations: Migration, Immigration, and the Politics of Places* (Ann Arbor: University of Michigan Press, 1999).

21. John Logan, *America's Newcomers,* Lewis Mumford Center Working Paper (Albany: Lewis Mumford Center for Comparative Urban and Regional Research, State University of New York at Albany, 2003).

22. Logan, Alba, and Yin Leung, "Minority Access."

23. Douglas Massey and Mitchell Eggers, "The Ecology of Inequality: Minorities and the Concentration of Poverty," *American Journal of Sociology* 95 (1990): 1153–88; Douglas S. Massey and Nancy A. Denton, *American Apartheid: Segregation and the Making of the Underclass* (Cambridge, Mass.: Harvard University Press, 1993); John Logan, "Ethnic Diversity Grows, Neighborhood Integration Lags," in *Redefining Urban and Suburban: Evidence for Census 2000,* ed. Bruce Katz and Robert E. Lane (Washington, D.C.: Brookings Institution Press, 2003); William H. Frey, "Melting Pot Suburbs: A Study of Suburban Diversity," in *Redefining Urban and Suburban,* ed. Katz and Lane.

24. Min Zhou, *New York's Chinatown: The Socioeconomic Potential of an Urban Enclave* (Philadelphia: Temple University Press, 1992); Frey, "Melting Pot Suburbs"; Logan, "Ethnic Diversity Grows"; John Iceland, "Beyond Black and White: Metropolitan Residential Segregation in Multi-Ethnic America," *Social Science Research* 33, no. 2 (2004): 248–71.

25. Xavier Briggs and Elizabeth Mueller, with Mercer Sullivan, *From Neighborhood to Community: Evidence on the Social Effects of Community Development* (New

York: Community Development Research Center, 1997); Prudence Brown, "Comprehensive Neighborhood-Based Initiatives," *Cityscape: A Journal of Policy Development and Research* 2, no. 2 (1996): 161–76; Robert Chaskin, "Building Community Capacity: A Definitional Framework and Case Studies from a Comprehensive Community Initiative," *Urban Affairs Review* (Sage Publications), 2001; Lorrie Frasure and Linda Faye Williams, "Civic Disparities and Civic Differences: Ethno-Racial Civic Engagement in the United States," in *The Democracy Collaborative,* Civic Engagement Working Paper 3, Research/Action Brief Prepared for Knight Foundation (College Park: University of Maryland, 2002); Lorrie Frasure and Linda Faye Williams, *Civic and Political Disparities in the United States: The Effect of Race/Ethnicity, Class, Gender, Age, and Geographic Context,* Research/Action Brief Prepared for Annie E. Casey Foundation (College Park: University of Maryland, 2004).

26. Robert Dahl, *Who Governs? Democracy and Power in an American City* (New Haven, Conn.: Yale University Press, 1961). Also see Raymond E. Wolfinger, "The Development and Persistence of Ethnic Voting," *American Political Science Review* 59, no. 4 (1965): 896–908; Raymond T. Wolfinger, *The Politics of Progress* (Englewood Cliffs, N.J.: Prentice-Hall Press, 1974); and Nelson W. Polsby, *Community Power and Political Theory,* 2nd ed. (New Haven, Conn.: Yale University Press, 1980). But see Pinderhughes for a critique of this model regarding African Americans; Dianne Pinderhughes, *Race and Ethnicity in Chicago Politics: A Reexamination of Pluralist Theory* (Urbana: University of Illinois Press, 1987).

27. Gimpel, *Separate Destinations;* Alba and Nee, *Remaking the American Mainstream.*

28. John Mollenkopf and Gary Gerstle, eds., *E Pluribus Unum? Contemporary and Historical Perspectives on Immigrant Political Incorporation* (New York: Russell Sage Foundation, 2001); Dennis R. Judd and Todd Swanstrom, *City Politics: Private Power and Public Policy,* 3rd ed. (New York: Longman, 2002); Michael Jones-Correa, *Between Two Nations: The Political Predicament of Latinos in New York City* (Ithaca, N.Y.: Cornell University Press, 1998); Michael Jones-Correa, ed., *Governing American Cities Interethnic Coalitions, Competitions and Conflict* (New York: Russell Sage Foundation, 2001); Massey and Eggers, "Ecology of Inequality"; Massey and Denton, *American Apartheid;* William J. Wilson, *The Truly Disadvantaged: The Inner City, the Urban Underclass and Public Policy* (Chicago: University of Chicago Press, 1987); William J. Wilson, *When Work Disappears: The World of the New Urban Poor,* reprint ed. (New York: Vintage Books, 1996).

29. Leland Saito, *Race and Politics: Asian Americans, Latinos, and Whites in a Los Angeles Suburb* (Urbana: University of Illinois Press, 1998); Fong, *First Suburban Chinatown;* Horton, *Politics of Diversity;* Sarah Mahler, *American Dreaming: Immigrant Life on the Margins* (Princeton, N.J.: Princeton University Press, 1995).

30. Wilbur Zelinsky and Barrett A. Lee, "Heterolocalism: An Alternative Model of Sociospatial Behavior of Immigrant Ethnic Communities," *International Journal of Population Geography* 4 (1998): 1–18.

31. Also see Samantha Friedman, Ivan Cheung, Marie Price, and Audrey Singer, "Washington's Newcomers: Mapping a New City of Immigration," Center for Washington Area Studies Paper, July 13, 2001; Michael Jones-Correa, "Reshaping the American Dream: Immigrants and the Politics of the New Suburbs," paper presented at American Political Science Association Meeting, Boston, August 30–September 1, 2002.

32. Cathy J. Cohen and Michael C. Dawson, "Neighborhood Poverty and African American Politics," *American Political Science Review* 87 (1993): 286–302.

33. Robert Huckfeldt and John Sprague, "Networks in Context: The Social Flow of Political Information," *American Political Science Review* 81, no. 4 (1987): 1197–1216; Robert R. Huckfeldt, "Political Participation and the Neighborhood Social Context," *American Journal of Political Science* 23 (1979): 579–92.

34. Paul Peterson, *City Limits* (Chicago: University of Chicago Press, 1981).

35. Juliet Gainsborough, *Fenced Off: The Suburbanization of American Politics* (Washington, D.C.: Georgetown University Press, 2001).

36. Chris Jenkins, "Picking Up a Spanish Influence," *Washington Post,* December 11, 2000; Ruben Castañeda, "Language Differences a Challenge for Courts," *Washington Post,* June 21, 2001; Eugene Meyer, "Majority Black District Proposed for Prince George's," *Washington Post,* October 10, 2001; Jo Becker, "Diversity Warrants Change, Panel Says," *Washington Post,* December 20, 2001.

37. Fong, *First Suburban Chinatown;* Stacy Harwood and Myers Dowell, "The Dynamics of Immigration and Local Governance in Santa Ana: Neighborhood Activism, Overcrowding and Land-Use Policy," *Policy Studies Journal* 30 (2002): 70–91; Neema Kudva and Pierre Clavel, "The New Melting Pot: How City Governments Respond to Increasing Diversity," paper presented at Association of Collegiate Schools of Planning Annual Conference, Baltimore, November 2002; Michael Jones-Correa, "Racial and Ethnic Diversity and the Politics of Education in Suburbia," paper presented at annual meeting of American Political Science Association, Chicago, September 2–5, 2004; Michael Jones-Correa, "The Bureaucratic Incorporation of Immigrants in Suburbia," paper presented at conference on "Immigration to the United States: New Sources and Destinations," Russell Sage Foundation, New York, February 2–3, 2005.

38. Dahl, *Who Governs?* Wolfinger, "Development and Persistence of Ethnic Voting."

39. Michael Lipsky, *Street-Level Bureaucracy: Dilemmas of the Individual in Public Services* (New York: Russell Sage Foundation, 1980); James Q. Wilson, *Bureaucracy: What Government Agencies Do and Why They Do It* (New York: Basic Books, 1989); Marissa Martino Golden, *What Motivates Bureaucrats? Politics and Administration during the Reagan Years* (New York: Columbia University Press, 2000); Steven Maynard-Moody and Michael Musheno, *Cops, Teachers, Counselors: Stories from the Front Lines of Public Service* (Ann Arbor: University of Michigan Press, 2003).

40. Martha Derthick, *Policymaking for Social Security* (Washington, D.C.: Brookings Institution Press, 1979), 30–31.

41. Jones-Correa, "Bureaucratic Incorporation of Immigrants."

42. These are 2000 data from the U.S. Census Bureau.

43. Frey, "Melting Pot Suburbs," 175, table 9A-1.

44. This research was supported by a grant from the Russell Sage Foundation and a fellowship from the Woodrow Wilson International Center for Scholars.

45. This field research on the impact of racial/ethnic change in suburbia, conducted with Lorrie Frasure and Junsik Youn, has resulted in several preliminary papers, on demographic change and its implications in suburbia (Jones-Correa, "Reshaping the American Dream"), on the response of suburban educational systems in the metropolitan Washington area to changes in the region's racial/ethnic populations (Jones-Correa, "Racial and Ethnic Diversity"), and on the 'bureaucratic incorporation' of racial/ethnic minorities in suburbia (Jones-Correa, "Bureaucratic Incorporation of Immigrants").

46. Marie Price, Samantha Friedman, Ivan Cheung, and Audrey Singer, "Mapping

Washington's Recent Immigrants: Residential Choices and Sociospatial Networks," paper presented at Geography Mini-Conference, George Washington University, Washington, 2002.

47. Audrey Singer, Samantha Friedman, Ivan Cheung, and Marie Price, "The World in a Zip Code: Greater Washington, D.C., as a New Region of Immigration," Center on Urban and Metropolitan Policy, Brookings Institution, Washington, 2002.

48. In addition to interviews with public officials, representatives of public agencies, and directors of nongovernmental organizations, the research team also interviewed representatives of Chinese, Korean, Latin American, and Iranian organizations.

49. Cf. Jones-Correa, *Between Two Nations.*

50. Jones-Correa, "Bureaucratic Incorporation," develops this argument in greater detail.

2

The Placelessness of Migrant Filipina Domestic Workers

Rhacel Salazar Parreñas

In global cities, widening disparities distinguish the lifestyles of the haves and have-nots. These inequalities manifest in the normalization of services between members of the haves, the productive service class of lawyers, accountants, and corporate consultants, and of the have-not class of personal service workers—the manicurists, housekeepers, and launderers—who cater to their needs. Decisionmakers of global capitalism have come to increasingly depend on low-wage migrant workers to provide services from manicures to housecleaning.[1] Made affordable by the low wages of workers, personal services that used to be luxuries are now necessities, leading the political economist Saskia Sassen to reflect on how the intensified inequalities in global cities far exceeds segmentation to encompass peripheralization. As she states: "We have long known about segmented labor markets, but the manufacturing decline and the kind of devaluing of nonprofessional workers in leading industries that we see today in these cities go beyond segmentation and in fact represent an instance of peripheralization."[2]

49

In this chapter, I examine the spatial integration of one group of these pe-ripheralized personal service workers in global cities: migrant Filipina do-mestic workers. Understanding their integration in global cities as migrant workers requires us to interrogate not just their social relations with, for in-stance, employers but also their negotiation of urban spaces. Space is a key lens for examining migrant experiences in host communities.

On any given day, approximately 2,531 workers leave the Philippines as overseas contract workers.[3] They join the estimated 7.38 million Filipinos who work and reside in 187 destination countries and territories.[4] Most of them are women who seek employment outside the country as domestic workers.[5] By domestic work, I broadly refer to the work of doing cleaning and caring services in private households. Filipino migrant women toil in private households in cities throughout the world, including Hong Kong, Taipei, Tokyo, Los Angeles, New York, Paris, and Rome, to name just a few. In looking at the case of migrant Filipina domestic workers in Rome and Los Angeles, I argue that the peripheralization in the labor market of which Sassen speaks manifests in the use of space and place by peripheralized mi-grants in the global city. The use of urban space by migrant Filipina do-mestic workers reflects not just their negotiation of the host urban commu-nity but also the relations of power that shape their everyday life both at and outside work.

In some capacity, the spatial peripheralization of migrant Filipina domes-tic workers emerges in their residential segregation on the urban periphery —poor migrants are pushed toward the urban periphery by gentrification and the escalating prices of real estate.[6] But by peripheralization, I speak less of their residential patterns of settlement or, in other words, their place in the city. This is because many migrant Filipina domestic workers are live-in workers who reside with their employers in urban centers.[7] As such, they tend to be dispersed throughout the global city. For instance, in Rome, Fil-ipinos reside in all twenty districts of the city. More precisely, by spatial pe-ripheralization, I refer to the limits in spatial action in everyday life and the social inequalities that shape the use of space.[8] I speak of the social bound-aries that embody the experience of spatiality with the notion that "the par-tition of space" reflects social inequalities.[9]

As I show in this chapter, the everyday practice of migrant life for Filip-ina domestic workers mirrors their spatial peripheralization by race and class.[10] We see this not only in their limited spatial movements in the work-place but also in the control of their actions in the public spaces that they occupy during their days off. Thus, the mobility—or in this case the limited mobility—of foreign domestic workers in the city reflects social inequalities of race and class. As the geographers Brenda Yeoh and Shirlena Huang have found in Singapore, employers limit the access of domestic workers to public spaces by denying them a day off or by choosing the activities that they would do during their days off. The spatial peripheralization that confronts Filipina domestic workers in Singapore usually manifests in the extreme form of their complete segregation in the private sphere. Moreover, of those with the actual freedom of a day off, spatial peripheralization also emerges in their concentration in "marginal, residual spaces and places associated with outsiders."[11] This limited temporal and spatial incorporation in public spaces confirms their racial subordinate status.

My examination of the peripheralization of migrant Filipina domestic workers stems primarily from the seminal work of the sociologist Judith Rollins on the spatial deference imposed on domestic workers by their employers, meaning the "unequal rights of the domestic and the employer to the space around the other's body and the controlling of the domestic's use of house space."[12] According to Rollins, domestic workers do not have the ability to move around freely in the home of employers. Instead, they have to spatially defer to them by making themselves invisible when their services are no longer needed. In this chapter, I extend the work of Rollins to show how the "spatial deference" of domestic workers in the workplace extends to the level of society. Albeit coming from the opposite direction, my analysis converges with the call by the social geographer Laura Liu for the "inclusion of immigration into place-based studies of race."[13] Conversely, I insist that the consideration of the place of migrants in urban spaces could likewise lead us to a better understanding of migrant processes and the ways that race and class constitute such processes.

As I show, race and class shape the politics of settlement for migrant Filipina domestic workers and determine their spatial incorporation in Rome and Los Angeles, cities with two of the largest populations of migrant Filipinos in Italy and the United States. As I had addressed in an earlier discussion, migrant Filipina domestic workers experience the dislocation of nonbelonging upon settlement, meaning that they experience settlement with a sense of constant discomfort in the host society.[14] In this chapter, I give greater emphasis to the spatial dynamics that characterize the dislocation of nonbelonging for migrant Filipina domestic workers and in so doing illustrate how the use of space as a framework for analysis magnifies the significance of race and class inequities in understanding their experience. Outside the workplace, two distinct sources of social exclusion engender feelings of nonbelonging among migrant Filipina domestic workers. For women in Los Angeles, it stems from the class stratification in the Filipino migrant community; and for women in Rome, it results from the racial prejudice in dominant Italian society.

I look at the politics of space by addressing two questions. First, how does geographical integration influence and shape feelings of incorporation for migrant Filipina domestic workers? Second, how do the politics of space and spatial movements extend our understanding of migrant settlement? It is in addressing these questions that I identified "placelessness" to define the spatial integration of migrant Filipina domestics in both the public and private spheres, or in other words in both their spaces of leisure (public) and work (private). By placelessness, I do not mean to imply that these women are nomadic. Instead, by placelessness, I refer to the absence of a fixed geographic space that migrant Filipina domestic workers could call their own as well as the denial of private spaces from them, spaces where they are free from "spatial deference" or surveillance either inside or outside the workplace. In short, placelessness refers to the social reality that migrant Filipina domestic workers are *without place*.

A quick example of what I mean by placelessness would, for instance, refer to the working-class niches occupied by migrant Filipina domestic workers in Los Angeles as being rarely geographically fixed spaces but instead tending to only be fleeting encounters in public spaces such as buses. Another example would be the places of gathering of migrant Filipina domestic workers in Rome being not just segregated from Italians but also being outside their view. Generally, placelessness refers to the spatial incorporation of migrant Filipina domestic workers as being constrained so as not to impose on the spaces occupied by dominant members of society, including their employers, middle-class members of the Filipino American community, and finally Italians. Notably, experiences of placelessness in dominant spaces of society are generally true among migrants. For instance, scholars have repeatedly shown the formation of geographically based ethnic enclaves as a place-based strategy used by migrants to counter their exclusion from dominant spaces in the host society.[15] Yet the shelter of an enclave has not been made available to migrant Filipina domestic workers in either Rome or Los Angeles. Consequently, they seldom can retreat from their experiences of placelessness in a particular geographic area free from public scrutiny. Still, migrant Filipina domestic workers—even if without a geographic place of their own—negotiate their marginality in urban spaces by creating a sense of community from their fleeting encounters with one another in urban spaces, whether at bus stops, in parks, or on buses.

My discussion of the placelessness of migrant Filipina domestic workers begins with a brief description of the cities of Rome and Los Angeles. I then describe my methodology and the characteristics of my sample. After which, I proceed to describe the placelessness of migrant Filipina domestic workers, first in the private sphere of the workplace and second in the public sphere. Due to sharp distinctions in the social characteristics of the Filipino immigrant communities of Rome and Los Angeles—with the former composed mostly of low-wage workers and the latter more diversified by class—I address the experience of placelessness in each city separately. In illustrating the "spatial deference" that embodies the integration of migrant Filipina domestic workers in Rome and Los Angeles, this chapter establishes how their spatial incorporation mirrors what Sassen describes as the labor market peripheralization of the increasing number of personal service migrant workers in global cities.[16]

Rome and Los Angeles

Filipino migration into Italy officially began in the 1970s, but Filipinos did not become a visible presence in Rome until the 1980s. By the late 1990s, Filipinos had become the largest migrant group in the city, representing close to 12 percent of the foreign population of Rome.[17] Local community members estimate the number of Filipinos to be close to 100,000, which is significantly higher than the figure of 24,000 given by the minister of the interior in 1996.[18] Since 1998, the annual deployment of overseas contract workers from the Philippines to Italy has reached 20,000 a year.[19] The destination of half these workers is Rome. Not being concentrated in any geographic area in Rome, Filipinos are residentially dispersed throughout the city. The largest proportion of them, 17.8 percent, reside in the northern periphery of Rome and in the areas close to the central train station, Termini, reaching 9 percent in the first district and 11 percent in the second district. The rest of the population is dispersed throughout the twenty districts of the city, with approximately 5 percent of the migrant population located in each of the rest of the districts.[20]

Most Filipinos in Rome are long-term legal residents of Italy. As a receiving state, Italy has generously granted amnesty to undocumented migrants, for example, awarding it in 1987, 1990, and 1995. In Italy, legal migrants hold a *permesso di soggiorno* (permit to stay), which grants them temporary residency. With its length of stay extending to seven years, residence permits for most Filipino migrants are renewable contingent on the sponsorship of an employer, the regular employment of the migrant, and finally the continual filing of income tax by the employer. Though the residence permit, with very few exceptions, generally restricts the labor market activities of migrants to domestic work, it grants them access to social and health services and rights to family reunification with spouses and children under the age of eighteen.[21] Notably, these rights were bestowed on migrants only upon the implementation of the 1989–90 Martelli Law.[22]

Although most Filipinos in Rome are documented workers, many societal constraints promote feelings of nonmembership among them. One factor is their restricted social integration in Italy, which is reflected in their avoidance of public spaces of leisure. For example, Filipinos are unlikely to go to the movies on their own in Rome, that is, without their employers or young wards. My own experiences also demonstrate the social segregation of Filipinos. To my discomfort, Italians often vocalized their surprise or just stared at me when I entered high-end clothing stores or even neighborhood Italian restaurants. I was not accorded this treatment when accompanied by my white friends—that is, Italians or Americans—for their presence established my identity as a "tourist" whose purchasing power abated my racial "Othering" as a Filipino. Though many Filipino domestic workers told me that they restrict their leisure activities in public social spaces so as to minimize their expenses (e.g., not eating in Italian restaurants), without doubt, the "self-imposed" restriction of leisure space among them is also influenced by their construction as perpetual foreigners in Italy.

In Rome, 98.5 percent of Filipinos are in domestic work.[23] In recent years, migrant Filipinos have ventured into other work, but for the most part they remain highly concentrated in low-wage service work, with most of them still in domestic service.[24] In contrast, Filipino migrants in Los Angeles occupy more diverse sectors of the labor market. With its roots predominantly tracing back to the post-1965 migration of professionals into the United States, the Filipino migrant community of Los Angeles has had considerable access to mainstream jobs. Marked class distinctions divide the Filipino community of Los Angeles. The class cleavage of the Filipino community can be described as bipolar, divided between the haves (the middle class) and the have-nots (the working class). From the perspective of domestic workers, the Filipino migrant community is centered on the middle class, which is a group not limited to those in the professional managerial class but also includes those employed in low-level professional occupations, such as records processors and office clerks.

Looking briefly at the employment characteristics and the geographical incorporation of migrant Filipinos gives us a glimpse at the class cleavage that defines the Filipino migrant community of Los Angeles. Migrant Filipinos are concentrated in wage employment.[25] The employment profile of the Filipino population is quite diverse, as it includes managerial, high- and low-level professional, blue-collar, and service workers. In Los Angeles, 25 percent of them hold managerial and professional jobs, an equal percentage hold low-level professional occupations, and the rest are in lower-end service and manufacturing jobs.[26] In its diversity, a class cleavage has come to define the migrant community of Filipinos. The community is distinctly divided between the haves and the have-nots, with migrants obtaining office work (even if low-level) considered the haves and migrants in low-level service occupations (e.g., hotel and domestic workers) included among the have-nots. The concentration of Filipinos in the wage labor market develops class hierarchies determining relations in the community. In the hierarchy of paid employment, domestic workers are clearly at the bottom. It is from this perspective that domestics view their "place" in the community.

Filipinos are the second-largest Asian immigrant group in Los Angeles. Despite this fact, they still do not have a visible ethnic enclave economy, meaning "a locational cluster of business firms whose owners and employees are (largely) co-ethnics."[27] Unlike most other Asian immigrant groups in Los Angeles, the Filipino ethnic economy is distributed throughout the city and is not contained within an identifiable enclave. The absence of a Filipino ethnic enclave economy can be attributed largely to their concentration in wage employment.

The geographical constitution of the Filipino community is more discernable by residential patterns. Residential clusters of Filipinos have developed in both the inner city and suburbs. Filipinos are the dominant ethnic group in the suburbs of Carson and West Covina. In the inner city, community insiders identify a few neighborhoods in the vicinity of downtown, for example, certain blocks of Temple Street, as Filipino Town. This neighborhood houses a small number of video rental stores and markets that cater to its predominantly Filipino residents. The other residential clusters of the community include Eagle Rock, Echo Park, and extend outside Los Angeles to Cerritos and Long Beach.

Interestingly, the class cleavage in the Filipino community of Los Angeles cannot be easily demarcated according to residential patterns. For most other Asian ethnic groups, inner-city residents are usually more disadvantaged than their counterparts in the suburbs. Yet urban planners have noticed that "inner-city Filipinos are the exception to this pattern."[28] Middleclass and working-class Filipinos reside alongside each other in both the inner city and suburbs. Because sharp geographic boundaries do not reflect the class division of the Filipino population, a working-class spatial niche does not cushion the entrance of migrant Filipina domestics into the community. Thus, in spaces of the community, migrant Filipina domestic workers, as members of the have-nots, experience the community from a contentious location, one that always carries a keen awareness of their lesser success than the haves of the community.

Notably, in Los Angeles, many of my interviewees are permanent residents of the United States, a status they obtained via marriage or labor certification. Yet they still are ambivalent about their permanent settlement in the United States. The opportunities in the United States—at the very least the possibility shown by the professional managerial class—give hope for mobility and instill desires for permanent settlement. However, the realities of not having similar opportunities as the middle class also enforce sentiments of temporary settlement. Significantly, the realities of domestic work seem to outweigh the possibilities of class mobility, for most of my interviewees claim to only be temporary migrants in the United States.

Methodology

This chapter is based primarily on open-ended interviews that I conducted with forty-six female domestic workers in Rome and twenty-six female domestic workers Los Angeles. I based my study on these two cities because they are two main destinations of Filipina migrants. To protect the anonymity of informants, I used pseudonyms for all my interviews. I taperecorded and fully transcribed each of my interviews, which were mostly conducted in Tagalog or Tag-lish (a hybrid of Tagalog and English) and then translated into English. I did not share my interviews with informants, who had knowingly volunteered to participate in my study. Notably, none had asked to see the interviews, but many requested and expressed their desire to be video-recorded instead of tape-recorded during our interview. Without adequate resources, I could not accommodate their request.

A little less than five months in Rome in 1995 and 1996 gave me ample time to collect forty-six in-depth interviews with Filipina domestic workers. The interviews ranged from one and a half to three hours in length. I collected an unsystematic sample of research participants by using chain and snowball referrals. To diversify my sample, I made sure to solicit research participants from various sites in the community (e.g., church, parks, and plazas). In Los Angeles, I collected a smaller sample of twenty-six in-depth interviews with Filipina domestic workers. These interviews range from one and a half to three hours in length. I collected these interviews between April and September 1996. My smaller sample is due to the fact that, unlike their counterparts in Rome, Filipina migrants in Los Angeles are not concentrated in the informal service sector. Another factor contributing to the smaller sample in Los Angeles is their relatively small representation among domestic workers. Although present in the ethnic community, Filipinas are but a minority among the larger group of Latina domestic workers in the area. This is not surprising because Latinos represent the largest racial-ethnic population in Los Angeles.

In the field research site of Los Angeles, tapping into the community began with the network of my mother's acquaintances, friends, and relatives. This network—which is based in a Catholic parish heavily attended by Filipinos, two different hometown associations, the Philippine consulate in Los Angeles, and the ethnic stores frequently visited by my mother—led me to a group of women that represented different regions of the Philippines. To further diversify my sample, I posted flyers in various ethnic enclave businesses. Two women responded to the flyers. Utilizing networks of domestic workers, the sample of interviewees was collected unsystematically through a snowball method. Participant observation provided a gateway to the community as I attended meetings of Filipino labor groups, the occasional Filipino town fiestas, and the more frequent Filipino family parties, and spent time with domestic workers at their own and at their employers' homes.

Characteristics of the Sample

Although there are distinguishing characteristics between my interviewees in Rome and Los Angeles, they also share many social characteristics. Differences between them include region of origin and median age. Interestingly, there are more similarities between them. First, most of them are legal residents of their respective host societies. In Italy, thirty of the forty-six interviewees have a *permesso di soggiorno,* which, as noted above, grants them temporary residency for seven years and allows them to sponsor the migration of their families. Nonetheless, most of my interviewees have chosen not to sponsor their children. Most maintain transnational families. In Los Angeles, fifteen of the twenty-six interviewees have legal documents. Most acquired permanent legal status via marriage or the sponsorship of a wealthy employer. Yet many have not been able to sponsor the migration of dependents because they had been caught in the legal bind of obtaining legal status only after their children had reached adult age, when they are no longer eligible for immediate family reunification.[29]

Another similarity between my interviewees in Rome and Los Angeles is their high level of educational attainment. Most of them have acquired some years of postsecondary training in the Philippines. In Rome, my interviewees include twenty-three women with college degrees, twelve women with some years of college or postsecondary vocational training, and seven women who completed high school. In Los Angeles, my interviewees include eleven women with college diplomas, eight women with some years of college or postsecondary vocational training, and five women who completed high school. In both cities, the majority of my interviewees had been professionals or semiprofessionals in the Philippines. Most had been teachers and office workers.

Finally, more than half my interviewees are married women with children, who as I noted above mostly remain in the Philippines. Only five of twenty-six interviewees in Los Angeles and fewer than half (nineteen) in Rome are never-married single women. Women with children in the Philippines constitute a greater portion of my sample: twenty-five of forty-six in Rome, and fourteen of twenty-six in Los Angeles. The median age of interviewees suggests that the children of women in Rome are fairly young and that in Los Angeles, the children are older. The median age of my interviewees in Los Angeles is surprisingly high, at fifty-two years. The youngest research participant is thirty-three, whereas the oldest is sixty-eight. What explains the extremely high median age of domestic workers in Los Angeles? We can surmise that younger immigrant Filipino women are not attracted to domestic work because of its isolating nature. They can choose to avoid domestic work, because compared with other immigrant groups, their knowledge of the English language gives them access to other types of employment. In Rome, the median age of interviewees is thirty-one years, significantly lower than my sample in Los Angeles. Though only four women fall under the age of twenty-five, the oldest woman is sixty-six.

Race, Class, and Space: The Place and Placelessness of Migrant Filipina Domestic Workers

Inside and outside the workplace, placelessness is how migrant Filipina domestic workers experience place. Three key features illustrate what I mean by placelessness: (1) the limits in the spatial movements of domestic workers in the workplace, (2) their segregation from dominant public spaces, and (3) the containment of the places that they can truly call their own to fleeting spaces of encounter such as buses and public parks.

Looking first at the politics of space in the workplace, the constricted spatial movement of domestic workers in their employer's home is telling of what I mean by placelessness. Employers control the spatial movements of domestic workers as they decide on the domestic's integration or segregation from the family. More often than not, they prefer segregation, as they, according to Julia Wrigley,[30] tend to hire those who will demand very few resources in terms of time, money, space, or interaction. Moreover, as noted above, employers expect the "spatial deference" of domestics. The access of domestic workers to household space is usually far more contained than for the rest of the family. In both Los Angeles and Rome, Filipina domestics, including nannies and elderly care providers, have found themselves subject to food rationing, prevented from sitting on the couch, provided with a separate set of utensils, and told when to get food from the refrigerator and when to retreat to their bedrooms.

With "spatial deference" so established in domestic work, Filipina domestics are often startled when employers fail to enforce segregation. This is reflected in the pride of one woman in Los Angeles, whose employers, she boasts, do not insist that she use separate utensils in the household:

> Here they are very nice. In other households, the plates of the maids and the cups and glasses are different from the employers. Here, it is not. We use the same utensils and plates. They don't care. . . .

Her surprise over her employer's lack of concern over crossing the boundaries of spatial deference is telling of its established pattern in the workplace.

The isolation of live-in employment, I should note, aggravates the spatial segregation of domestic work. In Los Angeles, most migrant Filipina domestics are live-in workers. In contrast, Latina domestic workers are concentrated in day work.[31] The difference between Latinas and Filipinas could be attributed not only to the smaller number of domestic workers from the Philippines, and thus their less extensive networks and lesser access to different employment opportunities, but also to the concentration of Filipinos in elderly care, which requires twenty-four hours of on-call labor. Likewise, Mexican elderly care workers in Los Angeles are likely to be live-in workers.[32]

In Los Angeles, we can assume that the recruitment of nurses from the Philippines has led to the creation of the health industry as an ethnic niche for Filipino migrants.[33] This in turn has led to the funneling of jobs and information in health care to the community. Consequently, migrant Filipinos can be found occupying various jobs in different levels of the health industry. They include medical doctors, physician's assistants, medical technicians operating X-ray machines in hospitals, registered nurses, licensed vocational nurses, and nursing aides, as well as home care workers for the elderly.[34] Though Latina domestic workers also do elderly care work, they are less concentrated in this type of job than are Filipinos.[35]

In Rome, a larger proportion of Filipina domestic workers are day workers but a sizable number of women are also live-in workers. According to Caritas Roma, 42.1 percent of Filipinos in Rome live in rented apartments, mostly located on the northern periphery of Rome, and 32.9 percent are live-in domestic workers.[36] Often feeling trapped, live-in domestics cannot help but see the enclosed space of the employer's home as a prison. Maria de la Luz Ibarra has made a similar observation of Latina domestic workers in California.[37] Counting the days until their day off is usually part of the everyday routine for live-in workers. Moreover, live-in domestics often do not have the freedom to leave their employer's home, for instance, to take a lunch break. Instead, they have to ask permission to do so. So, in addition to being subject to spatial segregation and deference, live-in domestic workers also face spatial constriction with their limited ability to decide on their bodily movements around their employer's home.

By being subject to the close scrutiny of employers, domestic workers are without privacy in the private sphere.[38] Privacy is only achieved in the anonymity of public spaces. Yet surveillance also takes place in public spaces occupied by migrant Filipina domestic workers. Thus, I found that the Filipino migrant community does not offer domestic workers an adequate escape from the sense of placelessness that they encounter in the workplace, which, to summarize, is defined by spatial deference and segregation. This is the case in both Rome and Los Angeles.

In Los Angeles, migrant Filipina domestic workers constantly experience a state of discomfort in the representative spaces of the Filipino community, which they see as centered on the middle class. I noticed this in the get-togethers I frequented with domestic workers. At these get-togethers, I found that their physical movements were constrained by an invisible class line that separated them from middle-class members of the community. For example, at one event I attended with three women, I noticed that they stayed at the far corner of the room and were removed from the rest of the crowd during the entire time we were there at a party hosted by their hometown association. Migrant Filipina domestics tend to feel discomfort in the middle-class spaces representing the community, despite the fact that their identity as domestic workers is not physically distinguishable. Avoiding the middle class in these spaces, however, gives them a sense of anonymity, which in turn eases their discomfort at being have-nots in the Filipino migrant community.

What leads domestics to question the romantic notions of the migrant community is the fact that they feel they do not garner support from their middle-class counterparts. As Cherry Jacinto, a domestic worker in Los Angeles, states:

> There are people here who I knew in the Philippines. I used to feel terrible that they were treating me differently than how they did in the Philippines. They treat you differently just because you are in this situation. They give you attitude. They act like you are below them, telling you that you are a domestic worker. They are not sensitive and don't remember that you were not like this in the Philippines. They don't treat you the same way. . . . It really registers in my mind. . . . What I want is a little bit of respect. There is nothing like that here.

Though some domestic workers describe the community as generally supportive, most feel an absence of camaraderie among Filipino migrants. As members of the have-nots in the community, domestic workers are acutely aware of its class divisions. It is an awareness that engenders their cautious behavior in the community and aggravates their sense of placelessness in the United States.

Unlike their counterparts in Los Angeles, migrant Filipina domestic workers in Italy do not have to contend with class identity conflicts whenever they leave the confines of the workplace. In Italy, migrant Filipinos are for the most part restricted to low-wage service work, particularly as domestic workers for individuals and families. Despite the lack of class stratification in the community, Filipino migrant women in Italy also have to contend with a sense of placelessness whenever they are outside the workplace. Like their counterparts in Los Angeles, they also have to behave with caution whenever outside the private sphere of the workplace. In Italy, migrant Filipina domestic workers have to negotiate with a xenophobic and less-welcoming host society. Even though Italy has historically been a country that sent workers to industrial centers of Northern Europe, the recent wave of immigrants has not resulted in compassionate understanding among Italians.[39] Instead, it has led to increasing sentiments of nationalism and xenophobia against foreigners, as shown for instance with the victory of the political party Lega in local elections in the North with an anti-immigration platform.

We can visualize the placelessness of migrant Filipina domestics outside the workplace in Rome by looking at the geographical constitution of the community. In Rome, the community is geographically situated in what I refer to as *isolated* pockets of gathering—pockets that are located in both public and private domains. These pockets include, in the private domain, church centers and apartments, and, in the public domain, bus stops and train stations. The term *pockets* aptly describe the community's geographic organization because it captures two central characteristics: (1) the segregation of the social space of migrant Filipina domestic workers, and (2) the geographic decentralization of Filipinos into multiple sites in the city of Rome.

Even though these pockets can be described as isolated—for example, those in the public domain are usually located in the periphery of the city and are without much pedestrian activities—Italians still resent the visibility of Filipinos, for I have even been yelled at on different occasions by an Italian in these spaces. One of these unprovoked racial incidents occurred in Termini, the central train station and collection of bus stops of Rome, but another occurred in a neighborhood on the periphery. My experience is not an exception. Many Italians across class backgrounds make their resentment of the use of public spaces by Filipinos known to members of the migrant community. It is a frequent and sore topic of conversation. For instance, members of the community were appalled but not surprised when I shared with them the story of how a middle-aged Italian man in a business suit who had been walking in my direction had spat on my face after I had failed to move aside and to his irritation had forced him to do so when we passed each other on the street. This Italian had let it clearly be known to me who was to act with spatial deference in the public space of Rome. My story provoked mixed reactions. Some members of the community told me that I should have also spat on his face, citing the expression "When in Rome, do as the Romans do." However, most thought it was better that I did not react at all to the assault and that I held my dignity by calmly walking away. For many, my experience raised nationalist sentiments, and they felt my "good behavior" signaled the cultural superiority of Filipinos.

With few exceptions, Filipinos tend not to gather in public spaces inhabited or frequented by Italians. Perhaps they do so to avoid confrontations such as the one I had the misfortune of encountering. Notably, Termini station is the only site in the city center where Filipinos impose on the public space of Italians. Yet, on any given day off, the bus stops of Termini are never congested with Filipinos in the morning and afternoon; they seem to congregate there only in the evening. One can imagine that the women crowding Termini at night are just delaying their return to their employer's home, staying a little bit longer, hoping they might run into a friend whom they have not seen in weeks. In general, most women do not spend an extended amount of time in pockets of gathering in the public domain such as Termini. They are often only fleeting spaces of encounter. On other occasions, Filipinos are not at all visible in these public spaces. Notably, they are only there on Thursday afternoons and Sundays, which are the standard days off for migrant domestic workers, but they are there in large numbers only at night.

In the public domain, the presence of food vendors essentially establishes particular spaces as official pockets of gathering. Ethnic enclave businesses among Filipinos in Italy are restricted to the informal sector. Food vending is a popular informal business. Vendors who are mostly women would prepack Filipino meals of rice and meat in separate plastic bags to sell to Filipino domestic workers. Using paper plates and plastic utensils provided by the vendors, customers would eat their meals sitting or standing around the pocket of gathering. Much monitoring of self and others occurs in these public spaces. For example, rarely do migrants litter, and when they do they usually get reprimanded by those around them. Migrants also keep an eye out for Italian pedestrians and more so Italian authorities. Vendors, because they carry their goods in duffel bags, are ready to run at the first sight of a law enforcement officer, who could fine them for illegally selling food products in violation of health codes.

Vendors are also known to use the trunks of automobiles. In a pocket of gathering, hidden in cars with slightly opened trunks would be industrial-size pots carrying a selection of dishes to eat for lunch or dinner. Members of the community would know that cars parked with trunks slightly ajar in a pocket of gathering are likely to be the stall of a food vendor. During my fieldwork, no other ethnic groups were known to sell prepared food informally in the public spaces of Rome. Polish domestic workers, I noticed, congregated at McDonald's and other fast food establishments, while Peruvians sometimes patronized the businesses of Filipinos. However, rarely did Peruvians and Filipinos socialize with one another.

One of the public pockets of gathering where vendors have historically gathered to sell Filipino food for domestic workers en route to work or on their day off is in the neighborhood of Mancini. At one point, Filipinos used to gather at the neighborhood's main bus stop. They were forced, however, to relocate as a result of the constant harassment of food vendors by the police, who would not only impose fines on them but also confiscate all their goods. Notably, the police had informed vendors that it had been complaints from Italian pedestrians that forced them to penalize the migrant vendors. As the actions of the police and the complaints of Italian pedestrians informed migrant Filipinos that they cannot impose on the public domain of Italians, they literally had to find a "hidden space" in a public place, meaning a site that, while in a public space, does not at all have a felt presence in the public social spaces of Italians. Hence, they eventually moved to a new site in the area, one assuredly not at all imposing, because it is located underneath an overpass by the Tiber River. It is not visible from the street level. This space is quite an unsanitary location, and I was told that it had been abandoned by Albanian refugees and had been filled with garbage and tall weeds when the Filipino migrants took it over.

This "public domain" has since been cleared, though it remains unpaved, and it now houses fifteen informal business enterprises—eating places, food stores, tailoring shops, and hair salons. These informal businesses are set up in wooden stands along the two structures of the overpass. There is also no running water in Mancini. In the evening, the stoves and portable gas tanks, the sewing machines, and the goods of the food stores are stored in padlocked wooden cabinets built at the premises. Mancini is a one-stop shopping bazaar. Hundreds of Filipinos patronize these businesses every day. This place of gathering under the bridge has given Filipino migrants of Rome a haven from the "public domain" *in* the "public domain." As such, the public enclave of Mancini speaks of the resistance and defiance of migrant Filipina domestic workers against efforts of dominant society to exclude them from public life in Italy.[40] Nonetheless, their very presence under the bridge serves as a reminder in the community that they do not belong in the public social space of Italian society. Their negotiation of the city of Rome limits their place in it to urban spaces invisible to the dominant society.

Filipino migrant domestic workers also spend their days off in the private domain, for instance in apartments and church centers. Church centers are working-class havens created by migrant Filipina domestic workers against the public domain, and they also frequently use these centers as alternative spaces for conducting petty retail trade away from the business establishments of Rome. Filipinos are often uncomfortable in businesses patronized by Italians, and they tend to avoid these public spaces. Many told me of their preference for buying clothes and perfume from other Filipinos rather than from a retail store, regardless of whether or not the items cost more from the Filipino entrepreneur. To negotiate their feelings of nonbelonging in various public retail venues, they make do with the informal businesses that are available in various gathering places in the community. Apartments, but more so church centers, are popular sites for informal small-scale retail enterprises. This is illustrated in my fieldnotes:

> In one church center, I notice that for a span of two hours I had been approached by at least 10 individuals soliciting various commodities. I was given catalogs of Amway and Avon. I was asked to look at a bag of sweaters, which are consigned by a domestic worker for her employer who owns a boutique. I was approached by a woman about shoes and bags that she sells and orders from a manufacturer in Napoli. A man inquired if I was interested in purchasing bootleg tapes that he had recorded from compact discs. . . . The selection of music ranges from artists such as Air Supply and Whitney Houston to Filipino artists such as April Boys.

Clearly, the church is not just a place of spiritual guidance for migrant Filipina domestic workers. They use it to counter their placelessness. Though places of gathering, church centers, however, are not truly places that they could call their own. The use of these places is limited to certain days and hours. Moreover, clergy often monitor the behavior and attire of domestic workers. For instance, members of the clergy impose a dress code and literally force those they think are dressed inappropriately to leave. An example are those wearing miniskirts. "Ill behavior" is also frowned upon.

For instance, domestics cannot smoke in these centers. Self-monitoring often takes places in these sites, which domestics tend to leave an hour or two immediately after Sunday morning church services.

After church services, the women usually move to a known public space of gathering or to an apartment, where they will spend the rest of their day off. In Rome, apartments provide migrant Filipina domestic workers with an intimate environment free of surveillance. In apartments, Filipinos can spend many nonworking hours playing card games, watching Filipino movies, and cooking Filipino dishes (notably, only nonsmelly Filipino dishes, so as not to attract the attention of Italian neighbors). Yet, apartments often tend to be crowded because of the system of bed spacing that is in place in the community. Among members of the community, beds and not rooms are what are rented out in apartments. Usually, four beds would be rented out per bedroom. Apartments are usually overcrowded and bustling with activity, as was the apartment where I stayed for one weekend. As I wrote in my fieldnotes:

The apartment is quite large with three bedrooms and one *salone* (living room) converted into a bedroom as well. Upon entering the apartment, the first thing I saw were three clothes lines hanging in the middle of the hallway. To enter the apartment, I had to walk around the wet clothes blocking the entryway.

Each room is separated in the center with large armoires. On each side is either a full-size bed or two twin-size beds. Couples, I learned, sleep on the larger beds, which usually fill up the entire space of their side of the room. The only space left is enough for one dresser with a TV and VCR usually on top of it. In one room, there were even two TVs, each placed in front of the two beds separated by two armoires, each facing a different side (or half) of the room. Like in the other rooms, four people live in this one room.

There is only one bathroom in the entire apartment, while there are fourteen individuals living in the apartment. The apartment was quite chaotic. There were always two sets of televisions on, sometimes set on the same channel, and stereos simultaneously playing from both sides of the house.

The kitchen, which is their only common area, is always full. Tenants take their turn eating, as the kitchen cannot accommodate everyone at the same time. There are pots of cooked food lined up on the counters. . . . I was asked to live in this apartment, . . . but I declined their offer for the reason that I wanted to have more privacy.

In apartments, the word *privacy* is usually not in the vocabulary of occupants. For example, people cannot escape to their own bedrooms but only to their side of the room. Though a haven from the spatial deference of the workplace, apartments tend to still spatially limit the movements of migrant Filipina domestic workers. Moreover, because migrant Filipina domestic workers are without privacy in apartments, they are not free from surveillance in these private spaces. They must constantly monitor their behavior so as to minimize their imposition on their roommates.

The geographic formation of the Filipino migrant community into intimate pockets—such as the place under the bridge in Mancini, church centers, or crowded apartments—speaks of the segregation of migrant Filipinos from the public spaces of dominant Italian society. On the one hand, the creation of these alternative spaces eases the process of settlement for migrant Filipina domestic workers because it gives them a space of retreat from dominant society. Yet, on the other hand, these spaces reveal the extension of their spatial deference in the workplace to the level of society. Consequently, these spaces and the segregation of domestic workers in these spaces reify sentiments of nonbelonging in Italy and consequently engender the experience of placelessness of migrant Filipina domestic workers. Indeed, many—as their citizenship is in fact limited to the status of temporary worker—perceive themselves as "guests" in Italy, meaning that they view themselves as fortunate guests graciously allowed by the state the privilege of earning the greater income its economy can offer and foresee an inevitable termination of their permit to stay once society no longer needs them. They often plan on being prepared for the possibility of their mass deportation, a sort of doomsday for temporary workers. This includes the domestic worker Luisa Balila, who describes her readiness for this possibility when she states, "If they send all of us strangers [or foreigners] away from Italy, even though my husband and I don't have much money, we have a house [a two-story structure with four apartment units] that we can go home to. . . . I want to be able to have a consistent income if we decide to go back to the Philippines. We can rent the apartments out."

Filipina domestic workers encounter a different kind of placelessness in Los Angeles compared with Rome. In Rome, they are displaced from the dominant spaces of Italian society; in Los Angeles, they are displaced from middle-class-dominated spaces in the Filipino community. Interestingly, in Los Angeles, migrant domestic workers—like their counterparts in Rome—are also able to form working-class havens from middle-class Filipinos. In Los Angeles, equivalent pockets of gathering could be found in retirement villages. Usually, domestics meet during their employer's nap times. Pro-

viding an example, Jovita Gacutan describes one such subcommunity of domestics:

> I was able to form a group. We helped each other out. . . . We would al-
> ways be in my room, which was informally referred to as the Filipino
> Center in the village. We gave each other moral support. It was because
> we were all just starting over in this country, and that is why it was in all
> of us to help each other out.

In other retirement villages, Filipina domestic workers would meet in front
of an employer's apartment or house. This is because most employers would
not tolerate domestics entertaining visitors.

On their day off, Filipina domestic workers usually leave the isolation of
their employer's home for other subcommunities of Filipinos. As I have
noted, the subcommunities that they enter as weekend visitors are usually
rendered middle-class spaces by the spatial configuration of the community.
Occasionally, they are able to form a subcommunity among themselves outside work. An example would be apartments in downtown Los Angeles,
where they would congregate on Sundays with domestics who they had met
on a bus or at work in a retirement village. I found that they are most comfortable in these truly private spaces, meaning spaces where they can act
without spatial deference. Likewise, this is the case in Rome. However,
these places, especially in Los Angeles, are rarely available to them. Family obligations usually take them to the more common middle-class–
centered spaces of the community.

The rarity of sharing private spaces with other domestic workers is more
of a reason why domestic workers take advantage of the moments when they
do meet other migrant Filipina domestics in public spaces. They make public spaces sites for building race and class solidarity. For instance, they use
buses as sites where they garner the information and resources that they need
to have greater control of their labor. As Mila Tizon of Los Angeles describes:

> Most of the people that I ride the bus with every morning are domestic
> workers. There are many of us [Filipinos]. There we compare our salaries
> to know the going rate. We also ask each other for possible job referrals.
> We often exchange phone numbers and contact each other.

Like for the domestic workers in Rome, public spaces such as parks and
buses are where Filipina domestics in Los Angeles forge a consciousness of

a collective struggle from their shared experience of marginality in the employer's home as well as the middle-class spaces of the community. This is where they establish standards of wages and evaluate the fairness of their working conditions. We should, however, note the fact that buses are only fleeting spaces of encounter and not permanent places that domestic workers can call their own.

Notably, these fleeting encounters do not extend to spark interracial solidarity with others in the margins, for instance Latinas in Rome and Los Angeles, with whom Filipinos do also cross paths in buses and parks. This tells us that interracial alliances cannot be assumed even among those who share an economically subordinate status. Language difficulties do pose a barrier, but more significantly perceived cultural differences discourage the Filipino domestic workers who I met from reaching out to the Latinas they encounter in public spaces. This is the case in both Rome and Los Angeles. Still, it should be emphasized that migrant Filipina domestic workers do attempt to counteract and appease their feelings of nonbelonging by finding support from one another. For instance, as noted above, they create alternative spaces to counter their placelessness in the workplace and migrant community. Yet it needs to be stressed that these spaces do not sufficiently counteract their sense of placelessness in the host society. This is because for the most part, as I noted, they are not geographically bound spaces or institutionalized spaces but instead are only temporary pockets of gathering. So, spurred by their placelessness, the discomfort of community life for migrant Filipina domestics is resolved by stressing their temporary membership in the host society. I found this to be true even if the women qualify for permanent residency, as is the case in Los Angeles.

Conclusion

In this chapter, I have looked at the politics of space in the lives of migrant Filipina domestic workers and in doing so have unraveled the placelessness that embodies their integration into the cities of Rome and Los Angeles. This sense of placelessness heightens feelings of temporary sojourn among them. Notably, the views on settlement of migrant Filipina domestic workers differ sharply from most other migrant women, for example Mexicans, who have a much greater tendency to view the receiving society as a permanent place of settlement.[41] In contrast to other migrant women, migrant Filipina domestic workers desire return migration. Their experience of placelessness is a central reason why they do so. The absence of a geographically rooted space that they can call their own metaphorically represents their stunted integration in Rome and Los Angeles.

Looking at space in analyzing migrant settlement shows us that race and class centrally determine the settlement desires of migrant Filipina domestic workers. Indeed, as Yeoh and Huang have argued, the construction of Filipina domestic workers as racialized others in Singapore manifests in the spatial and temporal restrictions of their activities in public spaces.[42] Ironically, in the literature on women's migration, discussions of race and class are often left on the back burner in our analysis of women's settlement. Instead, studies tend to reduce our understanding of women's desire for permanent settlement to gender by attributing this preference solely to the reward of "greater autonomy, resources, and leverage" that women gain upon migration.[43] Yet, looking at the spatial dynamics of settlement among migrant Filipina domestic workers underscores the centrality of race and class in understanding women's migratory processes. In the case of migrant Filipina domestic workers, race and class propel feelings of sojourn, which is in contrast to the dominant narrative in the literature on women's migration that says women prefer permanent over temporary settlement because of their "gains in status, autonomy, and resources relative to men" in migration.[44]

My discussion thus reminds us that in certain cases race and class also shape migrant women's settlement. To put it simply, race and class are also significant determinants of women's experiences and not just men's. By emphasizing racial and class inequalities in the lives of Filipino migrant women, I take heed of the observation of the feminist historian Joan Scott, who perceptively notes that while gender relations are a reflection of power relations, concepts of power are not always literally about gender.[45] Likewise, the processes of women's migration constitute and are constituted by gender but are not always literally about gender.

Notes

1. Saskia Sassen, *Cities in the World Economy,* 2nd ed. (Thousand Oaks, Calif.: Pine Forge Press, 2000).

2. Ibid., 140–41.

3. This figure is based on records of the Philippine Overseas Employment Agency. Danilo A. Arao, "Deployment of Migrant Workers Increasing," *Ibon Facts and Figures* 23, no. 8 (April 30, 2000): 8.

4. Destinations of Filipino migrants include territories of various countries such as the Pacific Island territories of the United States, British territories in the Caribbean, and

Hong Kong. Kanlungan Center Foundation, *Fast Facts on Labor Migration* (Quezon City: Kanlungan Center Foundation, 2000).

5. Rhacel Salazar Parreñas, *Servants of Globalization: Women, Migration, and Domestic Work* (Stanford, Calif.: Stanford University Press, 2001).

6. Sassen, *Cities.*

7. Salazar Parreñas, *Servants of Globalization.*

8. I use de Certeau's notion of space. As he states, "Space is a practiced place." Social inequalities manifest in the limits of spatial actions. Michel de Certeau, *The Practice of Everyday Life* (Berkeley: University of California Press, 1984), 117.

9. De Certeau, *Practice of Everyday Life;* Henri Lefebvre, "Reflections on the Politics of Space," in *Radical Geography,* ed. Richard Peet (London: Methuen, 1977), 339–52.

10. Brenda Yeoh and Shirlena Huang, "Negotiating Public Space: Strategies and Styles of Migrant Female Domestic Workers in Singapore," *Urban Studies* 35, no. 3 (1998): 583–602.

11. Ibid., 585.

12. Judith Rollins, *Between Women: Domestics and Their Employers* (Philadelphia: Temple University Press, 1985), 171; Seemin Qayum and Raka Ray, "Grappling with Modernity: India's Respectable Classes the Culture of Domestic Servitude," *Ethnography* 4, no. 4 (2003): 520–55.

13. Laura Liu, "The Place of Immigration in Studies of Geography and Race," *Social and Cultural Geography* 1, no. 2 (2000): 169–82; the quotation is on 176.

14. Salazar Parreñas, *Servants of Globalization.*

15. Ivan Light, Georges Sabagh, Mehdi Bozorgmehr, and Claudia Der-Martirosian, "Beyond the Ethnic Enclave Economy," *Social Problems* 41, no. 1 (1994): 65–79; Min Zhou, *Chinatown: The Socioeconomic Potential of an Urban Enclave* (Philadelphia: Temple University Press, 1992).

16. Sassen, *Cities.*

17. Carla Collicelli, Fabrizio Maria Arosio, Rosario Sapienza, and Fransesco Maietta, *City Template Rome: Basic Information on Ethnic Minorities and their Participation* (Rome: Fondazione CENSIS, 1997), www.unesco.org/most/p97rome.doc.

18. Ibid.

19. The number dipped to 12,000 in 2003. The source for these data is the Philippine Overseas Employment Administration.

20. Collicelli et al., *City Template Rome.*

21. G. Campani, "Immigration and Racism in Southern Europe: The Italian Case," *Ethnic and Racial Studies* 16, no. 3 (1993): 507–55.

22. Yasemin Nuhoglu Soysal, *Limits of Citizenship: Migrants and Postnational Membership in Europe* (Chicago: University of Chicago Press, 1994).

23. A. Venturini, "Italy in the Contest of European Migration," *Regional Development Dialogue* 12, no. 3 (1991).

24. Collicelli et al., *City Template Rome.*

25. Alejandro Portes and Ruben Rumbaut, *Immigrant America: A Portrait,* 2nd ed. (Berkeley: University of California Press, 1996).

26. Paul Ong and Tania Azores, "Asian Immigrants in Los Angeles: Diversity and Divisions," in *The New Asian Immigration in Los Angeles and Global Restructuring,* ed. Paul Ong, Edna Bonacich, and Lucie Cheng (Philadelphia: Temple University Press, 1994), 100–29.

27. Light et al., "Beyond the Ethnic Enclave Economy," 68.

28. Ong and Azores, "Asian Immigrants," 121.

29. For a more extensive discussion of loopholes in family reunification policies in the United States, see Rhacel Salazar Parreñas, *Children of Global Migration: Transnational Families and Gendered Woes* (Stanford, Calif.: Stanford University Press, 2005), chap. 7.

30. Julia Wrigley, *Other People's Children: An Intimate Account of the Dilemmas Facing Middle-Class Parents and the Women They Hire to Raise Their Children* (New York: Basic Books, 1995).

31. Pierrette Hondagneu-Sotelo, *Domestica: Immigrant Workers Cleaning and Caring in the Shadows of Affluence* (Berkeley: University of California Press, 2001).

32. Maria de Luz Ibarra, "Emotional Proletarians in a Global Economy: Mexican Immigrant Women and Elder Care Work," *Urban Anthropology and Studies of Cultural Systems and World Economic Development* 31, no. 3 (2002): 317–51.

33. Roger Waldinger, "The Making of an Immigrant Niche," *International Migration Review* 28, no. 1 (1994): 3–30.

34. Salazar Parreñas, *Servants of Globalization*.

35. Hondagneu-Sotelo 2001; Ibarra, "Emotional Proletarians."

36. Collicelli et al., *City Template Rome*.

37. Ibarra, "Emotional Proletarians."

38. Yeoh and Huang, "Negotiating Public Space"; Rollins, *Between Women*.

39. Giovanni Ancona, "Labour Demand and Immigration in Italy," *Journal of Regional Policy* 11 (1991): 143–48; John Veugelers, "Recent Immigration Politics in Italy: A Short Story," in *The Politics of Immigration in Western Europe,* ed. Martin Baldwin-Edwards and Martin Schain (Portland: Frank Cass, 1994), 33–49.

40. Supporting the observations of Yeoh and Huang in Singapore, public enclaves inhabited by migrant Filipina domestic workers such as Mancini should be seen as socially contentious spaces of dominance and resistance between the policing of activities of domestic workers, the defiance of domestic workers against spatial restrictions, and the creation by domestic workers of a space free from public surveillance. Yeoh and Huang, "Negotiating Public Space."

41. Nancy Foner, "Sex Roles and Sensibilities: Jamaican Women in New York and London," in *International Migration: The Female Experience,* ed. Rita Simon and Carolyn Bretell (Totowa, N.J.: Rowman & Allanheld, 1986), 133–50; Sherri Grasmuck and Patricia Pessar, *Between Two Islands: Dominican International Migration* (Berkeley: University of California Press, 1991); Pierrette Hondagneu-Sotelo, *Gendered Transitions: Mexican Experiences of Migration* (Berkeley: University of California Press, 1994); Terry Repak, *Waiting on Washington: Central American Workers in the Nation's Capital* (Philadelphia: Temple University Press, 1995).

42. Yeoh and Huang, "Negotiating Public Space."

43. Hondagneu-Sotelo, *Gendered Transitions,* 196.

44. Audrey Singer and Greta Gilbertson, " 'The Blue Passport': Gender and the Social Process of Naturalization among Dominican Immigrants in New York City," in *Gender and U.S. Immigration: Contemporary Trends,* ed. Pierrette Hondagneu-Sotelo (Berkeley: University of California Press, 2003), 359–78; the quotation is on 375.

45. Joan Scott, "Experience," in *Feminists Theorize the Political,* ed. Judith Butler and Joan Scott (New York: Routledge, 1992), 22–40.

3

"It's Just That People Mix Better Here": Household Narratives of Belonging and Displacement in Seattle

Serin D. Houston and Richard Wright

Immigration continues to transform the United States. The greatest influx of foreign-born people has occurred in the last hundred years; two out of three immigrants currently in the country arrived during the twentieth century.[1] Early waves of immigrants claimed European roots and a white heritage. In contrast, migrants today primarily arrive from Central America, South America, South Asia, and East Asia and usually self-identify as Latino or Asian. Newcomers directly influence the racial and ethnic composition of U.S. society for this and subsequent generations.

Cities commonly serve as destination points for new immigrants, so the changing demographics of the United States are a fundamental characteristic of urban places. It makes sense, then, to examine immigration-driven social processes within metropolitan contexts. The general account of urban-bound immigration portrays newcomers residentially clustering with similar others ("enclaved" in immigrant neighborhoods), working alongside co-ethnics ("niched" in particular types of employment), and forming households with similar others ("homogamous" partnerships). The underlying assumption in such tales is that newly arrived immigrants lead fairly isolated and segregated lives, meaning that interactions between groups are few, at least initially. Such claims adequately describe some historic patterns of immigrant settlement as well as some contemporary trends, but this dominant narrative glosses over other important geographies. In particular, we contend that cities are *both* places of segregation and places where lives interweave.[2] The scale of the mixed household—defined here as households headed by differently racialized partners, one of whom is foreign born—reveals the entanglement of lives and draws out the interplay of immigration and settlement processes within everyday life. Mobilizing the household as the primary entry point into our analysis enables us to broaden interpretations of immigrant experiences within urban spaces.

To add to this conceptual latitude, we adopt an expansive definition of households and consider the household as a geographic scale, a collectivity, and a set of practices, rather than just a mark of location and residence.[3] Household members may sleep in a specific location, but their lives are heterogeneous and involve interpersonal interactions all over town. Scholars often ignore mixing in households, but the immigration and settlement experiences embedded in mixed-nativity, mixed-ethnicity, and mixed-race households merit further attention.

Recognizing both the attraction of cities for newly arrived immigrants and the analytical possibilities evident within mixed households prompts us to peel back the prevailing assumption of immigrant separation in urban spaces to highlight the intermingling of people. We do this through a focus on contexts of belonging and displacement for three mixed-nativity and mixed-race households in Seattle, a city where nearly 10 percent of all reported marriages are mixed race. We ground our discussion in the narratives of these households for a number of reasons. The voices of people in mixed households, for instance, shed light on the complex lived reality of immigration. These stories also illustrate that settlement in a new city, much like participation in a mixed household, is not a singular occurrence but a continual practice. Taken together, the narratives of mixed households in Seattle point to the power relations and hierarchies of difference that inform the lives and settlement of immigrants *and* the native born.

Examining mixing in households allows us to poke some holes in the cultural myths of immigrant isolation as well. We are, of course, not the first to try this. Massey and Denton, for instance, use Thomas Philpott's reevaluation of immigrant concentrations in Chicago in the early twentieth century to take on Ernest Burgess's portrayal of the "immigrant ghetto."[4] Neighborhoods that Burgess described as "Czech" or "Polish," for example, turn out to rarely have contained majority Czech or Polish populations. In fact, the average number of nationalities per ghetto was twenty-two. In a more recent study, Ellis and colleagues investigate the residential patterns of a number of immigrant groups in Los Angeles. They conclude that the varying rates of clustering or dispersion for groups depends on a number of factors, including time in country, occupational status, English-language ability, and education, with exogamy being the most important explanatory variable. Indeed, the probability of living outside an immigrant residential concentration is most strongly associated with forming mixed-nativity partnerships.[5] What are known as enclaves and immigrant neighborhoods are thus not monocultural gateway places; they are embodied and negotiated spaces where mixing matters.

Finally, a household approach redirects attention away from individuals and toward *relationships between individuals.*[6] Rather than just reading immigration and settlement patterns through the standard lens of networks and enclaves (defined in terms of individuals or as a relatively homogenous collective), we challenge these normative logics by shifting scales to the mixed household and to the relationships encompassed within these households. This is important because, as Luke explains, "interracial families reconstruct their identities in relation to each other."[7] Focusing our attention in this way helps us extend the literature and unsettle presumed narratives of immigration and assumed narratives of settlement, both in Seattle and more broadly. Therefore, much like de Certeau, our interest veers away from "the production of difference" for immigrant groups writ large and instead highlights "different productions" of belonging and displacement for specific mixed households.[8]

The chapter unfolds in the following manner. To begin with, we outline some of the opportunities afforded through the household scale. We then briefly address mixing in the Seattle context. Our attention next shifts to the perspectives of mixed households themselves as we delve into the household narratives. The first vignette examines Tori's[9] and Bill's perceptions of home, whiteness, and fitting in. We then turn to Jack and Khiet's stories of borders and belonging. The third vignette foregrounds sexuality and highlights Steve and Juan's concerns with citizenship and activism. In the end, these examples question dominant paradigms and bring awareness to a new arena of research that ponders relationality within multiply mixed households. We do not offer these vignettes as authoritative accounts of all mixed households or as evidence of a deep ethnography of Seattle. On the contrary, we selectively excerpt from interviews with three mixed households to uncover some compelling insights gained through a household-scale analysis of immigration. By accenting mixing we hope to contribute to conversations that reimagine and reexamine social processes in ways that both trouble and augment some standard narratives currently circulating in the literature.

Mixing in Households

Although immigration-driven demographic change creates new possibilities for mixing in households, shifts in the legal landscape have also been important. For example, the implementation of the 1965 Immigration Act, which abolished restrictive immigration quota laws, occurred at roughly the same time as workplace desegregation and affirmative action hiring practices during the civil rights era; all reclaimed spaces and opportunities for associating with others.[10] The 1967 U.S. Supreme Court decision in *Loving v. Virginia* further enabled mixing by striking down the remaining anti-miscegenation laws in sixteen states. Indeed, this historic case made it possible for people of different races—and often nativities—to legally marry. These laws find tangible expression in the growing rate of mixed-race, mixed-ethnic, and mixed-nativity partnerships and households.[11]

The legal right to mix does not necessarily translate, however, into widespread acceptance of people forming partnerships with whomever they choose. The persistent stigmatization throughout the United States of households headed by mixed partners indicates the degree of unease that frames the pressing together of certain bodies; it is the union, the coupling, the sex, and sexuality that usually arouse opprobrium.[12] Entrenched heterosexism, racism, and nativism sculpt normative codes for what bodies can interact in what ways and in which places. These social forces frequently result in the hypervisibility of mixed households. The multiple languages often spoken within mixed households can amplify difference in notable ways. Accordingly, members of mixed households commonly make linguistic choices that seek to signify belonging and inclusion rather than displacement. As Bill explains,[13] "Because I have moved around the world so often, the need to settle down, to be able to figure out, express myself and interact in this new world has always become the most important for me.

So, for example, here my primary language is English. If I go back to China, . . . it would take me three or four days to become fluent again." Bill's comment makes plain that immigration and settlement processes are far from stagnant. Given the importance of language and context, we must consider racialized bodies in relation to and in connection with each other. The household provides a chance to do just that.

We interpret the household to be a scale in between the body and the neighborhood and use it to locate and extend discussions of immigration and settlement. Hartigan depicts the family, as we would describe the household, in the following way: "a distended and nebulous location, a scale of reference between individuals and the broader society that generates a great degree of variation in how racial [and we would add ethnic and nativity] categories gain and lose their significance."[14] In a different analytical vein, Jarvis, Pratt, and Wu deploy a household lens to study urban sustainability because the "household is more than the sum of its (reflexive) individual members. The emergent 'reality' of the household is constituted through the mediation of multiple overlapping institutions (including class and gender)."[15] Building on the ideas of Hartigan and Jarvis and colleagues, we suggest that the "overlapping" of nativity and race within mixed households in Seattle adds depth to current understandings of urban social processes.

We readily acknowledge that the household itself is not a new site of analysis. Indeed, examining households connects with a long-standing research tradition in urban studies, evident in the literatures on locational attainment, family migration, mobility, and residential decisionmaking.[16] Yet, much of this scholarship centers upon homogamous couples.[17] Our emphasis on *mixed* households arguably engenders a different set of considerations and realities. For example, individuals cannot divorce themselves entirely from household relations once they leave the door of the home. Although people might not go to school or work with members of their household, the experiences of the household and perceptions of the household still come to bear. As Twine points out, recognizing sets of relations within mixed households and understanding the influence of such connections within and beyond the home helps debunk stereotypes of the family as a "*racially unified*" grouping.[18]

Shifting the focus to relationships does not mean simply erasing or denying the importance of linking households with geographic locations. On the contrary, having rights to a particular space, and creating a home at that physical location, can directly shape feelings of comfort for mixed households. The simple statement "we live here, this is our home" marks a performance of a household in place, of a household that belongs. Feeling in place means that the household becomes "a term laden down with a baggage of multiple meanings: shelter, abode, hearth, heart, privacy, roots, paradise, and so on."[19] The very title of Billston and Valentine's chapter, "Wherever I Lay My Girlfriend, That's My Home," besides playing on the heteronormative assumptions assigned to the household, furthers the idea of the household as endowed with emotion and significance. It also suggests that household members mix in more places than just the physical residence.

This scale allows us to draw attention to the variety of assemblages that mixed households can assume. In contradistinction, statistical portraits of urban spaces tend to portray static and monoracial or monoethnic households. This is primarily because most analyses of racial segregation rely on counts of racialized individuals rather than counts of individuals in households. Maps of settlement based on such data rarely acknowledge racial mixing in households, and therefore they naturalize assumptions that distinct groups of individuals make up urban spaces.[20] Such projects reinscribe patterns of difference by depicting individuals as both spatially clustered and discrete. If we concentrate only on individual bodies, it becomes easier to perpetuate certain myths of group separation and distinct immigrant futures within cities. Yet, "the patterns of concentration by several different household types . . . tell other stories [about immigration to the United States]."[21]

Contemplating mixing (or segregation and diversity) at the scale of the household likely produces varied portraits of neighborhoods and nuanced takes on belonging. Neighborhood diversity, then, would not only derive from counts of bodies in neighborhoods, but also from counts of bodies in households. Asking questions about racial and nativity mixing at the household scale thus has the potential to alter, and perhaps upend, perceptions of places and urban forms. Altogether, we hope to show here in the following narratives that the mixed household, as a mobile and relational collectivity and a physical location, provides a dynamic framework for unpacking the immigrant city.

Mixing in Seattle

The household scale clearly offers many opportunities for engaging with immigration and settlement. To begin to open up these possibilities, we base this chapter on empirical data gathered during interviews with mixed households in Seattle. These interviews constitute the qualitative component of a larger project that examines mixed-race households in urban contexts throughout the United States. This broader project primarily relies on statistical analyses of residential location and individual identity in the biggest U.S. cities. The quantitative data illustrate noticeably different patterns of racial mixing in the West as compared to other regions of the country. For example, the rates of racial mixing in Seattle—like San Francisco, San Diego, and Los Angeles—are about twice the national average. Specifically, census data from 2000 show that opposite-sex mixed-race partnerships make up the following shares of marriages in Seattle: white-black (1 percent), white-Asian (3.5 percent), white-Latino (3 percent), white–Native American (1 percent).[22] These numbers would undoubtedly be much larger if long-term cohabiting and same-sex couples were included in the tally.

Of course, racial mixing does not necessarily indicate the mixing of nativity within households as well. Yet, nearly two-thirds of our interviews in Seattle involved mixed-nativity and mixed-race households. Given the histories of immigration and racial mixing in Seattle, this city offers a compelling site for the qualitative study of immigration and settlement and for engagement with household-scale research. As Khiet[23] explains,

> *It's just that people mix better here.* Seattle is very different, I find, from other cities—Ithaca, New York, from San Luis Obispo, Sacramento, San Jose—all those places, it's just different.

The partners who head the households highlighted in this chapter are just three of a sample of eighteen households interviewed in Seattle. Households volunteered to participate in this study and usually responded to recruitment flyers posted throughout the city or sent out on the Internet listservs of various race-based organizations. The people in the households live in a variety of neighborhoods within Seattle and its suburbs. The partners range in age from their late twenties to early eighties and demonstrate a fairly even spread across age cohorts. Fifteen of the households include opposite-sex partners and three include same-sex partners. Some of these couples have spent decades together, and others were recently married or partnered. The majority of the interviewees are in their first and only marriage or long-term cohabiting relationship.

In terms of racial mixing, the majority of the households involve one partner who self-identifies as white and another partner who self-identifies as black or Asian. Of the two remaining households, one includes a person who identifies as Asian and a person who identifies as multiracial (Asian-white) and the other includes a black-Asian pairing. Our sample obviously has tremendous breadth, but this diversity of experiences is important for our study of mixed households. Indeed, garnering insight from an array of interviewees exemplifies our point that mixed households hold the potential for confounding and altering singular narratives of settlement and immigration.

The "Odd Couple": In and Out of Place

As a mixed-race, mixed-nativity, and mixed-age household, Tori[24] and Bill[25] articulate in the interview the many lines of difference they navigate within their household and within urban spaces more broadly. They repeatedly discuss external appraisals of their relationship and mull over where and if they fit in. Their own self-designation as "an odd couple" (Bill) signals both Tori and Bill's feelings of displacement and the many negotiations necessarily undertaken by their mixed household. The prominent themes underpinning the interview speak to the central tenets of this chapter: (1) narratives of immigration and settlement are multiple and power laden; and (2) questions of belonging frequently vex households that do not conform to normative expectations. For example, in the following exchange, Tori and Bill consider how people might name or "know" their household:

Serin: Do you feel like you all have been very labeled by people, as like "Oh, they're this or that"?

Tori: How would we know?

Bill: Who would label us? It's got to be kind of hard to label us. . . . We don't ever belong to anything long enough for them to label us.

Tori: Exactly. And people often can't figure out what our relationship is.

Serin: Between the two of you? Oh really?

Tori: Yeah. I can't tell you how many times I've said "No, this is my husband" [laughs].

Bill: But that we encounter in China, too.

Tori: All over the place. Because age difference, race difference. It's understandable. It doesn't offend me. People label us as outsiders, that's true.

Bill: All the Chinese women look at you—

Tori: Oh, well, that—it's Chinatown.

Bill: Stealing handsome Chinese man away—they don't like that.

In this excerpt, Tori and Bill indicate that questions about their relationship emerge in several contexts, including each of their birthplaces (China and the United States). Bill also suggests that they do not belong to any group or place long enough to attain a label, and Tori mentions that they are often "outsiders." Through her marriage to a man who is different from herself in terms of age, nativity, and race, Tori becomes more bound up with immigration and settlement processes than she might be otherwise as a white woman in the United States. Indeed, Bill describes the scrutiny that Tori endures from "all" Chinese women as a result of purportedly "stealing [a] handsome Chinese man away." Such interactions, and other parallel experiences, would probably not be present in Tori's life if she was not a part of a mixed household. Similarly, Bill undoubtedly experiences certain challenges as a Chinese immigrant married to a white woman. Put differently, the reality of being in a mixed household is not something that just lingers in the background and becomes visible in spatially constrained moments. On the contrary, Tori and Bill imply that being mixed infuses their lives.

For Bill, his personal history of migration stirs up questions about home. Being in a mixed relationship—and not linked with cultural spaces, such as Chinatowns or international districts, that work to translate many aspects of the homeland to the United States—adds to the potency of such ruminations:

Bill: What I call my home?

Serin: Yeah, do you have like a little—

Bill: I don't—well, this is my home, but I don't consider Seattle my home.

Serin: Oh yeah?

Bill: I've been here ten years, but I have a feeling I'm not going to be here for the rest of my life.

Tori: We're not going to stay here. We don't feel like we belong here.

Bill: But then Shanghai, where I was born, is not really my home anymore so it's not just—if you ask me, I never know how to answer so that eventually I settled down with an easy answer. I said, "Well, I travel all over the world, but I only feel at home in San Francisco, since I've been there thirty years, so I give that, San Francisco."

Bill differentiates between place of birth, place of residence, and place of connection in his discussion of home. He and Tori both note that they do not belong in Seattle and that San Francisco was their most comfortable "home." Yet, as Tori clarifies, "when people ask where you're from or that sort of thing, both of us feel that that's contingent on where we are, first of all." This comment implies that context matters to perceptions of emplacement. Moreover, Bill's musings on not really being entirely at home anywhere and Tori's comments about not belonging once again illustrate the ongoing negotiations sparked by immigration.

The theme of being out of place regularly surfaces for Bill and Tori. At one point in the interview, for instance, Tori describes the racial discomfort she felt when the couple lived in Missouri. Even though she was born and raised in the United States, Tori takes on the language often reserved for immigrants in her story. She explains,

> We felt like foreigners, we really did, and we would never be assimilated. The one time I felt assimilated was he [Bill] was in San Francisco and a workman came over to fix my flue and . . . we have this little chat and he starts going on about how beautiful Missouri is and how it's the most beautiful place in the world, "didn't I think so?" And on and on in that vein—I don't know why I felt called upon, you know, to be a part of this, but I felt very strong pressure. And then a young woman came from the trailer park to clean the house when I was trying to sell it, and it was the same deal, about how we were basically white people together, and wasn't this a wonderful, wonderful place. It's hard to explain, but it was very, very oppressive.

In Tori's visceral and negative reaction to the assumptions of shared whiteness, she alludes to the internal discomfort she feels with the presumption that Missouri is wonderful and welcoming. Although she does not explicitly say so, it is clear that she does not feel comfortable "passing" as an assimilated part of the white majority since her marriage with Bill confounds such affiliations. Although the workman and young woman read her whiteness in particular ways, she feels unsettled by their categorization of her. She continues,

> I never felt so white in my whole life. I had never been interpellated as a white person. I had never been asked to stand with whites against everybody else. I'd never been included in those kinds of conversations

before, and it stupefied me actually. The real hatred between and among people. I'd never ever seen that before.

Tori's experiences in Missouri directly confront her sense of self as she feels both like a foreigner and like an assumed and assimilated part of the majority. In the end, neither of these dialectically opposed positionalities fully captures the dynamic realities of Tori and Bill's lives as a mixed household.

This couple negotiates their own personal identities as well as that of their partnership in a host of contexts. As a result, notions of home, displacement, and belonging hover in the wings of their daily lives. Furthermore, as Tori and Bill's comments elucidate, several narratives of immigration and settlement characterize this mixed household. Taking seriously this multiplicity can inform our interpretations of households—and by extension cities—as active sites of immigration and settlement. Moreover, attending to the relational attributes of mixing via a joint interview provides a window into the intricacies of displacement and belonging. These nuances would be left by the wayside if we only interviewed individuals or focused solely on broad-scale immigrant collectives and enclaves.

Borders and Belonging: Language Choices and Citizenship Concerns

In the first vignette, Tori and Bill discuss their perceptions of fitting in or not and reference the ways in which immigration continually informs their daily lives. Jack[26] and Khiet[27] add to this conversation by invoking the legal normative orders of belonging that shape their experiences. For instance, the crossing of national borders incites fear and concern for this mixed-nativity and mixed-race household. Khiet explains, "Even now I would have problems too. . . . If I did not have my passport, I don't think I could have gone through with just a photo registration. They [the Border Patrol] would have thought that I faked that." Jack adds, "it can happen either with the Canadians or with the Americans, either one can give a lot of grief to people who don't look or talk or act white American." Such negative experiences bring to the fore the interplay of immigration and social identities for Khiet and Jack. Additionally, their language choices within the household and broader family networks indicate another way that this mixed household negotiates feeling in place. This second vignette, therefore, draws upon Jack and Khiet's stories to flesh out how linguistic and citizenship decisions deepen interpretations of borders and belonging.

As a Vietnamese refugee—"I was one of those boat people that you heard about in the late '70s, early '80s. I arrived here in 1980, I left in '79, and so I'm one of those refugees, or was"—Khiet voices her gratitude to the United States for taking her in when she was in desperate straits. She worked hard to succeed in this new country, changing from just having "the clothes on my back and nothing else" to eventually achieving advanced degrees, citizenship, and a stable income. Yet, recent global events have caused Khiet to rethink her connection to the United States. She explains,

> I question my own citizenship here, whether I belong. Before that [September 11, 2001] I was here, I'm here, I'm an American and that was that. There was no question whatsoever. But since 9/11, and it wasn't right away, it was much later—when 9/11 happened, we were overseas. We found out at the airport overseas—it was a month or two later that I arrived back, two months later that I arrived back in the United States and the feeling, it was not the same place I left. That's a strange thing and that speaks to how the authorities can really set the tone for an entire country like that. . . . I never had any doubt that this is my home. . . . Now I'm not so sure.

Khiet's personal narrative includes several moments of dislocation and relocation. After she fled her homeland, she managed to establish a life for herself in the United States. She presents herself as feeling in place at that time, presumably accepted as an American. These binds of citizenship and belonging have become tenuous since 9/11, however, as Khiet copes with challenges at national borders and confronts a different social climate. In short, her experiences of immigration and settlement receded from her consciousness after twenty years of residence; they have now reemerged as prominent themes in her daily life.

The unraveling of Khiet's sense of belonging affects Jack's sense of belonging as well. He states, "as the representative of the dominant culture, I don't see anything. It's not—it really is almost invisible to me, and I see it through Khiet's reactions or Khiet's descriptions of things going on." His comment exemplifies how immigration narratives may become coauthored tales—even when one of the partners is native born. As Jack himself acknowledges, identifying as a native-born white male in the United States means that he is exempt from always having to justify himself or critically examine his place in society. Yet, he is also part of a mixed household, so he cannot live with blinders on. Indeed, as he mentions, he has come to see and understand society differently because of Khiet's experiences. Not only has Jack learned to interpret interactions in new ways due to his relationship with Khiet, but he has also engaged with questions of location and belonging as a result of this partnership. He notes,

> We were finding a place to be where . . . we'd have our network with my parents and family nearby, and we'd have the infrastructure we needed. We didn't want to go too rural. We didn't want to get lost in this big city. . . . So that was all part of the quest—again, the racial-ethnic-cultural mix that suited us at the time.

Khiet and Jack thought carefully about their residential location when they moved to Seattle. They wanted to live in a place that had enough of an Asian feel to make her comfortable, they wanted opportunities for their children to interact with multiple communities, and they wanted to be near his family. These concerns are ones most likely shared by scores of households; the mixing of nativity and race in Jack and Khiet's household, however, produces particular needs and sensibilities about what it takes to "belong." Furthermore, Jack's comments typify the twin arguments of this chapter, namely, that settlement and immigration are ongoing and that the household scale offers a productive site for examining such processes.

While Khiet and Jack negotiate the borders of societal inclusion, they also navigate decisions about language within the household and the broader family network. Jack is fluent in Vietnamese, but his extended family is not. As a result, Khiet often brushes up against the limits of acceptance when she speaks Vietnamese with their children. Jack and Khiet describe one such encounter:

> Khiet: We just came back from Vietnam and our little one spoke at the time only in Vietnamese. . . . Before that, with our oldest, they [Jack's family] thought it was all so cool that I tried to raise my kids bilingual and that I would be speaking Vietnamese to my kids. But now Dad [Jack's father] was very sick . . . and I was speaking to my youngest in Vietnamese and that bothered him -
> Jack: It was probably at the dinner table or something like that.

Khiet: Later he said to you on the side, he said, "Jack, would Khiet be offended if we ask her not to speak so much Vietnamese?" Or something to that—

Jack: And part of that is because—you know, they can catch the emotion out of the tone of voice, but they don't really know what's going on. And so there's that kind of—the monolinguist's discomfort with somebody saying something they don't know what it is, Americans are really—feel this way a lot.

This passage reveals the pressures that Khiet and Jack face because, on the one hand, they want to raise their children bilingual so as to maintain cultural links. On the other hand, it is clear that speaking English helps solidify belonging and acceptance. Presumably, if Khiet and Jack lived in an ethnic enclave or had married people of similar backgrounds they would not have to grapple with such choices or external responses. It is clear, then, that being in a mixed household directly informs a host of daily choices and experiences.

Questions about language not only affected conversations with Jack's extended family (there seem to be fewer confrontations with Khiet's relatives because he can speak Vietnamese), but also influenced decisions about the naming of the children. Khiet speaks passionately to this issue:

With the first one [child] I said I want him with an English name, a name that everybody know[s] how to pronounce, but that is pronounceable in Vietnamese so that my family can call him by the same name and not make up another name for him. . . . The second one, now during the time I sent [older child] to daycare and grade school and all that, he's had all kinds of friends with names I never heard of before and names that speak to who their parents are. And I thought what am I ashamed of? My kids are half Vietnamese—by golly they're going to have a Vietnamese name and they're not going to—a lot of Vietnamese choose to have an English or American name for the first name for their kids and a middle name of Vietnamese. I said that's hiding it, because nobody uses the middle name. So, I'm not ashamed of who I am. I'm not ashamed of my kids being half Vietnamese. By golly, this one is going to have a Vietnamese first name! And so when the name was decided, . . . [Jack's] brother said, what kind of a name is that?!

Khiet outlines her own odyssey of trying to blend in and belong—"assimilate"—while also honoring her own heritage in this tale of naming her children. For the first child, choosing an English name signified fitting in and settling into life in the United States. With the second child, Khiet wanted to more publicly acknowledge a Vietnamese legacy. This decision elicited some disapproval from Jack's family, though, as it challenged notions of homogeneity and uniformity within the family unit. Affirming Khiet's Vietnamese heritage seemingly threatened the borders of her acceptance and her children's inclusion within Jack's family. These examples are microexpressions of belonging and displacement and also mirror broader urban processes wherein immigrants perform new identities vis-à-vis linguistic choices and names.

Jack and Khiet's narratives make it obvious that Vietnam and the Vietnamese language are not distant memories, even though Khiet fled her country of birth years ago. Khiet and Jack exercise all kinds of flexibility as they navigate difference within their household. Their stories also indicate that the people with whom they interact—within national and familial contexts—do not necessarily share this broad view of acceptance; instead, these people often determine the very borders of belonging.

Sexuality and Status: Activism, Citizenship, and Speaking English

In this last vignette, language and citizenship remain at center stage. Three primary factors—pending citizenship for Juan, questions about "proper" English, and an accent on sexuality—differentiate the following narratives from the stories of Jack and Khiet. As a gay, mixed-race, mixed-nativity, and mixed-age household, Juan[28] and Steve[29] describe numerous contexts of displacement and belonging in the interview. The ways that sexuality and individual citizenship status coalesce in daily practices for these two men—evident in discrimination experienced at the workplace and in opportunities (or the lack thereof) for investing in real estate—outline another dimension of immigration and settlement. This last section, therefore, references moments when Steve and Juan talk about activism, citizenship, and speaking English.

Language often serves as a clear marker of inclusion and exclusion for immigrants. In Jack and Khiet's stories, the choice to speak Vietnamese with their children inspired ire and challenged inclusion. In contrast, Juan bumps up against some limits to acceptance due to the way he speaks English. In the following exchange, Juan describes moments when he feels "Othered" by language, and Steve notes one of Juan's linguistic slips that frequently positions him as foreign born:

> Juan: A friend of my brother visited us a few months ago and he asked me like how I adapt and all that. It's hard because sometimes if we talk, I mean my English is not perfect, it's not going to be the same way that Americans will say things. There are some words that we will pronounce differently just because of the upbringing. But if you talk that way, there is that whole communication barrier. . . . So, sometimes I will ask Steve or ask someone else, is this how you pronounce it? . . . Or will the "shold" be "should"? [laughter] There are a lot of those little things that it's just different.
>
> Steve: And there's something else different. Filipinos don't have a difference between he and she.
>
> Juan: We don't have pronouns for he and she.
>
> Serin: Oh!
>
> Steve: They don't have that. So, sometimes he'll be talking about a guy and he can say she.

Although this pronoun switching involves only a couple of words from the English language, it immediately marks Juan as a non-native speaker and thus not native born. Moreover, the assumptions conveyed by pronouns are key to spoken English, so these words carry significant weight. It is worth noting the wonderful irony in this excerpt as it is a gay man that mixes up the gender identities of people in his stories.

Juan's experience with speaking English shows that belonging and displacement are often predicated upon a few words. We can extrapolate from Juan and Steve's conversation that acceptance requires adherence to particular norms and standards. The numerous lines of difference woven throughout Steve and Juan's partnership make it difficult for this household to neatly fit into one box or normative definition of a household. In reference to aspects of this multiplicity, Juan offers the following story about how he fills out official forms on race and ethnicity. He notes,

> Juan: It [forms] will ask if you're Asian and all that and sometimes I don't want to answer that because I cannot identify. I don't want to be put in a box. I'm not AP, I'm an Asian Pacific Islander or I'm not Asian—I mean I'm Asian but I'm not—
>
> Steve: Asian is a whole bunch of different groups.
>
> Juan: Yeah, it is.

Steve: I hate those questions. I think that's the most annoying thing. . . .

Juan: So would I consider my race to be Hispanic because growing up in the Philippines I know we were so exposed. I mean, there's probably a part of us that's Hispanic because of all the interaction with the colonial, yeah. But then I'm not really Hispanic, but I have a Hispanic-sounding name [laughs].

Juan's comments carry this conversation on identity, presumably because as the immigrant of color in the household he is subject to great scrutiny within society. Steve, however, is quick to note how census categories of race, such as Asian, simplify heterogeneity. Ultimately, Steve is the one who repeatedly expresses frustration with systems of grouping because such categorization always works to exclude. He comments,

You can definitely see the doors that close. There are doors that close and it may not always be noticeable, but there are doors that close and whether it's just a gay couple or a gay mixed couple, different doors close. And when you're a white hetero couple, none of those doors are closed.

Most likely, Steve could have avoided personally experiencing the closing of doors if he had partnered with someone else. Instead, his commitment to Juan means that he intimately shares and experiences Juan's concerns with immigration, settlement, citizenship, and belonging. For example, the fact that Juan was not yet a citizen at the time of the interview influenced the couple's political activism. This situation indicates the meshing of sexuality and status within the household:

Steve: I was never political till we got together. I was going to vote for George Bush.

Juan: And I was like—I'm going to be down in San Francisco [laughs]! I am not going to bed with somebody who votes for George Bush!

Steve: It was funny.

Juan: So, that's a big example of what is political is personal!

Steve: Now since then, though, I've started to get involved, and I write letters all the time, for different reasons. Whether it's gay rights or whether it's just rights period, whatever is happening at the time.

Steve, as the native-born citizen in the partnership, becomes the spokesperson of sorts for the household. He and Juan make collective decisions about Steve's voting practices—"like even now when Steve votes, we will talk about issues that's going on, which initiative he will vote for, but it's like he's voting for the two of us" (Juan)—and Steve engages with political activism on their joint behalf. Despite Steve's role as the citizen for both men, Juan's pending status means that in public spheres Steve has to present himself as a sole voice. Steve offers the following explanation for why he does not ever mention Juan in his activism:

> Even like with the legal marriage alliance or me writing letters and stuff like that, that's all on me. He [Juan] can't, I wouldn't involve him in any of that because I even write the letters to George, and if he's [Juan] associated with that, those guys are blacklisted. So I don't involve him in any of that. Even on the gay side, you know, with gay issues and stuff like that, [Juan] totally stays out of it.

Clearly, the foreign born are not the only ones to negotiate immigration and settlement or to be intimately involved in such processes. Questions of citizenship status contour many decisions of this household, and this focus has a history within the partnership. Indeed, it was the lack of security for the relationship that prompted Juan's citizenship application. He states,

> I think for us it's also a secured [sic] for our relationship because it's weird because I can be, if I'm not a citizen I can be paying my taxes and all that for years and years and years, but I cannot have any benefit of that. . . . I mean, if you're a permanent resident you're not granted the full benefits. If something happens they can deport you so those are concerns of being in a relationship and being here in the United States.

Feeling at home in general entails more than gaining a particular legal status. Notions of acceptance and comfort frequently correspond with actual residential decisions. Although Juan and Steve generally enjoy life in Seattle, they do wonder about where else they might live. In such conversations, the multiple mixes in their household are front and center:

Juan: It's almost like it's not just the race that's the consideration but also our sexuality that factors in—

Steve: Because it's huge when the government doesn't accept you and you don't have rights, that's huge. We had to go to lawyers and get all kinds of papers because we have three houses now and all our other stuff, huge considerations. If something happens to one of us, you know?

Juan: Like after the [2004] election, we were talking like oh, I told Steve I will never travel anywhere in that whole middle part of America! I have a Hispanic name, I am gay, and I look Asian when they see me in person [laughter]!

Juan's final comment in this passage exemplifies that immigration and settlement are not singular and temporally limited experiences. In contrast, they are ongoing social processes that inform daily life for mixed households in a host of contexts.

Steve and Juan's narratives resonate with and incorporate many of the themes voiced by Tori and Bill and by Jack and Khiet. We close with this interview because it augments the other stories and elucidates the complexities inherent in negotiating life within U.S. cities. Altogether, these three vignettes underscore how the scale of the household foregrounds relationality and sheds light on diverse and multiple experiences.

Conclusion

The potent immigration history of the United States serves as a springboard for our discussion here because immigration helps power the transformations of our cities and households. The formation of mixed households is just one outcome of migration patterns, but we suggest that this scale offers exciting opportunities for studying displacement and belonging. Given the wide range of mixed households in the United States, our intention with this chapter is to participate in conversations about the multiplicity of life courses that immigrants enact within urban spaces rather than to provide some sort of comprehensive account. We do this by foregrounding the narratives of three mixed households in Seattle. Within this narrow sample, we find significant variability in the issues and concerns voiced by interviewees. Nevertheless, we can trace three common themes as well.

First, the individual experiences of one member of the household usually affect the other member to the extent that these mixed households coauthor narratives of belonging and displacement, despite racial and experiential differences. This finding mirrors the results offered by Petronoti and Papgaroufali on the "joint scripts" that Greek-Turkish couples compose in their mixed family contexts.[30] In our Seattle study, the shared narratives of mixed households stem from a variety of contexts. As Juan states,

Being in a mixed-race relationship, there are a lot of—there's a lot of that going on, a lot of—how would you say? Like we experienced things that a lot of couples will never experience and we will be open to a lot more things that other couples may not be that open. And it influences our decision every day, like where we go, where we eat, or where are we going to travel—. . . Like if I will not be comfortable in one place, then we won't go there, and the same thing for him.

Second, our research also suggests that issues of settlement and belonging are rarely foreclosed in mixed households; instead, immigration entails ongoing negotiations as mixed households have to simultaneously confront stereotypes of race and citizenship and race and partnership. Almost by the act of studying mixing in households, we disturb notions of singular belonging or standard norms for acceptance to show how people can both feel emplaced and displaced at the same time. Still, dominant norms of race and place hold tremendous sway and are often hard to dislodge. For example, despite the diversity of her household, Khiet's status, in the eyes of some, remains fixed and removed. Here she recounts a meeting with an African American woman:

We were talking something about around race and prejudice and discrimination, and suddenly she just said—"but, we are Americans. We," meaning the blacks, "are Americans and we deserve better than those people who just come here." Anyway, so there is also that within the minorities. There's also those of us who are true Americans and those of you who aren't.

Mixed households may certainly challenge presuppositions about the racial makeup of households, and even the nation, but this excerpt reminds us that this is an ongoing struggle.

Third, although it is almost painfully obvious, it bears repeating that the United States remains segregated and that de facto segregation continues to govern many aspects of daily life; this truism makes it even more worthwhile to study how differently racialized members of households successfully negotiate the perils and pressures of stereotyping and how different lives come together and become rescripted. In this chapter, we therefore highlight a narrative approach that draws out some of the complexity of integration, visible in the negotiations of mixed-race, mixed-ethnic, and mixed-nativity households. And just as these narratives draw attention to the joint reproduction of household members, the household scale requires that attention be paid to the multiple spaces of everyday life because "racial and ethnic identities do not exist in a vacuum; the places and space in which individuals and groups operate influence how race and ethnicity have come to be understood, expressed, and experienced."[31] As Berry and Henderson note, "The spaces and places that we exist in and create, simultaneously shapes and records the way life unfolds, including the lived experience of ethnicity and race. Experiences and identities, in turn, influence our interpretations and definitions of space and place."[32]

The household scale opens up space for inflecting dynamism into the concept of the household; rather than simply a residential address, it is a contested, expressive, and affective site. In an effort to reconceive standardized analyses of immigration, the household become the means for recognizing other scales, places, and microgeographies of difference and commonality. Mixing is happening—in cities, workplaces, schools, and bedrooms. Therefore, we need to stand up to the fiction that ethnic and racial groups lead separate and discrete lives to more fully imagine and explain the multiplicity of settlement patterns and the daily remaking of immigrant and native-born experiences in urban America.

Notes

1. R. Ueda, *Postwar Immigrant America: A Social History* (Boston: Bedford Books of St. Martin's Press, 1994).

2. S. Houston, R. Wright, M. Ellis, S. Holloway, and M. Hudson, "Places of Possibility: Where Mixed Race Partners Meet," *Progress in Human Geography* 29, no. 6 (2005): 700–17.

3. S. Buzar, P. Ogden, and R. Hall, "Households Matter: The Quiet Demography of Urban Transformation," *Progress in Human Geography* 29, no. 4 (2005): 413–36.

4. T. Philpott, *The Slum and the Ghetto: Neighborhood Deterioration and Middle-Class Reform, Chicago, 1880–1930* (New York: Oxford University Press, 1978); D. Massey, and N. Denton, *American Apartheid: Segregation and the Making of the Underclass* (Cambridge, Mass.: Harvard University Press, 1993).

5. M. Ellis, R. Wright, and V. Parks, "Spatial Assimilation and the Household: Partnership, Nativity, and Neighborhood Location," *Urban Geography* 27, no. 1 (2006): 1–19.

6. M. Ellis and R. Wright, "Representations of Difference: Mapping Immigrants or Immigrant Households?" *Proceedings of the National Academy of Sciences* 102, no. 43 (2005): 15325–30; R. Wright and M. Ellis, "Mapping Others," *Progress in Human Geography* 30, no. 3 (2006): 285–88.

7. C. Luke, "Global Mobilities: Crafting Identities in Interracial Families," *International Journal of Cultural Studies* 6, no. 4 (2003): 379–401; the quotation is on 380.

8. Quoted by I. Buchanan, "Introduction," in *The Certeau Reader,* ed. G. Ward (Malden, Mass.: Blackwell, 2000), 97–100; the quotation is on 99.

9. This, as with all names used in this chapter, is a pseudonym.

10. It is important to note that several other social processes aid in the formation of mixed households. E.g., the military is one institution often attributed with fueling interactions between different people. As Bill explains, "Yeah, military and war lead to miscegenation [laughter]. Very bad for racial purity! Right? . . . You send kids abroad for war, and then they come back and all the back and forth, it's bringing a lot of foreign elements."

11. K. Eschbach, "The Enduring and Vanishing American Indian: American Indian Population Growth and Intermarriage in 1990," *Ethnic and Racial Studies* 18, no. 1 (1995): 89–108; G. Nash, "The Hidden History of Mestizo America," *Journal of American History* 82, no. 3 (1995): 941–64; U.S. Bureau of the Census, "Race of Wife by Race of Husband: 1960, 1970, 1980, 1991, 1992" (Washington, D.C.: U.S. Bureau of the Census, 1998), http://www.census.gov/population/socdemo/race/interractab1.txt; D. Wong, "A Geographical Analysis of Multiethnic Households in the United States," *International Journal of Population Geography* 5 (1999): 31–48; M. Root, *Love's Revolution: Interracial Marriage* (Philadelphia: Temple University Press, 2001).

12. N. Zack, ed., *Race/Sex: Their Sameness, Difference, and Interplay* (New York: Routledge, 1997); J. Tyner, "Narrating Interracial Relations and the Negotiation of Public Spaces," *Environment and Planning D: Society and Space* 20 (2002): 441–58; J. Nagel, *Race, Ethnicity, and Sexuality: Intimate Intersections, Forbidden Frontiers* (New York: Oxford University Press, 2003).

13. Bill self-identifies as Chinese and Asian.

14. J. Hartigan, "Locating White Detroit," in *Displacing Whiteness: Essays in Social and Cultural Criticism,* ed. R. Frankenberg (Durham, N.C.: Duke University Press, 1997), 181–213; the quotation is on 184.

15. H. Jarvis, A. Pratt, and C. Wu, *The Secret Life of Cities: The Social Reproduction of Everyday Life* (London: Prentice-Hall, 2001), 89.

16. P. Rossi, *Why Families Move* (Glencoe, Ill.: Free Press, 1955); C. Stapleton, "Reformulation of the Family Life-Cycle Concept: Implications for Residential Mobility" *Environment and Planning A* 12 (1980): 1103–18; W. Clark and F. Dieleman, *Households and Housing: Choice and Outcomes in the Housing Market* (New Brunswick, N.J.: Center for Urban Policy Research, 1996).

17. See, as exceptions, C. Peach, "Ethnic Segregation and Intermarriage," *Annals of the Association of American Geographers* 70, no. 3 (1980): 371–81; M. White and S. Sassler, "Judging Not Only by Color: Ethnicity, Nativity, and Neighborhood Attainment," *Social Science Quarterly* 81, no. 4 (2000): 997–1013; and R. Wright, M. Ellis, and V. Parks, "Re-Placing Whiteness in Spatial Assimilation Research," *City and Community* 4, no. 2 (2005): 111–35.

18. F. W. Twine, "Bearing Blackness in Britain: The Meaning of Racial Difference for White Birth Mothers of African-Descent Children," *Social Identities* 5, no. 2 (1999): 185–210; the quotation is on 186, with the emphasis in the original.

19. L. Billston and G. Valentine, "'Wherever I Lay My Girlfriend, That's My Home': The Performance and Surveillance of Lesbian Identities in Domestic Environments," in *Mapping Desire: Geographies of Sexualities,* ed. D. Bell and G. Valentine (New York: Routledge, 1995), 99–113; the quotation is on 111.

20. R. Wright, S. Houston, M. Ellis, S. Holloway, and M. Hudson, "Crossing Racial

Lines: Geographies of Mixed-Race Partnering and Multiraciality in the United States," *Progress in Human Geography* 27, no. 4 (2003): 457–74.

21. Ellis and Wright, "Representations of Difference"; Wright and Ellis, "Mapping Others," 15,325.

22. U.S. Bureau of the Census, *Census of Population and Housing, Five Percent Public Use Microdata Sample Files* (Washington, D.C.: U.S. Bureau of the Census, 2000).

23. Self-identifies as Vietnamese.

24. Self-identifies as white.

25. Self-identifies as Chinese and Asian.

26. Self-identifies as white and Caucasian.

27. Self-identifies as Vietnamese.

28. Self-identifies as Asian.

29. Self-identifies as white.

30. M. Petronoti and E. Papgaroufali, "Marrying a 'Foe': Joint Scripts and Rewritten Histories of Greek Turkish Couples," *Identities* 13, no. 4 (2006): 557–84.

31. K. Berry and M. Henderson, "Envisioning the Nexus between Geography and Ethnic and Racial Identity," in *Geographical Identities of Ethnic America: Race, Space, and Place,* ed. K. Berry and M. Henderson (Reno: University of Nevada Press, 2002), 1–14; the quotation is on 3.

32. Ibid., 6.

4

Spatial and Symbolic Patterns of Migrant Settlement: The Case of Muslim Diasporas in Europe

Chantal Saint-Blancat

Space is not socially neutral. The settlement of urban territory is connected with the historical construction of the identity of social groups; but cities are also the point where differences meet. Cities are born and remain under the sign of multiculture.[1] Urban space is therefore characterized by a strong symbolic value; its symbolic control results in competition for the monopoly over territories that are at the same time social entities.

At the beginning of 1900, the Chicago School, which studied the various "moral regions" born of the typical metropolitan mechanisms of aggregation-segregation,[2] suggested reading difference as a value in itself, as a residue of traditionalism, which was, however, destined to be channeled into processes of production, of individual and collective mobility, and of the construction of a better society. The logic of the melting pot did not survive the demand for a widening of inclusion during the 1960s. In Europe, this universalistic dimension exploded during the 1980s with the march for equality of young Beurs in France (1983), a first sign of the crisis of assimilation policies and of the ensuing strong sense of deprivation.

With the debate on multiculture, the concept of difference is established as a constituent and fundamental value of the person and as an inalienable right. This, however, may lead to the risk of a return to defining difference as an absolute essence to be protected,[3] whereas belonging to a certain ethnocultural group does not automatically trace one's only destiny, as was clearly shown in *Street Corner Society* by William Foote White in 1943.[4]

The demand for acknowledgement of difference in contemporary society has been expressed by a request for differentiated visibility in the public sphere, above all among Muslims. European societies have to deal with the fact that, if they consider Muslims as citizens on equal terms,[5] they have to make room for them and open national urban spaces to their mode of behavior, in order to make them finally feel "at home." This concerns not only collective expression of religious belief but also attitudes toward food, music, and dress codes that do not necessarily coincide with national cultural traditions.

As a reaction to this "differing" presence, Enzo Colombo suggests analyzing how it is practically utilized in social interaction, by whom, in which contexts, and to which ends. Urban situations of confrontation with otherness, situations of everyday multiculture, are nowadays one of the spaces in which "difference is not completely imposed, but is the result of dialogue and conflict taking place in a condition of difference in power, capabilities and resources."[6]

As Goffman reminds us,[7] whoever distances himself or herself from normal and customary appearance causes the surrounding environment, taken for granted as safe, to turn into a source of alarm. A widespread sense of fear thereby arises,[8] leading to a demand for expulsion from the urban scene of all those who, although not infringing any law, disturb the "normality of appearances" by not respecting the habitual codes of everyday social interaction (noise, collective and differing occupation of public space, religious hallmarks as veils, beards). The triad of immigration-fear-security (with concerns about immigration being particularly sensitive for Muslims, especially since the September 11, 2001, terrorist attacks), also thanks to media amplification, marks everyday behaviors, political strategies, and local urban policies.[9]

In a recent survey, "Immigration and Citizenship in Europe: The Social Perception," 25 percent of the people interviewed declared that they were anxious about the process of migration for the following reasons: risk of public disorder (28 percent), threat of unemployment (27 percent), and challenge of cultural identity (25 percent).[10] Immigrants bring with them different cultural norms and values (family models, gender hierarchy, types of authority, relationship between social and private space) but also religious pluralism, thereby challenging the European exception so clearly set out by Grace Davie.[11]

Space is the result of a continuous process of social interaction, expressed through corporeal practices and the symbolic use of the territory. So space is always acquiring new meanings. Nowadays, it seems to have become a testing and training ground of sorts for multicultural coexistence.

We are witnessing a difficult acceptance and management of contemporary religious and cultural plurality in European urban space.[12] Through conflicts and negotiations, the redefinition of the symbolic utilization of urban territory is redrawing the lines of the borders of identity and is bringing forth new modes of interaction with "Otherness."

We will here consider two case studies concerning two types of request for visibility. One, of a more institutional nature, is the conflict born of the construction of mosques in European towns; the other pertains to the process of the reterritorialization of Muslim identities in public urban space, in particular the demands and visibility strategies of young Muslims born or socialized in European societies.

Mosques in the European Urban Public Space

The mosque issue is still a hot subject on the urban public agenda in some European countries, such as Italy, Spain, and even France. Despite all the efforts of the Muslim populations, the goodwill of many local bodies, and changes in public opinion, general suspicion and fear of cultural and religious diversity continue to fuel this type of urban conflict. In each national context, the mix of variables at stake is different. But misunderstandings, a lack of communication, and political ambiguity with respect to concrete pluralism continue to slow down the institutionalization of Islam in the European public space.

From Controversy to Negotiation

The religious dimension of Muslim immigration in Europe has long been invisible in European public space. In countries like the United Kingdom and France, Muslim populations have arrived since the 1950s from the ex-colonial empires; in the 1970s, they came to Germany from Turkey; and more recently, they have come to Italy and Spain. Mainly temporary male immigration was initially considered as an impermanent process both for the workers and the European states. It was just a convenient answer to reciprocal economic needs. The situation changed radically all over Europe at the end of the 1970s.[13] European societies discovered that, as a result of family reunification and of the arising of generations of young Turks, Algerians, or Pakistanis, born in Berlin, Birmingham, or Lille, most of them European citizens and socialized in their schools, Islam was by now a sedentarized and definitive presence.

Starting in the 1980s, praying rooms, which had long been hidden in suburban areas of European towns, sprung up in Europe's main cities—or, one should say, in those cities with a strong Muslim residential presence, like Bradford and Birmingham in Britain; Paris, Lyon, Lille, and Marseille in France; Brussels in Belgium; Berlin, Frankfurt, and Munich in Germany; Milan, Turin, and Rome in Italy; and Barcelona and Madrid in Spain. Urban topography reflects the different typologies of the ways in which migration has become established: concentrated in city centers in Brussels, Cologne, and Bradford; pushed out into the suburbs of Strasbourg and Lyon; and spread across the territory, "village style," in northeastern Italy, where the Muslim presence follows the polycentrism of the labor market.

Religious bookshops, *halal* butchers, ethnic shops, and recreational, sporting, and cultural associations flourish and provide evidence of the pluralism of the *umma* in the Muslim diaspora. The increasing number of mosques in the whole European urban territory between the 1970s and the 1990s reflects a public affirmation of identity as well as the internal pluralism of diaspora Islam. Rivalries between mosques reproduce the traditional ethnic divisions that are always present even in institutional and representative structures, between Algerians and Moroccans in France, and between Pakistanis and Bangladeshis in Britain.[14] Different places of worship reflect the various religious traditions: neo-bandi or barelvi in Britain; the Senegalese murid brotherhoods in Brescia, Northern Italy; or the more specifically ideological dividing lines related to different varieties of religious militancy (e.g., *tabligh* or *salafi* mosques, or mosques under the control of the Turkish state). In more recent times, mosques also bear the marks of generational differences.

This new development is related to two concomitant factors. The first is the domestic demands of immigrants, emerging from the realization that their presence in Europe no longer is going to be a simple interlude in their lives. It therefore becomes necessary to maintain one's system of values and beliefs, and to transmit it to the children. As a consequence of these demands follows the affirmation and the claim to one's own culture in a public space in which it had long been "hidden," self-censored, almost seen as a source of "shame."[15] To this first factor one has to add the strategy adopted by European public power structures: They see acknowledgement of the religious dimension, and hence the institutionalization of places of worship, as a possible means of political and social regulation for the critical issue of Muslim populations in urban areas, which are often characterized by alienation and socioeconomic discrimination.

Hence there is a still-unresolved ambiguity at the heart of some European urban and social policies: the tendency to "manage" the problem of migration with the help of Islam and that of spatial segregation in urban contexts by means of mosques.[16] Religious identity becomes the framework in which the issue of cultural and socioeconomic integration is dealt with. This approach is responsible for the fact that the "sociological Muslim," no matter what kind of relationship he or she has with Islam (whether secularized, cultural, or only related to respect for rites of passage, occasionally practicing, pietist, or integralist), is nevertheless somehow "confessionalized."

From the beginning of the 1990s, we therefore witness the following paradox: People of Turkish, Pakistani, or Moroccan origin are culturally absorbed into the "Muslim" category. Statistic surveys do not take the religious variable into account,[17] and this while religious identity, as in any other religious context, becomes more and more an individual choice instead of a passively inherited affiliation. So, instead of an ordinary case of town planning, building a mosque in Europe still remains in most cases a symbolic urban affair. What occurs (or does not occur) as mosques are built in European towns raises three issues:

- What is the status of Muslim populations, in the sense of their legitimacy to become visible within the urban space of the local and national arenas?
- There is a symbolic dimension of territory strongly connected with the construction and the maintenance of local and national identities. "The debate is woven around a generalized slippage from the theme of the 'mosque' towards the theme of social construction where Islam is directly linked to invasion, intolerance, and terrorism."[18]
- Finally, mosque controversies operate as a good interpretive framework for the delicate process of normalizing religious and cultural pluralism in urban space.

Local Negotiations: Contradictory Strategies

When the construction of a Muslim place of worship leads to resistance (or not), the interactions observed between municipal authorities (mainly the mayor and his deputies), Muslim associations, and local public opinion bespeak the level of Muslim integration in European towns. The actors' strategies in this process show the level of social regulation they have achieved: whether the issue acquires a religious, ideological, and political dimension or is instead faced as a normal professional and pragmatic case of ordinary town planning.

Three variables usually intervene in this process. The first factor is the relevance of the local level in the resolution of conflicts and in the management of negotiations. Even before becoming structured at the national level, Islam has already become an intrinsic part of the local space. Mayors, head teachers, and police chiefs find leaders of Muslim associations, or of youth community groups in secular associations, as credible and effective partners in the daily management of the territory.[19] The local level has been the first place for the management of Islamic issues in public urban space.

At times, local conflict can be at the center of a national controversy, orchestrated by political parties and by the media, as in the paradigmatic case of the Lodi mosque in Northern Italy near Milan; in 2000, its construction became the object of a national dispute for months. But everywhere in Europe, the request for Muslim worship areas or Muslim areas in cemeteries tends to be dealt with in the local arena, which has become the key location for the regulation and management of European Islam.[20]

The second variable is the kind of strategy chosen by local political elites, and in particular the mayor, who still is the real decisive leader in his own kingdom. The European context appears eminently contradictory in the political management of the visibility of Islam in the public sphere. The political orientation and the personal approaches of local leaders seem at times to play a determining role. It is apparent that the power held by local institutions over public space, and their autonomy in land management, can encourage certain social strategies rather than others, some of which contradict national trends and policies, especially in matters of immigration and cultural/religious pluralism.

The case of the mayor of Mantes la Jolie, Paul Picard, who played a crucial role in the building of France's first city mosque, belongs to the above-mentioned logic. He has been described as "proud to conduct this first major political battle to make Islam visible in the urban space," and his left-wing orientation and his militant past engaged in social causes, coupled with his stated agnosticism and respect for religious pluralism and the laity, proved decisive.[21]

In contrast with this judgment about the potential for social regulation offered by building a mosque, the persistent resistance (from 1973 to 1994) of the mayor of Schaerbeek (a borough of Brussels) to conceding any mosques to the Muslim population under his rule is also emblematic. A political personality can, therefore, sometimes determine the kind of relational model adopted in relating to Islam (e.g., mistrust or even hostility).[22]

Five years after the Lodi conflict, the mosque is still not built; and looking back at the events, the mayor of Lodi, Aurelio Ferrari, told us—trying to keep the whole experience at arm's length—that his actions were organized around three elements:[23]

- The legal necessity for equal treatment of citizens: Considering that other plots of land had previously been granted for use by a disabled persons' cooperatives and a young offenders' centers, then why would the Muslim community not be granted some land?
- There was a long-term political decision that Muslims must be socially integrated into the local social contract, reflecting the tradition of voluntary Catholic organizations aimed at "bringing back the lost sheep," for certain Muslims run the risk of remaining marginal and falling into well-established paths of deviant behavior.
- There was a completely personal consideration linked with his own Catholic beliefs.

This last approach contrasts with the attitudes of Northern European municipalities, where the local authorities tend to treat the problem not as a political or ideological issue but merely according to a professional and bureaucratic approach to town planning. "Islamophobic arguments against a mosque not only lack legal validity (and will even work against a person in Court, but until recently were also seen as politically incorrect."[24] One may ask if this depoliticized attitude of local politicians will last after the recent events of Pim Fortuyn's and Teo van Gogh's murders.

Why Communication Makes the Difference

The third crucial variable is the type of interaction between local administration and Muslim communities. In the mosque issue, the determination of Muslim populations as much as their capability to communicate with local authorities and neighborhood communities also plays a key role. In recent contexts of immigration like Italy, the exclusion strategy adopted by Lega-affiliated mayors obviously turns out to be a significant hurdle. However, even in municipalities that demonstrate reticence regarding Islam, the ability of Muslim representatives to obtain public legitimacy and financial credibility, as well as to form ties with local society, proves in fact to be decisive.[25]

Creating social networks and increasing social capital means that Muslim representatives develop the skills to work with a range of local institutions (e.g., city councils, police or trades unions). It means gaining the knowledge and confidence to interact with Christian colleagues or social workers. It also means dealing with issues on all fronts: being able to shift from the juridical resolution of conflict to social mediation. Leadership therefore requires the capability to change register, Goffman's famous "reframing."[26] Today, Muslim public figures in Italy, for instance, must demolish distrust and undo suspicion through the creation of networks and the employment of a calm yet assertive style of communication.

Because they are considered to be "nonintegrable," Muslims generally find it difficult to "efficiently communicate in a way that demystified those threatening representations of Islam so rooted in people's minds."[27] As Muslims came to the bitter and frustrating realization that there was a need for more efficient communication with the general public regarding their identity and the positive characteristics of the Islamic faith, some chose to withdraw from society (foreshadowing the threat of ghettoization), whereas others began fighting an often silent (but very effective) battle for a place in Italy's local social arena via various types of interaction with institutions and civil society.

Yet not all Muslims are treated as "problem cases." The emergence of a new Muslim young elite has radically changed the controversial landscape of mosque issues in Europe. Younger Muslim representatives have an easier, more self-assured, and even cynical approach to the types of relations one should create with the media. They know much better how to deal with journalists, thanks to accelerated experience "on the field." Theirs is an "active" perspective, contrasting with the relatively "passive" attitude of older representatives. Indeed, until recently the general tendency has been to protect the community and strengthen its own internal cohesion, rather than turn Muslims into actors involved in national and local public space. Now, young leaders know when and how to keep a low profile to project the im-

age of a moderate, nonviolent, and well-adjusted Islam. They tend to participate more and more in making local decisions and in public debates that do
not exclusively concern the Muslim population but affect the whole community, thus building up good working relationships and credibility. They
want to build a "national Islam" linked to the context of their daily life, distancing themselves from the first generations of traditional imams or from
the bureaucratic leaders (mainly Pakistani, Moroccan, or Turkish) sent by
their home countries.[28] Young European Muslims, as we will shortly see, are
the best example of the refusal of the Muslim specificity to which they tend
to be relegated. They lay claim to an ostensible but not ostentatious Islam.[29]

Fear of Losing Control of the Urban Territory or Fear of Islam?

The second issue is linked to the symbolic dimension of urban space. In
most cases, what is refused is the granting of a piece of communal land to
the "Other." Sometimes it is because of the fear that multiethnic and multi-
religious settings could change the social and power balance in urban areas.
But the excesses of intolerance observed (in Northern Italy for instance) are
more due to a reappropriation of space associated with fear of invasion and
pollution. The fear of Islam is real and present in all European societies, but
it develops and incarnates differently depending on the various political cultures. The obsession with the veil issue in France is, for example, an unknown phenomenon in Britain.

What is at stake? Borders, identities, or sense of peril? Symbolic violence is rare, but it did develop in the case of the resistance to the construction of the mosque in Lodi in Northern Italy. The excesses observed during
the march on Lodi organized by the Lega Party on October 15, 2000, were
a mixture of the ritual and the grotesque. They are part of a theatrical or-
chestrating a feeling of need for protection from the threat of an "Islamic
invasion." Notions of what is "pure" and "impure" are brought into use,[30]
and the staging of the religious dimension causes the fracture between
Christianity and Islam to grow deeper, and the "peril" to be made clear. The
flags (in the colors of the Lepanto battle) serve as a reminder of this current
renewal of such practices.

This obsession for reappropriation of space associated with fear of invasion and pollution echoes the statement made by Senator Michele Bucci (of
Forza Italia): "In a few years, Muslims will make up 10 to 15 percent of the
population, thus putting in danger the purity of our values. They aim to

marry our women, to convert them to Islam, and to bring down our society's structure from the inside."[31] Two actions in particular help highlight the way in which Lega very efficiently (in terms of symbolic/political communication) made use of the local group boundaries.[32] First, the land was physically "polluted" (with pig urine), a process that was willfully blasphemous toward the Muslim population—in no ambiguous terms—and that stirred up indignation throughout the country. Then, it was reconsecrated by a priest (Don Mario Carpeggiani), who said Mass on the very spot where the "mosque" was to be built, thus invalidating its sacredness. The importance of this marginal episode should not be overestimated; neither, however, should it be dismissed as irrelevant, for the feelings to which it gave rise are still held by certain sections of the population.[33]

Resistance to Cultural and Religious Pluralism in Urban Space

The third issue is Europe's cultural and religious pluralism, a crucial factor for the ongoing construction of its social and cultural cohesion. The mosque appears to be the symbol of the social construction of diversity at the heart of some European societies, and this indicates the degree of social visibility of new communities acceptable within the public space in a given context.

Muslims are facing the European exception, that is to say, the advanced degree of secularization that characterizes the continent as a whole, the general level of religious practice being considerably lower than in the United States. This does not mean that religious belief has disappeared or that religious traditions have lost all their cultural relevance. Danièle Hervieu Léger reminds us that the deregulation of institutional religion is the distinctive brand of the European trajectory of secularization.[34] But the massive Islamic presence in several countries, such as Germany, France, and Britain, calls for a reassessment of the relationships between religion and state, and religion and culture, in the various societies concerned. European societies are all facing the same problem, but they are giving different answers to the Muslim demand for recognition. This is due to the fact that each country is still modeled by its own specific religious roots, which have shaped symbolic structures and frameworks for thought and which remain a latent presence even after the decline of religious observance.

The content and style of public debate, the main ethical issues, the conception of private and public space, and even the concept of citizenship and the actual historical experience of religious pluralism all therefore vary highly from one European society to another. The various approaches to issues such as the wearing of veils at school or at work, or the construction of mosques in urban space, hence show how differently each society deals with the inclusion of its populations of Muslim origin.

What especially strikes the observer is the fact that religious pluralism is sometimes invisible and perfectly tolerated in the public space, while at other times it is the key factor of obsessions and fears. It is interesting to note in this regard that not all religious communities with foreign origins experience the same kind of discrimination. The last president of the European Commission, Romano Prodi, officially inaugurated the first Sikh temple (*gurdwârâ*) in Italy, on October 1, 2000, in Novellara (in the province of Reggio, in Emilia-Romagna; the town has approximately 12,000 inhabitants). The temple's opening took place in the name of the freedom of worship set out by the Constitution, and in the name of the need for religious pluralism. It was definitely a symbolic act that swam against the predominant current of immigration/insecurity themes, which was certainly strengthened by the events of September 11, 2001. The opening of this temple, located in an industrial neighborhood in the suburbs, led to no controversy, in contrast to the opening of mosques in many Italian towns.

Why? The history of the Sikhs—just as that of certain other Muslim, Hindu, or Irish Catholic groups—includes episodes of terrorism (notably the assassination of Indira Gandhi). Their nationalist demands have not been any the less virulent than those of other groups like Kurds and Palestinians. Moreover, they assert their identity by making religious demands (the wearing of a turban, the carrying of a weapon) that make them just as visible in the public arena, if not more so, than Muslims. However, neither their temples nor their turbans seem to upset anyone, nor do they threaten public order or local identity; they do not make people think of a mass invasion. In a word, they do not become the scapegoat to be used by Italian society to cover up a series of tensions and ambiguities that are particular to it.[35]

The Muslim presence apparently rouses all the historical, political, and religious contradictions specific to each European society. In the case of Italy, it shows the presence of religion in public space, traditionally monopolized by the majority religion (the Catholic Church), and the ambivalence of the so-called neutrality of the state. At present, Italy seems to be the place where a real shift toward religious pluralism seems most problematic. In France, it denotes the obsession of the *"laicité"* (laity) and the question of public space secularization, religion having been relegated to private space. The social representation of the separation of certain urban outskirt-quarters expresses a fear of *"communautarism"* and a lack of understanding when faced with changes in religious behavior and requests for sacred spaces in the public space (not only due to Islamic presence)— demands that are inconceivable for the French state and its usual definition of public space.

Conflicts over mosques are still to be found in some European countries, such as Italy or Spain; but they can also occur in France and Germany, where the recognition of the Muslim presence has become a reality. Nowadays, these examples of resistance, or even hostility, are being progressively resolved. It is presently difficult for a town councilor to deny the right to build a mosque. This is due to changes in public policies and public opinion. Mosque issues have succeeded in making Islam public and, despite the difficult processes of negotiation, have contributed to a legitimate Muslim presence in European urban space. Most conflicts reflect the diffidence and fears of local populations, which are still linked to a negative social representation of Islam at large.

With regard to this perception, still prevalent among European societies, it is interesting to observe the new strategies emerging among young European Muslims. The so-called Veil Affair in France has been above all interpreted as a risk of Islamization of the school system. It could also be read as an individual readjustment of identity (in terms of gender and generation). It belongs to the enactment of a new urban Muslim culture, in which an Islamic dress code and even Islamic "covers" of rap music are an active part of an Islamic way of life expressing a demand for differentiated visibility in public space. This will be the focus of our second point.

The Reterritorialization of Muslim Identities in European Cities

Since the end of the 1990s, young European Muslims have tried to find ways to gain a public recognition of their distinctive identity in the European public space. Their asking for visibility has become, as we will see below, an opportunity to renegotiate the usual external representation of themselves. Because most of them are also European citizens, they knew the rules that characterize each local and national context. Therefore, public space was an open field to conquer, with new social interactions with the larger European society, religious and political actions, and symbolic visibility. These new forms of visibility are always plural, often in competition between themselves, and even contradictory. As they become more visible, some young European Muslims focus on religious identity; others prefer a more secularized approach. But all of them question the meaning of being Muslim today in the European urban arena.

Young Muslims' Requests for Visibility

The real change in Muslims' stance toward their presence in European countries comes from the demand for visibility in public space by Muslim youths born and socialized in Europe. There is far too often a tendency to represent them as actors who seek refuge in their own communities, while in fact their needs set young European Muslims to demand an individualization of religious identification that is perfectly consonant with the secularized space where they grew up.

Young Muslims acknowledge the secularization of urban space, but they want to participate in it as Muslims and want to live in it as believers. They tend to think that their religion does not necessarily coincide with privatized religion. As Davie has pointed out, "They want to make their voices heard in public as well as in private debate."[36] Theirs is not a will to gain political power but a desire to transform the religious field itself. Perhaps this is exactly where the ambiguity of the contemporary debate on Islam has its source: Is Islam still perceived as a "different" religion, or is it a matter of more generally redefining the role of religion in society? Hence the debate on wearing the veil at school in France, because in that lay culture the state defines the usage of public space, and it does not accept a polysemous and privatized concept of urban space.[37] Reflecting on this issue of the visibility of religion in public urban space means first examining the changes observed since the 1990s in young Muslims' religious behaviors and practices.

From Self-Building to the Reappropriation of Islam: The Multiplicity of Approaches

Nowadays, it is rather difficult to assign categories to the various types of religious conduct among young Muslims in Europe. Moreover, it is rather challenging to try to quantify the various sociological profiles of this new Islamic claim to recognition. They all, however, have certain common traits. Two kinds of events—family migratory history and the emergence of radical Islam—constitute a shared experience that becomes sociologically

significant as it represents a common factor of emotional and symbolic socialization. As for the first kind of event, young European Muslims have in
common the fact that they are the sons and daughters of immigrants, but
their present and future belong in the country where they were born and not
elsewhere. Most of them indeed possess European citizenship (e.g., the
children of Pakistanis in Britain, of Algerians in France, of Moroccans in
Belgium) or have had to face this problem, as did German Turks after the
reform of the citizenship code in 2000. They have all experienced the impact of migration on the history of their community and their family, and
hence on their own lives. For some, like British Pakistanis and French Algerians, migration is also connected to a memory of the colonial experience,
an aspect that the parents and the nations involved, particularly France, have
long kept obscure.

The second kind of event is connected to the establishment of radical Islam, both in the societies of origin and in the Muslim diaspora. Young Muslims, or at least half of them, have witnessed it, though at different ages. All
have directly or indirectly faced events that were strongly symbolic for their
cultural contexts, the prominence of which was corroborated by the social
representation of Islam in general that followed. Young European Muslims
were hurled into a "shortened" historical time. Several key events need to
be mentioned here: the Iranian Revolution (1979); the Salman Rushdie issue (1988); the foulard affair (1989); the various Intifada and the never-
resolved Israeli-Palestinian conflict; the Gulf War (1991); radical Islamic
terrorism in the heart of the societies of residence (the terrorist attacks in
Paris, July and October 1995); the terrorist attacks in New York and Washington on September 11, 2001, in Madrid in March 2004, and in London in
July 2005; and finally the recent Iraqi conflict. For many young Muslims,
their response to the close succession of such violence and tension cannot
be neutral or painless and is objectively, if not subjectively, enough to assign them to a generational historical time. It is therefore no wonder that
young European Muslims distinguish themselves for certain behaviors of
social rebellion and cultural creativity that identify them as actors who contest the social construction to which they are subjected.[38]

However, young diasporic Muslims dwell in cultural discontinuity. Those
who turned twenty at the beginning of the new millennium inherited from
the previous cohorts contradictory approaches to identity and to social strategies. This is due to the inevitable evolution of the types of social interactions
in the European context. This legacy bears upon the difficulties and lack of
understanding they nowadays meet in their pursuit of social visibility.

All empirical research shows a manifold relationship of young people to Islam. The approach of each is shaped by one's biography, by the history of one's cohort, by one's original community—be it Turkish, Somali, or Algerian—but also by the European society one is living in, whether it grants Islam legitimacy in public space or not. Each and every young person then combines in a different way the communal, ethical, cultural, and emotional dimensions of his or her beliefs.[39] The approaches vary from religious "resocialization" as an answer to social exclusion to a transitory stage at which to regain balance and harmony, which enables one to better exploit his or her potential in terms of social and professional mobility. This reappropriation of Islam is not always followed by long-term observance. For young women and girls, it coincides with the retrieval of gender identity and the demand for the transformation of family roles. For others, the regaining of the self (i.e., great *jihad*) leads to political militancy, religious proselytism, or participation in local, national, and sometimes European citizenship. It could be stated that reinsertion into a line of faith bestows new life on a capital of memory, revisited and rendered dynamic by the need for individual self-realization.[40]

All these approaches are indeed journeys of self-building. But not all of them utilize Islam as social capital for social interaction or for the process of self-building. This variety of approaches indicates that religious reflection is no longer seen as a shelter for identity. Only a small minority is still linked to this strategy, as we will see below. Religious affiliation appears instead as a social card to play, and belonging to Islam is considered as a resource in social interaction. This turning point could not have been reached without the emergence and the gradual recognition of an elite cohort of youths who are the embryo of a European Muslim middle class.[41]

Becoming visible on the European urban stage does not mean necessarily performing as a "religious" Muslim but simply acting as a Muslim who asks for public recognition of a distinctive identity. Self-definition can be extremely diverse, but what counts is to interact with society at large as Muslims.

Since the 1990s, a period when identity was sought through religious difference, young European Muslims have gradually distanced themselves from the ethnic features of memory. Their reappropriation of their own "line of faith" in universalistic terms has step by step released them from the association of Islam with immigration and foreign origin. The young no longer partake of the silent Islam of their fathers and mothers, a prevalent feature of the first migratory cycles during the 1950s and the 1960s. They tend to refuse confinement in a labeling logic bound to an essentialist vision of Islam. They reject the stereotypes European societies assign them, and they activate rearrangements that move in all directions, thus making it difficult to distinguish which behavior entails religious modifications and which instead reflects new strategies of social interaction.

Muslim youth nowadays express a need for a new kind of citizenship, developed from concrete experiences in European local and national contexts. They share their aspirations with the whole of the European youth. It means distancing themselves altogether from traditional family culture, a closed communitarian ethnic life, and also from the negative representation of a normative, sometimes aggressive, and stigmatized Islam. It is a reappropriation of modern, urban, and secularized space, but along guidelines of Muslim distinctiveness, where religion, as also among Catholic or Protestants of the same age group, is associated with an individual search for meaning, distrust of institutional forms, challenging authority models, and a culture of consumption more than strict practice.[42] These strategies imply the end of marginalization and of the social construction of the "Muslim exception."[43] They also mean that young Muslims are expressing a demand for social recognition and participation.[44]

Young Muslims want to break Islam open. But they meet incomprehension in the process, above all in their pursuit of social visibility in urban space. They are faced with the enduring idea that their religious practice is incompatible with their involvement in public space; but it is exactly there that the new strategies are being developed.[45]

Strategies of Visibility in European Urban Space

How do these young Muslim actors make their entry into the European public sphere? We cannot take into consideration all the new formulations.[46] We will focus on the strategies that tend to build up a form of public presence (symbolic and concrete) in the European urban context.

Two types of strategies can be identified. The first one, adopted by *salafi* groups scattered among all European towns, a militant active minority, empowers the free choice of remaining isolated from European societies. The second one, which is dominant nowadays among young European Muslims, privileges new forms of social interactions with the local and the national society, and requests better access to European citizenship through a quiet affirmation of diversity.

The sectarian logic of the appropriation of public space adopted by *salafi* realities is very efficient in terms of clashing visibilities. The conduct of these sectarian groups is expressed in urban space by the creation of substitutive social spaces in order to break apart from an impure context. You do not eat or have physical contacts with "*haram*" people. This creates a sort of Muslim microsociety in urban space, reducing economic and professional contacts with French or British reality to the essential minimum. The ritualization of a sacredness that codifies all conduct in everyday life confines these groups in a world order that leaves no room for dialogue with other Muslims or with society as a whole, particularly in Europe. Belonging to this utopian *umma* can, however, only result in a "sectarian enclosure, or in death."[47] Olivier Roy employs a very effective formula to describe what neofundamentalism has to offer to "young born-again Muslims": "a legitimization of all enforced and accepted fragmentations: colonization, immigration, and alienation."[48] According to Samir Amghar, adepts are between fifteen and thirty-five years old, and they belong to an "Islam of exclusion," including converts who come from the working class and from unemployed youth. The power of seduction of this "class religiosity" is related to its ability to provide a dimension of social protest that legitimates the social failure of converts and all young *salafi*. It also feeds a logic of revenge and opposition against European society, which is anyhow destined to irreversible decadence. The *salafi* movement has a cathartic function for the frustrations of youths and reflects a confessionalization of social and economic problems. Amghar defines *salafi* preaching as an elitist *da'wa* (preaching) that overturns the real social conditions of its adherents.[49]

This exaggerated orthodoxy, however, maintains a minority radicalism, which may, if allowed to continue, in the long term compromise the restructuring strategies of young diaspora Muslims. It in fact confirms the social construction of an "unassimilable" Islam, and it contaminates the ongoing new models of social interaction. The *salafi* strategy, in one way or another, puts all Muslim endeavors in Europe under pressure.

This type of conduct obviously contrasts with those kinds adopted by new Muslim actors, both religious and secular, who divide on another conception of what it means to be a Muslim in European urban space today. Amel Boubekeur, reflecting on the concept of "public Islam," casts light on this transformation: "It is a highly fluid, individually reappropriable reality, which tends to promote the staging of a process of construction of a modern public Islamic identity in public space."[50] In general, Muslim youths socialized in Europe tend to look for a religious sociality where the pre-dominating social fabric can be chosen according to one's likings and where one listens to the preachers one esteems the most.[51]

The youths reject the right of judging and excluding, which some Muslims adopt concerning their feeling of belonging to Islam. It is the case of some members of *salafi* groups, as we have just seen. In particular, many see the definition of which conduct is *haram* (illicit) or not (rap music is a frequent instance in the interviews) as a detriment to their own autonomy and individual responsibility, a modern characteristic of a religion in which each and everyone reckons with God on his or her own. For example, Aïcha, one of the young Muslims interviewed by Marongiu, demands more tolerance: "Each directs his/her Islam as he wishes, respecting the principles. . . . I like this metaphor: God is the top of a mountain. There are many ways to reach it and each can choose to follow his or her own path."[52]

But even more than the content of religious conduct itself, these young Muslims use Islam as an individual and collective self-definition in the public arena. As mostly members of UOIF in France and UCOII in Italy, they identify themselves as practicing Muslims but are far from strict observance or traditional pietism.[53] They want to affirm a new Islamic alterity, which must not be aggressive, normative, or exclusive but simply "cool."[54] This reflects the emergence and the elaboration of a modern, urbanized Islamic culture, intent on expressing itself without complexes in a secularized European space. It is no longer an ethnicized minority culture, but a European phenomenon, although a different one.

Religious observance, by means of new forms of religiosity, translates into a logic of the privatization of symbolic capital. This new norm is expressed through body aesthetics and the consumption of "Islamic religious objects."[55] Basically, the public visibility of diversity is also expressed by the choice of eating *halal* in *halal* fast food restaurants (Mecca Burger, Mak'alal, Hala fried chicken), drinking Mecca Cola, listening to Islamic rap, and dressing *halal,* but according to Islamic fashion trends. The yearly meetings at Le Bourget near Paris, and those of other associations, represent spaces and times in which this kind of interchange can take place, this consumption of the "brands" that gives the products a differentiated identity, a licit character. Far beyond traditional religious spaces (mosques or associations), these young Muslims invest in their everyday life and lay claim to urban space.

Two birds are thus killed with one stone. On the one hand, the *halal* dimension escapes the dominion and the strict control of religious thought, which is traditionally in the hands of religious experts. On the other hand, there is an increase of a kind of "Islamic consumption," experienced as ethical militancy,[56] as well as a form of support for modern and competitive Islamic production. For instance, in Italian towns, kebab shops have become serious competitors with traditional pizzerias. This success of the kebab business shows not only the Muslim kebab sellers' entrance into the food marketplace and their rapid social mobility as free entrepreneurs but also their in-depth comprehension of the host culture. This is a striking example of successful social interaction, where Muslims' strategies reflect how these actors have been able to make their own culinary traditions attractive to others, in particular Italian customers, who are difficult and diffident regarding food. This is not only a mere social and economic climbing usually associated with the ethnic minority entrepreneurship. These Muslim businessmen want to show that they can build up a business that inspires trust and respect. This reflects an individual pride that does not act through ostentatious differentiation or politics but emerges as economic performance in the modern urban context.[57]

Halal meat belongs to this logic of consumption of a regularly commercialized product on which a religious value is, however, bestowed. The estimated consumption of *halal* meat in Europe is about €5 billion.[58] This market includes from 4 to 5 million potential consumers in France, and consumption has increased at a rate of about 15 percent a year since 1998, above all among youths. Originally controlled by Muslim butcheries, *halal* products are more and more widely distributed in chain shops and supermarkets (as ready-made dishes, meat, meat soup cubes, and homogenized baby foods). It is a particularly appealing market, above all for beef and mutton professionals and for poultry vendors.[59] Florence Bergaud, one of the few sociologists who has done research on the consumption *halal* products, points out that in less than twenty years a shift has taken place from the simple selling of *halal* meat to a *halal* food business. The increasing demand in the future will depend not only on private consumers but also on collective entities (refectories, canteens, hospitals, prisons). "The definition of *halal* brands is actually controlled by consumers, who endow them with specific qualities, including religious ones; by the capability of dealers to adapt to the demand, more than by the contradictory directives of religious institutions, which have lost control of production standards."[60]

This kind of urban culture appears neither as a problematic nor as an ethnicized phenomenon. We are witnessing a redefinition of Muslim identity by means of consumption practices that bestow "religiosity" on secularized behaviors. These types of conduct prove that urban space can become something other than a place of conflict: fertile soil for Islamic diversity, adopting logics of exchange and consumption, modern secularized criteria, that are partially shared by other European youths. Urban space is not appropriated in closed or exclusive terms. Visibility strategies turn instead into a means of communication and of quiet affirmation of diversity.

Conclusion

Social interactions between Muslims and local European populations are still "works in progress." Urban space has become the stage where Muslim actors are negotiating the legitimacy of their presence in the public sphere through conflict or negotiation. By means of their request for visibility, Muslims bring into play the acceptance of their concrete and symbolic diversity in European cities. But because the symbolic use of urban territory has to do with the distribution of power in public areas, this calls into question the existing balance.

The "mosque issue," as we have seen, is a way to confirm the institutionalization of Islam in European urban space and the recognition of the Other's definitive integration. Young Muslims' demand for visibility has more to do with the everyday life process of renegotiating identities. In both cases, visibility is linked to social interactions in a context where the public status of religion and the expression of religious identities have been traditionally controlled by public policies, in some cases with the approval of the majority religion, as in Italy.

The visibility of Islam in European urban public space denotes three changes. The first is a process of mutual acknowledgment. On the one hand, European societies show recognition through the institutionalization of Muslim representative bodies and through an increasing number of procedures for the building of mosques in European cities. This is, moreover, encouraged by European jurisprudence, which responds positively through judicial decisions to the demands regarding both individual and collective religious freedoms.

On the other hand, most Muslim populations, and first of all their leaders and representatives, have realized that European Islam is destined to operate in a specifically secularized public arena and that it cannot manage its everyday interactions with a totalizing interpretation of Islam. This is attested by the frequent initiatives of certain European mosque officials, who opt for public clarity by organizing "open mosque days" in Milan, Paris, and Barcelona to show to the national population at large that a mosque is not a den of terrorists or center of occult activities but a versatile structure offering social assistance, religious instruction, and community socialization structured around a place of worship, the same—no more, no less—as in a traditional Catholic parish building. Mosque conflict happens to be a difficult experience of citizenship for Muslims. It is also an opportunity to gain access to a public definition of their religion, culture, and system of values. Muslim actors have to negotiate with local opinion and authorities how to communicate their distinctiveness in order to reverse misunderstandings and suspicion. They often discover that this is not as easy task and that they have to rethink their external frontier.[61]

The second change is the growing religious pluralism in European public space. Not all European societies are prepared to cope with it, as we have seen. Religious tolerance does not only mean conceding to the Other the space and opportunity to survive. It also means negotiating and creating common values. Young European Muslims have understood this perfectly. This is reflected in their expression of a Muslim identity that is highly engaged in dialogic interaction with civil society and shows a clear will to increase social participation. These young Muslims are aware of the values of a pluralist society that recognizes their right to diversity. For them, social and political militancy is now being conceived as partnership with other European citizens in the fight against all forms of discrimination and in dealing with environmental issues and globalization. This search for a common social project demonstrates the affirmation of a German, British, and Italian, that is to say European, Muslim identity that is common to the different national situations but expressed in different modes.[62] It should, therefore, be no surprise that young Muslims' demand for visibility in European urban space reflects a new culture of consumption, trying to combine a culture of obligation, still largely imposed in family environments and by mosques officials, with the individualization of religious experience and their free choice to interact in public as "observant Muslims" or not. Some prefer to express their difference with corporeal self-presentations and visible markers, such as veils and beards; others, like kebab shop owners, sell *halal* meat to Italian customers for whom this has no meaning, while not renouncing something that has value for them and other Muslim customers. Urban space becomes the area where pluralism is concretely experienced and tested.

The Muslim demand for visibility also expresses a new conception of the employment of the religious dimension in public space. Moreover, it highlights new modes of the management of alterity in urban situations of daily interaction. The issue at stake is the visibility of religion in the public sphere. Muslim strategies question the features of a landscape, be it British or French, that is highly secularized and where the control of religious visibility has for a long time been taken for granted.

This situation is of concern to all religions, not solely Islam. The public visibility of religious observance increases its integralist dimension, surely not the general level of practice or the number of religious callings. Reflecting on these issues means examining the meaning of actual Muslim practices in European public spaces. Only in these terms it is possible to identify how Muslims, and youths in particular, intend to define the forms and spaces of secularization regarding Islam. Throughout history, every society has developed its own specific forms of secularization; thus, the British do not face the veil issue as polemically as the French, and the Swedes do not deal with the problem of *halal* meat with the same tolerance shown by the Italians or Belgians. It is therefore justifiable to expect Muslims to manage their inclusion in European society differently, depending on the context in which they live, because the process of secularization reflects the forms and transformations of religions. In doing this, young European Muslims will have to deal with the degree of legitimization they can enjoy in the public space, above all considering the terrorist attacks in Madrid and London of the past several years. They do constitute, with young entrepreneurs and new Muslim leaders, the dynamic fringe of the present process of interaction between Muslims and European societies. Through their assertive and new style of communication, they have certainly contributed to the progressive normalization of Islam in European urban space.

Notes

1. Max Weber, *Wirtschaft und Gesellschaft* (Tübingen: Mohr, 1992); and Georg Simmel, *Le metropoli e la vita dello spirito* (Rome: Armando Editore, 1995).

2. Robert E. Park, Ernest W. Burgess, and Robert D. McKenzie, *The City* (Chicago: University of Chicago Press, 1925).

3. On the front of traditionalism, this is what would happen in Italy with a party like Lega, which structures and strengthens the borders to defend original purity. This party, part of the last coalition in power, defends the idea of federalism. It also advocates the creation of a cultural identity, based on the specific values of the fictional "Padania region" (encompassing all of Northern Italy). On its radio station, as well as in its own newspaper, *La Padania,* and also in certain public statements made by the movement's officials, the party puts forward ideas that are strongly xenophobic and anti-Islamic.

4. William Foote White, *Street Corner Society* (Chicago: University of Chicago Press, 1943).

5. A recent European report—*Muslims in the European Union: Discrimination and Islamofobia* (Vienna: European Monitoring Centre on Racism and Xenophobia, 2006)—underlines that European Muslims (nowadays 3.5 percent of the total population of the Union) exhibit the highest rate of social discrimination in terms of employment, housing, and education.

6. Enzo Colombo, "Una generazione in movimento," in *Stranieri & Italiani,* ed. Roberta Bosisio, Enzo Colombo, Luisa Leonini, and Paola Rebughini (Rome: Donzelli Editore, 2005), 67.

7. Ervin Goffman, *Relations in Public: Microstudies of the Public Order* (New York: Basic Books, 1971).

8. Mike Davies, *Beyond Blade Runner* (Westfield, N.J.: Open Media, 1992).

9. See Chantal Saint-Blancat and Ottavia Schmidt di Friedberg, "Why Are Mosques a Problem? Local Politics and Fear of Islam in Northern Italy," *Journal of Ethnic and Migrations Studies* 31, no. 6 (2005): 1083–1104.

10. Ilvo Diamanti, "Immigration et citoyenneté en Europe: Une enquête," *Critique Internationale* 8 (2000): 73–95.

11. See Grace Davie, *Europe the Exceptional Case. Parameters of Faith in the Modern World* (London: Darton, Longman and Todd, 2002). Compared with the United States, the author stresses the lower degree of church-related religiosity in Europe and the fact that the majority of the population "belong" to the dominant religious tradition. In the United States, people tend more to choose and select their religious allegiance.

12. See Chantal Saint-Blancat, "Religious and Cultural Pluralism in Europe: The Process of Immigration," in *Welfare and Religion,* ed. Anders Bäckström (Uppsala: Uppsala Institute for Diaconal and Social Studies, 2005), 55–64.

13. Regarding the evolution of the Muslim presence, see Brigitte Maréchal, Stefano Allievi, Felice Dassetto, and Jorgen Nielsen, eds., *Muslims in the Enlarged Europe: Religion and Society* (Leiden: Brill, 2003); Chantal Saint-Blancat, *L'islam de la diaspora* (Paris: Bayard Éditions, 1997); and Yvonne Haddad, ed., *Muslims in the West from Sojourners to Citizens* (Oxford: Oxford University Press, 2002).

14. Regarding the long and troubled process leading to the establishment of the French Council for the Muslim Cult, see Malika Zeghal, "La constitution du Conseil Français du Culte Musulman: Reconnaissance politique d'un Islam français?" *Archives de Sciences Sociales des Religions* 129 (2005): 97–112. For the British case, see Philippe Lewis, "New Social Roles and Changing Patterns of Authority among British Ulamâ, *Archives de Sciences Sociales des Religions* 125 (2004): 169–89.

15. On the analysis of migration-related alienation and the paradoxes of alterity, see Abdelmalek Sayad, *La double absence* (Paris: Éditions du Seuil, 1999).

16. Olivier Roy, *La laicité face à l'islam* (Paris, Éditions Stock, 2005).

17. Only Great Britain has introduced, since the 2001 census, the variable of religious affiliation, as obligatory in Scotland and Northern Ireland, and as optional in England and Wales.

18. Saint-Blancat and Schmidt di Friedberg, "Why Are Mosques a Problem?" 1094.

19. Chantal Saint-Blancat, "Islam in Diaspora: Between Reterritorialization and Extraterritoriality," *International Journal of Urban and Regional Research* 26, no. 1 (2002): 146–47.

20. See chapter 9 in this volume by Schmitter Heisler on the German case.

21. Claire de Galembert, "The City's 'Nod of Approval' for the Mantes-la-Jolie Mosque Project: Mistaken Traces of Recognition," *Journal of Ethnic and Migrations Studies* 31, no. 6 (2005): 1149.

22. For a more exhaustive analysis of the different national cases regarding mosque conflicts, see the special issue of *Journal of Ethnic and Migrations Studies* 31, no. 6 (2005).

23. Saint-Blancat and Schmidt di Friedberg, "Why Are Mosques a Problem?" 1091.

24. Nico Landman and Wendy Wessels, "The Visibility of Mosques in Dutch Towns," *Journal of Ethnic and Migrations Studies* 31, no. 6 (2005): 1139.

25. Saint-Blancat and Schmidt di Friedberg, "Why Are Mosques a Problem?" 1096.

26. Ervin Goffman, *Frame Analysis: An Essay on the Organization of Experience* (New York: Harper & Row, 1974).

27. Chantal Saint-Blancat and Ottavia Schmidt di Friedberg, "Mobilisations laïques et religieuses des musulmans en Italie," *Cahiers d'Etudes sur la Méditerranée orientale et le monde turco-iranien* 33 (2002): 93, 106.

28. For a more complete analysis of the transformation of Muslim Leadership in Europe, see Jocelyne Cesari, *L'islam à l'épreuve de l'Occident* (Paris: La Découverte 2004); and Chantal Saint-Blancat and Fabio Perocco, "New Modes of Social Interaction in Italy: Muslims Leaders and Local Society in Tuscany and Venetia," in *European Muslims and the Secular State,* ed. Jocelyne Cesari and Sean McLoughlin (Aldershot, U.K.: Ashgate, 2006), 99–112.

29. Roy, *La laicité face à l'islam,* 12.

30. Mary Douglas, *Purezza e pericolo* (Bologna: Il Mulino, 1993).

31. Saint-Blancat and Schmidt di Friedberg, "Why Are Mosques a Problem?" 1089.

32. Frederic Barth, *Ethnic Groups and Boundaries* (Oslo: Universitetsforlaget, 1969).

33. Saint-Blancat and Schmidt di Friedberg, "Why Are Mosques a Problem?" 1090.

34. Danièle Hervieu-Léger, "The Role of Religion in European Construction: Looking for a 'Common Heritage,' " in *Welfare and Religion,* ed. Anders Bäckström (Uppsala: Uppsala Institute for Diaconal and Social Studies, 2005), 49.

35. Saint-Blancat and Schmidt di Friedberg, "Why Are Mosques a Problem?" 1100.

36. Davie, *Europe the Exceptional Case,* 137.

37. Roy, *La laicité faceà l'islam,* 137.

38. Farad Khosrokhavar, *L'islam des jeunes* (Paris: Flammarion, 1997).

39. Nikola Tietze, *Jeunes musulmans de France et d'Allemagne: Les constructions subjectives de l'identité* (Paris: l'Harmattan, 2002).

40. For an analysis of the diverse reappropriation of Islam by young European Muslims, see Chantal Saint-Blancat, "La transmission de l'islam auprès des nouvelles générations de la diaspora," *Social Compass* 51 (2004): 235–47.

41. See Catherine Wihtol de Wenden and Rémy Leveau, *La Beurgeoisie: Les trois âges de la vie associative, issue de l'immigration* (Paris: CNRS Éditions, 2001); and Valérie Amiraux, *Acteurs de l'islam entre Allemagne et Turquie* (Paris: L'Harmattan, 2001).

42. Saint-Blancat, "La transmission de l'islam."

43. Saint-Blancat and Schmidt di Friedberg, "Mobilisations laïques et religieuses."

44. For an analysis of the demands of young European Muslims, see Dounia Bouzar and Sonia Kada, *L'une voilée, l'autre pas* (Paris: Albin Michel, 2003); Dounia Bouzar, *"Monsieur islam" n'existe pas* (Paris: Hachette Littératures, 2004); Annalisa Frisina, "Giovani musulmani d'Italia: Trasformazioni socio-culturali e domande di cittadinanza," in *Giovani musulmani in Europa,* ed. Jocelyne Cesari and Andrea Pacini (Torino:

Edizioni della Fondazione Agnelli, 2005), 139–60; and Annalisa Frisina, "Musulmani e Italiani, tra le altre cose: Tattiche e strategie identitarie di giovani figli di immigrati musulmani," in *Giovani musulmani,* ed. Cesari and Pacini, 161–87.

45. Saint-Blancat, "La transmission de l'islam."

46. E.g., as a consequence of the institutionalization of Muslim representatives in Europe, new currents emerged and distanced themselves from practicing observant Muslim movements. Despite their lack of structure, however, they reflect a tendency to internal pluralism regarding, this time, a Muslim identity that is more cultural than religious. See Frank Fregosi, "Les musulmans laïques, une mouvance plurielle et paradoxale," *Maghreb-Machrek* 183 (2005): 33–44.

47. Farad Khosrokhavar, *Les nouveaux martyrs d'Allah* (Paris: Flammarion, 2003), 237–41.

48. Olivier Roy, *Les illusions du 11 septembre* (Paris: Éditions du Seuil, 2002), 78–79.

49. Samir Amghar, "Les salafistes français: Une nouvelle aristocratie religieuse," *Maghreb-Machrek* 183 (2005): 18, 28.

50. See Amel Boubekeur, "L'islam est-il soluble dans le Mecca Cola? Marché de la culture islamique et nouveaux supports de religiosité en Occident," *Maghreb-Machrek* 183 (2005): 47.

51. For a closer look on changes in the process of transmission (content and practices) and the problem of the search for religious authority and legitimacy among young Muslims, see Saint-Blancat, "La transmission de l'islam"; and Kadisha Mohsen-Finan, "La mise en avant d'une 'citoyenneté croyante': Le cas de T.Ramadan," in *De la citoyenneté locale,* ed. Rémy Leveau, Catherine Wihtol de Wenden, and Kadisha Mohsen-Finan (Paris: Ifri, 2003), 87–96.

52. Orengo Marongiu, "L'islam au pluriel: Étude du rapport au religieux chez les jeunes musulmans," PhD thesis in sociology, Université des Sciences et Technologies, Lille, 2002, 259. For a better understanding of the relationship between rap and Islam among young Muslims, see Samir Amghar, "Rap et islam: Quand le rappeur devient imam," *Hommes et Migrations* 1243, no. 6 (2003): 78–86; and the autobiographical work of the sufi Abd al Malik, *Qu'Allah bénisse la France!* (Paris: Albin Michel, 2004).

53. UOIF, and its Italian counterpart UCOII, are two Muslim associations, similar in their structures and affinities and considered as being close to the Muslim Brotherhood movement. They are both very active in their national public spaces, they interact with their governments and control several mosques. They lay claim to representing a large portion of practicing Muslims, especially those belonging to the middle class. Every year, UOIF organizes a summit in Le Bourget, near Paris, with the participation of young Muslims of different affiliations.

54. Boubekeur, "L'islam est-il soluble dans le Mecca Cola?" 45 n. 2.

55. For a thorough analysis of this phenomenon, see ibid.

56. Drinking Mecca Cola, considering that it took a clear stance against Israel and the United States, equals to making a political choice, and reminds one of the "Buy British" slogan.

57. For the results of this research on social interactions between kebab shopowners and their customers in the local public space of two medium-sized town such as Padua and Trevise, see Chantal Saint-Blancat, Khalid M. Rhazzali, and Paola Bevilacqua, "Il cibo come contaminazione: Tra diffidenza ed attrazione," forthcoming in a volume edited by Federico Neresini and Valentina Rettore to be published by Carocci in Rome.

58. This figure is from *Le Monde,* July 14, 2005.

59. Slaughtering is regulated by the November 6, 1982, convention, undersigned by the European Council with a directive by the European Union restating its terms, and it has to take place under veterinary control. Muslim sacrificers in France are licensed by three mosques (Paris, Lyon, and Evreux). The absence of illicit substances (*haram*) or of contamination with non-*halal* products, is guaranteed by the Codex alimentaires of July 17, 1997, which established the criteria later recognized by the World Trade Organization.

60. Florence Bergaud, " 'Qualité halal' and Social Definitions of Halal Quality: The Case of Maghrebin Muslims in France," in *The Quality of Food,* ed. M. Harvey, A. McMeekin, and A. Warde (Manchester: Manchester University Press, 2004), 94–107; the quotation here is on 97.

61. Chantal Saint-Blancat, "L'islam diasporique entre frontières externes et internes," in *Itinéraires européens: Nation(s) et religion(s) à l'épreuve du pluriel,* ed. Antonela Capelle-Pogacean, Patrick Michel, and Enzo Pace (Paris: Presses des Sciences Politiques, 2008).

62. For a complete analysis of Young Muslims' recent strategies in Europe, see Jocelyne Cesari and Andrea Pacini, eds., *Giovani musulmani in Europa* (Torino: Edizioni della Fondazione Agnelli, 2005).

5

Moving toward Uncertainty: Migration and the Turbulence of African Urban Life

AbdouMaliq Simone,
with Jean Pierre Sempabwa Gatarayiha

Africa is a space of intensified movement that broadly encompasses migration, displacement, and accelerated social mobility. A mixture of economic and geopolitical pushes and pulls is driving larger and more diverse populations into some form of migration to Africa's cities. This movement has become a multifaceted strategy of urban survival and accumulation. For many, migration is simply a practice of livelihood formation, social affiliation, and decisionmaking. Migrants engage the city as an embodiment of long-term aspirations and make concerted efforts to invest in an urban existence. In this process of negotiation, migrants have redefined urban space and relationships, changing the landscape of the contemporary African city.

In their very physicality, African cities do not have an overarching institutional logic or public discourse capable of tying their heterogeneous residents together with a sense of common belonging or reference. There are a wide range of discrepant notions about the built environment, how it operates, what it looks like, and what takes place within it. The sheer volatility of urban life means that interactions among people are "jumping" across sectors, territories, identities, occupations, and roles. Without strong connections to institutions that provide clear definitions of how people, things, and spaces are to be used and valued, urban quarters become patchworks of decay and renewal, economic vibrancy and implosion.[1] Cities in Africa provide a platform for residents to put together forms of belonging and social operation that transcend the particularities of identity and culture. No matter how resourceful residents of particular locality might be, they cannot go it alone. They cannot make a living simply by drawing from the locality itself. There must be connections outward—things coming in, things go on. The viability of any locality is contingent upon a circuitry of external relations.[2]

This chapter considers how urbanization has critically changed the dynamics of migration in Africa and, in turn, how migration has altered urban social life and economy across the continent. Drawing from research I have conducted over the past ten years, the chapter uses the migrant experience in inner-city Johannesburg to explore the complexities of the shifting relationship between urbanization and migration. Looking specifically at the case of the Congolese diaspora, I outline the trajectories of inward migration to the central city of Johannesburg and examine how migrants have shaped the city to create new forms of residency and livelihood. In the urban environment, migrant households rely upon a wide range of family and social networks as well as regional and ethnic ties for support. For the Congolese in Johannesburg, churches are one of very few institutions that mediate the challenges they face and their relationship with the city. As migrants face greater hardship with an overstretched urban fabric, they invest more time and resources outside formal institutions, challenging conventional concepts of regulation and governance. In this chapter, I try to capture what is taking place outside the purview of the state as migrants transform urban space and life through their daily interactions.

Inner-City Johannesburg: The Urban Economies of Piracy

Through a combination of the increased centralization of regional services, the domination of regional investment, and the continued expansion of unconventional resource flows, South Africa has maintained a strong comparative advantage in moving money, goods, and people across the continent.[3] This makes the country's major urban center, Johannesburg, a hub not only for the formal regional economy but also for a variety of other economies operating at different scales and degrees of legality. The city's sophisticated formal trading, services, and financial infrastructure has its counterpart in a more invisible, informal one. The latter is composed of diverse economic activities and actors at widely divergent scales and capacities, often drawing on illegal goods and the illicit exchange of conventional goods or services.[4]

As the urban economy becomes increasingly dependent upon a plurality of linkages across Africa, the associated economic infrastructure—such as the cultivation of local agents, clients, political networks, and staff—constitutes a platform for physical and financial movements between Johannesburg and other African cities. Migratory flows into South Africa from across the region are a by-product of the very structured formal economic incursions engineered by the South African economy.

Political and economic refugees from across Africa usually consider South Africa the most accessible place of either asylum or opportunity, and they work hard to identify constantly shifting points of permeability in the conjunction of immigration policies and policing apparatuses that attempt to regulate these inward flows. The level of demand has marked out a series of routes, bureaucrats "on the take," provisional jobs, and temporary places of residence that attain some consistency, or at least have sufficient flexibility to shift in the face of assorted crackdowns. Thus, during the past fifteen years, not only has Johannesburg harbored increasing numbers of migrants from every African nation but it has also served as an arena where various African nationals put together collaborative schemes and networks.

Johannesburg has been a place of overlap, where Somali, Senegalese, and Nigerians, for example, with little history of economic association, aim for speculative synergies from trying to put together their particular areas of expertise. Thus one finds not only a great deal of activity that falls outside the law, formality, or official regulation but also individual schemes that are folded into each other and then spun out into various domains of operations with networks of substantial reach and diversity. This situation makes it difficult for any regulatory authority to assert order, let alone adequately understand the processes at work.

The inner city of Johannesburg has become a significant platform for the proliferation and entrenchment of what could be called "economies of piracy." Though this notion strongly conveys economies centered on theft and looting, it is not limited to these activities. The inner city has also been a place of substantial infrastructure development—large apartment blocks, with some buildings containing hundreds of units; hotels with swimming pools and sophisticated communications facilities; entertainment complexes; and large underground parking garages. Through systems of unconventional economic use, this infrastructure has either been extended beyond its capacity or converted into uses never intended. These economic systems are informed by specific kinds of habitation, entrepreneurship, and social collaboration that do not necessarily coincide with the prevailing normative conceptions of households, social networks, and so forth.

Additionally, these economies are not driven by large-scale mafias or syndicates, even when they sometimes have the capacity to act as if they are. Rather, in my research, I have found that an important factor in the proliferation and reach of this variegated unofficial trade has been the interaction of household and entrepreneurial segments organized according to conventional ethnic identity and/or nationality and heterogeneously composed segments that cross these ascriptions. In situations where an ethnic, religious, political, or even national identity produces vulnerability, migrants try to keep things as ambiguous as possible as to how they will be perceived by others around them.[5]

Yet, at the same time, migrants need to center their associations and dependencies on those with whom they share some language of recourse—that is, where a familiar set of moral references and social practices exist that do not require a lot of work to maintain or negotiate, and that can be counted on as an anchor in uncertain situations. In part, it is the very act of attempting to reconcile these tensions between extensive and intensive affiliations that make various unofficial economies dynamic.

Finally, if formal employment and production possibilities are limited, then migrants have to make the most extensive use of whatever they can get their hands on. Living spaces, as well as cars, social occasions, documents, information, and equipment, have to be shared and used for many different purposes. This multiplication of uses is made possible through an ability to put together different combinations of people with different skills, perspectives, linkages, identities, and aspirations. Tensions and conflicts will ensue, and participants will have to spend significant time working out disputes; but even in this process, new opportunities are often worked out.

The Congolese Community:
An Example of an Inner-City Diaspora Economy

The Congolese represent a significant portion of the African diaspora in Johannesburg. Immigrants from the Democratic Republic of the Congo (DRC) have been in Johannesburg for many years, the first wave arriving as medical doctors in the late 1980s when visas were not required to enter South

Africa. The rapidly expanding number of entries into the country, together with the fact that many never returned home, has led to the enforcement of stringent visa requirements. Visas are very difficult to obtain and require a deposit of $1,000 upon application. These constraints have opened a route for business people to smuggle friends and family across the border.

Most Congolese seek refugee status in order to remain in the country, putting them in difficult financial circumstances because they are not eligible to work or seek education until their asylum status has been resolved. Officially, this process is supposed to take six months, but it can often last up to three years. The bulk of Congolese reside in Yeoville, Berea, Hillbrow, Parktown, Bertrams, Malvern, Turfontein, and in the many other suburbs around Johannesburg. Their chief concerns center on residency papers, access to work, and adequate housing. There are many Congolese organizations and networks, but none has formal status and they are, for the most part, informal political, ethnic, or religious groups. Football matches, basketball games, and other social events are organized at an informal level, and teams organize sporting equipment and gatherings after games. Medical doctors are the most organized group of professionals. Their network provides assistance to newly arrived doctors, helping them find work, obtain papers, and pass the examination they must take to practice in South Africa. Theirs is still an informal organization, but due to the nature of their work, it tends to be more structured. Accommodation is arranged, and interim work will be provided, because many Congolese doctors have opened their own practices.

Congolese citizens are inclined to assume that just because they hold the same passport, they will receive help from fellow nationals. But there is a big rivalry, for example, between people from Kinshasa and those from Lubumbashi, as well as among those from the newer feeder cities such as Bukavu, Butembo, Goma, and Bunia. They have different associations, different religious groups, and separate support networks. There is little trust between them. They often hide information about jobs, papers, or other opportunities and information about different opportunities from one another. The size of each subcommunity is large, however, and this helps the groups to operate independently.

Renegotiating Urban Space: Accommodation and Livelihood

Because the municipal authorities of Johannesburg have been unable to impose viable forms of regulation of how space is occupied and managed, a wide array of tenancy and subtenancy arrangements have proliferated. More and more households are composed of highly provisional arrangements among unrelated individuals, often with complicated informal financial arrangements among them. In addition, residential buildings increasingly house informal businesses—one of which is the provision of short-term accommodation itself. Also, a substantial informal economy is made available to the middle class through which to hedge its consumption expenses and even its access to investment resources.

The sheer diversity of the quality of housing stock—its ownership, regulatory structures, and its availability to distinct populations—constitutes a field of intricate interplay. Despite the volatility of the inner city, this interplay manages to stabilize different kinds of residents, from different backgrounds and with very different occupations. Within this context, churches provide an important node of mediation.

Few Congolese have any intention of returning to Kinshasa or Lubumbashi in the near future. They prefer renting flats or houses that they can share with friends rather than staying in one of many cheap hotel rooms scattered across the inner city of Johannesburg. Their reasoning is that they will share these apartments and contribute with food. Take, for example, Didier, living in an apartment at 16 Skyway on Pope Street. The building has eight three-bedroom flats occupied by Congolese from Kinshasa, each accommodating at least ten adults and seven children. Didier rents a room where he lives with his wife, who just recently had a child. Two men who work as security guards at the OK Bazaar supermarket share the second room; and two women who braid hair occupy the third. The men occupying this flat all hold university degrees yet have not been able to find formal work. Didier is currently unemployed, as is his wife. He helps out at the weekly Rosebank Craft Market to earn a little money, selling artifacts on behalf of Congolese traders who own the stall.

Another flat in the building is rented out to a woman who braids women's hair to earn a living. She rents out the three bedrooms (two people per room), and four sleep in the living room (including her). The rent for each flat is R1,600, and she rents each room at R500 per room and R200 for a mattress in the lounge.[6] This allows her to supplement her income from hair braiding, covering rent and services for the flat, with some extra for herself. The maximum number of people officially allowed in each of these flats is six, and the caretaker of the building is not aware of the number of people living in each flat—or certainly turns a blind eye and does not report it to the owner.

Most of the Congolese from Lubumbashi live in the inner city. They have been here longer, have managed to find work, and some have even moved to more suburban residential areas. Their network is very strong and they take care of each other, helping new arrivals find work. Historically, there have been strong connections between Lubumbashi and Johannesburg in the past, based on connections through the mining sector, political intrigue, and Greek trading syndicates.

The Congolese from Kinshasa seem to take longer to form strong networks outside their immediate community. They may live and network together, but they do not readily seem to be able to find each other work. It is also important to note that many of the Congolese from Kinshasa do not intend to stay permanently in South Africa. Many have family in Europe, Canada, or the United States and are using South Africa as an interim destination. These Congolese often receive money from their families abroad to help them live.

Other examples of Congolese settlement arrangements include a house in Berea on Heddon Road bought by Nzimbi, who was an army general under Mobutu Sese Seko. The house is left to manage itself, and whoever arrives to stay will stay. "La loi du plus fort" is how this place is run. People arrive and rent a mattress for R10 to R15 per night. Similarly, newly arrived Congolese will rent a mattress for R5 per night at an abandoned house on Houghton Road called Saint Jose. Didier stayed at Saint Jose when he first arrived in the city from Kinshasa. These two houses are "landing spots" for new Congolese arrivals to Johannesburg. Only the Congolese without a contact or family member to take them in will use these houses as a point of entry.

The degradation of much of the inner-city housing stock has led to compromises and new solutions within the apartment rental market, making it easier for new arrivals to find accommodations. Agencies are increasingly managing the buildings according to the new population and close their eyes to issues such as overcrowding and legal status, as long as they get their money. Some foreigners are buying apartment blocks and are accommodating fellow nationals. Where leasing requires proof of nationality, South Africans are paid a fee to secure apartments. Some rental agencies are now accepting refugee documentation, and there is a widespread system of subletting bedrooms, beds, and living rooms across the city.

Bolengu Botondo, a banker in Kinshasa, moved his family to South Africa and bought a block of flats, Montero Vetero, on Pope Street in Yeoville that his wife is comanaging with the original owners, Leeco Property Limited. The building is four stories high, with twenty-seven different types of apartments. The official criteria for obtaining a flat are a valid identity document, a pay slip from work, three months of recent bank statements, and a deposit of R2,000. Still, the building is inhabited mainly by Congolese residents because it is easier for the Congolese woman who manages the apartment to deal with her people because, as she puts it, at least she knows what to expect from them. "When they don't pay I know what measures to take; I understand that most of them have no real regular income and have to sublet to afford the rent and I can control that. The real issue for me is to find Congolese that will at least keep the building clean."

There is an important convergence between specific forms of livelihood and the construction of spaces for various transactions. For example, Congolese taxi drivers can be found waiting for Congolese patrons on Houghton and Tudhope roads in Berea, where at any given time there are about twenty taxis waiting in line. The corner is an important gathering place for information exchange. Hairdressers and taxi drivers become props for supporting Congolese interactions, facilitating connections to secure fraudulent immigration papers or obtain under-the-counter cell phones or accommodation. There are many networks to help new arrivals through various hurdles of regularization, whether it be arranging payoffs to police and immigration officials or arranging marriages with South African citizens. For the marriage business, R500 is charged when someone brings their own contacts to marry and R2,500 when they have to find a contact. Nigerians, Cameroonians, and Ghanaians are the primary players in these marriage networks, but all the migrant communities have their own networks.

Social class and educational background play a significant role in the trajectories of immigrant livelihoods. Most upper-class Congolese still benefit from financial support from home, meaning that they can survive without odd jobs or they have the opportunity to study further. Most important, many have grown up outside the DRC and are better prepared to make their way in South Africa. They live in better conditions, often not in the inner city. They can learn English and find a job; they often have money to get their papers in order.

Yet in recent years, the interchanges among nationals of various backgrounds, sometimes centered on codependencies and complementarities forged elsewhere, have been particularly important. During the years of war in the Great Lakes Region, many of the former elite lost everything, while others involved in various aspects of the war economy made a great deal of money. These oscillations sometimes corresponded to ethnic backgrounds and their relationships to particular trades—such as trucking, mineral extraction, hoarding of essential supplies, and smuggling. Political contestation in the region had to be funded, and the fight over resources was often the basis for such political contestation. The various intelligence and security operatives, as well as militias, were well entrenched in these economies, particularly those of Uganda and Rwanda with their various Congolese allies.

Many of these dynamics have been transplanted to Johannesburg in an extension of these variegated economies of the Great Lakes. Some intelligence operatives can reach deep into certain South African ministries and major enterprises, and at the same time, can "string along" hundreds of migrants in precarious affiliations. Documents, funds, and opportunities can be used and then quickly withdrawn. Still, assets from conventional and unconventional economic pursuits circulate spatially across Johannesburg, from inner city to suburbs and back, as well as far beyond, as both inner-city and suburban residential neighborhoods attempt to stabilize each other.

Despite the difficulties, there are efforts on the part of Congolese to try and establish the semblance of formal businesses. Let us look at some examples.

Salon Ilunga La Coiffure, owned by Ilunga Mbuyi on Saint George Street in Bellevue, opened in July 2002. Ilunga, from Kinshasa, is married and has a son; he has lived in Johannesburg since 2001. His wife and son joined him in 2004, traveling from Kinshasa to Lubumbashi, and then to Zambia, Zimbabwe, and finally South Africa. He is a professional hairdresser with twenty years of experience. He runs his business in a transformed garage of a Congolese-owned apartment block facing the street and pays a rental of R350, plus electricity and water. He says he manages to feed his family but also has to deal with shakedowns from the police, intimidation from local residents, and demands for assistance from fellow nationals.

Bellevue Laundromat and Dry Cleaner on Cavendish Road, Yeoville, is owned by Charles Lomba, who bought this business that had already existed for four years. He employs a Congolese manager, two South African women, and one Angolan woman. He pays his employees roughly R800 per month and R3,000 rent, while earning roughly R8,000 per month.

Full Service Agency at 54 Regent Street in Yeoville is owned by Gaby Pindi, who resides in Kinshasa, and it is managed by another Congolese, Guy-Tshibangu. A Mr. Dambana, the owner of the building, also lives in Kinshasa. The agency has operated since November 2000 and offers freight, money transfer, and communication services. The agency employs thirteen people, all from the DRC. They pay R3,300 for rent and electricity per month, which is paid to the owner's wife, who resides in Johannesburg. The business possesses the full gamut of necessary documents and regularly pays all taxes. Still, the agency faces continuous harassment from the police. It has managed to open several branches in South Africa—in Johannesburg, Cape Town, and Durban—in addition to offices in Kinshasa and Lubumbashi. There are also branches in Luanda, Cotonou, Lagos, Brazzaville, and Pointe-Noire as well as in London, Paris, and Rotterdam.

Silken on Hunter Street in Yeoville is managed by Zamoy Mozagba and is owned by another Congolese, Yves Mukenge. The business has been in operation since 2003, and its activities, again, include freight, money transfer, and communication. It employs six people, all married, living with their families, and originally from the DRC. Like the previous example, the premises are owned by Mr. Dambana, who charges the same rent that is in turn received by his wife. The business is fully legal. The majority of clients are from DRC and Angola.

Tony Security was started by a Congolese, who has lived in Johannesburg for a decade and is married to a South African woman. The majority of the nearly 200 people that work for him are Congolese, although he also hires Nigerians and Ghanaians. He negotiates security contracts with shops, companies, warehouses, restaurants, and nightclubs at reduced rates, in part because he produces fake security licenses for his employees. Salaries are negotiated with employers, with Tony taking a cut of the eventual pay. When obliged by the employer to have a firearm before starting work, Tony will buy a stolen firearm with no license for his employees, putting them in jeopardy. Though his employees have been arrested for possession of an illegal firearm, Tony has sufficient connections to usually get them out of trouble. Although he subjects his employees to often exploitative conditions, many educated Congolese attempt to get employment here because the work provides them with an opportunity to impress employers with their skills and thus access different kinds of employment opportunities.

In addition, there are many informal economic activities. Patrick and James are both Congolese from Lubumbashi whose job is to translate from French to English on Sunday at Pastor Kipa's church. They also participate with eight others in a business that buys secondhand cars in Johannesburg and sells them in Lubumbashi. The eight initially pooled their money to buy one car, but now they purchase up to five cars at one time. They have also gained access to secondhand cars in Dubai for less that $1,000. Now they do not buy without orders from people in Lubumbashi, selling three to four cars per month, and they have recently expanded their business into Zambia. The main transaction cost entails circumventing immigration and customs officials as they do not have the necessary licenses to move vehicles across the various borders.

Many Congolese are involved in *ngulu,* a Lingala term used to describe smuggling people across borders. One smuggler has been living in Johannesburg since 2001, he himself having been smuggled into South Africa from Kinshasa via Angola and Namibia. Because it has become exceedingly difficult to secure legal travel documentation, many different groups deal in this highly profitable business. In addition to the Kinshasa-Luanda-Namibia route, there is the Kinshasa-Lubumbashi-Lusaka-(Mozambique or Zimbabwe) route. The business relies on contacts in Kinshasa who identify people willing to travel. The contact organizes passports for the trip, which commences when there are fifteen to twenty people ready to go. The average cost is $750 per person. As the trip can take up to three months, depending on the difficulties that the group encounters en route, the process is strenuous and financially difficult because, in addition to the fee, travelers have to pay for their food and accommodations. Many arrive in South Africa with no money left to survive the first months. Borders are difficult to negotiate as officials change all the time, which then requires negotiations for bribes to begin anew.

Kayba Mamie is one woman who was smuggled into the country. She is from Kinshasa, worked as a receptionist, is divorced, and is financially responsible for a child, mother, and sister in Kinshasa. Unable to cope with her divorce and unwilling to return to live with her mother, she paid $500 for the trip to South Africa. The group consisted of eighteen people, six women, two babies, and ten men, with ages varying between twenty-five to thirty-five years. The trip started from Kinshasa to Lubumbashi by military plane, because it is less expensive than regular commercial flights. The group was prepared to depart from Lubumbashi at any time because the flights are irregular and the smuggler needs to negotiate with the military for space on the plane. Once in Lubumbashi, the smuggler organized accommodation while waiting for information about the guard at the Zambian border. When preparations for the next leg of the trip were ready, the group took a bus and then a truck that was going to Lusaka via Kasumbalesa, a border town with the DRC. The group spent four days in Lusaka before leaving for Mozambique, where they spent some weeks because negotiations with the South African agent failed. Eventually, they crossed the South African border with a Mozambican guide through a game park. The entire trip took three weeks. Kayba ran into trouble in Zambia, where she ran out of money and was compelled to become the smuggler's girlfriend for the remainder of the journey.

Phenomene bana ya asie is a type of check fraud that uses fake postal orders and stolen checks to open up bank accounts in Asia with "legitimate funds" transferred back into South African accounts. It is a scheme that attracts many young Congolese and is similar to the better-known "419" scams associated with Nigerians. The fraud is usually organized by Congolese syndicates operated by more worldly elder members who have experienced in a wide range of unconventional economic activities. They train young men to attempt high-risk endeavors. Sometimes this fraud is centered on the hedging of particular commodities, such as the gem trade in Bangkok, where fake bills of sale are issued for large jewelry deliveries that circulate among a network of complicit retail outlets. These items are then used as collateral for the purchase of other commodities that are bought and sold.

The visible presence of a Congolese nightlife has also consolidated an opportunity for Congolese with some money to exert a wider influence over the extended community. Sankayi, owned by a Congolese, was the first African club to open in the northern suburbs. It has been open for four years and still attracts many people. Its clientele is composed primarily of foreign African professionals. But it is a very diverse place where Europeans living in South Africa as well as South Africans are in contact with African migrants. The owner used to be close to the Mobutu regime and is well known for serving as the president of the Congolese Football Associations.

Chez Ntemba is well known throughout Southern Africa as the club with the best Congolese music. The owner, from Lubumbashi, has branches in Angola, Mozambique, and now two in Johannesburg. Unlike Sankayi, his clientele is not from the upper class but rather composed of a cross section of people who love Congolese music. La Reference in Yeoville is a bar with typically male clientele that stays open from early morning to late night serving Congolese cuisine. Village Kin Malebo opened in Yeoville during 1996 and was the first Congolese restaurant, closing in 1999 but then reopening at a different location three years ago. It is owned by Ruphin, who arrived in Johannesburg eight years ago and is married to a South African woman. He employs fifteen people—five men and ten women, most of whom are South African. He is still working on securing his licenses yet pays all government taxes. Nazaire, from Brazzaville, owns La Congolaise Bar/Restaurant on Rockey Street in Yeoville. He works at a freight agency and bought the restaurant from a Congolese woman (Madame Corrine) in 2002, who was immigrating to the United States. He employs ten people, eight men from Congo Brazzaville and two South African women. He manages to make R5,000 on weekdays and R7,000 on weekends. The monthly rent, water, and electricity charges amount to R8,000. He is regularized with all the licenses and taxes, but he still faces occasional police raids and gives them money to stop the harassment of his customers. The majority of his clientele are from Brazzaville and Kinshasa, who frequent his restaurant to listen to the Congolese music he plays. Since his opening, he has been the victim of two armed robberies and tear gas has been thrown into the club on several occasions. He pays R1,400 per month to male employees and R1,100 for the women. Because the majority of his clientele have little money, he offers a low-cost menu of pap, stew, and fish, which in turn enables him to expand his clientele beyond the Congolese community because these dishes are South African staples.

The Church: A Platform for Urban Mediation and the Insertion of the Migrant into the City

Churches are also important gathering places. Congregation members come from all over Johannesburg to attend Congolese church services in Yeoville, Berea, Hillbrow, and Parktown. Churches tend to be divided according to one's city of origin. For example, Pastor Muteba from Lubumbashi is head of the main Congolese church in Berea, which attracts a large congregation of Congolese who are mainly from Lubumbashi. He was the first Congolese pastor in Johannesburg in the early 1990s and started his church in the massive residential tower known as Ponte City. He then moved to Joubert Park as the popularity of his services increased throughout the Congolese community. Now he runs his church in Berea. Unlike the nightclubs and other public spaces for gathering such as hair salons, church congregations are not segregated along educational or social divides.

What is particularly important here are the ways in which these churches operate as an extended family for migrants whose domestic household arrangements can often be quite fluid. Also critical is the fact that these churches draw upon individuals with different relationships to the city and its urban economy. In other words, the congregations may initially start by drawing individuals from the same country, city, and even a particular neighborhood in the city of origin, but these are individuals who are both rich and poor, employed in both the formal and informal sectors. This heterogeneity provides not only an environment where different perspectives from various vantage points within Johannesburg can be exchanged but also a range of opportunity for collaboration.

Similar to extended family systems, the churches encourage concrete acts of mutuality and support. They differ from extended families in the intensity of obligation and the hold that individual congregants exert over one another. In addition, the churches provide a range of flexible times and occasions for affiliation. As a result, they have become critical places of mediation—managing stable social supports but at the same time dealing with people who make their living in a range of ways and have access to very different kinds of networks.

I have identified about sixty such churches across the inner city of Johannesburg, and there are undoubtedly more. Let us look at each of the major Congolese congregations.

The Victory Gospel Ministry, "God City of Power," located at Minor and Honey Streets in Berea, created in 2002, hosts frequent services and a variety of activities. Both pastors, Fils Kabongo and Isaac Mafuka Kilunda, are from Kinshasa and studied theology at the Protestant University of Kinshasa. The church has an executive committee headed by the pastor and his representative and 10 members from the church on a voluntary basis. They serve as mediators with the different members of the church in case of illness, argument, or need. Although the majority of the 120 members are from the DRC—most unmarried, with a fairly equal distribution of men and women—there are about 30 South Africans and others.

Dynamique de la Foi, at 6 Becker Street in Yeoville, was founded by Pasteur Benson Mputu in 2003. The majority of the church's twenty-two members are young single men and women, eighteen to thirty-five years old, from the DRC, although the pastor hopes to open up the church to broader participation. Like the Victory Gospel Ministry, it organizes many different times and kinds of opportunity for worship.

World Life Assembly, at the corner of Kenmere and Hunter streets in Yeoville, was founded in December 2000 with Ernest Kipa as pastor. The church employs French, English, and Lingala and draws upon roughly 450 members. It has purchased a school, part of which serves as a clinic and an orphanage that houses children who have lost their parents to HIV/AIDS. It also provides accommodation and food for members who have no other place to go. It helps its members find work and provides information about accommodation vacancies. It helps pay fees for training and education courses so that its members may find work or create employment. The pastor has lived in Johannesburg for more than ten years, originally working with another clergyman before establishing his own church. Initially he used his own apartment, then rented a room in a building in Hillbrow, and then sublet premises from a Nigerian minister. He rapidly established himself within the Congolese community, which helped him acquire enough money to purchase a former synagogue as the site of the present church.

Tabernacle des Vainqueurs uses the Blue Room at the Yeoville Recreation Center. Albert Mputu created the church in November 2002 with forty Congolese members, most with families. The church runs a local pharmacy and raises money to purchase medical equipment for different hospitals in Kinshasa. It enjoys the patronage of a well-known South African businesswoman, who has made substantial contributions to the church.

Word of Faith Mission, at Fortesque and Hunter streets in Yeoville, was established ten years ago and is served by the Reverend Placid Mwamba. The congregation consists primarily of Congolese and Angolans, although there is a growing contingent of South Africans among its 300 members. The pastor has been living in Johannesburg for the past ten years and has been working on his church since his arrival. He claims that his church is an international church, as there are branches elsewhere in Africa, in Europe, and America. He started his evangelic mission in Kinshasa; the next churches were in Zambia and then South Africa. He recently created missions in the United States, Kenya, Tanzania, and the United Kingdom. He recently bought an old synagogue, having operated in various Hillbrow locations over the years. Twice a year, he tours all his different churches, allowing him to monitor the growth of his church and maintain contact with the congregants.

There are a number of similar Congolese churches that average approximately one hundred members. Moreover, an increasing numbers of Congolese have begun to attend a largely Anglophone congregation known as the Amazing Glory Covenant Church International Partakers Chapel, located in a large house at 33 Bedford Road in Bellevue, with Joseph Cosmos as pastor. Most of the congregation consists of Nigerians, Zambians, Ghanaians, Ugandans, and South Africans. The church has started a range of small enterprises to maintain itself, as most its worshippers have very limited means. The church opened a nursery and two small hairdressing salons that bring in money. The Nigerian minister is married to a South African woman who contributes to the church and helped obtain the house used for prayers. The minister initially worked as a security guard for a Nigerian compatriot who owns a shop in the city.

As is clear from these examples, churches bring together various social opportunities, serve as platforms to incubate entrepreneurship, acquire property, operate as "switchboards" for networking across Johannesburg and cities elsewhere, and serve as a legitimate context for the accumulation and distribution of funds. Some churches are even involved in various smuggling activities. As evangelical Christianity has made vast inroads across Africa, coupling guaranteed material gains in an afterlife with the promise that self-discipline and self-reliance will generate material as well as spiritual gains, these churches in Johannesburg act as a crucial domain where migrants can manage their insertion into a largely cutthroat urban economy. Given the composition of the Africa Diaspora in Johannesburg, with its mélange of shifting political alliances, motivations, and initial reasons for emigration, migrants face many uncertainties, particularly about whom they can trust and deal with. The world of the church, which is comfortably circumscribed yet made up of various links, personalities, and networks, offers both a sense of stability and possibility.

Possibilities and Constraints

Taking migrant economies together with the highly circumscribed movements of inner-city residents navigating open-ended games of chance, deception, and trickery, the inner city of Johannesburg is the intersection of narrow spaces of operation with porous vectors of external connectivity. Such an intersection poses many challenges to conventional paradigms of urban governance, particularly if municipal institutions lack the policy instruments to engage it, let alone the analytical instruments to develop some functional understanding of the economic and social dynamics involved.

Everyday survival for inner-city residents requires a diversity of strategies employed to secure basic needs, for example, simultaneous participation in formal and informal economies, dispersion of dependents across different localities, and diversifying sources of borrowing and evasion. These practices cultivate particular economic and social practices that can weaken customary modalities of social affiliation and support. Policy efforts to constrain the mobility of domestic private capital and to attract and maintain mobile external capital have had the effect of intensifying the mobility of the poor. This, of course, is not upward but rather lateral mobility—movement within and between townships and informal settlements, cities, and regions, all in an incessant hunt for livelihood.

The extent of demographic shifts in some areas, such as the inner city of Johannesburg, is unprecedented in contemporary urban history. Also unprecedented is the degree to which social boundaries are marked by spatial arrangements in high-density quarters and the ways in which the physical trappings of wealth and security can be penetrated by "roving bands" of "opportunists" that take whatever they can. The intense levels of contestation over who has the "right" to do what in African cities produce a situation where things can happen very quickly. Urban dwellers do not, as a result, feel constrained by the sense that specific places and resources belong to only certain kinds of uses or identities. There are constant and often violent arguments in apartment blocks, on streets, in taxis, in schools, and in stores about who can do what where. Such disputes lead to greater flexibility in the use of urban space but can also break down a sense of propriety and the integrity of places, which in turn makes them vulnerable to incursions and distortions of all kinds.

In the midst of these fluidities, there are also efforts to eke out some basic coordination of livelihood practices and simply manage the activities of everyday life. These collective efforts are not only expressed in the forms of organizations, local institutions, and associations but also at their intersections—or often when certain associations such as churches operate on many different levels. Indeed, across urban Africa, a multiplicity of small democracies are at work, where exchanges and complementarities continue to be renegotiated, as people try to make vital lives wherever and however they can.

Notes

1. D. Malaquais, "Anatomie d'une arnaque: Feymen et feymania au Cameroun," *L'Études du Ceri* 77 (2001); C. Gore and D. Pratten, "The Politics of Plunder: The Rhetorics of Order and Disorder in Southern Nigeria," *African Affairs* 102 (2004): 211–40; C. Moser, "Urban Violence and Insecurity: An Introductory Roadmap," *Environment and Urbanization* 16 (2004): 3–16. D. Anderson, "Vigilantes, Violence, and the Politics of Public Order in Kenya," *African Affairs* 101 (2002): 531–55; Human Rights Watch, "The Bakassi Boys: The Legitimatization of Murder and Torture," *Human Rights Watch Reports on Nigeria* 14, no. 5 (2002): 2002.

2. Ash Amin and Nigel Thrift, *Cities: Reimagining the Urban* (London: Polity, 2002).

3. P. Gastrow, *Penetrating State and Business: Organized Crime in Southern Africa*, Monograph 89 (Pretoria: Institute for Security Studies, 2003).

4. K. Harrison, "Falling Down the Rabbit Hole: Crime in Johannesburg's Inner City," *Development in Practice* 16 (2006): 222–26; M. Shaw, "West African Criminal Networks in South and Southern Africa," *African Affairs* 101 (2002): 291–316.

5. R. Brubaker and F. Cooper, "Beyond "Identity," *Theory and Society* 29 (2000): 1–27.

6. The current exchange rate of the South African rand hovers around R8 to $1.

Part II

The Renegotiation of Urban Citizenship

6

Immigrants in a Sunbelt Metropolis: The Transformation of an Urban Place and the Construction of Community

Caroline B. Brettell

The study of immigration in the United States is often associated with four cities—Los Angeles, New York, Chicago, and Miami—and indeed these four metropolitan areas still have the largest foreign-born populations according to the 2000 census. In recent years, however, second-tier metropolitan areas in the Midwest, West, and Northwest (Minneapolis–Saint Paul, Denver, and Portland), in the South and Southwest (Atlanta, Dallas–Fort

The research for this chapter was supported by the Cultural Anthropology Program of the National Science Foundation (NSF/BCS 0003938). The coinvestigators on the project were James F. Hollifield (political science, Southern Methodist University), Dennis Cordell (history, Southern Methodist University), and Manuel Garcia y Griego (Center for Mexican American Studies, University of Texas at Arlington). The author also acknowledges the work of two anthropology graduate students, Lisa Greenman and Jose Santos. Any opinions, findings, conclusions, or recommendations expressed in this chapter are those of the author and do not necessarily reflect the views of the National Science Foundation. A more extended discussion of the development of the Asian Indian community is included in "The Spatial, Social, and Political Incorporation of Asian Indian Immigrants in Dallas, Texas," by Caroline Brettell, *Urban Anthropology* 34, no. 2 (2005).

Worth, Phoenix), and even in some areas of the East (Washington, as Jones-Correa notes in chapter 1 of this volume) and the Southeast (Nashville, Raleigh-Durham) have received large numbers of new immigrants, making them more ethnically diverse than ever before.

This trend has led the demographer Audrey Singer to formulate a new model that distinguishes six types of gateway cities: former gateways, such as Cleveland and Buffalo; continuous gateways, like New York and Chicago; post–World War II gateways, like Los Angeles and Miami; emerging gateways, such as Atlanta, Dallas, and Washington; reemerging gateways, like Seattle, Denver, and Minneapolis–Saint Paul; and preemerging gateways, like Salt Lake City and Raleigh-Durham. Singer's work needs to be placed within a larger body of new research, in the United States and elsewhere, that is attempting to compare cities as contexts for late-twentieth and early-twenty-first-century immigration.[1]

My own interest in the different ways in which immigrant populations enter into and transform urban environments dates back more than thirty years when, in early multi-sited ethnography, I found myself contrasting the settlement and employment patterns of Portuguese immigrants in Toronto with those in Paris. I have returned to this topic more recently, developing an analytical framework for how we might approach the comparative study of cities as contexts for immigration and how different urban contexts might affect the process of incorporation for various immigrant populations.[2] This framework focuses on four areas.

The first area is *the temporal and spatial dimensions of cities*. This includes the historical depth of immigration and whether or not a city has defined itself for some time as a "city of immigrants" as well as the contrasts that can be drawn between cities laid out in concentric zones—the old Chicago School model—as opposed to those that grew up with the motor car as suburban cities.

The second area is *the social context*. This includes an analysis of how heterogeneous a city is, how divided it is, whether one ethnic group hold the reins of local power, how different ethnic groups relate to one another, and when, where, and how identity politics emerge.

The third area is *the urban labor market / the immigrant labor market*. This includes assessments of how differences in local economic structures (including variations in entry-level earnings) can result in diverging patterns of opportunity for both the native and the foreign born as well as nodes of attraction for particular immigrant populations—for example, those with high human capital.

The fourth area is *the cultural ethos of cities*. This includes an examination of whether or not a city projects a dominant set of values that shapes political, economic, and institutional life, and hence both the incorporation of and attitudes toward immigrants. This ethos can emerge from a specific history of economic and political growth. It can also derive from the larger state or national context or a larger cultural context. To some extent, ethos is also about the way a city looks at itself, represents itself, or constructs its identity.

It is with an interest in new cities of immigration and the concept of "city as context" for the incorporation of immigrants that I explore here one particular emerging gateway city—Dallas—where a team of researchers has been engaged in studying several different immigrant populations. I discuss the city of Dallas in relation to the Dallas–Fort Worth metroplex (henceforth, DFW).[3] By using the term "metroplex," which is used locally, I want to suggest that, in exploring cities of immigration in the late twentieth and early twenty-first centuries, we need to think carefully about our units of analysis and about the relationships between cities and their suburbs—a point equally made by Jones-Correa in chapter 1 of this volume. Although it is interesting to look at the city of Dallas itself, the city of Fort Worth itself, the cities of Arlington or Irving that lie between Dallas and Fort Worth, or the northern city of Plano (one of the fastest-growing suburbs in the United States in the 1990s), ultimately we need to consider the broader metropolitan region as a whole to grasp fully what is going on and what is at issue in studying the spatial, economic, and social incorporation of immigrants in this Southwestern Sunbelt metropolis.[4] The pivotal questions that I explore here, in relationship to the central theme of this volume, are how immigrant populations engage in processes of place making and cultural citizenship, and why some groups are more active than others in claiming space in urban contexts.

I begin the chapter with a brief historical overview of Dallas that pays particular attention to the growth of the foreign-born population in relation to the native born as well as the timing of shifts from a biracial to a triethnic to a multiethnic urban metropolis. I then turn to a discussion of data drawn from the 1990 and 2000 U.S. censuses, as well as from other economic data, to explore the process by which Dallas, and DFW by extension, has become a new city of immigration as well as some of the spatial dimensions of this transformation. In the final section, I address some of the implications of the rapid transformation of urban metropolises such as DFW for the study of immigrants and/in cities. I pay particular attention to the relationship between geographic space on the one hand and social, cultural, and political spaces on the other. In this discussion, I use examples from my fieldwork with Asian Indians in DFW to explore how public spaces are claimed and used by immigrant newcomers as well as how communities are constructed when an immigrant population is residentially dispersed. What are the places of encounter that these immigrants create that give them a sense of spatial belonging in the absence of residential enclaves?

The Founding and Growth of a City:
Dallas 1840–1980—from Biracial to Triethnic

The city of Dallas was founded by John Neely Bryan in the early 1840s on a crossing of the Trinity River. Historians have routinely pointed to the emphasis, accurate or misguided, that has been placed on the founding of a city where no city should have existed, because the river was essentially unnavigable. But Bryan's boosterism for the place, the reputedly rich soil, and a deal established between the Republic of Texas and the Texas Land and Emigration Company to establish the Peters Colony in North Texas attracted settlers.[5] By 1846, Dallas County was organized, and the town was surveyed, platted, and later chartered in 1856. In 1850, Dallas County had a population of 2,753; of these, 163 lived in town. The residents were largely farmers, many originating in states to the East—Tennessee, Missouri, Georgia, and Alabama.

Fort Worth, by contrast, was originally founded as a camp (never a fort) where U.S. troops under Brevet Major R. Arnold could keep a watchful eye on the Indians. It was named to honor General William Jenkins Worth, a hero of the Mexican War. Gradually, the Indian populations were driven out of the area as Anglo settlers began to move in, bringing their slaves with them.

Dallas grew quickly. In 1860, the population of Dallas County was 8,665 and the city's was 678. By 1880, the county's population had grown to 33,477 and the city's to 10,385. This growth was largely due to internal migration from Arkansas, Missouri, Tennessee, and Louisiana and was fueled by the cotton industry and the railroad. Cotton brought slaves who, in 1860, constituted 12 percent of the population. The expansion of the railroad, which arrived in Dallas in 1872, led to further population growth, including the arrival of African American freedmen who came to the city to work as common laborers, boilermen, trackmen, and engineers.[6] In 1880, "Negros" made up 19 percent of the Dallas population, and the foreign born were 12.8 percent of the population. Promotional literature described a city that does remunerative business "in dry goods, groceries, blacksmithing, foundrying, wagons, buggy, plow, cultivator and saddlery making, milling, wool carding, cotton ginning, brickmaking, concreting, etc."[7] The *Dallas Morning News* began publication in 1885 and the *Times Herald* in 1888.

If Dallas became a center for cotton, Fort Worth became an important trading and supply center for the cattle drives. It remained a frontier settlement with a couple of hundred inhabitants; but in the early 1870s, in anticipation of the arrival of the railroad, the population began to grow. However, in 1873, the year the city was incorporated, the company that held most of the liens against the railroad, as well as a large portion of the property in Fort Worth, failed. The city's population declined rapidly, from 5,000 to 1,000. When the railroad finally arrived in 1876, the population began to grow again. Fort Worth became a center for the cattle trade and later for meatpacking. Swift and Armour started operations in Fort Worth in 1903. After 1917, further growth was fueled by the oil industry and a short time later by the aviation industry.

Dallas also continued to grow and by 1910 had become the dominant city in North Texas, with a larger population and twice as many manufacturing firms as Fort Worth. This boomtown image, solidified in 1914 when a branch of the Federal Reserve was established, drew a range of ethnic groups, albeit in small numbers.[8] German Jewish merchants moved into the city to set up dry goods and other general stores and to create a host of new white-collar jobs. German immigrants were joined in the 1880s by immigrants from Switzerland, Italy, and Mexico. "By the turn of the century, Mexican Americans were working as grocers, vendors, cotton buyers, printers, candy manufacturers, and tailors. Tamale vendors were seen on the streets in the 1880s, and the first Mexican restaurant opened."[9]

By 1900, the population of Dallas had quadrupled to 42,638. African Americans were just over 20 percent of this population, and they lived in their own neighborhoods, as did the Jews. Table 6.1 shows the composition of the population between 1900 and 1930 by nativity and race for the city of Dallas as well as the city of Fort Worth and for the four counties (Collin, Dallas, Denton, and Tarrant) that today constitute the core of population growth in the area. This corresponds to the height of the so-called third wave of immigration nationwide.

Although the native-born white population dominated the area, there were significant proportions of Negro/colored populations. However, this

Table 6.1. Population of the Dallas–Fort Worth Area, 1900–30

Population Unit	Total Population	Native-Born White		Foreign-Born White		Negro/Colored/Black	
		Number	Percent	Number	Percent	Number	Percent
1900							
Collin County	54,993	49,767	90.5	309	0.6	4,914	8.9
Dallas County	110,046	78,522	71.3	4,204	3.8	27,320	24.8
Denton County	38,157	27,790	72.8	528	1.4	9,839	25.7
Tarrant County	63,911	50,075	78.3	2,301	3.6	11,535	18.4
Dallas City	42,638	30,230	70.9	3,381	7.9	9,063	21.2
Fort Worth City	26,688	20,651	77.4	1,766	6.6	4,271	16.0
1910							
Collin County	49,021	40,555	95.0	250	0.5	2,206	4.5
Dallas County	135,738	105,137	78.0	6,201	4.6	24,355	17.9
Denton County	31,258	28,557	91.4	484	1.5	2,210	7.1
Tarrant County	108,572	88,168	81.2	4,913	4.5	15,418	14.2
Dallas City	92,104	68,816	74.7	5,264	5.7	18,024	19.6
Fort Worth City	73,319	55,839	76.1	4,209	5.7	13,280	18.1
1920							
Collin County	49,609	45,499	91.7	399	0.8	3,711	7.5
Dallas County	210,551	168,664	80.1	10,398	4.9	31,397	14.9
Denton County	35,355	32,319	91.4	454	1.3	2,580	7.3
Tarrant County	152,800	125,287	82.0	8,637	5.7	18,730	12.3
Dallas City	158,976	126,158	79.4	8,730	5.5	24,023	15.1
Fort Worth City	106,482	83,107	78.0	7,350	6.9	15,806	14.9
1930							
Collin County	46,180	42,052	91.1	149	0.3	3,979	8.6
Dallas County	325,691	266,845	81.9	10,889	3.3	47,879	14.7
Denton County	32,822	30,290	92.3	373	1.1	2,159	6.6
Tarrant County	197,553	167,305	84.7	5,526	2.3	24,660	12.5
Dallas City	260,475	212,230	81.5	9,391	3.6	38,742	14.9
Fort Worth City	163,447	136,282	83.3	4,890	3.0	22,234	13.6

Sources: U.S. Census, 1900, 1910, 1920, 1930.

proportion declined as native-born whites from other states moved in during the first three decades of the twentieth century. The proportion of foreign-born whites declined between 1900 and 1930, although it was always higher in the urban areas than in the surrounding rural counties. Among the largest groups of foreign-born whites in 1900 were individuals born in Germany, Ireland, England, France, Canada, Russia, and Switzerland. These were not, for the most part, the same foreign-born populations that were moving in massive numbers into the cities of the East Coast at the turn of the twentieth century.[10] Similar foreign-born populations were among the largest in 1910 as well, although in that year 338 Italians were also counted in Dallas city and there were also immigrants from Norway and Austria. Darwin Payne reports that the numbers of Italians helped to launch an Italian language newspaper, *La Tribuna Italiana,* in 1913.[11] By 1920, Poles and Greeks were also present. Among the larger populations in Fort Worth at this time were Russians, Germans, English, Irish, Greeks, Canadians, and Italians. In 1930, the only foreigners added to the mix were Czechs and Swedes. Despite this diversity, the numbers of any of these nationality groups was generally under 500 in both cities.

During this period, individuals born in Mexico who were not "native indigenous" were included in the foreign-born category. Although their numbers were larger than any of the other foreign-born populations, they were not sizable. In 1920 the U.S. Census counted 3,378 Mexicans in the city of Dallas and 3,785 in the city of Fort Worth. By 1930, the number in the city of Dallas had increased slightly and in Fort Worth had declined appreciably. Living conditions for the Mexican population, native or foreign-born, were bad. Hazel notes that between 1934 and 1936 the highest death rate from tuberculosis in Dallas was in Little Mexico.[12]

In the period spanning the decades between 1930 and 1970, Dallas became increasingly segregated, achieving what Schutze has referred to as an accommodation between the white population on the one hand and the African American and Hispanic populations on the other.[13] The white elite that came to power in the 1930s "ran Dallas like an efficient corporation in which the authority of the board of directors was not questioned. The management of Dallas concerned itself with the wealth and prosperity of the business community. The city's African American and Latino populations continued to suffer from severely limited employment opportunities and an ongoing shortage of decent housing. Migrants from rural areas who came to the city with few skills received some of the lowest wages of any urban workers in the country."[14]

Following World War II, Dallas became one of the fastest-growing Sunbelt cities in the United States, offering jobs in aviation and electronics, among other industries. It had a population under 300,000 in 1940, but by 1960 its population had more than doubled to 680,000. Nationally, the doors to immigration were closed, and the second and third generations of largely white European immigrants grew to maturity and were absorbed into the dominant white fabric of the city. In 1970, only 1.4 percent of the population of the Dallas–Fort Worth Consolidated Metropolitan Statistical Area was foreign born (the comparable figure for the city of Dallas was 2.1 percent).

The population of Hispanics in the city of Dallas began to expand in the

1960s. They numbered 29,464, or 4 percent of the total population of the city of Dallas, in 1960; but by 1970 the number had increased to 67,902, or 7.6 percent of the Dallas population. This represented a 130 percent growth rate, as compared with 62.7 percent for blacks and 8.7 percent for Anglos. Achor points out that in 1960 Dallas was at the top of a list of Southwestern cities in the index of dissimilarity—scoring 85 (where zero is a randomly distributed population and 100 is a totally segregated population). In 1970, there were nineteen census tracts in Dallas that were 95 to 100 percent black; nine more were 90 percent black, and twelve were 75 percent black.[15]

In Dallas, segregation was fueled by rapid suburbanization in the postwar period. The suburban spread began in the 1960s and rose dramatically in the late 1960s. New commuter suburbs grew up in Richardson and Garland.[16] The City Planning Department reported that 100,000 had fled to the suburbs during this period. As busing in the city was launched concertedly in the early 1970s, white flight accelerated. Established black communities to the north were displaced, and Little Mexico was progressively razed as a new downtown with a circumference of freeways emerged to fill the Texas sky. Eventually, a triethnic committee composed of white, black, and Hispanic members was appointed to oversee desegregation and the power of the Citizens Council began to erode as minorities became increasingly empowered. The first African American and Mexican American to serve on the city's formal governing body were elected in 1969, and in 1975 the form of city council elections changed. In 1980, the population of the Dallas Primary Metropolitan Statistical Area (PMSA) was 74 percent white, non-Hispanic; 15.8 percent black, non-Hispanic; and 8.6 percent Hispanic (all races). The foreign born were 4.5 percent of the population. Table 6.2 provides the breakdown by race/ethnicity for the central city of Dallas and the suburbs in 1980 and shows the changes in these proportions in the succeeding two decades. It is to these changes that I now turn.

Boom Town, Boom Growth: The Growth of a Multiethnic Metroplex, 1980–2000

In the early 1980s, the media began to notice the urban transformation of major American cities. Dallas was featured with New York, Detroit, and Los Angeles, and a local journalist was recorded to say that "a person caught in a time warp for the past 20 years, even the past 10, would not recognize the place today. You walk four blocks and move through five cultures—upscale

Table 6.2. Race/Ethnicity and Foreign Born as Percentage of Total Population, Dallas Primary Metropolitan Statistical Area (PMSA), Central City, and Suburbs, 1980, 1990, and 2000 (percent)

Category	Dallas PMSA	Dallas Central City	Dallas PMSA Suburbs
White, non-Hispanic	1980, 74.2	1980, 57.1	1980, 87.6
	1990, 67.8	1990, 47.9	1990, 80.8
	2000, 56.2	2000, 34.6	2000, 69.0
Black, non-Hispanic	1980, 15.8	1990, 29.2	1980, 5.4
	1990, 15.6	2000, 25.6	1990, 7.3
	2000, 14.9	1980, 29.2	2000, 9.4
Other races, non-Hispanic	1980, 1.5	1980, 1.5	1980, 1.4
	1990, 3.9	1990, 2.6	1990, 3.0
	2000, 5.8	2000, 4.2	2000, 6.3
Hispanic (all races)	1980, 8.6	1980, 12.2	1980, 5.6
	1990, 13.6	1990, 20.3	1990, 8.9
	2000, 23.0	2000, 35.6	2000, 15.3
Foreign born	1980, 4.5	1980, 6.1	1980, 3.0
	1990, 8.8	1990, 12.5	1990, 5.8
	2000, 16.8	2000, 24.4	2000, 11.7

Note: For the 2000 data, only those persons identifying themselves as "white alone" and "black or African American alone" are categorized as "white, non-Hispanic" and "black, non-Hispanic," respectively. "Other races, non-Hispanic" includes those who identified themselves as "Asian alone," "Native Hawaiian and other Pacific Islander alone," "American Indian and Alaska Native alone," "some other race alone," or of more than one race.
Source: U.S. Census.

white, low-income white, black, Hispanic and Asian."[17] The transformation, which continued through the 1980s and the 1990s, was fueled by an economic boom in the late 1970s and early 1980s.

The new Dallas City Hall, designed by I. M. Pei, was opened in 1978, and the new Dallas Museum of Art, designed by Edward Larabee Barnes, in 1984. According to Payne, 29.3 million square feet of new office space was created in the city in 1983 and 1984. "The metroplex, a new term coined to encompass Dallas–Fort Worth, and the growing suburban areas, now ranked third behind New York and Chicago as headquarters for companies with more than $1 million in assets."[18] Although there was a financial setback in the latter 1980s, the boom was restored by the 1990s as the economy became more diversified, moving away from an overdependence on oil, gas, and real estate.

According to the Greater Dallas Chamber, DFW ranked first in the nation for employment growth in the 1990s—760,600 new jobs were created.

Atlanta, another emerging gateway city, was second. In 1999 alone, Dallas gained 96,300 new jobs; and in 2000, DFW led the nation by creating over 102,000 jobs. The economy of the city was growing at 4.8 percent annually in the late 1990s, outpacing the national average. The total gross domestic product for DFW passed $250 billion in 2001.[19] Several important companies moved to the area in the 1990s, including ExxonMobil and JC Penney. The telecom corridor grew to the north of the city as companies such as Alcatel, Nortel, and Ericsson built major facilities in Dallas and Collin counties. Companies like Nokia and Verizon built offices in Irving. In 2000, and before the recent downturn, Dallas had more information-sector jobs than all but two other U.S. cities. California's Milken Institute ranked DFW in the late 1990s as the number two technology center in the country, lagging only the Silicon Valley.[20]

By the end of the 1990s, the metroplex had a highly diversified economy with between 5 and 30 percent of the workforce in each of the major industrial sectors. More specifically, 31 percent of the population of the city, according to Dallas Chamber of Commerce data, worked in services; 24 percent in wholesale/retail; 13 percent in manufacturing; 11 percent in government; 8 percent in finance, insurance, and real estate; 7 percent in transportation, communications, and utilities; and 5 percent in construction. At the end of 1999, *Fortune* magazine ranked Dallas first on a list of the best cities for business and *Site Selection,* a corporate relocation magazine, named Dallas the top labor market in the country in 2001.[21]

Other characteristics that fueled the economic boom were the airport, a low population density compared with other large metropolitan areas, and a relatively low cost of living for a large metropolitan area.[22] People were spending on average 20 percent of their income on housing, compared with over 40 percent in San Francisco and New York. Zinsmeister captures the "bigger as better" in Dallas by referring to the fact that there are more shopping centers in this city than in any other U.S. locale—retail space per capita is 42 percent above the national average. There are also more restaurants per capita than New York City. He also notes that a progressive attitude in the local Federal Reserve branch supports free trade and high technology, and that the deregulation of business sustains the booming new economy.[23]

This economic growth had a significant impact on demography. In 2000, 5.2 million residents were counted in the Dallas–Fort Worth consolidated metropolitan district. The PMSA of Dallas had 3.5 million residents, and that of Fort Worth 1.7 million. DFW experienced a growth rate of 29 percent between 1990 and 2000. Only Los Angeles and New York, with much larger populations, had higher growth rates. Much of this overall growth was also fueled by immigration. It was the economic climate of the 1980s and 1990s that made DFW attractive to new immigrants—both those with low human capital who found employment in the service and construction sectors and those with high human capital drawn by the telecommunication and financial industries.

Researchers at the Lewis Mumford Center ranked the Dallas PMSA 14th out of 331 metropolitan regions in attractiveness to immigrants in 1990 and 8th in 2000 while the Fort Worth–Arlington PMSA was ranked 31st in 1990 and 30th in 2000. Table 6.3 shows these rankings, together with the proportion of the foreign born in 1990 and 2000 for the two DFW PMSAs as well as for two other emerging gateway cities—Atlanta and Phoenix-Mesa.

For the entire Dallas–Fort Worth Consolidated Metropolitan Statistical Area, the increase in the proportion of the foreign born was from 7.9 percent of the total population to 15 percent. In all these emerging gateway cities, the foreign-born population essentially doubled (and in one case more than doubled) in a decade.

Another way to assess the dramatic change that occurred in the 1990s is to look at census data for the year of entry of the foreign-born population. Table 6.4 provides these figures by county for DFW. In all cases, half or

Table 6.3. Ranking of Attractiveness to Immigrants and Proportion of Foreign Born, Four Emerging Gateways, 1990 and 2000

Primary Metropolitan Statistical Area	Ranking of Attractiveness to Immigrants[a]	Percentage Foreign Born
Atlanta, 1990[b]	24	3.9
Atlanta, 2000[b]	10	10.3
Phoenix-Mesa, 1990[c]	21	7.2
Phoenix-Mesa, 2000[c]	11	14.1
Dallas, 1990[d]	14	8.8
Dallas, 2000[d]	8	16.8
Fort Worth–Arlington, 1990[e]	31	6.2
Fort Worth–Arlington, 2000[e]	30	11.4

a. This ranking is for 331 cities, by the Lewis Mumford Center for Comparative Urban and Regional Research, State University of New York at Albany.
b. Nineteen counties are included in the Atlanta Primary Metropolitan Statistical Area (PMSA).
c. The Phoenix-Mesa PMSA includes Maricopa and Pinal counties.
d. The Lewis Mumford Center and the U.S. Census include the following counties in the Dallas PMSA: Collin, Dallas, Denton, Ellis, Henderson, Hunt, Kaufmann, and Rockwall.
e. The Fort Worth PMSA includes Hood, Johnson, Parker, and Tarrant counties.
Source: Lewis Mumford Center.

Table 6.4. Year of Entry of Foreign-Born Population, Dallas–Fort Worth Primary Metroplex, Various Time Periods (percent)

Period	Collin County	Dallas County	Denton County	Tarrant County
1995–March 2000	33	37	32	32
1990–94	20	20	18	19
1980–89	26	27	27	27
1970–79	14	11	16	14
Pre-1970	7	5	7	7
Total number of foreign born	65,279	463,574	40,591	183,223

Source: U.S. Census, 2000.

slightly more than half of the foreign born had arrived since 1990, and generally a third since 1995. Indeed, more than half (56 percent) of the foreign born in the Dallas PMSA entered after 1990.

The county figures are worth examining more closely (figure 6.1 locates these four counties and major cities in the area). These data are included in table 6.5. The foreign-born population in Dallas County doubled from 1980 (when it was 5.1 percent of the total population) to 1990 and almost doubled again in the next decade to reach 20.1 percent of the total population. Tarrant County experienced similar growth—its foreign-born population in 1980 was 3.6 percent, but by 2000 it was 12.7 percent of the total population. The change in suburban Collin County was even more dramatic. There, the foreign-born population was 2.9 percent in 1980, but by 2000 the figure was 13.3 percent. Finally, in more remote Denton County, the foreign-born population rose from 3.8 percent of the total population in 1980 to 5.4 percent in 1990 and 10.1 percent in 2000.

Table 6.5 not only provides the percentage of change between 1990 and 2000 for the foreign-born population as a whole but also the changes for broad regions of origin. Suburban Collin County experienced the most dramatic growth in its foreign born across all groups, including Hispanics. The comparisons with city figures are instructive because in both Dallas and Fort Worth the percentage changes in the foreign born were much more modest than in Collin and Denton Counties.[24] For the Dallas PMSA, the proportion of the foreign born in the central city increased from 12.2 percent of the total population in 1990 to 24 percent in 2000. In the suburban areas of the Dallas PMSA, the foreign born increased from 5.8 to 11.7 percent. Comparable figures for the Fort Worth–Arlington PMSA are an increase from 8.5 to 15.9 percent in the central city and from 3.6 to 6.6 percent in the suburban areas.

Figure 6.1. Map of the Dallas–Fort Worth Metroplex

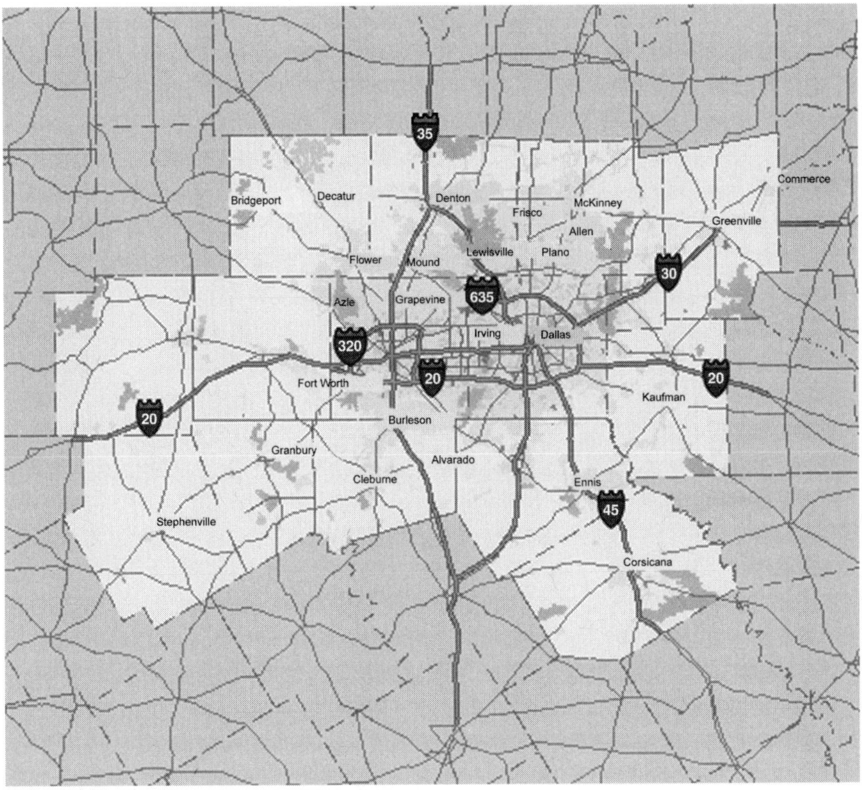

The settlement of immigrants in suburbs (as the first point of entry) is a phenomenon that has recently been noted by several scholars studying late-twentieth-century U.S. immigration, including several other contributors to this volume. As Wood has written, "Like other American frontiers in other generations, suburbs are now the geographical spaces in which Americans of all sorts of origins are creating America."[25] Using national-level data from the 2000 census, the demographer William Frey notes that in 65 of the 102 largest metropolitan areas, minorities account for most of the suburban growth. More than half of Asian Americans in large metropolitan areas reside in the suburbs, as do half of Hispanics, but only 39 percent of blacks.[26] The foreign-born population in suburban Atlanta, another emerging gateway, increased from 4 percent of the total population in 1990 to 10.7 percent in 2000, while comparable figures for the central city were 3.4 and 6.6

Table 6.5. Changes in Foreign-Born Population, Dallas–Fort Worth Metroplex, 1990–2000

Jurisdiction	Total Population	Percentage Foreign Born of Total Population	Percentage Foreign Born from Asia	Percentage Foreign Born from Latin America	Percentage Foreign Born from Africa
Collin County, 1990	264,036	5.9	39.0	33.6	2.9
Collin County, 2000	491,675	13.3	43.7	34.9	3.7
Percent change, 1990–2000	86.2	318.2	361.6	334.4	423.4
Dallas County, 1990	1,852,810	10.6	21.6	61.5	3.4
Dallas County, 2000	2,218,899	20.1	16.4	74.8	3.7
Percent change, 1990–2000	19.8	136.1	79.4	187.0	152.9
Denton County, 1990	273,525	5.4	40.2	35.8	4.4
Denton County, 2000	432,976	10.1	34.2	50.1	3.1
Percent change, 1990–2000	58.3	176.2	134.9	286.4	93.6
Tarrant County, 1990	1,170,103	6.8	29.0	51.3	3.4
Tarrant County, 2000	1,446,219	12.7	23.8	63.7	3.8
Percent change, 1990–2000	23.6	130.9	89.3	186.7	157.8
Dallas City, 1990	1,006,831	12.5	14.7	69.5	3.5
Dallas City, 2000	1,188,204	24.4	10.5	81.1	3.7
Percent change, 1990–2000	18.0	130.8	64.2	169.3	147.2
Fort Worth City, 1990	447,619	9.3	16.4	69.8	2.4
Fort Worth City, 2000	535,420	16.3	13.3	79.3	1.4
Percent change, 1990–2000	19.6	116.2	75.7	145.5	25.3

Source: U.S. Census, 2000.

Table 6.6. Household Income and Housing by County, Dallas–Fort Worth Metroplex, 1999

Income or Housing Measure	Collin County	Dallas County	Denton County	Tarrant County
Total population	182,245	808,268	159,062	534,019
Percent with income under $49,999	31	57	42	53
Percent with income $50,000–$99,999	37	29	36	32
Percent with income over $100,000	30	14	21	13
Median family income	$81, 856	$49,062	$69,292	$54,068
Proportion owner-occupied housing units	69	52	64	61
Proportion housing built 1990–March 2000	50	14	40	20

Source: U.S. Census, 2000.

percent. In Phoenix-Mesa, the comparable suburban figures were 6.5 percent in 1990 and 9.9 percent in 2000, but this metropolitan area saw an even more dramatic increase in the central city, from 7.6 to 16.4 percent. These differences may have something to do with the composition of the immigrant population in any particular city, as well as with the nature of the urban core, and the housing stock, among other factors. Such comparisons require much more in-depth comparative research, but table 6.6 does present some differences in income and housing stock by county for DFW.

What about the composition of the foreign-born population in DFW and its residential distribution? As indicated on table 6.5, the proportion of the foreign-born population that is Asian grew in Collin County but declined in all other counties as well as in the two major cities. By contrast, the Latin American populations grew dramatically in all four counties and in the cities, although the growth was extremely modest in the most suburban and wealthiest county, Collin County. Further differences emerge if we look the distribution of native and foreign born within the broad Asian and Hispanic/Latino ethnic categories. These data are contained in table 6.7.

Only in Dallas County do the foreign-born Hispanic/Latinos outnumber the native born. This table also indicates that despite the fact that a much higher proportion of the total Asian population is foreign born (74.7 percent, by comparison with 42.2 percent of Hispanics/Latinos), more than twice as many foreign-born Asians have naturalized (41.5 percent) by comparison with foreign-born Hispanic/Latinos (18.1 percent).

Table 6.7. Place of Birth and Citizenship of Asian and Hispanic Residents, Dallas–Fort Worth Metroplex, 1999

Place of Birth and Citizenship	Collin County	Dallas County	Denton County	Tarrant County	Total
Asian total	33,606	87,446	17,110	51,202	189,364
Native-born Asian	8,692	20,731	4,827	13,536	47,786
Foreign-born Asian	24,914 (74.1%)	66,715 (76.3%)	12,283 (71.8%)	37,666 (73.6%)	141,578 (74.8%)
Foreign-born / naturalized	10,507 (42.2%)	25,655 (38.4%)	5,439 (44.3%)	17,224 (45.7%)	58,825 (41.5%)
Foreign-born / not a citizen	14,407	41,060	6,844	20,442	82,753
Hispanic total	50.262	663,125	52,365	285,338	1,051,090
Native-born Hispanic	28,747	322,197	32,804	171,553	555,301
Foreign-born Hispanic	21,515 (42.8%)	340,928 (51.4%)	19,561 (37.3%)	113,785 (39.9%)	495,789 (47.2%)
Foreign-born / naturalized	4,339 (20.2%)	55,540 (16.3%)	4,675 (23.9%)	25,277 (22.2%)	89,831 (18.1%)
Foreign-born / not a citizen	17,176	285,388	14,886	88,508	405,958
Total foreign-born	65,279	463,574	40,591	183,223	752,667

Source: U.S. Census, 2000.

Table 6.8 breaks these broad categories out by nationality group—specifically the six largest foreign-born populations in DFW in 2000.[27] The 2000 census enumerated 433,534 individuals born in Mexico in the four-county DFW—57.6 percent of the total foreign-born population. This population increased by a little more than 200 percent in a decade. Of these, 295,678 (or 68.2 percent) resided in Dallas County and 104,438 (or 23.9 percent) in Tarrant County. In Dallas County, this represented a 197.4 percent increase from 1990; and in Tarrant County, a 194.1 percent increase. The city of Dallas gained more than 130,000 Mexican residents between 1990 and 2000. In 2000, immigrants from Mexico accounted for 71 percent of the foreign-born population in the city of Dallas.[28] Finally, 63 percent of the Mexicans in Dallas County lived in the city of Dallas itself. This is a more urban immigrant population.

Yet, it is certainly also worth noting the rate of change of the Mexican population in more suburban Collin and Denton counties. Indeed, for all groups, the suburban settlement pattern was particularly characteristic of the decade of the 1990s and most characteristic of Indians (with a 718 percent rate of increase) and Chinese (with a 709 percent rate of increase).

Settlement patterns vary by immigrant population. Let me use four examples from among the six largest foreign-born populations in the area. Mexican settlement is dense, widespread, and centered, as suggested above, around the urban cores (with some expansion into inner-ring suburbs), and in the cities between Dallas and Fort Worth in areas south of Highway 183, one of two highways that passes the Dallas–Fort Worth Airport and connects Dallas and Fort Worth. Indeed, an even greater proportion are settled south of Interstate 30, which runs north of Arlington. The Vietnamese, who first arrived in the mid-1970s (Dallas was a refugee staging area), increased by 132 percent during the 1990s. In 2000 they showed three nodes of residential concentration. One node is right in the urban center of Dallas, in what is known as the Oak Lawn area, where many of the initial refugee generation were settled and where they have remained. A second node is in Garland, an inner-ring suburb that developed in the 1970s. It is in this area that the Vietnamese have built their community center, where first-generation Vietnamese immigrants, those with strong anticommunist sentiments, gather. The final node is in South Arlington, a city between Dallas and Fort Worth with a lower cost of living and affordable housing. By contrast with some of the other large Asian groups in the city, the Vietnamese, who continued to arrive under refugee status in the 1990s, have a lower income and

Table 6.8. Foreign-Born Population, Dallas–Fort Worth Metroplex, 1990 and 2000

Jurisdiction of Residence	Total Population	Total Foreign-Born Population	Born in Mexico	Born in Vietnam	Born in India	Born in El Salvador	Born in China	Born in South Korea
Total four counties, 1990	3,560,475	305,996	142,078	15,746	10,347	9,663	4,866	8,177
Total four counties, 2000	4,589,769	752,667	433,534	36,522	30,030	26,271	14,379	14,001
Percent change	28.90	146.00	205.14	131.94	190.22	171.87	195.49	71.22
Collin County, 1990	264,036	15,611	3,617	586	703	250	696	546
Collin County, 2000	491,675	65,279	17,479	2,675	5,753	841	5,634	2,265
Percent change	86.20	318.20	383.20	356.50	718.34	236.40	709.50	314.80
Dallas County, 1990	1,852,810	196,328	99,411	8,084	6,408	8,235	2,451	5,347
Dallas County, 2000	2,218,899	463,574	295,678	16,934	16,030	22,351	5,223	7,333
Percent change	19.80	136.10	197.40	109.5	150.15	171.40	113.1	37.10
Denton County, 1990	273,525	14,674	3,541	1,000	758	423	466	664
Denton County, 2000	432,976	40591	15,939	2,038	2,911	834	941	1,764
Percent change	58.30	176.20	350.10	103.80	284.00	97.20	101.90	165.70
Tarrant County, 1990	1,170,103	79,363	35,509	6,076	2,478	755	1,253	1,620
Tarrant County, 2000	1,446,219	183,223	104,438	14,875	5,336	2245	2,581	2,639
Percent change	23.60	130.90	194.10	144.80	115.33	197.40	106.00	62.90
Dallas City, 1990	1,006,831	125,862	75,507	3,772	2,256	4,271	1,296	1,803
Dallas City, 2000	1,188,204	290,436	208,688	6,235	5,339	10,443	3,101	2,686
Percent change	18.00	130.80	176.40	67.70	136.65	144.50	139.30	49.00
Fort Worth City, 1990	447,619	40300	26,068	2,129	646	391	342	390
Fort Worth City, 2000	535,420	87,120	64,469	4,195	1,417	946	565	897
Percent change	18.00	116.20	147.30	97.00	119.34	141.90	65.20	130.00

Source: U.S. Census, 2000.

are more insular. This appears to be reflected in their settlement patterns.[29] The Vietnamese in 2000 were 2 percent of the foreign-born population of Dallas County, and 37 percent of this population lived in the city of Dallas itself.

The Indians, one of the fastest-growing minorities in the United States, are largely settled in the suburbs in a half circle north of the city of Dallas and east in Irving north of Highway 114. This settlement pattern reflects the higher mean income of Asian Indians by comparison with other immigrant groups, and their concentration in the hi-technology sector. They live in the vicinity of where they work—EDS, Texas Instruments, and the major telecommunications company headquarters are all to the north or the east in the town of Irving near Las Colinas. Though slightly more than half of Asian Indians lived in Dallas County in 2000, this includes the city of Richardson, an inner-ring suburb where some of the first Indians who came to DFW settled. The major grocery store for this community, Taj Mahal Imports, is in Richardson. A secondary node for Indian settlement is in Mesquite, a near southeast suburb in Dallas County. Many Indian Christians from the state of Kerala live there, and it is where the offices of the Kerala Association are located. Of those Asian Indians living in Dallas County, only 40 percent lived in the city of Dallas itself. Nearly 20 percent of Asian Indians lived in Collin County in 2000.

The Salvadorans, the second largest Hispanic group in the metroplex, and a population that grew by 172 percent during the 1990s, are concentrated in two areas that are relatively close together. One runs just north of Loop 12, the innermost highway ring around the Dallas urban core, and the other just to the east of that, out toward Irving but in the city of Dallas. These are areas of very-low-cost housing, more urban than suburban, and also very Hispanic—Mexicans are equally concentrated in these areas. Salvadorans were 3.6 percent of the foreign born in the city of Dallas in 2000; and of the Salvadorans in Dallas County, 47 percent resided in the city of Dallas itself. Indeed, a small but dense group of Salvadorans settled in East Dallas, a very-low-income area near some of the organizations that may have initially handled Salvadorans who came to escape the political turmoil in their country and who have often applied for political asylum. Many Salvadorans in the area are currently in Temporary Protective Status. It is important to note that the Salvadoran consulate is located on Mockingbird Lane near Harry Hines Boulevard in the heart of the city and certainly not far from the nodes of settlement for this population.

Table 6.9. Selected Foreign-Born Population Groups, Selected Suburban Cities, Dallas–Fort Worth Metroplex, 1999

Group	Richardson	Garland	Plano	Carrollton	Arlington	Irving	Grand Prairie	Mesquite
Total population	91,635	215,991	222,301	109,215	332,695	191,611	127,049	124,578
Total foreign born	17,274	43,588	37,923	21,796	50,911	50,696	20,841	11,409
Percentage foreign born of total	18.8	20.1	17.0	19.9	15.3	26.4	16.4	9.1
Born in Mexico	3,770 (22%)	22,307 (51%)	8,271 (22%)	8,234 (38%)	22,547 (44%)	22,353 (44%)	12,827 (61%)	5,452 (48%)
Born in Vietnam	1,415	5,420 (12%)	1,481	1,876	7,274 (14%)	1,394	1,738 (8%)	271
Born in India	1,684	1,959	3,524	2,176 (10%)	1,636	4,295	440	1,648 (14%)
Born in China	2,239 (13%)	866	6,557 (17%)	431	2,191	1,070	179	85
Born in Salvador	302	2,150	630	868	978	6,005 (12%)	609	205
Born in South Korea	921	973	1,647	833	779	1,825	216	96

Source: U.S. Census, 2000.

Table 6.9, the final table, presents the figures for selected foreign-born populations in several suburban cities in DFW. Richardson, one of the earliest suburbs, is largely in Dallas County, but its northernmost section extends into Collin County. Garland, another close-in and early suburb, is located to the north and east of central Dallas in Dallas County. Plano is further north in Collin County and, as mentioned above, was one of the fastest-growing suburbs in the United States in the 1990s. Carrollton is to the northwest of the city of Dallas, with its southern half in Dallas County and its northern half in Denton County. Arlington, Irving, and Grand Prairie are to the west in the mid cities area between Dallas and Fort Worth. Irving and Grand Prairie are largely in the westernmost portion of Dallas County, and Arlington is in the easternmost portion of Tarrant County; Mesquite is to the southeast. The Mexicans are the largest foreign-born group in all these cities, and above 50 percent in two of them—Garland and Grand Prairie. In two cities, Richardson and Plano, the Mexicans and the Chinese are the largest groups, but together they do not constitute 50 percent of the foreign-born population, indicating much greater diversity in these areas. The same is true for Carrollton, although here the second-largest foreign-born group is Asian Indian. Grand Prairie is clearly a very Hispanic suburban area.

To summarize, immigration to metropolitan areas of the United States increased dramatically during the 1980s, but particularly during the 1990s. Many cities that had not experienced much immigration before this time became rapidly diverse, although in many of these cities it was the growth of the Mexican population that was most dramatic. DFW is such an area, changing from a triethnic to a multiethnic urban metropolis in a very short period of time. Equally characteristic of this period in U.S. immigration history is the suburbanization of immigrant populations, many settling directly in suburbs rather than in inner cities first and then moving up and out. DFW also illustrates this trend. However, different foreign-born populations experience different patterns of settlement that can be related to their distinct immigration histories; to their human capital, which relates in turn to their position in the metropolitan labor market; and to the type of housing they can afford. These settlement patterns pose interesting questions about the impact of immigrants on urban spaces, the process by which new immigrants construct communities when they are residentially dispersed, and how new immigrants are incorporated and become citizens—not merely in the sense of naturalization but also in the sense of civic engagement. It is to some of these broad issues that I now turn.

Immigrants in Cities / Cities of Immigrants: Place Making, Communities, and Civic Engagement

The literature on globalization has in some sense spawned a counterliterature on localism, place making, and the construction of community and identity in the face of the forces of homogenization.[30] Localism is about the significance of place, something clearly germane to the study of immigrants in cities and cities of immigration. Community has myriad definitions, some of them rooted in "place"; but in its broadest sense it is about "forms of collective cultural consciousness,"[31] something certainly apposite to questions of immigrant incorporation.

Locality has been addressed in two ways in immigration research. The first is the comparative study of cities as different places—the city as context issue mentioned above. This is the approach that Zhou takes to locality by suggesting that different places offer "different sets of localized opportunities and constraints at different points in time. Such constraints and opportunities interact with the dynamics of migration and, as a result, influence the mix of immigrant groups and their strategies in adapting to the local environment."[32] Zhou argues that this aspect of locality in immigration research is "under theorized" despite a handful of comparative studies of New York and Los Angeles.[33] Min, who also focuses on New York and Los Angeles, poses the interesting question of why Koreans in New York City have entered a particular sector of the urban economy—the small grocery store business—whereas in other cities this is not the case. He links the difference to spatial issues—in a city like New York, where residential and commercial zones are compressed together and people pick up produce on the way out of subways or off buses when they come out at night, small grocery stores can be lucrative. In an automobile city like Los Angeles, this is not the case, and hence the focus is on businesses in underserved or abandoned minority areas where overhead is less expensive.[34]

Casting a broader net, Logan and his colleagues pose the question of why some groups and some cities are characterized by ethnic enclaves (a form of localization) while others are not. These scholars suggest that "concentrated minority business centers are most common in those metropolitan areas in which a group has the largest numbers"—a conclusion that may be valid in some urban contexts but perhaps not in those where there is much greater diversity and where other kinds of arrangements emerge.[35]

Here I have suggested that DFW may be a different kind of urban place from New York or Los Angeles (and one without classic enclaves), and that these differences should be brought into a broader comparative framework. Certainly, this is precisely what the Metropolis project is doing, although rarely does one see collaborative projects that address precise comparisons that might move us further theoretically on this issue. Such projects should raise questions about incorporation—spatial, social, economic, political, and cultural—across time as well as space. In doing so, they should be mindful of both bottom-up and top-down perspectives. By the former, I mean looking at the immigrants as agents; and by the latter, I mean looking at what institutional structures urban and suburban governments themselves construct to receive and incorporate immigrants. For example, in the 1980s the Association of Dallas Schools created an Asian American Advisory Committee to address the increasing diversity in their schools. Over ninety different languages are spoken in Dallas area schools, and one of the charges of this committee was to address the teaching of English as a second language. Though the institutional approach has not been a focus of my research, it certainly is one that other contributors to this volume address.

The bottom-up perspective also addresses a second aspect of localism—how communities and ethnic identities are constructed or, as Stephen Castles has put it, "How contemporary immigrants are re-territorializing identity at the level of the city."[36] Communities, including urban communities, are generally thought to be based on neighborhood and co-residence. But what if co-residence is not characteristic of an immigrant population—as is the case for the Asian Indians in DFW? How do Indians in DFW construct their community in a suburban metropolis, and how is their community different from that of the much larger and hence more concentrated Mexican community? In other words, what is the nature of place making in the city and how are urban spaces being modified by new immigrants?

Zelinsky and Lee's concept of heterolocalism offers us a "place" to begin to answer this question. Heterolocalism refers to "recent populations of shared ethnic identity which enter an area from distant sources, then quickly adopt a dispersed pattern of residential location, all the while managing to remain cohesive through a variety of means."[37] What are these means? Zelinsky and Lee suggest that "much of the glue that holds [the deterritorialized ethnic community] together exists in the shape of ethnic churches, business associations, athletic leagues, social and service clubs, bars, cultural centers, festivals, and other institutions that may or may not be situated in neighborhoods where some modest degree of clustering can be detected."[38] To this list I would add retail centers (grocery stores, strip malls, and other enterprises) that can become gathering places but which are not ethnic enclaves in the traditional sense of the word. Wood describes a process of place making among the Vietnamese in the suburbs of Washington that is similar to the process that has emerged among the dispersed Indian, Chinese, and Korean populations in DFW.[39] Each group has taken over old shopping centers and converted them into ethnic malls with large "anchor" grocery stores selling products from their respective home countries. In these malls one can also find restaurants, clothing stores, travel agencies, and, in the case of the Indian strip mall in DFW, a Bollywood film video rental store. The Indian and Chinese malls are in Richardson, where some of the earliest immigrants of these populations settled. But today many members of these groups who are residentially dispersed throughout the metroplex come to these malls on the weekends to do their shopping and meet with other members of their groups. The Korean mall is on the northwestern rather than the northeastern side of town along Harry Hines Boulevard. This is the place where the head office of the Greater Dallas Asian American Chamber of Commerce has been located. Indeed, this is a revitalized area designated by the city of Dallas as an Asian Trade District, but the Koreans are the group that have established their business enterprises in the district to a much greater extent than other Asian groups. It is a little Korea without the name and with no Koreans residing in the area.

In December 2002, DFW South Asians opened another "place" for their community several blocks to the east of this strip mall. It is a 32,000-square-foot community center called FunAsia, which houses three movie theaters where Bollywood films can be shown, an Indian restaurant, a banquet hall, a disco-club facility, and a small clothing store called Maharani's Closet. The banquet hall and disco club can be rented out for community or family events. For example, this author once attended an Indian bridal wear fashion show set up in the big banquet hall and on another occasion a panel discussion and dinner where the topic was religious pluralism. Interestingly, it was in this facility that representatives from a host of communities gathered together in the aftermath of the tsunami disaster to share with one another what they were contributing to the relief effort. FunAsia has been so successful that an expansion was announced in the spring of 2005. A 6,500-square-foot banquet hall opened in the northern suburb of Carrollton, and a 15,000-square-foot theater together with a 4,500-square-foot banquet hall and meeting room were planned for a shopping center in Irving.

Clearly, the strip mall and other centripetal commercial centers for immigrant communities in suburban contexts are not the only ways in which place making occurs. Religious institutions are another.[40] In DFW, one of the most important religious institutions is the DFW Hindu Temple, located in Irving between Dallas and Fort Worth. In 1979, members of the Indian community in Dallas began to discuss building a temple. They realized that they had a social and political organization in the India Association of North Texas, but no religious organization other than the Hare Krishna Temple, which was devoted solely to the worship of Krishna. Their idea was to found a temple where all deities could be worshiped. This decision was made in recognition of the fact that different people from different regions and with different personal gods and different rituals were moving to the area. They needed an "umbrella" temple. As one founder put it, "This was a radical idea—normally you would have a temple dedicated to a single god with a small icon in it." It took some time to find the best location and to raise the funds, but finally in 1991 the temple was inaugurated, and since then a cultural center has been added to the compound. In the most recent phases of construction, a rather plain building has been "Indianized" with elaborate carving over the main entry door.

Not only is the DFW Hindu Temple a place for a dispersed immigrant population to gather, particularly on the weekends and on important holidays; it has also contributed to the construction of a new pan-Indian identity in the United States. One of the founders noted that what has happened is that people who come to the DFW Hindu Temple learn about the gods of their compatriots from other regions and they learn about particular festivals celebrated in other regions of their country. Together, they engage in what Peggy Levitt, writing about a group of Gujarati Patidars in the Boston area, has described as "migrant-community affirming events."[41] Indeed, while the founders of the temple were motivated primarily by the desire to have a place where their children could learn about the Hindu religion, the DFW Temple has become a community center. It sponsors programs for the entire DFW Hindu population and various regional associations, including those like the Kerala Association whose membership is largely Christian, use the cultural hall for their own festivals. The tendency for such temples to become secular social spaces as well as sacred spaces is one that has been described for other U.S. cities where Asian Indians have settled.[42]

However, in the immigrant cities of the twenty-first century, we need to consider not only the geographical spaces and places that are claimed and constructed by immigrants but also the virtual spaces. Appadurai refers to Internet neighborhoods, defining a neighborhood as a "context or a set of contexts within which meaningful social action can be both generated and interpreted."[43] By far the most important Internet neighborhood for Indian community in DFW is Ek Nazar (the word means "a glimpse"), an electronic bulletin board founded in 1998 by an Indian who was studying at the University of Texas at Dallas at the time. He began by putting up information for other Indian students on his personal Web site. He was getting a lot of hits, and when the volume became too great, he decided to create a Web site (actually, a collection of Web-based yellow pages) that would be available to the broader Indian and South Asian community in DFW. He discovered that no one had tried this before in any U.S. city where there is a large Indian population. Ek Nazar was registered as a C-corp in 1999 and, although started as a community service, within a few years it began to turn a small profit, mostly through advertisers. As the site grew, the founder brought in more people to help him, and by 2003 six young men, all information technology professionals, were working on it in their spare time. The growth of the site parallels the rapid growth of the South Asian and particularly Indian population in the area, and concomitant with that growth the expansion of the business sector within this community. The site reaches a targeted audience, and businesses that advertise on it understand its reach—that it is a place of encounter.

The Ek Nazar Web site has several sections in addition to the business advertising. One of the most active sections is the classifieds. "People put up private sale items at no cost. They have a very rapid turnover. "People have sold their automobiles in a day. There is no overhead this way. People sell furniture, even their homes. If they are moving back to India, which many people have done recently, they must sell everything fast." In the absence of a geographic neighborhood, Ek Nazar creates a cyberneighborhood where yard sales can proceed. According to the founders, every day fifty to a hundred items are bought and sold.

The second most popular section of Ek Nazar is the forum, a discursive space for the exchange of ideas and opinions. In an interview, one of the site operators made the following observation:

> If someone has been to the Anand Bazaar and wants to comment on it, he can post his opinion in the forum. The site is a powerful tool for linking people. They can learn about an event, buy their tickets on the site, attend the event, and then post their opinions afterwards. It offers a forum for constructive discussion and the organizers of events get instant feedback.

Ek Nazar has a database of 20,000 individuals, and each week an e-mail goes out about upcoming events. In an interview, one of the site operators observed that people log on to see what is going on and then decide what they want to do on the weekend, what movies and cultural events. They can find the restaurants they need—the ones that serve vegetarian food. It is all a convenience to the users. It offers people flexibility. Old-timers who have been here some time say when their first came they never knew people and it was hard to meet one another. Now there is this facility, and people can feel part of a group. They come together to share feelings with one another. They meet together in cyberspace.

Another popular thing to do on Ek Nazar is to post notices about elderly family members who are traveling to and from India. People want to find out if someone else is going to be on the same flight so that they can watch out for a parent. People also post information on carpooling, on neighborhood events, on availability for babysitting, and on informal gatherings.

The latest expansion of Ek Nazar is national, concomitant with some of the layoffs in DFW. People working here were transferred, and wherever they have ended up, they did not find an equivalent site. This has prompted the site's operators to test out other markets, beginning in cities with large Indian populations—Atlanta, Houston, Detroit, the San Francisco Bay Area, and Newark. If it works, it will bring the broader national U.S. Indian community together. They began this expansion by forming partnerships with students at area universities, who gathered the data. Additionally, businesses and other advertisers have contacted them about getting on these local sites.

Creating community (i.e., habitual places of contact, congregation, and confirmation) in a heterolocal urban context involves not simply the formation of commercial nodes, the development of organizations and institutions, and the creation of internet neighborhoods but also the celebration of cultural events. Each year the Indians take over the racetrack (Lone Star Park immediately to the west of downtown) for the Anand Bazaar, an event that celebrates Indian Independence Day (August 15, 1947). More than 20,000 Indians gather in the late afternoon and evening—the food, the clothing booths, the music, and the heat remind them of home! In some sense, these activities are precisely what Rosaldo is addressing when he writes about cultural citizenship. "Cultural citizenship refers to the right to be different (in terms of race, ethnicity, or native language) with respect to the norms of the dominant national community, without compromising one's right to belong, in the sense of participating in the nation-state's democratic processes."[44]

At the Anand Bazaar, and at other events sponsored by the Indian community in DFW, the symbols and practices of hybrid identity are ever-present—the U.S. and Indian flags, the Pledge of Allegiance, the U.S. and Indian national anthems, the lighting of oil lamps. These events need to be examined as a form of civic engagement and then compared with other forms of civic engagement with which new immigrants are involved. Establishing or negotiating cultural presence in the city may be as significant as establishing political presence. Where and how does it occur, in what institutional and noninstitutional contexts, in what forms, by which groups, and with what success?

What is needed is more comparative and cross-cultural research on the processes of claiming space and making place by immigrants in cities as well as an exploration the impact of these activities on more general urban life. To what extent, for example, is the general population even aware of what is occurring? How have local institutions responded to increasing diversity? How, in other words, are cities assimilating new immigrants, and how are they incorporating a new multiculturalism into their urban identity or urban ethos? In DFW, the mainstream media have hired immigrant community members (often first-and-a-half or second generation) to "cover" "ethnic" news. The number of articles in the *Dallas Morning News* that cover "ethnic events" or that narrate stories of immigration increased significantly through the 1990s.[45] As mentioned above, local school districts have formed diversity committees that are reaching out to many of the new Asian populations. The Dallas and Fort Worth police departments have hired Southeast Asians, specifically Vietnamese, to help reach out to these communities and address some of the problems they have faced in adapting to U.S. society.

What is the role of such initiatives and of the place making associated with it, not only in creating community and constructing ethnic boundaries but also in transgressing boundaries? Where do immigrant groups come together in other spaces that surmount differences? Where do immigrants come together with the native born? In Dallas, we might look to the Asian Charity Ball or at the functions of an umbrella organization (run largely over the Internet) called Dallas International, which sponsors an annual festival in which a breadth of groups, including the native born, participate. It is a fascinating forum for cultural encounter. These are a few of the shared spaces of immigrant interaction in the city, but there are others—large Catholic cathedrals, where Central Americans and Mexicans come together; and the mosque in Richardson, which gathers Middle Eastern, South Asian, African, and African American Muslims. Equally, in the workplace, diversity programs that reach out to a broad spectrum of groups have been established—in the Dallas area, by important companies such as Texas Instruments and American Airlines. Members of different groups sometimes sponsor lunchtime festivals to introduce all employees to their culture and their cuisine. Finally, there are private initiatives, such as the Foundation for Pluralism, which attempts to bridge the divides across all the faiths in the metroplex and create a different kind of unity. In this case, the shared space is a Web site and an early morning radio program launched by a South Asian.

Why do some immigrant populations engage in this process of place making and cultural citizenship while others do not? Miyares tells us that the Central American population in New York is invisible in terms of making its mark on the urban landscape.[46] This is equally true of Salvadorans in Dallas, although they were among the five top immigrant groups in 2000. Is this because they are absorbed by the larger Mexican population, or does their place making occur on the soccer field and other sports activities? When does place making based on class or common occupation usurp place making based on ethnicity, indicating the development of different localities of meaning and experience?

In her monograph on Native Americans in Los Angeles, Weibel-Orlando asks how Native Americans maintain community identity in a complex urban society. She outlines several aspects of "community" that are well worth considering for other populations, including new immigrants. These are community as collective rights and responsibilities, community as institutional integrity, community as cultural continuity, community as cultural calendar and public ritual, community as communications network, community as longevity and shared history, community as locality, and community as ethnic group membership. In addition, her framework recognizes individual differences in levels of participation (what I have referred to above as engagement). There are core members, selective members, peripheral members, and those who are nonassociated.[47] All immigrant groups will be characterized by these variations. Recognizing both individual and group differences is essential to a more complete understanding of how new immigrants negotiate the city and hence how they are incorporated economically, socially, politically, and culturally.

Notes

1. Audrey Singer, *The Rise of New Immigrant Gateways* (Washington, D.C.: Center on Urban and Metropolitan Policy, Brookings Institution, 2004). Perhaps best known for the study of immigrants and cities is the International Metropolis Project (http://

www.international.metropolis.net). For an example of a study that has emerged from the metropolis framework, see Jorge Malheiros, and Francisco Vala, "Immigration and City Change: The Lisbon Metropolis at the Turn of the Twentieth Century," *Journal of Ethnic and Migration Studies* 30 (2004): 1065–86.

2. See Caroline B. Brettell, "Is the Ethnic Community Inevitable? A Comparison of the Settlement Patterns of Portuguese Immigrants in Toronto and Paris," *Journal of Ethnic Studies* 9 (1981): 1–17; reprinted in Caroline Brettell, *Anthropology and Migration: Essays on Transnationalism, Ethnicity and Identity.* (Walnut Creek, Calif.: Altamira Press, 2003); Caroline B. Brettell, "Urban History, Urban Anthropology, and the Study of Migrants in Cities," *City and Society* 12 (2000): 129–38; and Caroline B. Brettell, "Bringing the City Back In: Cities as Context for Immigrant Incorporation," in *American Arrivals: Anthropology Engages the New Immigration,* ed. Nancy Foner (Santa Fe: School of American Research, 2003), 163–95. Jeffrey Reitz presents a somewhat similar framework; Jeffrey Reitz, "Host Societies and the Reception of Immigrants: Research Themes, Emerging Theories and Methodological Issues," *International Migration Review* 36 (2002) :1005–19. For an analytical framework to understand migrant policy development in local urban contexts, see Michael Alexander, "Local Policies toward Migrants as an Expression of Host-Stranger Relations: A Proposed Typology," *Journal of Ethnic and Migration Studies* 29 (2003): 411–30, as well as the other chapters in this volume.

3. When "metroplex" is used in this chapter, it includes the four counties of Collin, Dallas, Denton, and Tarrant.

4. The Fort Worth–Arlington Primary Metropolitan Statistical Area is also included in Audrey Singer's list of emerging gateway cities—some of the fastest-growing centers of immigration in the 1990s; Singer, *Rise of New Immigrant Gateways.* Other cities on this list, in addition to Dallas and Fort Worth–Arlington, are Atlanta, Las Vegas, Orlando, Washington, and West Palm Beach–Boca Raton.

5. Michael V. Hazel, *Dallas* (Austin: Texas State Historical Society, 1997).

6. Robert Prince, *A History of Dallas from a Different Perspective* (Dallas: Nortex Press, 1993), 37.

7. Hazel, *Dallas,* 15.

8. Michael Q. Hooks, "The Struggle for Dominance: Urban Rivalry in North Texas, 1870–1910," PhD dissertation, Department of History, Texas Tech University, 1979; Patricia Evridge Hill, *The Making of a Modern City* (Austin: University of Texas Press, 1996).

9. Hazel, *Dallas,* 22.

10. The small numbers of Chinese, Japanese, and Native Americans were classified as colored and included with the Negro population.

11. Darwin Payne, *Big D: Triumphs and Troubles of an American Supercity in the 20th Century* (Dallas: Three Forks Press, 2000).

12. Hazel, *Dallas,* 45. The Hispanic population is hard to estimate before 1960 because Mexican Americans before that time were listed as white in the census and hence were not enumerated separately.

13. Jim Schutze, *The Accommodation: The Politics of Race in an American City* (Secaucus, N.J.: Citadel Press, 1986).

14. Hill, *Making of a Modern City,* 126.

15. Shirley Achor, *Mexican Americans in a Dallas Barrio* (Tucson: University of Arizona Press, 1978), 50. Segregation was equally characteristic of the city of Fort

Worth. In 1950, ten census tracts contained 84.5 percent of the total Negro population. In that year, 8,139 persons with Spanish surnames were counted in the city—2.9 percent of the total population. These individuals were concentrated in twelve census tracts close to downtown. Of the 8,139 persons with Spanish surnames, 1,509 (less than 20 percent) were born in Mexico. These individuals constituted slightly more than 36 percent of the total foreign born in Fort Worth in 1950. See Robert H. Talbert, *Cowtown-Metropolis: Case Study of a City's Growth and Structure* (Fort Worth: Texas Christian University Press, 1956), 83.

16. Hazel, *Dallas,* 50.

17. This is as quoted by William L. Chaze et al., "Our Big Cities Go Ethnic," *U.S. News & World Report,* March 21, 1983, 49–53.

18. Payne, *Big D: Triumphs and Troubles of an American Supercity in the 20th Century,* 423. For a wonderful more tongue-in-cheek assessment of late-twentieth-century Dallas see Willard Spiegelman, "Dallas On (and Off) My Mind," *Parnassus* 28 (2005): 365–87.

19. The author thanks Lyssa Jenkens, an economist with the Dallas Chamber of Commerce, for providing much of these data.

20. Karl Zinsmeister, "Land of the Meat Eaters," American Enterprise Institute, http://www.theamericanenterprise.org/tae00a.htm, 2000, 9.

21. In 2003, *Forbes Magazine* ranked Dallas 9th out of 150 major U.S. metropolitan areas on a list of "Best Places for Businesses and Careers Survey."

22. Anne Fisher, "The Best Cities for Business," *Fortune,* December 20, 1999, 214–23.

23. Zinsmeister, *Land of the Meateaters,* 9.

24. But it also appears that had no immigrants settled in the central cities, the populations of both Dallas and Fort Worth might themselves have declined given the rather modest rates of growth—under 20 percent.

25. See Richard Alba, John Logan, Brian Stults, Gilbert Marzan, and Wenquan Zhang, "Immigrant Groups and Suburbs: A Reexamination of Suburbanization and Spatial Assimilation," *American Sociological Review* 64 (1999): 446–60; Richard Alba, John R. Logan, and Brian J. Stults, "The Changing Neighborhood Contexts of the Immigrant Metropolis," *Social Forces* 79 (2000): 587–621; Wei Li, "Anatomy of a New Ethnic Settlement: The Chinese Ethnoburb in Los Angeles," *Urban Studies* 35 (1998): 479–501; Sarah J. Mahler, *American Dreaming: Immigrant Life on the Margins* (Princeton, N.J.: Princeton University Press, 1995); Audrey Singer, *At Home in the Nation's Capital: Immigration Trends in Metropolitan Washington* (Washington, D.C.: Center on Urban and Metropolitan Policy, Brookings Institution, 2003); and Joseph Wood, "Vietnamese American Place Making in Northern Virginia," *Geographical Review* 87 (1997): 70–71. The media has also picked up on suburban settlement patterns of immigrants; e.g., see Samira Jafari, "Atlanta Suburb Seeing Diverse Population," *Washington Post,* June 20, 2003; Nina Bernstein, "Recent Immigration Is Changing the Face of New York's Neighborhoods," *New York Times,* January 24, 2005; and *The Economist,* March 31, 2004, 31–32.

26. William H. Frey, *Melting Pot Suburbs: A Census 2000 Study of Suburban Diversity* (Washington, D.C.: Center on Urban and Metropolitan Policy, Brookings Institution, 2001), 5; see also Bruce Katz, *The New Urban Demographics* (Washington, D.C.: Center on Urban and Metropolitan Policy, Brookings Institution, 2003).

27. It is important to set the trends in DFW in the context of statewide trends. In

Texas, the largest group of foreign born were from Mexico, followed by the Vietnamese, whose numbers increased by slightly more than 50,000 in a decade. The next largest foreign-born population in Texas were Salvadorans, whose numbers increased by 52,330. Salvadorans were followed by Indians, whose numbers grew by 46,219 in a decade. The Chinese round out the top five groups, with an increase of almost 30,000 between 1990 and 2000.

28. Again, comparisons with Atlanta and Phoenix are intriguing. In Maricopa County, Arizona (one of the two main counties of metropolitan Phoenix), Mexicans were 64.6 percent of the foreign born in 2000; in the city of Phoenix itself, they made up 73.8 percent of the foreign born—a figure like that of Dallas. By contrast, in Atlanta, Mexicans were only 32.3 percent of the foreign-born population in the city and 26.8 percent of the foreign-born population in DeKalb and Fulton counties.

29. It is worth noting, however, that second-generation Vietnamese have done well in school.

30. Vered Amit, ed., *Realizing Community: Concepts, Social Relationships and Sentiments* (New York: Routledge, 2002); Vered Amit and Nigel Rapport, eds., *The Trouble with Community: Anthropological Reflections on Movement, Identity and Collectivity* (London: Pluto Press, 2002); Arjun Appadurai, "Disjuncture and Difference in the Global Cultural Economy," *Public Culture* 2 (1990): 1–24; Arjun Appadurai, *Modernity at Large* (Minneapolis: University of Minnesota Press, 1996); Akhil Gupta and James Ferguson, "Beyond 'Culture': Space, Identity, and the Politics of Difference," in *Culture, Power, Place: Explorations in Critical Anthropology,* ed. Akhil Gupta and James Ferguson (Durham, N.C.: Duke University Press, 1997), 33–51.

31. Vered Amit, "Reconceptualizing Community," in *Realizing Community,* ed. Amit, 6.

32. Yu Zhou, "How Do Places Matter? A Comparative Study of Chinese Ethnic Economies in Los Angeles and New York City," *Urban Geography* 19 (1998): 532.

33. See, e.g., John Mollenkopf, "Urban Political Conflicts and Alliances: New York and Los Angeles Compared," in *The Handbook of International Migration: The American Experience,* ed. Charles Hirschman, Philip Kasinitz, and Josh DeWind (New York: Russell Sage Foundation, 1999), 412–22; Roger Waldinger, *Strangers at the Gates: New Immigrants in Urban America* (Berkeley: University of California Press, 2001); and Philip Kasinitz, John Mollenkopf, and Mary C. Waters, "Becoming American / Becoming New Yorkers: Immigrant Incorporation in a Majority Minority City," *International Migration Review* 36 (2002): 1020–36.

34. Pyong Gap Min, *Caught in the Middle: Korean Communities in New York and Los Angeles* (Berkeley: University of California Press, 1996).

35. John R. Logan, Richard D. Alba, and Thomas L. McNulty, "Ethnic Economies in Metropolitan Regions: Miami and Beyond," *Social Forces* 72 (1994): 691–724; the quotation here is on 718.

36. Stephen Castles, "Migration and Community Formation under Conditions of Globalization," *International Migration Review* 36 (2002): 1159.

37. Wilbur Zelinksy and Barrett A. Lee, "Heterolocalism: An Alternative Model of the Sociospatial Behaviour of Immigrant Ethnic Communities," *International Journal of Population Geography* 4 (1998): 281. Some scholars have questioned Zelinsky and Lee's model; e.g., see Richard Wright and Mark Ellis, "Race, Region, and the Territorial Politics of Immigration in the US," *International Journal of Population Geography* 6 (2000): 197–211. In this chapter, I am not addressing issues of assimilation but rather

the agency of place making and multicultural expression among groups who are residentially dispersed in single metropolitan contexts. In this regard, I think it is both useful and appropriate to consider heterolocal or multicentered immigrant communities and the institutions and events that sustain this form of urban and suburban incorporation. In other words, my interest is not merely in where immigrants live but also in how they construct community and become civically engaged when they do not necessarily live next door to one another.

38. Zelinsky and Lee, "Heterolocalism," 288–89.

39. Wood, "Vietnamese-American Place Making."

40. See Charles Hirschman, "The Role of Religion in the Origins and Adaptation of Immigrant Groups in the United States," *International Migration Review* 38 (2004): 206–34; Robert A. Orsi, *Gods of the City: Religion and the American Urban Landscape* (Bloomington: Indiana University Press, 1999); and R. Stephen Warner and Judith G. Wittner, *Gatherings in Diaspora: Religious Communities and the New Immigration* (Philadelphia: Temple University Press, 1998).

41. Peggy Levitt, "Migrants Participate across Borders: Toward an Understanding of Forms and Consequence," in *Immigration Research for a New Century,* ed. Nancy Foner and Ruben Rumbaut (New York: Russell Sage Foundation, 2000), 470.

42. E.g., see Monish Das Gupta, "What Is Indian about You?" A Gendered, Transnational Approach to Ethnicity," *Gender and Society* 11 (1997): 572–96.

43. Appadurai, *Modernity at Large,* 184.

44. Renato Rosaldo, "Cultural Citizenship, Inequality, and Multiculturalism," in *Latino Cultural Citizenship: Claiming Identity, Space, and Rights,* ed. William V. Flores and Rina Benmayor (Boston: Beacon Press, 1997), 57.

45. Mainstream institutions have also asked for time with the immigrant media. After the September 11, 2001, terrorist attacks and two hate crime murders in the area, one of the victims a Hindu gas station / convenience store operator from Gujarat, the local FBI worked closely with a local South Asian radio station in an effort to reach out to the immigrant community. They took telephone calls and educated the public.

46. Ines M. Miyares, "The Changing Latinization of New York City," Department of Geography, Hunter College, New York.

47. Joan Weibel-Orlando, *Indian Country, L.A.: Maintaining Ethnic Community in Complex Society* (Urbana: University of Illinois Press, 1999).

7

Postmulticulturalism?

David Ley

We live in an era of "posts": postindustrial, postfordist, postmodern (or is it now postpostmodern?), postnational, poststructural, post-Marxist, post-colonial, and so it goes on, as theorists rush to be first to the post, as it were, in identifying a new economic break, political transition, or social transformation to warrant the creation of new conceptual and discursive space. Whether constant innovation and societal reinvention is truly our lot or whether there is a more capricious creation of discursive novelty by the chattering classes for our own purposes is a matter worthy of reflection.

Nonetheless, in this chapter I suggest the existence of a multicultural world moving ideologically toward postmulticulturalism. The chapter considers the current crisis of multicultural policy in both theory and practice before presenting an empirical vignette that demonstrates the continuing value of multicultural planning as a tool for the negotiation of cultural conflicts over land use in metropolitan areas where immigrants and the native born find themselves contesting the shaping of urban space. Though the argument is grounded in Canada, and the case study occurred in Vancouver, the task of managing diversity is much broader, and the earlier and later stages of the discussion consider first the status and finally the necessity for some form of multicultural governance in a world where growing cultural diversity *within* nation-states, and particularly within gateway cities, is an unavoidable certainty.

Starting Point: The Theoretical Assault

Intellectual response to multicultural policy has frequently been surprisingly ambivalent, if not hostile. From the political left has come the challenge that the posture of equality upheld by multiculturalism is a veil that conceals significant economic and political inequalities, and from the right has come the anxiety that multiculturalism is an exercise in postmodern identity politics that fragments the national project. Both are partial truths, and I shall try to suggest that such criticisms do not exhaust the potential capacities of multiculturalism.

Critical judgments are abundant. The charges of national fragmentation with "the proliferation of problematic diversity" are widespread even in Canada,[1] while in the United Kingdom multiculturalism is seen by some to encourage a "competitive agenda . . . multicultural turf wars are everywhere."[2] In the United States, Samuel Huntington has weighed in with anxieties about the fragmentation of American identity in light of growing cultural diversity.[3] On another front, Lisa Lowe is one of many theorists who have argued that the gaiety of multicultural festival (in her case, in the United States) is a sedative that dulls the senses to the continuing marginalization of immigrants from the economic and political mainstream of national life.[4] Indeed, the celebration of cultural exoticism marks participants as ethnic exhibits in a display orchestrated by, and ultimately intended for, a mainstream Caucasian audience. To this Ghassan Hage has added an intricate Foucauldian analysis of multiculturalism in Australia as a project of the old Anglo-Celtic elite to classify and arrange the appropriate niches for new Australians.[5] The old elite are the social and spatial engineers who continue to shape the nation and control access to its privileges. As guardians of the national space, they alone, writes Hage, claim the right to worry about the multicultural status of Australia. In a strategy of divide and conquer, new immigrants are sorted into groups predicated on cultural difference, an essentialization of identity that hearkens back to older and more pernicious models of ethnoracial classification.[6] From this perspective, it is only a small step to see multiculturalism as a more sophisticated version of earlier racisms, "a 'racism with a distance,' " similar to the imperialist project of classification and containment of "native" cultures.[7]

As an American scholar writing about Canada, Katharyne Mitchell adds a separate indictment of bad faith, for beyond false claims to equality, a takeover of multiculturalism by elites has occurred for economic purposes.[8] In a neoliberal era, with the market in ascendancy, multiculturalism is pragmatically regarded as a benefit to international trade and foreign investment, and thereby as a tool that may be employed to lower barriers to capital flows.[9] Multiculturalism enables elites to play the ethnic card as a sign of their worldly cosmopolitanism, to capitalize on what Australians call an ethnic advantage—an advantage referenced in public policy and fully deployed in Sydney's bid for the 2000 Olympic Games.[10]

Although these theoretical challenges are true, they are not fully true, and multiculturalism may yet escape in perhaps a narrower but more precise form for its exposure to them. Four main points can be made here. First, the attack from the right claiming that multiculturalism is an invitation to a politics of fragmentation is usually parried by the response that multiculturalism is widely regarded by the public as a distinctive Canadian value, and is thereby a source of national identity and unity, not disunity.[11] Similarly, in Britain, Bhikhu Parekh's defense of multiculturalism is to argue that it comprises an integral part of British identity: "What unites us and makes us all British is . . . our common commitment to respect our differences and forge commonalities in a civilised dialogue."[12]

Second, though Lowe and others are correct to claim that cultural equality should not trump economic inequality, it is too limiting to define the symbols and practices of cultural celebration as the exclusive content of multiculturalism today. To be sure, this was its origin, but as Kobayashi detailed more than a decade ago, multiculturalism, at least in Canada, has advanced from its celebratory beginnings and has moved squarely into the territory of citizenship rights.[13] Few Canadian critics would limit multiculturalism today to the aestheticization of heritage cultures. Instead, it enjoys the legal status afforded in the 1988 Multiculturalism Act, while it attained constitutional status in the 1982 Constitution Act, where article 27 of the Canadian Charter of Rights and Freedoms asserts a declaration of rights "in a manner consistent with the preservation and enhancement of the multicultural heritage of Canadians." As such, multiculturalism provides an underpinning to rights-based claims before the state and civil society in such domains as welfare, policing, immigration policy, and equal opportunity in employment. Among its successes would be the 1988 Redress Settlement that included an apology and compensation to Japanese Canadians for the abrogation of their rights, including confiscation of property and subsequent internment, during World War II.[14] More recently, in 2006 the government of Canada apologized, adding a nominal cash award, to survivors and their families for the head tax collected as a deterrent to block Chinese immigration for four decades from the 1880s to the 1920s, when it was replaced by invidious legislation enforcing Chinese exclusion altogether. The purpose of these redress settlements is not only to remove the stigma of past social exclusion but also to testify to such exclusion as a historic error, thereby underscoring the contemporary commitment to an open inclusive society. Like Canadian multiculturalism more generally, the intent is the social integration of ethnic diversity.

Third, Hage's assertion that multiculturalism is simply a project of existing elites to manage unruly ethnics is weakened in Canada not only by the weighty legacy of Pierre Trudeau's inclusivity, sustained by immigrant support in electoral politics, but also by the government's practice of appointing an immigrant, including in recent years two women of color, as federal minister responsible for multiculturalism. Far from being marginalized, the immigrant voice is heard in cabinet discussion. Two other immigrant women of color have been selected as the most recent appointees to the Office of the Governor General, acting as the official representative of the Queen of England in Canada's constitutional monarchy. Indeed, Irene Bloemraad has documented the unusual access of immigrants to Canada to political inclusion and legislative office in comparison with the United States, seeing such inclusion as a reason for the high naturalization rates among immigrants and refugees to Canada.[15]

Fourth, the economic appropriation of multiculturalism as ethnic advantage does not eliminate access by minorities to citizenship claims. Indeed, quite the opposite is true, for when a state disseminates an image of itself in terms of its multicultural identity it then legitimates both expectations and claims to citizenship rights on precisely those terms. Moreover, not only elites profit from the commodification of multiculturalism. Minority groups are willing and able to play the same game for commercial gain, as we see daily in Little Italy, Chinatown, or Olde England branding in products and neighborhoods. For example, both historic and contemporary immigrant cohorts from China have shown a willingness to trade in orientalist genres when it is commercially advantageous to do so.[16]

But it is precisely this essentialization of national origins that has provided perhaps the most influential critique of multiculturalism in the Canadian context. Though this objection has been raised by a number of scholars (see Abu Laban for a response),[17] its most potent deployment has come from more populist sources within the immigrant community. Reacting against what he sees as a multicultural requirement to display his Trinidadian background in his Canadian present, Neil Bissoondath has railed against such a barrier to expressing his own identity as an unhyphenated Canadian.[18] This challenge went to the heart of the federal bureaucracy, because so ingrained is multiculturalism in Canadian institutions that in the national census until the 1990s it was almost impossible to declare one's ancestral identity as Canadian.[19] The cues in the census form led toward writing in an identity as a hyphenated Canadian instead. Bissandooth offered a vigorous rebuttal to government mantras, arguing that multiculturalism aids the containment, marginalization, and ghettoization of essentialized immigrant identities.[20]

Such challenges led to a direct response by the Department of Canadian Heritage. In a series of releases with the authoritative title "The Evidence Series: Facts about Multiculturalism," the department rejected the charge of "ghettoization" and offered the official position that "multiculturalism has been a vital policy promoting citizenship acquisition, participation and integration."[21] Another release in the series led with the calming message that "ethnic identity reinforces attachment to Canada."[22] Clearly, the climate of public skepticism was sufficient to require this unusually direct defense.

Rallying Point: Public Attacks on Multiculturalism

The most damaging opposition to multiculturalism has, however, been populist rather than intellectual, and has frequently been associated with the international rise of nativist parties on the right. More isolated early warnings, such as the Le Pen movement in France, have now consolidated into major political reactions across many European welfare states, leading to political breakthroughs for anti-immigration groups in Austria, Denmark, and the Netherlands, and to their rise to significant minority standing elsewhere.[23] Social democratic governments in Britain and even Sweden have backpeddled in the face of grassroots opposition to immigration and multiculturalism.[24] The murder of controversial filmmaker Theo van Gogh in Amsterdam in November 2004 by a Dutch Muslim extremist led not only to civil disorder but also to marked criticism of multicultural policy by intellectuals as well as the general public, prompting additional moves toward assimilationism by the Dutch government. The two London bombing incidents of July 2005, and the discovery that all the bombers were British residents, first- or second-generation members of minorities from the developing world, prompted a visceral reaction by the popular media and public opinion against multiculturalism, which was seen as enhancing sociocultural segregation, shutting out "British values" while finding space for the reproduction of a hostile alternative. Even before these catalytic events, the tide of resistance to multiculturalism had been rising,[25] and gathered around the much-publicized declaration in April 2004 by Trevor Phillips, the son of Guyanese immigrants and chair of the Commission for Racial Equality, that multicultural policy in Britain had outlived its usefulness and was encouraging not integration but separation.

Western Europe experiences at least two of the three conditions that Kymlicka has suggested are predictors of a retreating multiculturalism: a high proportion of asylum seekers among its immigrants, taxing the treasury of the welfare state; and a significant share of Muslims, who are perceived to challenge some of the presuppositions of Western liberalism.[26] These conditions are less prevalent in New World immigrant-receiving countries. Australia followed Canada in its pursuit of multiculturalism after the abandonment of the White Australia Policy in the 1970s. By the 1990s, however, significant resistance had arisen, leading to the creation of the restrictionist One Nation Party, which was opposed to multiculturalism and immigration from nontraditional source counties. Though a short-lived fringe group, One Nation drew sufficient popular support to drive the conservative Liberal Party, led by John Howard, further to the right, a position rewarded by its success in 1996 and subsequent elections. Howard eliminated or curtailed multicultural programs, closing the Office of Multicultural Affairs, and he proved so unfriendly to multicultural policy that the term was commonly referred to as the "M-word."[27] In the 2001 election, the Howard government skillfully if cynically used the issue of illegal boat landings as a hot button issue to galvanize electoral support.[28] In an anxious and divided nation, openness to and tolerance of diversity—minimal expectations of multicultural policy—have been compromised.

North American societies are also turning to earlier models of self-identification. In the United States, public apprehension concerning immigration contributed to the punitive measures in the 1996 welfare reform legislation.[29] Simultaneously, the discourse of assimilation, seemingly side-lined by pluralist ideology, has made a return in academic work.[30] Multiculturalism, frequently understood as the provision of schooling in heritage languages (notably Spanish), is associated with a dangerous tendency toward separation, even balkanization of the national territory.[31] As Roger Waldinger has written, "Long in disgrace, assimilation is now back in style."[32] The United States, of course, never made the same ideological commitment to multiculturalism as Canada, and significantly assimilation has not yet been revived in Canadian discussion. Canada, after all, has a Multicultural Act and a federal Charter of Rights and Freedoms that institutionalize not only respect for difference but also the rights to be different.[33] Nonetheless, some erosion has occurred. The federal and provincial governments have downsized and in some cases closed multicultural offices, settlement benefits for immigrants have been cut back, and government rhetoric has moved from multiculturalism toward a normative language of social cohesion and integration, positions that could easily blend into a disguised assimilationism.[34] Even in the nation where it was first enunciated and most fully institutionalized, multicultural policy is on the defensive.

The international withdrawal from a confident multiculturalism is illustrated by the shift in Leonie Sandercock's important work on multicultural planning.[35] In *Towards Cosmopolis: Planning for Multicultural Cities,* published in 1998, she gives a number of uplifting examples of multicultural practices drawn from cities on several continents. But by 2003 and the appearance of her book *Cosmopolis II: Mongrel Cities of the 21st Century,* the examples have become less robust and less persuasive. Moreover, two meritorious cases she nominates in this text, Rotterdam and the Aboriginal settlement of Redfern in Sydney, have seriously deconstructed since 2003, with nativist mobilization opposing immigration in Rotterdam and an antipolice riot by Aborigines in Redfern. There are, it seems, few multicultural certainties that remain.

Counterpoint: Multicultural Policy and the Negotiation of Urban Spatial Conflict

In this bleak contemporary period, it is important to look for more hopeful indicators as a way forward, so I now present an extended example of multicultural problem solving in Vancouver, a Canadian city of 2 million, which has been transformed from a European-origin metropolis to a significantly

Asian-origin one in the space of thirty years. In a demographic equation that is becoming increasingly common in the global North, low fertility levels and limited net domestic migration mean that population growth is largely achieved through immigration. In Vancouver newcomers have arrived primarily from Asia, led by population flows from the two dominant population cores of Greater China (including China, Hong Kong, and Taiwan) and the Indian subcontinent (including India, Pakistan, Bangladesh, and Sri Lanka). It is highly probable that this migration regime will continue for the foreseeable future.

While seeking new sources of investment during the recession of the early 1980s, Canadian policymakers saw significant prospects in the burgeoning economies of East and Southeast Asia. A series of neoliberal initiatives encouraged trade, investment, and migration from these countries, with revisions to Canadian immigration policy that envisaged a significant stream of economic migrants, including business-class families whose entry would be fast-tracked according to the scale of their human capital measured by successful business experience and available financial capital.[36] Between 1983 and 2001, some 310,000 immigrants entered Canada through the Business Immigration Program. With Hong Kong accounting for one-third of the landings, and Taiwan and South Korea another 20 percent, business immigrants are disproportionately concentrated in the Vancouver region. They brought significant financial capital with them. Liquid assets per household disclosed to immigration officials exceeded on average $1 million (Canadian) and commonly $2 million, leading to a burst of consumer spending on arrival.

The economic growth of Hong Kong in particular has been characterized as a property-based regime of public and private accumulation, with land sales and related taxes accounting for 30 percent of total government revenues in recent years, while the largest companies, with 40 to 50 percent of the capitalization on the Hong Kong stock market, are primarily property developers.[37] With insecurities rising with the approaching return of Hong Kong to China in 1997, wealthy households sought a safe haven and responded to Canada's invitation to migrate. Embedded in the social, cultural, and economic significance of property, wealthy East Asian families sought to deploy their assets in family and portfolio investment in the Vancouver land market.[38] The result, particularly in the 1988–94 period, was a staggering inflation of prices.[39] With understandable hyperbole, Mitchell identified the local housing market during this period as "the hottest real estate in the world. It was a city on fire."[40]

The wealthiest immigrant households not surprisingly sought out the blue chip, elite neighborhoods, in particular the spacious, older central districts of Shaughnessy and Kerrisdale.[41] These areas had for decades been the untroubled home of an Anglo-Canadian middle class and upper middle class. Their mature landscapes were leafy and manicured, and the houses were in various European revival styles, especially the neo-Tudor that was prominent in bourgeois circles during the 1910–30 period. Landscape and identity mutually reinforced each other in a sympathetic anglophilia. But this landscape ethic had no meaning for hypermodern business immigrants embedded in a domestic economy that first placed a premium on the size of residential space,[42] and second saw property in terms of improvement and exchange value rather than of heritage and symbolic value. So old elite properties were bulldozed and yards were clearcut of trees and shrubs, with all replaced by large, modern structures on minimally landscaped lots. So was born the "monster house" conflict in Vancouver's old elite districts that reverberated throughout Canada and beyond in the early 1990s.

There is not space here to detail the ensuing conflict and its negotiation.[43] Vigorous protests emerged among the old elite, leading to unsuccessful remedial attempts by the city to tinker with existing bylaws and building codes. The failure of these efforts aggravated growing tension, as the conflict threatened to erupt into overt racialization. The old elite, however, were well organized, and in 1992, prompted by heightened anxiety and activism by long-established residents, the city called a public hearing with an intended plan, approved by the old elite, to aid preservation through a downzoning that would make housing demolition and redevelopment less economically attractive.

Due to the large number of briefs, the public hearing was stretched over several successive nights in a large hotel ballroom. The space was packed, with television cameras and prominent national and international media creating a sense of spectacle. A totally unexpected development was the politicization and mobilization of the new immigrants. They established an ad hoc organization, the South Shaughnessy Property Owners' Rights Committee, and at the hearings speaker after speaker challenged the proposed downzoning, usually speaking through interpreters. Emphasizing their group's self-identification as property owners with rights, they adroitly steered the conflict into the arena of citizenship rights.[44] The economic and cultural understanding of property transported from Hong Kong lent a strong orientation toward the privileging of property rights. As one speaker saw it:

We have large lots [in Shaughnessy] and nice houses can be built on these lots. Land value is dropping and there is a reduction of deals. There is evidence investors are scared away. We have to attract more investors. We should do our best to maintain land values and all parts of the community will profit and the country will grow prosperous.

But onto a neoliberal concern with property rights and a Hong Kong preoccupation with unit size was skillfully grafted a recognizably Canadian preoccupation with democratic political rights:

I live in Shaughnessy and we built a house very much to my liking. The new zoning would not allow enough space for me. . . . I strongly oppose this new proposal. Why do I have to be inconvenienced by so many regulations? This infringes my freedom. Canada is a democratic country and democracy should be returned to the people.

And again:

I oppose (the) changes. Is it right to deny the rights of these people? Is it right for government to force rights? Canada is a free country. We decided to build our own dream house for our own family needs. It was a family project. Everyone was excited by our new house. Now the children will have to sleep in the basement.

In this final rendition, the just society is defined in terms of the family unit on their own property claiming political rights against an overly intrusive state.

These interventions by new immigrants astutely adopted the discourse of citizenship rights, the rights of all Canadians regardless of culture or longevity of tenure. In vain, the old elite presented the argument of guardianship of the landscape over the decades, of a historically grounded authority. They claimed, too, that society was defined not just by families but by neighborhoods, that an ethic of care stretched beyond the single family lot:

The house across the lane was bought by Orientals. Soon after they moved in, two 200-year-old Douglas firs were cut down. *It felt to me like one of my children was dying.* . . . The English family who originally built the house and had lived there for fifty years had asked me especially to protect those trees, the tallest in the whole neighborhood. (emphasis added)

The communitarian care and anguished sense of loss in neighborhood change, an ethic successfully argued in the past,[45] was unable to carry the day. When the city council tallied up the briefs at the end of six boisterous nights of presentations, it discovered that over 60 percent of speakers had rejected the downzoning plan presented by city planners and approved by the old elite. The proposal could not be carried in its existing form.

The conflict, however, remained, and had indeed escalated through the existing management process, with polarized cultural groups vociferously articulating opposed positions. Dangerous and opportunistic charges of racism were being leveled, while widespread media coverage, not merely local but also national and international, was inciting the racialization of the impasse. In response, the city council moved behind closed doors, out of media range, thereby attempting in ensuing months to dampen emotions that had been aroused by public deliberation. A special committee was formed that included a range of stakeholders, including not only the old elite but also new immigrants and members of the property industry. This group was facilitated in a negotiating process by city planning staff and charged to come up with a landscape solution.

After six months of committee work, and much fuller mutual understanding, a compromise solution was reached. A modest reduction in the size of new houses was agreed upon, following the direction of city council's earlier proposal, but this could be annulled by a space bonus, permitted if new house design was selected from a palette of styles drawn from the existing European revival idiom in the neighborhood. In this scenario, builders could construct houses to the permitted maximum size, buyers could purchase new properties, and long-settled residents would benefit from landscape continuity because the new houses would match the style of the old ones. This outcome was also reinforced by a realization among new buyers (and hence builders) that resistance by traditional buyers to unsympathetic, boxy mansions would limit the property resale market. At the same time, to mitigate the rawness of new development and to maintain the existing urban woodland canopy, tree protection was also secured. For the past decade, the first sign of new development in Shaughnessy and Kerrisdale has been the appearance of protective orange netting placed around trees on a lot that is to be redeveloped.

This neat negotiated solution effectively ended the conflict over monster houses in Vancouver's elite districts. In 1998, a reexamination of letters to the city found fewer than ten complaints had been received in the intervening five years, in contrast to the hundreds that were sent in the tense years at the beginning of the decade.[46] Though the arrival of wealthy immigrants has continued, Vancouver's elite districts have returned to a somnolent state, once again protected behind regulatory barriers from unwanted land use change, while the troubling ethnic division and polarization of the early 1990s have been contained. A review of the new zoning protocols in Shaughnessy, Kerrisdale, and other upmarket districts in 1999 pronounced them to have achieved their goals. The mayor of Vancouver declared with relief: "I'm not getting nearly as much mail as I was. There's much less anxiety and concern throughout the city. . . . I think this has been a good program and has helped a lot."[47]

Endpoint: The Necessity for Multicultural Policy

Although the Vancouver monster house conflict has been widely documented, much less has been said about its resolution. But in the long term, it is the solution that matters more, showing as it does the potential efficacy of multicultural diversity management in negotiating a settlement between immigrants and long-established residents over conflicting values and practices concerning urban landscape and land use. The language of political compromise that achieved conflict resolution in Shaughnessy may be translated into another rhetoric, that of integration or hybridity, both of which imply a mutual adjustment of values in a multicultural society. The charge that with multiculturalism it is only the immigrants who have to make accommodations is in this instance far from the mark.[48] The sense of disrupted identity accompanying landscape change led to a palpable sense of loss among long-settled residents. But their long-term tenure of space did not give them monopoly rights over the use of that space. New Canadians were able to contest the definition of place precisely because they articulated and implemented the same citizenship rights. Their astute mobilization of the discourse of property and political rights provided legitimacy in a legal and political tussle. Their claim had to be acknowledged, for it was a claim that was integral to Canadian self-definition. The extension of what would have been an annoying but inconsequential clash over landscape taste into a rights-based claim to be heard at the negotiating table brought legitimacy, even though it sidetracked the arguments of an existing elite with close political linkages at city hall.

The case of the monster houses is only one local—albeit transnational—example of conflict resolution in multicultural planning. As such, it is an incomplete counterpoint to the flood of opinion marshaled against multiculturalism. But it is possible to muster other cases of a messy, argumentative, but nonetheless consistent move toward integration outcomes in cultural land use conflicts.[49] There is no common template for successful outcomes, and local micropolitics define conflict trajectories, but nonetheless, in the present crisis of diversity management in the global North, such precedents are significant as case studies to show that a democratic, rights-based process leading to conflict resolution is possible within the rubric of multiculturalism.

One thing *is* certain: Demographic multiculturalism will be an ever-increasing feature in cities in the global North during the twenty-first century. The extraordinary regionalization of global fertility and population growth has created an irreversible migration gradient. The specter of underpopulation due to a lack of replacement through natural increase in the global North, compared with overpopulation due to high natural increase relative to development in the global South, reinforced by a wide income gap, designate a movement potential that cannot be contained in an ever-more-mobile world. Population decline is not a policy option entertained with any enthusiasm by national governments in the developed world, although occasionally politicians make gestures to a population steady state at some distant point in the future.[50] More important, it seems, the economy continues to need growing numbers of workers and consumers, while the state requires more taxpayers to cover its rising expenditures. Immigration from the South to the North, whether legal or illegal, is a sine qua non for the North's own continuing development.

Population growth throughout the global North today is being sustained by immigration. In Canada, by the mid-1990s, 50 percent of population growth and 70 percent of labor force growth were attributable to immigration,[51] and these figures are rising annually. Barriers to immigration, such as those being assembled in "fortress Europe," provide no answer to this demographic imperative. Natalist experiments have rarely been successful, and without a significant reorientation of resources to increase local fertility, with no guarantee of success, immigration is the only route to population replacement. This is creating major social challenges outside as well as inside Europe and North America. Confronting plummeting fertility levels,

Singapore is welcoming "foreign talents" as quasi-citizens but is seriously limiting the freedoms of less-skilled workers who are granted temporary visas and minimal rights.[52] But Japan faces the most severe challenges. With a restrictionist and nativist citizenship policy, it has been opposed to immigration for those who cannot claim some Japanese ethnic heritage. Moreover, the fertility collapse in Japan has led to an aging population and labor shortages, with a recent UN report estimating that the country would have to admit an immigrant workforce of 640,000 every year to maintain its labor stock or else face a 6.7 percent annual fall in gross domestic product.[53] Here, then, is the demographic *and* economic necessity for multicultural planning.

One response, of course, is to admit demographic multiculturalism but dismiss rights-based multiculturalism. This is the old and also the new model of the melting pot and assimilation. But France's assimilationist republican model, with its deliberate nonrecognition of cultural groups, has tended to conceal immigrant inequality to a greater degree than states where there is an identification of difference—until social exclusion reaches the explosive levels that fired the suburban riots in October 2005 in Clichy-sous-Bois, a poor immigrant *banlieue* in the eastern outskirts of Paris, demonstrations that subsequently diffused to many other parts of the country over the next three weeks. Employment equity policies require the identification of ethnocultural groups that may be confronting systemic marginalization, and the republican model has no mechanism here for remedial intervention.

Moreover, though few immigrants would reject economic assimilation to the middle class, is cultural assimilation a fully viable option? Is a public culture of mass consumption welcoming enough to submerge divergent cultural values? With the religious tenor of so many recent immigrants—including Catholic and Pentecostal Latinos, Middle Eastern and African Muslims, and Indian Sikhs and Hindus—the promises of secular consumer culture may not be good enough. In contrast, the policy of multicultural recognition in Canada, extending to rights and not just tastes, has led to acceptance of the *hijab,* of Sikh police wearing turbans not hats, and even serious consideration in Ontario—eventually not adopted—of limited aspects of *shariah* family law.[54] It has also led to political activism and the pursuit of citizenship rights in such areas as antiracism, policing, education, housing, and welfare services. The debates in Quebec in 2007 over the appropriate level of "reasonable accommodation" toward cultural diversity indicate that multiculturalism in Canada remains an unfinished work in progress in demarcating intergroup relations in public space.

Commonly, the conjunction of multiculturalism with the maintenance of non-Western religions in immigrant enclaves has generated the most marked anxieties, particularly in the post–September 2001 environment. The fear that multiculturalism will aid and abet sociospatial segregation that encourages not just the preservation of cultural difference but also the cultivation of hostile difference has created considerable backlash, notably in Britain, where it has been encouraged by Trevor Phillips's much-publicized anxiety, as chair of the Commission for Racial Equality, that the country is "sleepwalking toward segregation." But such fears are perhaps guilty of an oversimplification of minority identities.[55] The longer-settled Jewish communities in Britain and Canada have shown great aptitude in sustaining spatial concentration and a heritage culture that includes support for homeland religion and politics, while fully integrating into the economic and political mainstream of national life. Not coincidentally, Jewish organizations like the Canadian Jewish Congress have also been strong advocates of multiculturalism. The Jewish case could well provide an important precedent for the trajectory of current non-European immigration of self-defined religious minorities, and parry the observation that though multiculturalism worked for an earlier immigrant population that was primarily European and secular, it is overextended for contemporary immigrants with strong religious identities.

The umbrella of multicultural recognition has created a space for cultural difference that is important for immigrants but is also equally, perhaps more, important for the Canadian public imagination and, hence, its political culture.[56] It is notable that Canada, the nation that has most fully institutionalized multiculturalism, is also the nation with the most positive public responses to immigration.[57] Multiculturalism has become a defining Canadian value, socialized as a norm through school curricula and public expectations. From this multicultural platform has emerged an institutionally welcoming face to immigrants that includes significant (if inadequate) settlement services. Bringing mainstream civil society closer to immigrant everyday life, these programs are delivered not by bureaucrats but by nongovernmental organizations (NGOs) with co-ethnic staff, and provide not only services but also jobs and volunteer positions to recent arrivals. The intent here is to create bridging social capital with immigrant groups through their NGOs and thereby aid the integration process.[58] Volunteering provides some Canadian experience on a résumé that is so often critical to success in the labor market. The United Chinese Community Enrichment Services Society (known as SUCCESS), the largest immigrant-serving NGO in Vancouver, claims not only a staff of 200 but also 7,000 volunteers.[59]

Irene Bloemraad has developed an intriguing, if not yet fully tested, thesis on one consequence of the presence of such a multicultural umbrella for immigrants.[60] She interviewed a quasi-matched sample of Portuguese immigrants and Vietnamese refugees in Toronto and Boston to try to explain a growing divergence in naturalization rates between Canada and the United States, which evolved from a position of parity in 1970 to a large gap by the late 1990s, with American naturalization rates falling to 35 percent and Canadian rates rising to 72 percent. Her interviews led to the conclusion that multiculturalism and settlement policy in Toronto provided bridging and linking social capital, openings to economic and political inclusion that encourage political incorporation and a sense of national belonging. Her Boston interviews, in contrast, suggested that Portuguese and Vietnamese co-ethnics felt less enfranchised and more marginalized from the political mainstream. Here, then, is some confirmation that the devolution of settlement programs to NGOs as part of a national multicultural policy does establish points of identification and potential integration.

Increasingly, in large North American cities, the ethnographic exploration of cultural diversity and senses of inclusion and belonging can emerge from conversations in taxicabs, a self-employment niche now filled almost entirely by immigrants. So I end this chapter with a recent taxi story that provides some sense of Canadian multicultural belonging.

On the long rush-hour journey to Toronto's airport from a downtown meeting, I struck up a conversation with the taxi driver, a young man who had been born in Ethiopia and landed in Canada as a boy in the 1980s. He had completed a two-year community college program in Web design in British Columbia and taken an initial job with a parking corporation that provided funds for his cab purchase. He escaped the Toronto winter, he informed me, by renting out his cab and working for five months each year in Kenya, where he had a small Web design company in Mombasa and an Internet café managed by his brother. The conversation turned to the recent Athens Olympic Games, and I asked him about his (and my) dual allegiances, which revealed an elaborate transnational family project for the future. Though his two sons were still very young, he had dreams for them to become middle- or long-distance runners in the tradition of Ethiopian and Kenyan athletes. It was his plan to send them to private school in Kenya in their teens and ensure that they would be rigorously trained as distance runners, a program he regarded as more advanced in East Africa than in Canada. So I asked, who would his boys run for, Kenya or Ethiopia? Oh, neither, he replied. They would return to Canada and run for Canada. With

East African training, his sons might make a distinctive contribution as Canadian citizens in their own specialty. He dropped me off with the wish that I might live long enough to see them win Olympic medals! Among the several themes that could be extracted from this interchange—including immigrant enterprise, transnational linkages, and family aspirations—I note an intent to use ethnic resources to leave a mark, not just in local family or heritage associations but rather as a full member of a national society.

Notes

1. R. Day, *Multiculturalism and the History of Canadian Diversity* (Toronto: University of Toronto Press, 2000).

2. Y. Alibhai-Brown, "Beyond Multiculturalism," *Canadian Diversity / Diversité Canadienne* 3, no. 2 (2004): 51–54; the quotation here is on 51–52. Also see Y. Alibhai-Brown, *Who Do We Think We Are? Imagining the New Britain* (London: Allen Lane, 2000).

3. S. Huntington, *Who Are We? The Challenges to America's National Identity* (New York: Simon & Schuster, 2004).

4. L. Lowe, "Imagining Los Angeles in the Production of Multiculturalism," in *Immigrant Acts,* by L. Lowe (Durham, N.C.: Duke University Press, 1996), 84–96.

5. G. Hage, *White Nation: Fantasies of White Supremacy in a Multicultural Society* (Sydney: Pluto Press, 1998).

6. K. Anderson, "Otherness, Culture and Capital: 'Chinatown's' Transformation under Australian Multiculturalism," in *Multiculturalism, Difference and Postmodernism,* ed. G. Clark, D. Forbes, and R. Francis (Melbourne: Longman Cheshire, 1993), 68–89.

7. S. Zizek, "Multiculturalism, or, the Cultural Logic of Multinational Capitalism," *New Left Review,* September–October 1997, 28–51; A. Pred, *Even in Sweden: Racisms, Racialized Spaces and the Popular Geographical Imagination* (Berkeley: University of California Press, 2000).

8. K. Mitchell, "Multiculturalism, or the United Colors of Benetton?" *Antipode* 25 (1993): 263–94; K. Mitchell, *Crossing the Neoliberal Line: Pacific Rim Migration and the Metropolis* (Philadelphia: Temple University Press, 2004).

9. Y. Abu-Laban and C. Gabriel, *Selling Diversity: Immigration, Multiculturalism, Employment Equity and Globalization* (Peterborough, Ont.: Broadview Press, 2002).

10. P. Murphy, B. O'Brien, and S. Watson, "Selling Australia, Selling Sydney: The Ambivalent Politics of Entrepreneurial Multiculturalism," *Journal of International Migration and Immigration* 4 (2003): 471–98.

11. P. Li, "The Multiculturalism Debate," in *Race and Ethnic Relations in Canada,* ed. P. Li (Don Mills, Ont.: Oxford University Press, 2003), 148–77.

12. B. Parekh, "Multiculturalism Is a Civilised Dialogue," *The Guardian,* January 21, 2005.

13. A. Kobayashi, "Multiculturalism: Representing a Canadian Institution," in *Place/Culture/Representation,* ed. J. Duncan and D. Ley (London: Routledge, 1993), 205–31.

14. A. Kobayashi, "The Japanese-Canadian Redress Settlement and Its Implications for 'Race Relations,' " *Canadian Ethnic Studies* 24 (1992): 1–19.

15. I. Bloemraad, *Becoming a Citizen: Incorporating Immigrants and Refugees in the United States and Canada* (Berkeley: University of California Press, 2006).

16. On the historic cohorts, see K. Anderson, *Vancouver's Chinatown: Racial Discourse in Canada, 1875–1980* (Montreal: McGill–Queen's University Press, 1991). On the contemporary cohorts, see A. Ong, *Flexible Citizenship* (Durham, N.C.: Duke University Press, 1999).

17. Y. Abu-Laban, "Liberalism, Multiculturalism and the Problem of Essentialism," *Citizenship Studies* 6 (2002): 459–82.

18. N. Bissandooth, *Selling Illusions: The Cult of Multiculturalism in Canada* (Toronto: Penguin Books, 1994).

19. The share of census respondents claiming Canadian identity rose from 1 percent in the 1986 census to nearly 40 percent in 2001. An analysis of those who self-identified as unhyphenated Canadians in the 2001 census showed unexpectedly that the highest level of respondents was living in Quebec. J. Mahoney, "More Folk Calling Selves Canadian: French Speakers More Likely to Claim the Ancestry Than English Speakers," *Globe and Mail,* March 9, 2005.

20. Bissandooth, *Selling Illusions,* 111.

21. Department of Canadian Heritage, *Multiculturalism Promotes Integration and Citizenship,* Evidence Series: Facts about Multiculturalism, vol. 3 (Ottawa: Government of Canada, 1998).

22. Department of Canadian Heritage, *Ethnic Identity Reinforces Attachment to Canada,* Evidence Series: Facts about Multiculturalism, vol. 1 (Ottawa: Government of Canada, 1998).

23. R. Baubock, "Farewell to Multiculturalism? Sharing Values and Identities in Societies of Immigration," *Journal of International Migration and Immigration* 3 (2002): 1–16; C. Joppke, "The Retreat of Multiculturalism in the Liberal State: Theory and Practice," *British Journal of Sociology* 55 (2004): 237–57; C. Joppke and E. Morawska, eds., *Toward Assimilation and Citizenship: Immigrants in Liberal Nation-States* (Basingstoke, U.K.: Palgrave Macmillan, 2003); B. Prins and B. Slijper, "Multicultural Society under Attack," *Journal of International Migration and Immigration* 3 (2002): 313–28.

24. Pred, *Even in Sweden.*

25. L. Back, M. Keith, A. Khan, K. Shukra, and J. Solomos, "New Labour's White Heart: Politics, Multiculturalism and the Return of Assimilation," *Political Quarterly* 73 (2002): 445–54.

26. Kymlicka's third condition is a high level of undocumented immigration. Clearly this would be a key issue in the United States. In terms of Kymlicka's argument, it is relevant to note the generally negative media attention given to Islamic communities in Australia (per Poynting et al.) and the infamous scrutiny attended to undocumented entry (per Marr and Wilkinson). See W. Kymlicka, "The Uncertain Futures of Multiculturalism," *Canadian Diversity / Diversité Canadienne* 4, no. 1 (2005): 82–85; S. Poynting, G. Noble, P. Tabar, and J. Collins, *Bin Laden in the Suburbs: Criminalising the Arab Other* (Sydney: Sydney Institute of Criminology, 2004); and D. Marr and M. Wilkinson, *Dark Victory* (Crows Nest, Australia: Allen and Unwin, 2003).

27. I. Ang and J. Stratton, "Multiculturalism in Crisis: The New Politics of Race and National Identity in Australia," in *On Not Speaking Chinese: Living between Asia and the West,* ed. I. Ang (London: Routledge, 2001), 95–111.

28. K. Betts, "Boatpeople and the 2001 Election," *People and Place* 10, no. 3 (2002): 36–54; Marr and Wilkinson, *Dark Victory.*

29. K. Mitchell, "Geographies of Identity: Multiculturalism Unplugged," *Progress in Human Geography* 28 (2004): 1–11.

30. R. Alba and V. Nee, *Remaking the American Mainstream: Assimilation and Contemporary Immigration* (Cambridge, Mass.: Harvard University Press, 2003); R. Brubaker, "The Return of Assimilation? Changing Perspectives on Immigration and Its Sequels in France, Germany and the United States," *Ethnic and Racial Studies* 24 (2001): 531–48.

31. W. Clark, *The California Cauldron* (New York: Guilford Press, 1998).

32. R. Waldinger, "The Sociology of Immigration: Second Thoughts and Reconsiderations," in *Host Societies and the Reception of Immigrants,* ed. J. Reitz (San Diego: Center for Comparative Immigration Studies, University of California, 2003), 21–43; the quotation is on 23.

33. W. Kymlicka, "Immigration, Citizenship, Multiculturalism: Exploring the Links," *Political Quarterly* 74 (2003): 195–208.

34. P. Li, *Destination Canada: Immigration Debates and Issues* (Don Mills, Ont.: Oxford University Press, 2003).

35. L. Sandercock, *Towards Cosmopolis: Planning for Multicultural Cities* (Chichester, U.K.: Wiley, 1998); L. Sandercock, *Cosmopolis II: Mongrel Cities of the 21st Century* (London: Continuum, 2003).

36. D. Ley, "Seeking *Homo Economicus:* The Canadian State and the Strange Story of the Business Immigration Program," *Annals of the Association of American Geographers* 93 (2003): 426–41.

37. A. Smart and J. Lee, "Financialization and the Role of Real Estate in Hong Kong's Regime of Accumulation," *Economic Geography* 79 (2003): 153–71.

38. K. Olds, *Globalization and Urban Change: Capital, Culture and Pacific Rim Mega-Projects* (Oxford: Oxford University Press, 2001).

39. D. Ley and J. Tutchener, "Immigration, Globalisation and House Prices in Canada's Gateway Cities," *Housing Studies* 16 (2001): 199–223.

40. Mitchell, *Crossing the Neoliberal Line,* 3.

41. D. Ley, "Between Europe and Asia: The Case of the Missing Sequoias," *Ecumene* 2 (1995): 185–210.

42. H. Cheng, "Consuming a Dream: Homes in Advertisements and Imagination in Contemporary Hong Kong," in *Consuming Hong Kong,* ed. G. Mathews and T-L. Lui (Hong Kong: Hong Kong University Press, 2001), 205–36; Mitchell, *Crossing the Neoliberal Line.*

43. See Ley, "Between Europe and Asia"; and Mitchell, *Crossing the Neoliberal Line.*

44. Ley, "Between Europe and Asia." The quotations in the text below of speakers at the public hearing are taken from this source.

45. J. Duncan, "Shaughnessy Heights: The Protection of Privilege," in *Neighbourhood Organizations and the Welfare State,* ed. S. Hasson and D. Ley (Toronto: University of Toronto Press, 1994), 58–82.

46. D. Ley, "Multicultural Planning: Whose City, Whose Identity?" paper presented at Fourth International Metropolis Conference, Washington, D.C., December 1999.

47. K. Krangle, "Vancouver's 'Monster' Houses Tamed By New Zoning," *Vancouver Sun,* September 15, 1999.

48. See Li, *Destination Canada.* The 2002 Immigration and Refugee Protection Act addresses the need for integration processes to be a "two-way street" requiring adjust-

ments by both immigrants and the native born. J. Biles, E. Tolley, and H. Ibrahim, "Does Canada Have a Multicultural Future?" *Canadian Diversity / Diversité Canadienne* 4, no. 1 (2005): 23–28.

49. E. Isin and M. Siemiatycki, *Fate and Faith: Claiming Urban Citizenship in Immigrant Toronto,* CERIS Working Paper (Toronto: University of Toronto, 1999); A. Germain and E. Gangnon, "Minority Places of Worship and Zoning Dilemmas in Montreal," *Planning Theory and Practice* 4 (2003): 295–318.

50. P. Ruddick, "The Coalition Government's Position on Immigration and Population Policy," *People and Place* 7, no. 4 (1999): 6–12.

51. L. Bourne and D. Rose, "The Changing Face of Canada: The Uneven Geographies of Population and Social Change," *Canadian Geographer* 45 (2001): 105–19.

52. B. Yeoh, "Bifurcated Labour: The Unequal Incorporation of Transmigrants in Singapore," *Tijdschrift voor Economische en Sociale Geografie* 97 (2006): 26–37.

53. T. Tsuda, Z. Valdez, and W. Cornelius, "Human versus Social Capital: Immigrant Wages and Labor Market Incorporation in Japan and the United States," in *Host Societies and the Reception of Immigrants,* ed. Reitz, 215–42.

54. A report commissioned by the provincial government of Ontario, made public in December 2004, recommended limited use of Islamic shariah family law to avoid costly litigation, particularly in divorce settlements. The recommendation, empowered by a 1991 Act, was supported by the Islamic Institute for Civil Justice but angrily rejected by Canadian Muslim women's groups. See C. Mallan, "Report Called 'Betrayal' of Women," *Toronto Star,* December, 21, 2004. After protracted debate, and even hostile demonstrations outside Canadian embassies overseas, the premier of Ontario withdrew the proposal in September 2005, even though this would mean also terminating Jewish and Christian arbitration procedures that had been in motion since the 1991 legislation. There has been no mention yet of intervention in another alternative justice system, the use of Aboriginal healing circles, where victim and culprit are brought together in a cathartic community meeting. It remains to be seen whether the proposal of shariah law represented the high-water mark of Canadian multiculturalism, from which political pressure will force withdrawal on many fronts. Recent opinion polls do suggest a cooling of public support for multiculturalism, though such support has been cyclic in the past as well. See D. Munro, "Is Multiculturalism on Deathbed?" *Toronto Star,* August 18, 2005.

55. D. Phillips, "Parallel Lives? Challenging Discourses of British Muslim Self-Segregation," *Environment and Planning D: Society and Space* 24 (2006): 25–40.

56. R. McGown, *Muslims in the Diaspora: The Somali Communities of London and Toronto* (Toronto: University of Toronto Press, 1999), 165.

57. D. Hiebert, "Winning, Losing and Still Playing the Game: The Political Economy of Immigration in Canada," *Tijdschrift voor Economische en Sociale Geografie* 97 (2006): 38–48.

58. H. Duncan, "Multiculturalism: Still a Viable Concept for Integration?" *Canadian Diversity / Diversité Canadienne* 4, no. 1 (2005): 12–14.

59. United Chinese Community Enrichment Services Society, *1998 Annual Report* (Vancouver: United Chinese Community Enrichment Services Society, 1999).

60. I. Bloemraad, "Institutions, Ethnic Leaders, and the Political Incorporation of Immigrants: A Comparison of Canada and the United States," in *Host Societies and the Reception of Immigrants,* ed. Reitz, 361–402; Bloemraad, *Becoming a Citizen.*

8

"Community" Health and Transnational Communities: Undocumented Andean Migrants and Tuberculosis Control in a New Immigrant Gateway

Jason Pribilsky

From my fieldnotes: When Octavio Pomaguiza[1] reached the Guatemala/ Mexico border, he had already been away from his home in the Ecuadorian Andes for almost a month and a half. After enduring a three-week boat trip, smuggled in the cargo hold of a retired fishing trawler with little food or water, he made his way through Mexico—by car, hidden inside a truck, and by walking. The trip north dampened his spirits and left him with a great *dolor de corazón* (heartache) for his wife and children. However, he also looked forward to making money in the United States. He recalled feeling sick—overcome with fever, back pain, and cough—soon after illegally crossing into the United States. In fact, he attributed the sickness to the long time he had spent in the frigid waters of the Rio Grande. Not knowing how to swim (like many Ecuadorian migrants), he had trouble keeping his head above water and took in considerable fluid. The migrant smuggler who had secured Octavio's passage told him he was suffering from malaria and gave him some unknown tablets while he rested in a safe house in Los Angeles. When he felt temporarily better, he made off for New York by bus. Once in

197

Spring Valley, he started feeling weak again—experiencing high fevers and a persistent cough. Despite his poor health, Octavio quickly found work as a day laborer, taking what jobs he could find off the street at $10 an hour. His cough persisted to the point where he was spitting up blood, which he hid from his coworkers using a bandana to mask his reddened mouth. He knew he was very sick and should seek treatment but fretted about missing work. He called home to his wife, who sent numerous vials of injectable vitamins she had secured at an Ecuadorian pharmacy without a prescription. When the treatment offered little more than a palliative, he sought the help of a healer in Queens who suspected he had tuberculosis but said that that he could not cure him. The healer encouraged him to orally consume Vick's vapor rub and take a steam bath in order to clear up his respiratory problems. Finally, so exhausted (*tulluyahshca* in Quichua) that he collapsed on a construction site, Octavio was taken to the hospital and soon after was diagnosed with severe pulmonary tuberculosis—what he simply called *pulmón* (or, "lung"). Because he had such advanced TB, the public health department ordered that Octavio be under hospital quarantine until his infection could be controlled. The contact investigation that followed the detection of his case found that Octavio was living in a household with eleven other men in a two-room apartment—four of them also had active TB and were put on medication. It was determined that he had been battling active TB for two months before he collapsed.

Background and Overview

Although overall rates of tuberculosis (TB) have declined in the United States since the early 1990s, the disease has remained at epidemic levels among foreign-born populations and specific racial and ethnic groups. In 2004, just over half of all reported TB cases were found among foreign-born persons, an increase of over 20 percent from the previous decade.[2] The demographic profile of TB in the United States not surprisingly mirrors patterns of new immigration, with respect to both the countries of origin of new migrants and the geography of new migration settlements. In the past decade, the United States has seen increased immigration from countries with high incidences of TB, especially from underdeveloped regions of Asia and Latin America, as well as from the former Soviet Union. TB rates are also higher in areas currently experiencing increased immigration, including so-called new immigrant gateways."[3] As evidenced by the 2000 U.S.

Census, a large proportion of these new points of entry are suburban areas and midsize cities, whose experience with both immigrants and immigrant health issues are limited.[4] The fieldnotes above are drawn from a large TB outbreak in one such new immigrant gateway, Rockland County, New York, an expanding suburban area northwest of New York City. Between 1990 and 2000, Rockland's population grew by over 8 percent, a figure largely attributable to an influx of new immigrants. In raw numbers, the county's foreign-born population ballooned from 20,422 to 54,766, constituting 19.1 percent of its total population of 286,753.[5] In addition to Ecuadorians—the primary focus of this chapter—Rockland County has received recent immigrants from Haiti, the Dominican Republic, India, Guatemala, El Salvador, the former Soviet Union, and Mexico.[6]

A sharp rise in TB rates has accompanied the increase in Rockland's immigrant population. Though TB had historically been given a low-priority status by the Department of Health, by the late 1990s Rockland County was witnessing the second highest countywide disease rate in the state after New York City. In 2000, the county's TB incidence rate registered at 10.1 per 100,000 persons, compared with New York City's rate of 16.6. Additionally, while Rockland Country's incidence rate was lower than New York City, the percentage of cases found among foreign-persons was significantly higher. In 2000, 83 percent of TB cases in the county were among foreign-born persons, while in New York City only 65 percent of the cases fell into this category.[7]

In 2001, I was contracted by the Rockland County Department of Health as an applied medical anthropologist to help investigate the rising rates of TB among newly arrived Ecuadorian migrants. That year, Ecuadorians were already squarely on the public health TB radar screens because they constituted the largest number of foreign-born cases of TB in the New York City metropolitan area. In the New York City borough of Queens alone, 51 of the year's 129 active cases were identified as Ecuadorian.[8] Though health officials were generally preoccupied by the increased incidence of TB in their county, specific characteristics of the outbreaks and subsequent findings of the contact investigations raised special concerns. Outbreaks among Ecuadorians were, by public health standards, exceedingly large, requiring extensive contact investigations to locate all the potential individuals who might have been exposed or infected by active cases.

The large number of detected cases, combined with the fact that there were an unusually high number of late presentations with active TB (many infected migrants were discovered in extremely sickened conditions and on the verge of death), led public health officials to surmise that cultural barriers played a significant role in the TB problem. Though other immigrant groups from areas with high rates of endemic TB did not exhibit similar outbreak patterns, health officials zeroed in on specific cultural factors and language barriers to help explain why migrants from Ecuador would frequently delay care, misdiagnose their symptoms, and often downplay the severity of their illnesses. Moreover, health officials found themselves largely unprepared to grapple with the living conditions of undocumented migrants; the fact that migrants survived by clustering together in small dwellings and occupying multiple dwellings at the same time, in the experience of health workers, muddied the accuracy of contact investigations. Finally, as explored in greater detail below, the ethnicity of the Ecuadorian population in Rockland County also posed new challenges to a region with a limited immigration history. Most new immigrants were indigenous peoples from the Andean highlands, whose cultural beliefs and practices did not conform neatly to what health workers took to be a "Latino" model of TB, intensifying the belief that understanding cultural differences was the key to controlling tuberculosis, and immigrant health more generally, in the county.

This chapter closely analyzes the interface between undocumented migrants[9] from Ecuador and the Health Department of Rockland County, utilizing data generated through ethnographic fieldwork and clinical care among migrants and public health practitioners. The carte blanche freedom I was given to ferret out the "cultural factors" responsible for the production of poor migrant health held a special appeal for me, coming from anthropology—a discipline famous for trafficking in theories of culture and the privileging of local knowledge. However, as I argue in this chapter, the emphasis the health department placed upon these cultural factors—from health officials down to clinical staff and outreach workers—often served to buttress an exclusionary definition of what a "new immigrant" should be.

Rockland County, like its other northern suburban neighbors, has shown a tremendous flexibility to build "cultural competence" and "transcultural" practices and protocols into its public health initiatives and outreach with new immigrants. Such programs, which no doubt facilitate public health and hospitals staffs to become more sensitive to cultural difference, also unwittingly tend to homogenize the immigrant experience. With respect to the Ecuadorian context, such assumptions tend to downplay the political economy of undocumented migration and to obscure the persistence and importance of transnational ties that structure many migrants' lives. Indeed, when health departments put funds toward translation services and culturally appropriate education programs only to find migrants not adhering correctly to treatment regimes, they grow easily frustrated with groups they conclude are woefully "noncompliant." By contrast, an ethnographic investigation of migrant life suggests that the management of health has as much to do, and perhaps more to do, with the abilities (or inabilities) of new migrants to negotiate their way in suburban America and maintain the demands of transnational ties than it does with cultural beliefs and practices. Cultural differences are, of course, still important for health practitioners to consider, yet how they factor into migrant health—and TB outbreaks in particular—are structured by the constraints and agency of migrant lives spanning borders.

As the title of this chapter suggests, I explore these issues by partially highlighting competing understandings of "community" that arise in the context of providing public health services, especially as they illuminate the ways governmental and nongovernmental institutions in new immigrant gateways are conceptualizing the nature and needs of their newest residents. Among public health practitioners working in the past two decades, "community health" has become a catchall term that encompasses many things—medical interpretation services; the hiring of native health promoters; culturally appropriate health education for physicians, nurses, and outreach workers; and collaboration with local leaders, churches, and other entities that serve to define "community."[10]

In this chapter, I suggest that these largely well-intentioned efforts to promote a community approach often produce "meanings of community" that diverge significantly from the ways transnational migrants themselves understand and use the concept.[11] In one instance, while public health conceptualizes urban space to be bounded by specific communities (e.g., neighborhoods, churches, and workplaces), many migrants living in a highly transnational age may envision and talk about community as extending back to their homelands. Moreover, different senses of community affect not only the *spatial* assumptions public health practitioners make about immigrant populations but *temporal* ones as well. Many community health approaches dealing with new immigrant groups operate under an implicit assumption of acculturation, that is, a model of unidirectional cultural change. With respect to health, migrants over time are thought to abandon their native health beliefs and practices adopt those of their host society. This approach, however, fails to account for the actual movement of migrants as well as the enduring connections they maintain with their homelands. In both cases, a community health perspective runs the risk of glossing over the existence and importance of transnational communities and networks.

My ethnographic treatment of the transnational lives of Ecuadorian migrants and their encounters with the public health system of a new immigrant gateway begins with a discussion of the fieldwork methods employed in this study. I then move to a comparative discussion of the development of indigenous communities as sending communities and the historical development of Rockland County as a immigrant receiving community. Following the critical medical anthropologist Merrill Singer's call for a political economy of health, the first main section below aims to specify the "form and degree to which macroprocesses are manifested at the microlevel," particularly as factors such as housing, spatial dispersal, transportation, and working conditions and sites structure migrant lives.[12] In the second main section, I focus specifically on the issue of immigrant TB and the production of poor health. The third and last main section deepens my argument that community health must look at transnational factors by challenging the notion of acculturation. Before addressing these themes, however, it is important to distinguish the transnational approach I utilize in this study and to articulate the utility of this perspective for understanding the globalization of migrant health.

Transnationalism and Migrant Health in Focus

Since the late 1980s, a number of researchers have used the term "transnational migration" (or "transmigration") to delineate a host of characteristics that challenge standard assumptions of migration as a unilineal process of movement.[13] Through the acceleration of global connections, facilitated in part by the explosion of telecommunications (e.g., cheap telephone cards, cellular telephones, and the Internet), rapid transportation, and the ease by which remittances and other money transfers can occur, researchers have trained their focus on the ways migrants "forge and sustain simultaneous and multi-stranded social relations that link together their societies of origin and settlement."[14]

In its most forceful articulation, scholars understand the practice of transnationalism as creating a sense of a single transnational community—in the minds of both migrants as well as those they leave behind in their home communities. As the daily activities of both migrants and nonmigrants begin to span borders, the separation between locales dissolves, opening up new possibilities for people to rethink meanings of community and conceptions of "home." However, attention to transnational linkages and processes has not led researchers to dismiss the importance of borders, nation-states, or the everyday experiences of individuals rooted in specific locations. As Guarnizo and Smith argue, understanding transnational relations requires studying the mundane and routinized ways peoples lives span borders: "Transnational practices and discourses are those which are an *habitual* part of the *normal* lives of those involved. [They] are considered to be part of the normal life of an individual when their absence will impede or drastically disrupt her/his habitual pattern of activities, whether social, economic, cultural, or political."[15]

Moreover, beyond simply the "continuous circulation of people, money, goods, and information," to borrow the anthropologist Roger Rouse's description,[16] transmigration as practiced by poor households of highland Ecuador constitutes a survival strategy to negotiate the insecurities of the global economy. As economic opportunities have eroded in the both the "sending" areas of Ecuadorian highlands and the receiving areas of the United States, and immigration policies have become ever tightened, migrant households struggle with the inability to secure a full livelihood in either locale. By keeping open multiple options, families somewhat unwittingly create transnational households within transnational communities.

Part of the "normalcy" that Guarnizo and Smith and others argue develops around transnational practices invariably includes the ways people make health care decisions and seek out cures and remedies by crossing borders. In an age of hypermobility, there is a flourishing of options for addressing health problems beyond what might be locally available: Documented (and sometimes undocumented) Mexican migrants in the United States frequently think nothing of slipping back over the Mexican border to consult with traditional healers or obtain pharmaceuticals unavailable to them in the United States without a prescription or health insurance; affluent Yemenis seek out high-technology surgeries in Jordan; elderly Americans of all class strata orchestrate bus trips to Canada to obtain inexpensive medications in bulk.[17] With respect to undocumented migrants whose access to health services is severely curtailed by their "irregular" status and persistent lack of worker-provided health insurance, calling home for medications, health information, and advice, and in some cases transnational consultations with "traditional" healers, constitute what I refer to as a "transnational hierarchy of resort."[18] When migrants get sick, they put into place a plan of action that combines resorting to both local and afar services. Choosing and prioritizing different options requires weighing a number of factors—including pragmatic ones, such as expense, time lost from work, and safety; and more meaning-laden ones, such as the "power" of a particular remedy, the source of the health knowledge, and the influence of family members back home. When Ecuadorian migrants become ill, they often seek out care thousands a miles away first before accessing the services of a free public clinic just a few blocks from where they live and work. As I explore below, the fact that migrants' health care decisions have become unmoored from local contexts has serious implications for how officials charged with providing public health services grapple with the needs of new immigrant populations.

Fieldwork and Methodology

This chapter draws from the intermittent ethnographic fieldwork I conducted between 2001 and 2004, including, most important, twenty-two in-depth and semistructured interviews with indigenous Ecuadorian migrants residing in the villages and towns of Rockland County. My sample consisted of nineteen men and three women, all of whom entered the United States after 1999. These migrants ranged in age from eighteen to thirty-four years, with an average age of twenty-six. All interviewees were either undergoing treatment for active TB disease or were receiving preventative drug treatment after being exposed to TB, all under the supervision of the Rockland County Department of Health (RCDOH). I supplemented interviews with four focus groups—comprising both Ecuadorians and other migrants from Guatemala, Honduras, and Mexico—to collect general information about health care services and everyday life in Rockland County. All the Ecuadorians with whom I spoke for this project were undocumented migrants.

The necessity for migrants with undocumented status to remain clandestine and guard their movements often thwarts the use of random sampling, complicated surveys, and other highly systematic fieldwork methods. Similar to research with other "hidden populations," I relied heavily upon participant-observation methods aimed at working with migrants in their natural environments as much as possible; I also identified study participants through "snowball" or opportunistic sampling.[19] Initial contact with study participants was made possible by the RCDOH, most notably through the assistance of the director of TB control and her staff of outreach workers. Because most of the Ecuadorians I interviewed had come to trust the RCDOH (even if they did not always seek out their services), my affiliation with it greatly facilitated the rapport necessary to conduct sensitive interviews and gain entry into the partially clandestine lives of migrants. Additional contacts were located by tapping into the friendship and kinship networks of the study participants. Lengthy interviews (between one and three hours) were supplemented by shorter informal conversations and "hanging out" with groups of migrant as they waited for work on Rockland County roadways and street corners and at a popular day laborer center housed in the basement of Spring Valley church.

This day laborer center, El Proyecto Humanitario para Jornaleros / the Jornaleros Project, where migrants congregated for free breakfasts on cold mornings when work was slow and hard to come by and attended English language classes taught by community volunteers, proved to be an especially helpful location for holding conversations in a relaxed setting. In rarer instances, I joined migrants during moments of leisure, typically at pickup soccer and volleyball games in local parks and abandoned parking lots or over drinks and joking in their apartments and places of work. These often fleeting and informal encounters were invaluable ethnographic moments, allowing me to contextualize interview materials and clarify frequently used colloquialisms and jargon. Study participants who sat for an interview or participated in a focus group received $25 grocery vouchers or long-distance phone cards for assisting with the project.

My research also entailed collecting data about public health efforts with migrant groups. In addition to brief interviews and participant observation with staff (including attending physicians, nurses, and nurse's aides) in a free public health clinic run by the RCDOH, I spent a number of days "out in the community" with two Spanish-speaking outreach workers on their routine visits to the homes of migrants. I recorded their interactions with patients as they administered medications, answered questions, and provided other health services. Finally, I draw on fieldnotes gathered at community forums on immigration and migrant services coordination meetings attended by hospital staff members, public health workers, and social workers, as well as at two large TB screenings at area churches.

My data collection in Rockland County was also informed and contextualized by my previous ethnographic research on Ecuadorian transnational migration, including fieldwork among undocumented migrants living in the borough of Queens, New York City, in 2000 and 2001. To a lesser extent,

I utilize fieldnotes and interview data from new research initiated in Ecuador in 2004–5 addressing traditional medicine and the indigenous health movement. This research has included fieldwork trips to natural medicine markets to learn about nonbiomedical tuberculosis remedies and cures, interviews and clinical observation of native healers (*yachacs*), and ethnographic interviews with indigenous Ecuadorians about tuberculosis and the perceived health risks associated with undocumented migration.

From Andean Highlands to Spring Valley: The Making of a Transnational Community

The community names of Socarte, Herba Buena, Gallorumi, Chontamarca, and Tiopamba, among others, show up on almost no map of Ecuador that you can get in the United States. Even Cañar—the name of both a province and county seat—is a semi-obscure geographic locale. Yet, in the late 1990s, these place names began appearing with increasing frequency on the clinical intake forms RCDOH nurses and health workers were filling out on their newly arriving patients from Ecuador. If pinpointed together on a map, the communities would demonstrate a new trend in Ecuadorian migration to the United States—a significant shift from a largely mestizo population (i.e., persons of mixed Spanish and indigenous heritage) to an indigenous, or native Andean, one. Starting in the mid-1960s, mestizo Ecuadorians began entering "old immigrant gateways" in the United States, first to Chicago and then increasingly to the New York City boroughs of Queens and Brooklyn.[20] The bulk of these migrants originate from Ecuador's south-central Andes (an area named El Austro), which comprises the provinces of Azuay and Cañar.[21] Apart from the city of Cuenca (population 500,000) in Azuay Province, the region is primarily rural and is dotted with thousands of small farming communities.[22] Although they share a similar rural background and agricultural livelihood, Rockland's migrants differed significantly from this first waves of mestizo migrants in terms of ethnic background, culture, and, to some degree, their vulnerability.

The majority of migrants in Rockland self-identify as indigenous, and in particular, as belonging to the "*pueblo* Cañari" ("Cañari people"), whose communities correspond to the northern reaches of Ecuador's Cañar Province. All the Ecuadorians I interviewed were also from the *parroquias* ("parishes," small administrative units below the county level) of Chontamarca and General Morales, the poorest and most marginalized regions of the Cañari territory. Although significant differences exist between communities, the Cañari collectively represent one of a handful of distinct highland indigenous groups of Ecuador, who are identifiable by their use of the Indian language Quichua and a distinctive type of dress.[23] Women wear brightly colored and embroidered gathered skirts called *polleras* (common to much of the Andes) and woolen shawls pinned at the breast with decorative silver and nickel-plated pins (*tupus*). Though it is women who consistently wear "traditional" clothing, men also typically maintain an indigenous appearance through their long hair (kept neatly back in a single braid and often adorned with colorful ribbons) and white felt "bowler" hats with small colored pom-poms, which are also worn by women.

Most rural Cañari combine a subsistence livelihood, including the production of a wide array of crops (e.g., corn, barley, potatoes, wheat) and the raising of animals, especially cattle for milk production, with sporadic wage labor. Predominantly, Cañari men work as *jornaleros* (agricultural day laborers) and in local construction—building houses for migrants and returnees. An incipient professional class of indigenous people has also emerged, finding work as school teachers, nurses, and local government employees. Still, indigenous Cañari struggle along with other Ecuadorians with the uncertainty of the country's chronically unstable economy. In the past five years, families have seen significant declines in the market value of their agricultural products, while the price of inputs (e.g., fertilizers and irrigation) have increased under dollarization and the privatization of resources such as water. Migration—both to the United States and Spain—has become one of the only ways people recognize to get ahead ("*salir adelante*") and escape poverty. Many Ecuadorians I interviewed in Rockland shared with me their migration goals of making enough money to purchase land in their home communities, to build houses, and more generally to secure a agricultural future for themselves and their families. The vast majority had anticipated realizing these goals within two or three years (and then return to Ecuador), yet many who had been in the United States for longer conceded the difficulty of such an idea.[24] Overwhelmingly, migrants hoped to return soon to Ecuador (within two years); only two participants of my sample expressed a desire to stay in the United States indefinitely.

A major obstacle that hindered the migrants I interviewed from "getting ahead" in the timely fashion they imagined were the crippling amounts of debt they brought with them to New York. Undocumented migrants must seek passage to the United States from smugglers (*pasador* or *coyotero*) whose services carry a high price tag: between $10,000 and $15,000, depending on the reputation of the smuggler, the difficulty of route taken, and the person being smuggled.[25] To fund their journeys, would-be migrants invariably rely on a quasi-legal system of loan making (*chulco*) that typically requires immediate and extended families to put up land and other valuable types of collateral (e.g., livestock, automobiles, and jewelry) to fund their surreptitious trip north. Each loan carries an 8 to 10 percent interest rate compounded monthly. Once abroad, migrants must make regular monthly payments to *chulqueros* (moneylenders) anywhere in the range of $200 to $500. If a migrant misses a payment or if his or her family cannot make up the difference, *chulqueros* often resort to violence and intimidation. Threats to seize land and harm family members (and, in some cases, even kidnap them) are common. Because the loans themselves are legitimate (even if smuggling is not), households have no legal recourse when they enter into default. If months go by without payment—be it from a migrant's sickness or crop failure in Ecuador—*chulqueros* often increase interest rates, making payments astronomical and impossible to make.

In some cases, the migrants I interviewed had also arrived in Rockland as the virtual indentured servants of their employers. Some Rockland business owners, usually of restaurants and construction companies, who were happy with a particular migrant would pay the smuggling costs to have other reliable workers brought from Ecuador. Once in the United States, these migrants would have to work off their debts, thus ensuring loyalty to their employer. Though these situations were often described to me as preferable to having to mortgage the land of the family and extended family, this was not always the case. As one migrant told me, "I don't feel like I can leave the job or my boss will turn me into the *migra* [Immigration authorities]. While he was very nice at first and helped me, now, even when I am late to work he threatens me."

Although it is not the goal of this chapter to explore family and other types of obligations and debt agreements in rural Ecuador, stressing the stakes of migrants serves to highlight the kinds of structural pressures under which men and, increasingly women, find themselves. Beyond the affective transnational ties migrants maintain with family members back in Ecuador, a kind of economic transnationalism (in the form of debt) affects how and where these migrants look for work, their ability to change jobs, and their patterns of movement around the county. Sickness, including chronic weakness and fatigue, being bedridden, and the cost of curing oneself not only jeopardize employment but also increase the very real potential for rural households to spin further into poverty and physical danger.

Therefore, finding work and paying debts structures nearly every action migrants take upon their arrival in Rockland. As Antonio, an indigenous migrant from Herba Buena, explained to me: "I couldn't think of anything when I didn't know where I was. But I had to get working. For three days I did could not find work. I was overcome by fear." The feelings of fear and being overwhelmed that Antonio and others shared with me were compounded by their entry into Rockland County, a new immigrant gateway with few established migrant services and a hardly distinguishable community of migrants.

In their comparative study of immigrant incorporation in the United States, Portes and Rumbaut plot the successes and failures of new arrivals up against local "contexts of reception."[26] Such contexts chart migrants' potential agency and constraints vis-à-vis various factors, including government policies, labor market conditions, "ethnic typification," and the makeup of the preexisting immigrant community. Caroline Brettel similarly pushes migration researchers to think about the "city as context." Distinct from Portes and Rumbaut, however, she stresses the cultural dimensions of urban places—what she calls "the cultural ethos of cities." Researching an urban ethos "includes an examination of whether or not a city projects a dominant set of values that shapes political, economic, and institutional life, and hence both the incorporation of and attitudes toward immigrants."[27] Though migrants can rely on their own human capital (e.g., networks, skills, and language abilities), contexts of reception deeply influence how successfully that capital can be employed. Such contexts—when they work against the forming of a strong immigrant community—can foster the necessity of building and strengthening transnational linkages and ties with home communities. As the brief recounting below stresses, a history of limited housing, unstable work options, and a spatial layout antithetical to the creation of local community all contribute to the importance of strong transnational communities for undocumented Ecuadorian migrants. As we will see, these same factors also affect the health of migrants and structure the health-seeking actions they do or do not take.

New and Old Immigration in Rockland County

Rockland County is (with the exception of the five boroughs of New York City) the smallest county in New York State in area. Despite its close proximity to New York City, Rockland's history is largely a rural one, well into the twentieth century. Specific geographical features of the region, including the Ramapo/Highlands mountain chain and the exceedingly marshy Hudson River, worked to keep Rockland isolated for most of its early history. White foreigner settlement in the county began in 1686 as Orangetown, an English provincial town of Orange County. In 1798, as the fledgling New York State was erecting borders and dividing up its administrative territories, Orangetown split from Orange County and become present day Rockland. Yet geographical obstacles continued to hinder the county's economic development. It would be another thirty years before the region would become connected with the railroad and turnpike systems.[28]

Once Rockland had attained the requisite infrastructure and transportation improvements, industry began to flourish. Quickly, the county built a reputation for its expansive quarries, as well as the manufacture of bricks, tools, and cotton goods. It was under these conditions that the county began experiencing its first waves of significant immigration. Rockland's immigrant history begins with the movement of Jewish traders from Poland and eastern Europe into the region in 1830s and 1840s. By the late 1800s, synagogues and Jewish businesses (mainly small stores and manufacturing centers) were prominent fixtures in the towns of Spring Valley, Haverstraw, and Nyack,[29] attracting more permanent settlers to the region from New York City. Rockland's first housing developments on the so-called Jew Hill in Spring Valley were erected in this period and have remained the locus of immigrant housing ever since. Today, these early Jewish settlements have been greatly overshadowed by the growth of a sizable Hasidic Orthodox Jewish community (the largest suburban Hasidic community in the country), mainly concentrated in the village of Monsey.

Latino immigration to Rockland began with less prominence and much later, with trickles of Puerto Ricans, Dominicans, and Cubans entering the region in the 1930s to escape the pronounced effects of the global depression. Soon, affluent Puerto Ricans and other well-established Hispanic immigrants living in the Bronx and Harlem moved out to what they celebrated as the "country." Quickly, however, the town of Haverstraw, and North Rockland County more generally, became recognized Latino areas and took on a more urban character. Most early migrants found manufacturing jobs (producing dye and bedding) at a handful of factories. As one immigrant reflected on the early development, it felt "like a little city."[30]

Despite its urban pockets, Rockland did not become a "suburb" in the sense of intensifying networks and links with a larger urban area until the building of the Tappan Zee Bridge in 1955. The bridge, spanning the three-mile breadth of the Hudson River and connecting Rockland with Westchester County and New York City, was touted as a remedy for isolation. Prophetically, a newspaper promotion for the bridge in 1954 (there was significant opposition to what was considered the excessive cost of the project) trumpeted "Wake Up!! Rockland County. The Tappan Zee Bridge and New York State Thruway Will Make Rockland County Grow . . . and Grow." The bridge allowed for an increase in a commuter traffic and the ability of the county to entice city folk to the country.

One group of "city folk" that expanded into the region, and would have a profound effect on the immigrant "ethos" of the country, were the Haitians who began commuting to factory work and domestic jobs. Over time, a number of the Haitian commuters settled in Rockland, first in Nyack and then in greater numbers in Spring Valley, occupying housing abandoned by Jewish residents who had moved to deeper and more affluent reaches of the county.[31] The Haitian settlement of the county, and especially the degree to which they bought up real estate in Spring Valley, has a legacy for immigrant housing today. In the 1970s, Rockland became a primary destination for Haitian citizens escaping the reign of terror of "Baby Doc" Duvalier. Most refugees settled in Spring Valley, where longtime Haitian residents converted their existing homes into apartments, rented them to new arrivals, and used the rent to purchase new and larger houses for themselves outside of town. Although Rockland, like neighboring Westchester County, has moved to restrict large housing projects in favor of single family dwellings, the migrants I interviewed were able to take advantage of the myriad "slap-dash conversions" performed on homes to convert them to multiple apartments.[32] Most of these conversions were done illegally (without permits) and contained shoddy and dangerous construction work.

Rockland County Today: A New Immigrant Gateway

Although it is small in terms of area (516 square kilometers), Rockland County today feels like an endlessly sprawling suburb anchored only by an axis of county highways running north-south and east-west. Among the patchwork of small towns and villages clustered along these roadways, none can rightfully be called the core of the county. In other words, there is no well-established center, and much of the county's commercial activity takes place in "strip malls" along the main county roadways where one town spills into the next. Similarly, though the stamp of immigrant life is evident throughout Rockland in the presence of myriad Indo-Pak food stores, Latino supermarkets, and ethnic restaurants, no particular immigrant clustering is evident. With respect to Ecuadorian settlements, the major towns of Spring Valley, Haverstraw, Nyack, and Nanuet, among others, hold roughly equal concentrations of Ecuadorians, without any one particular town rightfully assuming a position as an enclave or immigrant nucleus.

In my interviews with migrants, a preoccupation with place, or more specifically with the "placelessness" of Rockland County, permeated our discussions.[33] Though migrants felt marginalized from what they perceived to be mainstream society, largely by their inabilities to speak English (and in many cases to even to speak an unbroken Spanish when they were primarily Quichua speakers) and by a lack of both time and money to be able to participate in activities they perceived as occupying most people's leisure—going shopping, seeing movies, and the like—they equally expressed feeling of being marginalized or isolated from other Ecuadorians. Indeed, on a few occasions I was struck by a situation where, after completing interviews, a migrant would query me about the other Ecuadorians I was interviewing for the TB project. They were curious to know how other migrants lived, where they lived, and from where exactly in Ecuador they came. The migrants I knew maintained very small friend and family networks, and some of these networks only consisted of the people with whom they shared apartments but because of busy work schedule rarely saw or did not consider "knowing well." In many cases, their closest friends and relatives lived in Queens or Brooklyn, or in nearby states (New Jersey and Connecticut). To the extent that they could, travel to these locations constituted a significant way for them to stay connected to other Ecuadorians.

The migrants living in Rockland who had visited Queens or Brooklyn were also quick to point out the differences, and they often bemoaned the lack of an identifiable Ecuadorian community in Rockland. Absent from Rockland is anything comparable to the community anchor that Roosevelt Avenue provides to Queens residents, with its rows of Ecuadorian restaurants, money-sending agencies, and specialty shops selling everything from Andean fruits and vegetables to *sanjuanito* and *huayno* music CDs.[34] As one migrant told me, "Rockland is just one long road that I travel on. There is no plaza, no center, no place for us to go. Nobody has neighbors. . . . I don't know even know the person who lives [in the apartment] next door." Feelings of isolation, of being sealed off, were especially acute for rural Cañari who were accustomed to spending much of their time working out-of-doors in public areas, and where workdays would be punctuated by visits from neighbors.

The migrants registered feelings of placelessness and isolation most prominently in their discussions of work. In Queens and Brooklyn, albeit with a large migrant population, Ecuadorians have arguably not fallen into one single "labor niche" but have maintained diverse employment in the garment industry, as employees of Korean-owned groceries, and as restaurant workers.[35] By contrast, the Rockland migrants I knew primarily found work as day laborers, and to a lesser extent as restaurant help in tasks that require little in the way of English language proficiency. In restaurants, migrants were typically relegated to "back work"—serving as dishwashers and busboys.[36] Most of the work was described to me as solitary, and because it focused a lot on cleaning up, it typically included working late into the night after the restaurant had closed and other staff had gone home. Contrary to what migrants hoped would be the case, restaurant work was lonely.

Day laborer work was not described as much better. Once picked up, workers (known as *esquineros* or "corner guys") told of being shuttled off to work in semiclandestine construction sites where they would labor away from the watchful eye of labor inspectors and construction codes. Many times, migrants noted that they did not even know if they were in Rockland when they were working. Waiting on the street for work also proved isolating. Although men are strangely public while they wait for potential employers to stop, the space is simultaneously removed from public life. *Jales,* as migrants referred to the waiting spaces, consisted of roadways and parking lots along Route 59, one of the main arteries of the county. They are areas where the boundaries between public and private spaces are blurred and constantly contested. Though migrants attempted to stay on public sidewalks, their numbers invariably pushed them onto the property of local businesses. As I observed a number of times, business owners would often force migrants back on to the sidewalks or, more preferably, send them walking to camp in front of another business. In a couple of the most heavily congregated areas when men look for work—in front of a gas station minimarket and a McDonald's restaurant—migrants earned squatter rights by pooling their change and buying endless cups of coffee. Indeed, through the long months of the New York winter, there was little else to do to keep warm as one waited for work.

The migrants found the street traffic to be only slightly more welcoming. As the morning wears on (after being on streets since around 6:00 a.m.), migrants must become more aggressive, watching closely as each car passes by. At the slightest hint that someone may be stopping to secure workers, migrants wave their arms and gesticulate to get attention. Sometimes the cars that slow down or stop are not looking for workers but rather are there to hurl anti-immigration sentiments and racial slurs out their windows. Migrants also reported to me incidences where fights broke out between men waiting for work and local residents antagonistic to their presence. With nowhere else to go, one migrant told me how they struggled to appear worthy of respect (*respeto*) with the few resources at their disposal. For some, this meant standing up tall, keeping their clothes clean as much as possible, and smiling at those who passed by. For the indigenous migrants, attempts to get respect on the road also entailed cutting off their long ponytails and discarding all outward trappings of indigenous identity if they had not already done so during their trips north.[37]

In the final analysis, the only nonisolating aspect of looking for work as a day laborer would seem to be the camaraderie of being with other migrants also seeking work. Intense competition on the street, however, often served to undermine the kinds of relationships that might form during the long hours of waiting. As Jacinto, a twenty-two-year-old *esquinero* from Chontamarca, explained to me: "Everyone is nice that you meet on the street until work comes along. Then it is pure chaos. Your best friend can become your greatest enemy when *plata* [money] is concerned."

Indeed, day labor wages vary considerably both from season to season and week to week, thus requiring the migrants to be extremely vigilant with respect to finances. Average hourly wages range from $6 per hour to over $10, depending the type of job and a day laborer's individual skills. During a particularly "good month," migrants reported netting earnings of nearly $1,400. However, during the winter season, or under other low-demand conditions, monthly averages could be as slim as $500—less than a third of what can be earned in a "good" month.[38] In addition to fluctuations in labor demands, migrants also reported having to contend with unscrupulous employers who refused to pay migrants for their work or would dole out less than the prearranged amount.[39] Such variability made it necessary for migrants to stay in close contact with their families back home to inform them when remittances would be slight or nonexistent. Though it goes almost without saying, day laborers also lacked any kind of employer-provided health insurance, nor did employers take any concerted interest in their worker's health. Because many migrants would work for an employer only once (a single day's work), a migrant's long-term health was of no consequence as long as they could perform well on the day they were hired.

In Rockland, as informants told me, community life overall was compartmentalized and hemmed in by the demands of work. Jobs as day laborers, dishwashers, and busboys, or as domestics in the case of women, found migrants dispersed throughout the county depending on the job they are doing on any given day. Many migrants maintained multiple jobs (or in the case of day laborers, they looked for work at multiple *jales*) and had to find a way to move between their different work locales. Rockland residents travel mostly by private automobile or by foot; public transportation is reportedly confusing, unreliable, and inconvenient. Along the main roadways, there are no enclosed bus stops to shelter patrons from the harsh winter weather. Transportation, consequently, was presented to me as one of the greatest obstacles of living in the county. Migrants also identified that in the absence of other face-to-face forms of community, there were no media outlets such as an Ecuadorian radio station or newspapers that would aid in the "imagining of community."[40] Community life, in short, was often described to me as being fleeting. A day off from work may afford the opportunity to take part in a volleyball game or to attend a special event at the local Catholic church, but rarely did such events translate into a sustained social life.

Although Rockland has a long history of immigration, it arguably does not embody the "ethos" of a historic immigrant community.[41] Its immigrant history is deep—extending back to the mid-1800s—yet its development has gone largely unrecognized or, more to the point, has escaped local criticism. A partial reason for this is the lack of well-defined immigrant neighborhoods or communities (on the scale of Queens, for instance). Also, two of the county's most prominent immigrant populations, Jews and Haitians, have proven to been "model immigrants." Following the standard immigrant narrative, these two groups, after a period of struggling financially in cramped and dilapidated housing in the town centers of Spring Valley and Haverstraw, have moved out of the poorer areas to the county's more affluent, wooded outskirts, building large homes and making significant contributions to their communities.

This acceptance of immigration seemed to be changing by late 1990s, and especially after the release of the 2000 U.S. Census data showed dramatic increases in the county's foreign-born population.[42] These immigrants, at least from an outsider's perspective, seemed to differ considerably from already established groups. In the very public image of the day laborer, new migrants appeared to be unproductive (as they loitered on the street waiting for jobs), single men without families, and, at times, aggressive (as they tried to flag down cars in their pursuit of work). In the case of Cañari and other Quichua-speaking migrants from Ecuadorian highlands, the fact that they spoke very little or no Spanish at all put them in a liminal category—appearing to be Latino, yet not conforming to the stereotypes associated with this larger group.

In early 2005, anti-immigration sentiments in the county intensified after an undocumented migrant from Guatemala with severe mental illness murdered his female employer while on a landscaping job. Though it was later learned that the migrant was suffering from delusions at the time of the killing, local reactions captured in the area's newspaper, the *Journal News,* constellated primarily around the migrant's undocumented status (a justification for more border patrol) and the claim that new immigrants were not making the same contribution as those who had come before them.[43] Despite such sentiments, since the late 1990s Rockland has also supported an Immigrant Coalition consisting of local political leaders, clergy, social workers, and various health agencies that work to identify and meet the needs of the county's expanding immigrant population. Also, a local church in Spring Valley operates the day laborer's center El Proyecto Humanitario para Jornaleros mentioned above, which offers a variety of services such as trying to recoup unpaid wages, offering free breakfasts, and providing English language classes two days a week.

On the basis of a content analysis of local newspapers, coupled with the informal conversations and interviews I conducted with county leaders and workers at social service organizations, it often seemed that Rockland County officials have had to struggle with how to balance meeting the needs of new immigrants without making the county appear as actively encouraging new immigrant settlement. A case in point was a debate surrounding a proposal (and promise) by the mayor of Spring Valley to address complaints about the hordes of day laborers along major roadways in the county. In particular, businesses owners along the roadways where day laborers waited for work started complaining that the groups of *esquineros* were discouraging customers from patronizing their shops and stores, as well as contributing to a litter problem. To remedy this situation, the mayor's office proposed to build a covered shed area where day laborers could wait and negotiate work in a public place without disturbing private property. Although the plan was applauded by some as a way to consolidate day laborers into a central location and give immigrants a safe place to meet with potential employers, others opposed the project on grounds that it "sent a wrong message" to immigrants that off-the-books work carried out by undocumented migrants is sanctioned by the county. Similar efforts to provide immigrant services have had to tiptoe around public opinion in Rockland. Efforts to address the county's migrant TB problem, however, had not met with the same scrutiny. Although the disease's outbreaks made front-page headlines in local and regional newspapers, cultural competence training—the most well-publicized response to immigrant needs in the public health system—was seen as incurring few costs and thus as more palatable than the construction of new physical structures.

Although county residents were apt to see immigrants as demanding new services and overtaxing preexisting ones, they remained largely unaware of the ways new migrants were placing significant demands on their home communities through the flexing of transnational ties. Before the advent of transnational theory in migration studies, the sociologist Michael Burawoy compared the dynamics of undocumented Mexican migration to California to labor migration in apartheid-era South Africa.[44] His comparison illuminated how, as migration separates labor migrants from their families, the receiving labor market essentially shift the burdens of reproducing its labor force to sending communities. In the case of undocumented Ecuadorian migrants in the United States, the costs associated with raising children, maintaining households, provisioning health, and taking care of the elderly are transferred to sending communities in Ecuador. The employers of day laborers and local restaurants pay none of these costs. To ensure this process works, remittances flow back to home communities, while migrants in the United States struggle to minimize costs, maximize productivity, and avoid illness and injury. Part of this strategy forces migrants to rely on their home communities for different kinds of support not found in their new surroundings.

In the absence of a strong local community, affective ties help to foster a "community of mind" with families and friends in sending villages.[45] With respect to maintaining good health, such ties allow migrants to practice a level of health care sorely constrained by the migrant life. Receiving medications and health information from abroad, relying on traditional cures, and delaying care are all ways migrants enact a transnational hierarchy of resort when it comes to dealing with health issues like TB. However, where health workers have seen these ties as representative of "enduring cultural beliefs," the migrants themselves understand and experience these ties as critical forms of survival.

The Political Economy of Health: Migrants and TB

During one of my phases of fieldwork in Rockland, I accompanied a middle-aged female doctor (an immigrant herself from South Asia) on her clinical rounds in the county's public hospital. We stopped off at the room of a Ecuadorian patient from the small community of Socarte. The patient was a young woman in her early twenties who spoke primarily Quichua and could only understand Spanish if she were spoken to very slowly. She had been admitted to the hospital three days before with advanced signs of active pulmonary TB and was placed in an isolation room. During an interview I conducted with her before the visit with the help of a Quichua interpreter, she told me about a harrowing month-long trip to the United States and how she had felt sick along the way. Since arriving in America, she had spent the previous two weeks on the couch of an aunt living in Newark, who, with a combination of home remedies and over-the-counter pain and cough medications, tried to nurse her back to health. Taking up the woman's chart, the doctor registered the facts of the case. As she read the chart, I filled her in with information from the interview. She interrupted me and asked for clarification, "She got sick on her way from Ecuador? Isn't that only a five- or six-hour flight?" Though not all hospital staff knew so little about the Ecuadorian population in their midst as this doctor, her comments did reflect a larger ignorance about the importance of surreptitious journeys in the production of poor health.

From a biomedical perspective, TB is the result of a bacterial infection (*Mycobaterium tuberculosis*) that is highly contagious and easily spread by air droplets and takes advantage of conditions of poverty—malnutrition, overcrowded housing situations, and physical stress. In the literature on immigrant TB, the reasons given for high rates of foreign cases often focus on the fact that immigrants come from countries with high rates or latent (or inactive) disease. Though people who are healthy (yet infected) do not typically present with active disease (and may spend their whole lives free of symptoms), the conditions of migrant life place significant stressors on the body and thus can often trigger active disease. As such, TB in host countries is often treated as an imported problem, like migrants themselves.[46] Though this chapter is not about the processes of undocumented migration per se, this perception of TB had a significant impact on how migrants interacted with the RCDOH and how it interpreted the actions of its migrant clients.

In his important history of TB, the microbiologist-turned-historian René Dubos summarily pronounced, "Tuberculosis was, in effect, the first penalty that capitalistic society had to pay for the exploitation of labor."[47] Indeed, the high rates of TB among undocumented Ecuadorians in Rockland can scarcely be separated from the labor demands and poor working conditions migrants must endure in the United States. For particularly vulnerable indigenous migrants in Rockland, their risk for TB is structured long before they get to the United States and begin working. In some cases, migrants described having TB-like symptoms (in particular, severe coughing and fever) before leaving their home villages, as well as during their illegal trips north. (In 2003, an epidemiologist in Ecuador's Cañar Province also reported to me that he had recorded a number of TB patients that migrated before finishing their TB treatment regimen.)

Although a molecular epidemiological study may be the only way we can learn exactly where transmission is taking place, migrants' own descriptions of their dangerous journeys north speak volumes of the health threats illegal migration poses. The clandestine journey typically consists of being stowed away in an aged fishing trawler or banana boat on a dangerous trek from the coast of Ecuador to Guatemala. From there, migrants usually travel by land (*"por la pampa"*; *"caminando"*) through Mexico and into the United States. The boat trips are described as particularly dangerous and unhealthy. Migrants are stowed in holds that are nearly airtight with upward of 200 other migrants. Many migrants endure the journey while sick, often described as having a persistent cough that may indicate TB infection. In the holds of smuggling vessels, they often must resort to sleeping in inches of fetid water polluted with vomit and human waste that collects over the course of the trip. Their nutrition aboard the boats is equally unhealthy. Migrants are typically fed only once a day (women receive more food than men) with a diet consisting of enriched white rice, crackers, and bananas. Though only approximately 10 percent of persons with latent TB infection form active disease, the stresses and strains of human smuggling greatly amplify one's chances of becoming sick. The difficulty of human smuggling can make an infected person (with latent TB) develop active disease as well as expose uninfected persons to the disease for the first time. Still, as most of my informants agreed, the risk of getting sick—even with TB—is a small price to pay in the context where migrants not infrequently perish during their perilous journeys north.

Clandestine journeys and the dangers they incur structure the biological risk of becoming sick with TB. The stress and malnutrition associated with undocumented migration compromise immune systems while at the same time exposing migrants to multiple vectors for TB infection or the aggravation of latent disease as they make their way north. In addition to boat experiences, migrants invariably find themselves commingling with other smuggled persons from throughout the world in safe houses, detention centers, and jails. Biological risk is accompanied by a kind of socioeconomic structuring shaped by the demands of transnational labor migration.

As I have explored elsewhere, these structures entail important gendered aspects that shape the demands migrants place on themselves to generate remittances for families back in Ecuador.[48] In the highland Andes, as partible inheritance no longer ensures young men land to start their own autonomous households, both young men and women have looked to migration as a saving grace. In the Cañari communities (home to the bulk of Rockland's Ecuadorian migrants), men's eighteenth birthdays are frequently equated with the time for a rural youth to "*cumplir su destino*" ("fulfill his destiny") and migrate north. Though many men do migrate, they do not do so without first getting married and often without having children—setting the foundation for their return years later. In the remittance economy, many households have suspended other income-earning strategies, including agriculture and artisan production. In this context, migrant men face pressures unknown to previous generations of men. Their fathers were "co-managers" in their households and agricultural livelihoods, but these men stand out as solitary breadwinners. Being able to provide both monetarily and to "produce their locality" back home, to borrow Arjun Appardurai's concept, is extremely important to maintaining their status and ensuring their eventual (and hopeful) reentry into Andean society.[49] In this context, sickness of any kind poses a serious threat to the already tenuous migrant life. Victor Mizurambay, a thirty-three-year-old father of five, shared with me how TB sidelined him from working and sending money home:

> I got sick, I was filled with *pena* [pain] and *verguenza* [shame]. I worked hard and now I couldn't. . . . What did I do? Some guys are always drunk, miss work and then lose their jobs. That wasn't me. I was sick, but my boss didn't know that.

For migrants like Victor, the situation presents itself as a doubly painful dilemma. While economic necessity and the community pressures have structured rural Ecuadorians to "fulfill their destinies in the United States," their role as fathers demands they should be at home with children. Many migrant men I interviewed described to me how they tried to hold these contradictory demands together through the dignity of not drinking, adhering to a strong work ethic, and sending home money. When one has been stricken with TB, however, the delicate emotional balance often cannot be maintained.

Balancing debt payments with household remittance obligations also forced men to seek out extremely low-cost living situations that inadvertently increase their susceptibility to TB infection. Many migrants living in "slapdash" housing joined between four and nine migrants in cramped, frequently windowless, studio apartments. In this context, public health advice to keep spaces well lit and ventilated (sunlight kills TB bacteria) often goes unheeded, for migrants have little choice in the matter. In one case, a migrant told me how he had wished to air out his clothing to kill the germs (*microbios*) he believed were in his clothes (as advised by the RCDOH). But his landlord forbade him to hang his clothing out his only window and ventilation source, lest the housing authority learn of his illegal construction job.

Public Health, Migrant Lives, and Cultural Competence

More so than other public health practices and interventions, TB contact investigations bring health workers into the intimate folds of daily immigrant life. When a case is brought to the attention of health departments—usually when a migrant presents him or herself to a clinic or emergency room with advanced stages of the disease (as the first case study demonstrates) or is reported by an employer—a frantic investigation is touched off to locate all potential active cases based on household data, including residential patterns, number of roommates, and interactions with neighbors and other guests. The relationships that form between health outreach workers (often entry-level staff with little or no medical training) and migrants extend far beyond the contact investigation.

Since 1980, federal public health mandates have required that TB patients must be treated following Direct Observation Therapy (DOT), whereby a health care worker observes the intake of every dose of a medication regimen to ensure the completion of treatment and to prevent the chance of the emergence of multidrug resistance. The standard therapy is a "short-course" six-month chemotherapy regimen starting with daily doses and shifting to biweekly doses after four months. Individuals who have been exposed to someone with active disease but are asymptomatic are also placed on a preventative therapy course that does not require direct observation. For TB

patients (migrant or not) and the health outreach workers assigned to administer DOT, coordinating times to receive and administer medications
can often be a headache. Cultural differences and language barriers become
a complicating layer in this interaction.

I began my consultancy with the RCDOH by reviewing contact investigations that involved Ecuadorian migrants. I interviewed outreach workers
who had participated in investigations and were assigned to administer
DOT. I later followed up with visits to the households of the migrants involved. The homes I have visited all reflect the necessities of saving money
and keeping costs down. Beyond crowding, the quality of housing is often
such that dwellings not infrequently lack heat and adequate water and are
in a general state of disrepair. Outreach workers were often shocked at the
hardscrabble lives they were exposed to during contact investigations. The
crowding and bed sharing shocked them. They dwelled on the fact that migrants seemed to subsist on almost nothing but parboiled white rice and a
few overcooked vegetables (thus removing their nutritional content, as they
pointed out). In one case, in a house that I visited numerous times for my
work, outreach workers were fascinated by a bathtub that was being used
to raise ten or so guinea pigs, an Andean culinary specialty (*cuy*) to be
roasted at a Christmas feast. The urine from the animals produced an almost
unbearable stench.

Although they could grow easily frustrated with migrants who did not
actively follow through with their DOT regimen, for the most part outreach
workers demonstrated a genuine compassion for the Ecuadorians they en-
countered in their jobs and expressed an eager desire to "know their culture." Rockland's two full-time outreach workers for TB were native Spanish speakers (both *mestizas* from Colombia and Guatemala) who were
selected largely for their language abilities and their presumed cultural similarity to the Ecuadorian population. These hires were part of a larger move
to put "cultural competence" measures into public health practice with new
immigrant groups in the county. At its core, cultural competence, according
to the National Center for Cultural Competence, seeks to "(1) value diversity; (2) conduct self-assessment; (3) manage the dynamics of difference;
(4) acquire and institutionalize cultural knowledge; and (5) adapt to diversity and cultural contexts of communities they serve."[50] In short, health
workers were trained to see the obstacles of immigrant health as problems
of tackling cultural difference.

Although such measures are without a doubt a critical component of
working with new immigrant populations with vastly different ethnomed-

ical systems from Euroamerican biomedicine, the reaction to "know Ecuadorian culture" and understand their work through cultural lenses often had the unintended consequence of keeping outreach workers from identifying the fact that migrant lives are in many ways structured by economic necessities and overarching political and economic structures. A focus on beliefs can easily erase the fact that migrant groups often lack the ability to change their situation or improve their health, and it is these factors, not cultural beliefs in and of themselves, that structure risks for poor health. Indeed, outreach workers who knew something of the diet in Ecuador often took the fact that migrants subsisted off rice to be evidence of a cultural preference *for* rice. Similarly, keeping guinea pigs in a bathtub was interpreted as "tradition" of living closely with animals, rather than anything to do with the limited choices migrants have with respect to living arrangements and available space. Positioning cultural difference before economic situations, moreover, often served to inhibit the possibility that health workers could identify commonalities between the living situations of migrants and other underserved poor and U.S. minority populations whose health is also compromised by disparities in access to care and a lack of economic choices.

A similar case in point demonstrating the ways cultural competence training colors public health perceptions of immigrant life was revealed in the frustration outreach workers expressed to me over trying to get accurate housing information after disease outbreaks. Unfortunately, it was my own introduction of cultural factors into the mix of interpretations that further colored their perceptions and narrowed their analyses. When I began my work, the outreach workers expressed a strong need to understand why migrants seemed elusive during contact investigations and why they provided what they considered to be "false information" about housing arrangements and domestic occupancy. As one outreach worker put it, "When we asked X where he lived, he gave one address, an apartment on Violet Street. When we asked him about other people he had potentially come into contact with, he listed a different group of people he lived with and then gave us another address where he claimed he resided. They all give multiple addresses." Outreach workers, in some respects, anticipated this kind of elusive behavior from undocumented migrants, especially in the post-9/11 climate. To be sure, health workers see as one of their major obstacles migrants' fear of immigration enforcement and the potential of deportation. Though fear of *la migra* has been demonstrated to have only a limited effect upon migrants' use of public health services,[51] outreach workers were further puzzled by the fact that all the information migrants furnished was correct—each household contained who they said it did and the addresses all checked out. If this was the case, why would migrants give so much conflicting information regarding their housing patterns?

In late 2001, I gave a short talk on my preliminary results at the RCDOH that I later came to regret. To answer the question regarding why Ecuadorian migrants were giving multiple addresses during contact investigations, I floated a hypothesis that the problem was not fear of immigration services but rather had to do with how public institutions like health departments conceptualize household formation. Contact investigation forms borrow terminology from conventional census models, which typically insist that "each person belongs to a single domestic group, and locates that 'household' in a single spot on the map in an identifiable 'community.'"[52] By contrast, I argued that Andean definitions of household are based less in notion of bounded units and more within different notions of "corporateness." In the Andes, household corporateness is invariably conceptualized not by where one necessarily sleeps but rather where and with whom one eats. Households, in short, are constituted by the sharing of hearths.[53] Because the migrants I interviewed expressed a certain fluidity in their movements, sharing meals with one or two friends or relatives (and their roommates) they had in Rockland, it was logical that they would define "their household" differently than outreach workers working with standardized contact investigation forms.

Under the guise of cultural competence, my remarks about household formation were quickly translated by outreach workers to be cultural differences and barriers. What I had failed to communicate in my talk were the reasons for the housing pattern. In the Andes, defining households as they do is structured by a need to pool resources, including food, cooking responsibilities, and child care. It is largely a sociocultural adaptation to an economic necessity. There were no reasons to believe that the patterns the Ecuadorian migrants interviewed in contact investigations were not also conforming to the economic necessities of migrant life on the margins. Indeed, as many migrant informants told me, moving around and staying at different domiciles helped migrants to hold down multiple jobs in different locations of the county (and outside the county) and ensure they would make it to work on time. In Rockland, the spatial layout of the town and villages—coupled with the lack of adequate public transportation—often translated into migrants maintaining multiple residences. (Among the lore of migrants is the idea of the *cama caliente* (literally, "hot bed"), a reference to sharing beds. As one migrant gets up to leave for a work, another is just returning, perhaps from an evening shift, just in time to take over the warm covers of the recently slept-in bed.) As I later tried to argue to a group of health workers, if divorced from an overemphasis on cultural beliefs, paying closer attention to this sociocultural adaptation to the structural constraints of living in a region without adequate transportation or full-time work could possibly lead to expanded and improved TB control.

Beyond Cultural Beliefs: Self-Medication in a Transnational Community

When the migrants I interviewed began feeling sick from the symptoms of active TB, their first instinct was to avoid their symptoms and continue working. Working as "*agotados*" (exhausted ones) often entailed coping with illness while on the job. With TB, many mistakenly (or hopefully) assumed that they had a bronchial infection and took advantage of an informal dispensary of antibiotics sold by Dominican immigrants who have medications sent from the Caribbean. As one migrant told me, "Whenever I felt sick, I would pop another pill. I can't afford to stop working."

However, persistent illness often called for a different hierarchy of resorts, one that did not necessarily involve seeking the aid of physician or attending a public health clinic, despite migrants' knowledge and previous use of these services both in the United States and in Ecuador. Rather, migrants first seek out their own remedies, cures, and practices of self-medication. Though self-medication is informed, at one level, by cultural beliefs about health and illness (ethnomedicine), it is perhaps best viewed as occurring at the intersection of two sociocultural systems of therapy management: the cultural background of migrants and the political and socioeconomic context in which they find themselves in receiving societies. Cultural competence approaches to public health, however, often privilege the former without fully taking the latter context into consideration when devising outreach programs.

To understand the logic of migrants' therapeutic decisionmaking processes requires a brief discussion of Andean ethnomedicine and, in particular, Andean-specific beliefs and health behaviors regarding TB (known as "*pulmón*"—simply, "lung"—in Spanish; or "the coughing sickness," *umkusha unguy,* in Quichua). At a very general level, TB is understood as caused by the imbalance of body heat (between hot and cold). Specifically, being exposed to cold winds, water, or other symbolically cold-identified forces can all structure one's susceptibility to TB. As such, many sick migrants who crossed illegally into the United States think that crossing the frigid waters of the Rio Grande made them sick.

Hot/cold (humoral) illnesses in Ecuador are attended to using a host of home remedies (*remedios caseros*). Being harmed by cold elements ("*resfrío dañado*") requires a complementary "hot" remedy. One of the simplest measures employed by sick migrants is to literally work through an illness by generating a great sweat. But it is more common to seek the aid of family members back home and enlist their knowledge of remedies. Ecuadorians employ various strategies of health care in a transnational hierarchy of resort. In the traffic of consumer goods and remittances between the United States and Ecuador also flow medicines. Through the same agencies that handle remittances, families in Ecuador send sick loved ones a host of *remedios,* including syrups, vitamin B complex injections, herbs, and tinctures. Families also send biomedical pharmaceuticals, such as antibiotics, which are easily obtained without a prescription in Ecuador. Transnational medical practices also include consultations, and sometimes healings, by Ecuadorians traditional healers (*curanderos/as,* Spanish; *yachaks,* Quichua). In these instances, family members take photographs of migrants to *yachaks* to be diagnosed with traditional methods using candles, eggs, and guinea pigs as diagnostic tools. *Yachaks* also provide transnational healings by curing sick migrants using the photo as a proxy.

When the migrants I interviewed get sick, their actions and health-seeking behaviors were heavily influenced by the shaping of their transnational communities, much to the consternation of health officials. As I mentioned above, health officials worry about not just the size of an outbreak but also its severity. The severity of a case upon detection suggests the degree to which migrants delay care. For public health officials, the response to the extreme severity of a number of detected TB cases (including pediatric cases) suggested problems related to cultural barriers to access. In the hierarchy of resort, biomedicine ranked low, not because of a fear of medical practices or barriers to access but largely because of its equation with missed work. Because of their heavy debt loads, migrants worried that missing even a couple of days of earnings would seriously compromise their abilities to make loan payments and care for their families back home. This kind of logic served to make rational the choice to delay care as long as possible. In some cases, even the choice of returning to Ecuador for treatment was a therapy option in the context of transnational community life. Some migrants described how they delayed seeking care for as long as possible with the eventual plan to simply return to Ecuador and their families when they became too sick.

New Immigrant Gateways, Transnational Migrants, and the Challenges for Public Health: Beyond Acculturation Models

Clinic staff, emergency room attendants, outreach workers, and other types of health care providers are often the first individuals undocumented migrants encounter as they maneuver their way through city, county, and state institutions and services. Whether it is migrants themselves who seek out health care—for example, to give birth; to obtain Women, Infants, and Children Program (WIC) services; or to get help for sick children—where health workers seek out migrants, public health broadly defined often serves as the critical interface between governing institutions and immigrant populations. City and county public health departments are unique in the sense that they are charged with ensuring the well-being of immigrants and other underserved populations while at same time ensuring the "public" is in good health. In a climate of Proposition 187–like measures that seek to restrict health services to undocumented persons, public health workers often find themselves in the dual role of providing services to migrants and assuring them they can take advantage of these services without recrimination.

Public health departments are at the forefront of efforts by expanding regions, such as New York's Rockland and Westchester counties, to embrace their roles as "new immigrant gateways." They have worked to remove standard barriers to health care access, attending to interpretation services and the printing of culturally sensitive education materials. Indeed, cultural competence has become a mantra of immigrant health programs. As described in a recent overview of immigrant health initiates in New York City, cultural competence or "cultural sensitivity" is "presented as part of a general understanding of immigrants' sociocultural context and its impact on health care behaviors." Health workers learn to "address language barriers and how to work with interpreters, entitlements and legal issues, previous experiences with the health care system, and *the influences of culture on health care practices and provider-patient interaction.*[54]

Although the implementation of these programs is to be applauded—indeed, they are a great improvement over the "cultural incompetence" of health care of the past[55]—health officials and policymakers must scrutinize how the culture concept and models of cultural barriers shape public health initiatives and programs. Even calls for "transnational competence" that seek to make educators, health workers, and social work agencies more attuned to issues of immigration tend to overlook the ethnographic reality that transnational migration is, in most cases, an economic survival strategy rather than a cultural preference.[56] As I have stressed throughout this chapter, such efforts are an important component of an immigrant health program attuned to the political and economic factors of migration. Still, such apparitions of culture should not stand in for templates of migrants' lives and daily struggles, nor should they form exclusively the idea of "community" in community health. Culture is not a monolithic feature of ethnic and racial groups; it is a process that is fluid and adaptive to new situations, as anthropologists have long argued.

During my interactions at the RCDOH, I came to realize that public health workers were not entirely bound by such monolithic constructions of culture as some of the literature in my own discipline had suggested.[57] Indeed, in meetings of the county's Immigration Coalition and other migrant health coordinating committees, members often found solace in the "newness" of migration. In their understanding, new immigrants such as Quichua-speaking *indígenas* (indigenous peoples) from rural Ecuador were different, but they were also recent arrivals who were green to American society, culture, and beliefs in biomedical healthcare. "Over time they will give up their cultural beliefs" was a oft-repeated declaration I heard in the meetings. Similarly, a local news article about the "Hispanicization" of New York's northern suburbs quoted a social worker from a Hispanic community center discussing a series of wellness programs for new immigrants: "We had a yoga session and there were a couple of [Latino] men there. This is a sign of acculturation."[58]

In my interviews and observations with clinic staff, I often heard discussions of "acculturation" as the public health answer to dealing with new immigration populations. "Noncompliance," a frequent description pinned on migrants who did not finish their TB medications, was framed as a cultural problem (rather than a structural one), and one that would be remedied with immigrant acculturation. As the explanation often went, with time, migrants would adapt, learn the procedures and "culture" of biomedicine, and become more compliant. The role of cultural competence training, then, was to help migrants on to the path of becoming acculturated.

Such nods to a theory of acculturation, however, often missed the dynamic way the formation and perpetuation of transnational communities shaped migrant identities and practices. Though, for example, a pamphlet about biomedical symptoms and treatments for TB written in Quichua that I helped to develop may no doubt assist in educating some migrants to watch for symptoms, such acts of subtly forced acculturation will likely not stymie transnational practices of health care. As the vignette that opens this chapter suggests, the contrary may be true: many migrants experience an *intensification* of cultural identity as they look to home for health remedies. For many young migrants, calling home and learning about "traditional medicine" put them in touch not only with their families but also with a set of cultural practices and beliefs to which they had not paid very much attention in their youth. In the context of a transnational community, what looks like acculturation may more often be *en*culturaltion as migrants' affinities to their home communities strengthen in the context of feelings of isolation and marginalization.

Conclusion

The transformation of suburban areas into "new immigrant gateways" has been one of the most surprising and perplexing findings of the 2000 U.S. Census. The introduction of new immigrants into these areas is both profoundly reshaping long-held definitions and understandings of what constitutes a suburban area and transforming the ways local governments conceptualize their roles in these spaces. In Rockland County, New York, constant immigrant settlement throughout the latter part of the last century has created an urban mosaic on what is still largely a suburban geography. In this chapter, I have traced the challenges and responses of public health officials to address the vexing problem of immigrant TB among newly arrived indigenous Andean migrants from highland Ecuador. By focusing primarily on the lives of the migrants themselves, I have tried to show the importance of placing public health initiatives within a transnational perspective. Doing this, I have argued, helps to illuminate both how migrants themselves conceptualize, use, and transform urban landscapes and to elucidate how local governments and social service institutions can better anticipate and adapt to these changes.

In the context of public health, however, responses to the needs of immigrants have long been incorporated into practice. As discussed above, community health initiatives and cultural competency training are common fixtures of accommodating new immigrants. Though these efforts should be lauded and their obvious benefits can be demonstrated, in this chapter I have argued for a cautionary stance toward the wholesale acceptance of these models with respect to the day-to-day realities of many new immigrants. The recognition that transnationalism is more than a theoretical model to explain new patterns of migration—that it is an important survival strategy for migrants living without essential resources—has significant implications for understanding the how and why new immigrants use health services. In suburban areas like Rockland, for instance, the maintenance of kin ties to home communities thousands of miles away is a crucial means for migrants to foster the kinds of support structures that allow them to live and earn money to be sent home as remittances. How transnational practices affect the lives of migrants, however, often flies in the face of the common approaches public health and other essential services put in place to meet the needs of a diverse immigrant population. Yet by questioning narrow definitions of community (as used in "community" health) and by interrogating the implicit understandings of assimilation that accompany cultural competency training, it is possible to see how these otherwise positive initiatives may not serve the populations they hope to reach.

Notes

Acknowledgments: This research was conducted under the auspices of the Rockland County Department of Health during intermittent fieldwork between 2001 and 2004. My sincere thanks to the entire staff working in the division of TB and Communicable Diseases at the RCDOH—the physicians, nurses, outreach workers, epidemiologists, and other public health staff that gave the generosity of their time and expertise. For purposes of anonymity, I have chosen not to mention individuals by name. Additional fieldwork funding was provided by research and travel funds from North Central College and Whitman College. A special thanks to Sixto Masaquiza, my Quichua interpreter in the field.

1. All proper names used in this chapter are pseudonyms; however, they are similar to the variety of first and last names found in south-central Ecuador.

2. Centers for Disease Control and Prevention, "Trends in Tuberculosis—United States, 2004," *Mortality and Morbidity Weekly Report* 54, no. 10 (2004): 245–49. In 2004, 14,511 confirmed cases of tuberculosis (4.9 cases per 100,000 population) were reported to the Centers for Disease Control and Prevention. Though this number represents a 3.3 percent decrease over 2003, rates for foreign-born persons have been steadily rising since the mid-1990s.

3. Audrey Singer, *The Rise of New Immigrant Gateways* (Washington, D.C.: Center on Urban and Metropolitan Policy, Brookings Institution, 2004).

4. William H. Frey, *Melting Pot Suburbs: A Census 2000 Study of Suburban Diversity* (Washington, D.C.: Center on Urban and Metropolitan Policy, Brookings Institution, 2001); Richard Alba, John Logan, Brian Stults, Gilbert Marzan, and Wenquan Zhang, "Immigrant Groups and Suburbs: A Reexamination of Suburbanization and Spa-

tial Assimilation," *American Sociological Review* 64 (1999): 446–60. For an ethnographic treatment of this phenomenon, see Sarah J. Mahler, *American Dreaming: Immigrant Life on the Margins* (Princeton, N.J.: Princeton University Press, 1995).

5. Jack R. Logan, "The New Latinos: Who They Are, Where They Are—Report on Metropolitan Racial and Ethnic Change, Census 2000," Lewis Mumford Center for Comparative Urban and Regional Research, State University of New York at Albany, 2001; Julie Moran Alterio, "New York Suburbs are Magnet for Immigrants," *Journal News,* March 20, 2005.

6. Ecuador, El Salvador, Guatemala, and Haiti are all countries with "severe case rates" of TB (over 85 per 100,000 cases); Pan American Health Organization, "Pan American Health Organization Tuberculosis Control Report 2004."

7. These data are courtesy of the New York State Department of Health Bureau of Tuberculosis Control and the Rockland County Department of Health.

8. These data are from the Queens Department of Health, 2001. See also Barbara J. Fleck, "Battle against Tuberculosis: Number of Cases among Ecuadorians Alarms Health Officials," *Newsday,* January 1, 2003.

9. A note regarding terminology is in order. Following conventions in the transnationalism literature, I use the terms "migrant" and "migration" rather than "immigrant" and "immigration" throughout this chapter to stress the transitory status of Ecuadorians in the United States, whereas "immigration" assumes a unidirectional movement. In most cases, I reserve the term "immigration" for discussions of government policy toward migrants, including public health services. My use of the term "undocumented migrant" loosely follows the definition provided by Chavez and his colleagues: "individuals who are living or working in the United States with out permission from Immigration and Naturalization Services (INS). They are not permanent legal residents of the United States. They typically entered the country without passing through a standard INS check for passports, visas, and entry permits . . . [or] they presented false documentation." For a extended discussion of this definition, see Leo R. Chavez, Estevan T. Flores, and Marta Lopez-Garza, "Undocumented Latin American Immigrants and U.S. Health Services: An Approach to a Political Economy of Utilization," *Medical Anthropology Quarterly* 6 (1992): 6–26. The INS, of course, has now been subsumed and reorganized under the Department of Homeland Security.

10. Linda Stone, "Cultural Influences in Community Participation in Health," *Social Science and Medicine* 35 (1999): 409–17; Lynn M. Morgan, "Community Participation in Health: Perpetual Allure, Persistent Challenge," *Health Policy and Planning* 16 (2001): 221–30; R. Jewkes and A. Murcott, "Meanings of Community," *Social Science and Medicine* 43 (1996): 555–63; Susan J. Shaw, "The Politics of Recognition in Culturally Appropriate Care," *Medical Anthropology Quarterly* 19 (2005): 290–309; Lenore Manderson and Pascale Allotey, "Storytelling, Marginality, and Community in Australia: Immigrants Position Their Difference in Health Care Settings," *Medical Anthropology* 22 (2003): 1–22.

11. Jewkes and Murcott, "Meanings of Community," 555.

12. Merrill Singer, "Reinventing Medical Anthropology: Toward a Critical Realignment," *Social Science and Medicine* 30 (1990): 182.

13. Linda Basch, Schiller, Nina Glick, and Constance Szanton-Blanc, *Nations Unbound: Transnationalized Projects and the Deterritorialized Nation-State* (New York: Gordon and Breach, 1994); Michael Kearney, "The Local and Global: The Anthropology of Globalization and Transnationalism," *Annual Review of Anthropology* 24 (1995): 547–65;

Roger Rouse, "Mexican Migration to the United States: Family Relations in the Development of a Transnational Migration Circuit" PhD dissertation, Stanford University, 1989.

14. Nina Glick Schiller, Linda Basch, and Cristina Szanton Blanc, "From Immigrant to Transmigrant: Theorizing Transnational Migration," *Anthropology Quarterly* 68 (1995): 48.

15. Luis E. Guarzino and Michael P. Smith, "The Locations of Transnationalism," in *Transnationalism from Below*, ed. Michael P. Smith and Luis Guarzino (New Brunswick, N.J.: Transaction Publishers, 1997), 9; original emphases.

16. Roger Rouse, "Mexican Migration and the Social Space of Postmodernism," *Diaspora* 1 (1991): 14.

17. Jen Plypa, "Self-Medication Practices in Two California Mexican Communities," *Journal of Immigrant Health* 3 (2001): 59–75; Cecilia Menjívar, "The Ties That Heal: Guatemalan Immigrant Women's Networks and Medical Treatment," *International Migration Review* 36 (2002): 437; De Ann Pendry, "Crossing Borders with Information and Resources for the Treatment of Diabetes," in *The Survival Strategies of Families in Poverty in the United States Border Region / Estrategía de sobrevívencia de families pobres en la region fronteriza de México y Estados Unidos,* ed. David M. Austin and Manuel Ribeiro Ferreira (Austin and Monterrey: School of Social Work, University of Texas, Austin, and Facultad de Trabajo Social, Universidad Autónoma de Nuevo León, 1998), 121–55; Norah Anita Schwartz, "Childhood Asthma on the Northern Mexican Border," *Medical Anthropology Quarterly* 18 (2004): 214–29; DeAnne K. Hilfinger-Messias, "Transnational Health Resources, Practices, and Perspectives: Brazilian Immigrant Women's Narratives," *Journal of Immigrant Health* 4 (2002): 183–200; Beth Kangas, "Therapeutic Itineraries in a Global World: Yemenis and Their Search for Biomedical Treatment Abroad," *Medical Anthropology* 21 (2002): 35–78.

18. My term is a an adaptation of the concept coined by Romanucci-Ross. See Lola Romanucci-Ross, "The Hierarchy of Resort in Curative Practices: The Admiralty Islands, Melanesia," *Journal of Health and Social Behavior* 10 (1969): 201–09.

19. For useful discussions of methodological approaches to studying undocumented migrant and other "hidden" populations, see Wayne A. Cornelius, "Interviewing Undocumented Immigrants: Methodological Reflections Based on Fieldwork in Mexico and the U.S.," *International Migration Review* 16 (1982): 378–404; Merrill Singer, "Studying Hidden Populations," in *Mapping Social Networks, Spatial Data, and Hidden Populations,* ed. Jean J. Shensul, Margaret D. LeCompte, Robert T. Trotter II, Ellen K. Cromley, and Merrill Singer (Walnut Creek, Calif.: Altimira Press, 1999); and Paul Stoller, "Globalizing Method," *Anthropology and Humanism* 17 (1997): 81–95.

20. The paucity of both well-established immigrant neighborhoods and only a lukewarm immigrant-friendly environment prompts the question of why migrants would come to Rockland in the first place. How did a stream of Ecuadorians end up in suburban New York rather than the more established Queens or Brooklyn? Interviews with migrants revealed the importance of kinship and friend networks in this regard. In most cases, migrants had a close relative that told them about the area or offered to help them once they arrived. In most cases, migrants had only the dimmest understanding of geography and sometimes only knew the specific town name where they wanted to go. (New York looms so large in the Ecuadorian imagination that relatively far away places where Cañari migrants have also ended up (e.g., Connecticut and Massachusetts) are thought to be parts of New York in the same way Queens or Brooklyn are. The distinction between "suburb" and "city" and "inner city"—let alone "new" and "old" immi-

grant gateways—meant nothing to migrants I interviewed. In some cases, migrants expressed a belief that wages were higher in the suburban areas and they were less crime ridden. See the similarities in Mahler, *American Dreaming.*

A clue to what made Rockland appear "immigrant" friendly to new groups entering in the 1990s came from members of the Immigrant Coalition and the Jornalero Project that I interviewed. They identified the roots of the county's immigration explosion in the Sanctuary Movement that helped thousands of undocumented refuges from war-torn Central America to safely enter the United States. Although such efforts won admiration for local church groups they also sparked considerable controversy. There is a common perception in Rockland that the Sanctuary Movement was responsible for the massive explosion of immigrants in recent years and the perception of their taxing of county services.

21. Jason Pribilsky, *La Chulla Vida: Gender, Migration, and the Family in Andean Ecuador and New York City* (Syracuse: Syracuse University Press, 2007).

22. The 2000 U.S. Census enumerated 122,472 Ecuadorians in New York State, the majority (nearly 60 percent) concentrated in the New York City metropolitan area. This figure, when adjusted for undercounting (given that an estimated 70 percent of the population is undocumented), is likely closer to 250,000. These data are contained in "New Latinos," by Logan. See also Brad Jokisch and Jason Pribilsky, "The Panic to Leave": Economic Crisis and the 'New Emigration' from Ecuador," *International Migration* 40 (2002): 75–101.

23. A good introduction to the Cañari is Hugo Burgos Guevara, *La Identidad de Pueblo Cañari: Deconstrucción de una nación étnica* (Quito: Ediciones Abya-Yala, 2003). Also see Lynn Hirshkind, "History of the Indian Population of Cañar," *Colonial Latin American History Review* 3 (1995): 311–42.

24. Because Rockland's Ecuadorian migrant population has arrived only recently, it is too early to make predictions about permanent settlement patterns or the average length of stay. Based on research with undocumented migrants in Queens, most migrants stay between two and five years before returning home. After returning, a number of men in my Queens sample made return trips to the United States. See Pribilsky, *La Chulla Vida,* for elaboration of these data. See also Jokisch and Pribilsky, "Panic to Leave," 75–101.

25. Smuggling women tends to cost more than men and, in the rare cases that it happens, the smuggling of children can almost double the price.

26. Alejandro Portes and Rubén Rumbaut, *Immigrant America: A Portrait* (Berkeley: University of California Press, 1996).

27. This quotation comes from Brettell's contribution to this volume. Also see Caroline B. Brettell, "Bringing the City Back In: Cities as Context for Immigrant Incorporation," in *American Arrivals: Anthropology Engages the New Immigration,* ed. Nancy Foner (Santa Fe: School of American Research, 2003), 163–95.

28. Useful works on the history of Rockland County include Frank B. Green, *History of Rockland County* (New City, N.Y.: Historical Society of Rockland County, 1886); Linda Zimmerman, ed., *Rockland County Century of History* (New City, N.Y.: Historical Society of Rockland County, 2002); and Joyce Ghee, *History Keepers' Companion: Guide to Sites and Sources of the Lower Hudson Valley and Western Connecticut* (N.p., n.d.).

29. Harold L. Larrof, "The Beginnings of Rockland's Jewish Communities, " in *Rockland County Century of History,* ed. Linda Zimmerman (New City, N.Y.: Historical Society of Rockland County, 2002), 15.

30. Randi Weiner, "The Beginnings of Hispanic/Latino Communities," in *Rockland County,* ed. Zimmerman, 16.

31. Morton Marks, *Haitians on the Hudson: The Formation of the Haitian Communities of Rockland County* (New City, N.Y.: Historical Society of Rockland County, 1993), 12–13.

32. James S. Duncan and Nancy G. Duncan, *Landscapes of Privilege: The Politics of the Aesthetic in an American Suburb* (New York: Routledge, 2004): 177–80.

33. See chapter 2 in this volume by Salazar Parreñas.

34. *Sanjuanito* and *huayno* are two musical styles popular with Andean peoples. Many of the songs of these genres have migration themes popular with Ecuadorians in the United States.

35. Pribilsky, *La Chulla Vida,* chap. 5.

36. See Sharon Zukin, "Artists and Immigrants in New York City Restaurants," in *The Cultures of Cities* by Sharon Zukin (Oxford: Blackwell Publishers), 153–86.

37. Women, who never work as *esquineros* tended to shed their indigenous dress more slowly. Women often continue to wear *polleras* yet pair them with "Western" clothing, including fleece jackets and T-shirts.

38. Abel Valenzuela Jr. and Edwin Meléndez, "Day Labor in New York: Findings from NYDL Survey," report from Center for the Study of Urban Poverty, University of California, Los Angeles, and Community Development Research Center, New School University, New York, 2003.

39. See Ron Gumucio, "Day Laborers Finally Get Money from Contractors," *Journal News,* December 13, 2003.

40. Here I am thinking of Anderson's emphasis on media as fostering a sense of community. See Benedict Anderson, *Imagined Communities* (New York: Verso, 1983).

41. Brettell, "Bringing the City Back In."

42. Indeed, the census revealed that one than one-third (34.7 percent) of the county's foreign-born population had entered since 1990. The anti-immigration organization Federation for American Immigration Reform (FAIR) made publication of these data in popular media outlets a top priority.

43. Though I have not carried out fieldwork in Rockland since this incident to ascertain the effects the ensuing anti-immigration sentiment has had on the Ecuadorian population, anecdotal information received from health department workers suggest that the impact has been substantial. A number of Ecuadorian patients have left the area to settle in suburban areas of Boston, another receiving community for Cañari migrants. Some migrants abandoned their TB treatment when they moved out of the county (personal communication, director of TB Control, RCDOH).

44. Michael Burawoy, "The Functions and Reproductions of Migrant Labor: Comparative Material from Southern Africa and the United States," *American Journal of Sociology* 8 (1976): 1050–87.

45. Sherry B. Ortner, "Reflections on Fieldwork in the Postcommunity," *Anthropology and Humanism* 22 (1997): 61–80.

46. See also the work of Ming-Jung Ho for a similar argument. Ming-Jung Ho, "Migratory Journeys and Tuberculosis Risk," *Medical Anthropology Quarterly* 17 (2003): 442–58; Ming-Jung Ho, "Sociocultural Aspects of Tuberculosis: A Literature Review and a Case Study of Immigrant Tuberculosis," *Social Science and Medicine* 59 (2004): 753–62. For a historical treatment of the relationship between TB and migration in the United States, see Alan M. Kraut, *Silent Travelers: Germs, Genes, and the "Immigrant*

Menace" (New York: Basic Books, 1994).

47. René J Dubos, with Jean Dubos, *The White Plague: Tuberculosis, Man, and Society* (New Brunswick, N.J.: Rutgers University Press, 1996; original ed.: London: Gollancz, 1953), 10.

48. Pribilsky, *La Chulla Vida.*

49. Arjun Appadurai, *Modernity at Large: Cultural Dimensions of Globalization* (Minneapolis: University of Minnesota Press, 1996).

50. T. L. Cross, B. J. Bazron, M. R. Isaacs, and K. W. Dennis, *Towards a Culturally Competent System of Care: A Monograph on Effective Services for Minority Children Who Are Severely Emotionally Disturbed* (Washington, D.C.: Georgetown University Center for Child Health and Mental Health Policy, CASSP Technical Assistance Center, 1989).

51. Steven Asch, Barbara Leake, and Lillian Gelberg, "Does Fear of Immigration Authorities Deter Tuberculosis Patients from Seeking Care?" *Western Journal of Medicine* 161 (1994): 373–76.

52. Richard Wilk and Stephen Miller, "Some Methodological Issues in Counting Communities and Households," *Human Organization* 56 (1997): 64.

53. See, e.g., Mary Weismantel, "Making Breakfast and Raising Babies," in *The Household Economy: Reconsidering the Domestic Mode of Production,* ed. Richard Wilk (Boulder, Colo.: Westview Press, 1994), 52–72.

54. Heike Thiel de Bocanegra and Francesca Gany, "Providing Health Services to Immigrant and Refugee Populations in New York," in *Health and Social Services among International Labor Migrants,* ed. Antonio Ugalde and Gilberto Cárdenas (Austin: University of Texas Press, 1997), 33–34; emphasis added.

55. Jennifer S. Hirsch, "Anthropologists, Migrants, and Health Research: Confronting Cultural Appropriateness," in *American Arrivals,* ed. Foner.

56. Peter H. Koehn, "Global Politics and Multinational Health-Care Encounters: Assessing the Role of Transnational Competence," *EcoHealth* 1 (2003): 69–85.

57. See, e.g., Janelle Taylor, "The Story Catches You and You Fall Down: Tragedy, Ethnography, and 'Cultural Competence,' " *Medical Anthropology Quarterly* 71 (2003): 159–81; and Vilma Santiago-Irizarry, *Medicalizing Ethnicity: The Construction of Latino Identity in a Psychiatric Setting* (Ithaca, N.Y.: Cornell University Press, 2001).

58. Leah Rae, "Hispanics Transform the Region," *Journal News,* March 25, 2003.

9

Local Authority Responses to Immigrants: The German Case

Barbara Schmitter Heisler

The vast majority of immigrants in advanced industrial societies live in cities. Cities are the places where immigrants find work, housing, schools, support services, and religious and leisure facilities, and where their own social networks are located. Though national laws and policies establish the legal framework for migration, determining who may or may not come and who may or may not be permitted to settle, it is in cities that immigrants make prolonged contact with the host society, its institutions, and its people.

Although the laws and regulations pertaining to migration are codified and tend to be relatively unambiguous (I do not imply that they may not be subject to challenges from groups or individuals, and that they change over time), beyond national laws pertaining to access to political citizenship, most immigrant societies lack clear and consistent national policies for immigrant integration.[1] In this context, the "incidental collision, conflicts and fusion of peoples and of cultures" accompanying immigration take place at the local level where local authorities must negotiate the increasing cultural and political diversity of their resident populations.[2]

The growing literature on cities and immigration has tended to focus on a handful of large cities, in particular those defined as "global cities,"[3] or "gateway cities."[4] Though these conceptual categories illustrate and perhaps magnify many of the characteristics and issues associated with the presence of large immigrant populations (immigrant settlement)—that is, their spatial concentration, their concentration in low-skill jobs at the bottom of the economy, education and language disparities between them and native populations—the conditions and processes observed in these cities may or may not be similar to those occurring in other, perhaps less glamorous cities that have tended to be relegated to the sidelines of immigration theory and research.

In this chapter, I focus on how German cities have negotiated the challenges posed by immigration. As is the case elsewhere, Germany's immigrant population is predominantly urban. Eighty percent of the foreign population lives in large cities (*Grossstädte*) with populations above 100,000.[5] Though the average proportion of immigrants in such cities is about 15 percent, it ranges from a high of almost 30 percent in Frankfurt to a relatively low 10 percent in Essen.[6]

The German case is particularly interesting for several reasons.[7] First, until recently, the German government had been reluctant to recognize that Germany had become a country of immigration. As a consequence, Germany had been lacking both immigration and immigrant policies.[8] The presence of large numbers of immigrants was an unintended consequence of guest worker recruitment and settlement, asylum and refugee policies, and special policies for ethnic Germans from Eastern Europe (*Aussiedler*) and for Jews from the former Soviet Union.[9]

Until recently, German citizenship laws based on the principle of jus sanguinis (a child's citizenship is determined by its parent's citizenship) made access to political citizenship, generally deemed a necessary (if not sufficient) condition to immigrant integration, difficult for the former guest workers and their descendents, who represent the largest contingent of Germany's immigrant population.[10] Although recent (2000) changes in citizenship and naturalization laws liberalizing previous restrictive policies and the passage of a historic immigration law may change the dynamics of immigrant host society interactions, in the past thirty years, the interaction between German institutions and newcomers has taken place in a context of what Dietrich Thränhardt has called "an undeclared immigration country."[11]

Second, Germany has had a well-balanced system of cities displaying considerable variety in terms of size and social and physical makeup. They include industrial cities (Rhine–Ruhr Valley), media and publishing cities (Hamburg), cities of culture and high technology (Munich), cities of banking and finance (Frankfurt), cities of wholesale and trade insurance (Cologne and Düsseldorf), and cities shaped by their universities and research institutions.[12] Though the Ruhr Valley is often identified as the industrial center of Germany, compared with other European countries, western Germany's industrial structure is geographically more balanced, to include a variety of industrial centers. In addition, Germany has lacked a regionally dominant capital, a fact Thränhardt attributes to German historical development, in particular since World War II, including, until 1989, the relative isolation and strangulation of Berlin.[13]

Third, local authorities, including cities (*kreisfreie Städte*)[14] occupy a unique legal/structural position in the German federal system. The German political system, based on the principle of "subsidiarity" (*Subsidarität*), allocates much of the responsibility and administration of federal and state laws and policies to local authorities, which are thus charged with implementing 80 percent of state and federal policies.[15]

Fourth, and related, Article 28 of the federal Constitution (Basic Law, *Grundgesetz*) assigns to local authorities the specific mandate of "managing the affairs of resident population." It is important to note that the article refers to "resident population," not "nationals" or "citizens."[16] This constitutional mandate is complemented by the "German model" of the "social city" responsible "for socially balanced local living conditions and opportunities."[17] An important goal of city policies throughout the twentieth and early twenty-first centuries has been the promotion of the "social blending" (i.e., class integration) of residents at the neighborhood level.[18]

Despite considerable variation in city size and function and the size of their immigrant populations, all German cities have had to manage the consequences of national policies over which they have had no control. They have done so within the fiscal and legal constraints imposed by the Constitution and by their traditional creed as socially responsible actors. Recognizing the fact that the legal and constitutional constraints imposed on German cities are greater than those in other European countries, the Independent Commission on Immigration charged with studying immigration to Germany concluded in its final report released in 2001 that local authorities had put forth great efforts to promote the integration of newcomers.[19]

The commission also noted that there had been no systematic and comprehensive study and assessment of the integration efforts made by local communities. Though the German literature includes several studies that fo-

cus on specific aspects of integration policies in particular cities, this literature is exceedingly fragmented and unsystematic.[20] Comparative studies
of European cities have tended to focus on those in the United Kingdom,
the Netherlands, Belgium, and France and have often excluded German
cities.[21] The existing English-language literature on German cities has
tended to focus on two cities in particular, Frankfurt and Berlin. Both are
generally included among global or gateway cities.[22]

Although the attention given to Berlin and Frankfurt is not surprising
given their respective prominence as the capital of reunited Germany and as
its financial powerhouse, the literature often highlights the progressive policies pursued by these two cities, suggesting that they are unusual (for German cities in particular) and that other German cities are more conservative
and less tolerant. Thus, for example, Koopmans notes: "In Germany, for instance, there is a clear difference both in the rhetoric and in the practice of
'foreigners politics' between more liberal cities such as Berlin and Frankfurt
and conservative Southern states such as Bavaria."[23] While Koopmans seems
to be comparing different political entities—a city-state (Berlin), a city located in a traditionally more liberal state Hessen (Frankfurt), and a state
(Bavaria)—he also implies that cities in such comparatively conservative
states as Bavaria must be more conservative by definition.[24]

Patrick Ireland's detailed comparative research on local immigrant
politics in selected cities in three countries—Germany, Belgium, and the
Netherlands—challenges such assumptions.[25] Comparing the actions and
activities of four German cities—Essen and Nürnberg and two city-states,
Berlin and Bremen—Ireland found that Nürnberg, located in conservative
Bavaria, was not only among the first German cities to set up a foreigners'
council (in 1973) and the first to have such a council elected directly by the
immigrants themselves; the city was also among the first to embrace a multicultural policy.[26] This suggests that the question of whether cities in more
conservative states pursue a more conservative policy than those in liberal
states remains open.[27]

The purpose of this chapter is to broaden our understanding of how German cities have responded to the consequences of national policies over
which they have had no control while placing them at the forefront of having to respond to and negotiate the increasing cultural and political diversity of their resident populations. More specifically, this analysis focuses on
the changing "immigrant policies" pursued by two German cities, Stuttgart
and Munich.

After providing a brief outline of the legal and institutional context of local government action, I turn to a detailed analysis of the changing immigrant policies of Stuttgart and Munich. I have chosen these two cities for two reasons. First, despite the fact that they rank second and third in the percentages of their foreign populations (Frankfurt ranks first), their immigrant policies have not received much attention in the academic literature. Second, although Stuttgart and Munich are located in conservative states (respectively, Baden-Württemberg and Bavaria), their immigrant policies have been decidedly progressive, suggesting that despite German cities' fiscal and to some extent legal dependence on their state, location in a conservative states tells us little about their immigrant policies.

German Cities: The Structural Context

As noted above, German cities are not independent political units. They are embedded in three political levels, each affecting their abilities to act: the European Union, the federal government, and state governments. Though EU economic, social, and cultural decisions have increasing repercussions at the local level,[28] it is the German federal system that structures local authorities' abilities to act.

As indicated above, in Germany local authorities are charged with carrying out a large variety of administrative and legal tasks for federal and state governments, including the administration and execution of laws and the maintenance of infrastructure, as well as a variety of other tasks that vary somewhat from state to state.[29] Though it specifically allocates to cities the responsibility to "manage the affairs" of its residents, the German Constitution does not recognize local authorities as independent political units. They are part of state government and must fulfill their obligatory tasks within the German federal system.[30] Their major discretionary tasks are in the area of culture and recreation; that is, they maintain museums, organize festivals, and maintain sports facilities and parks. Unlike their American counterparts, German local authorities have only limited opportunities to raise their own revenue and are highly dependent on federal and state funds to carry out their obligatory and discretionary tasks.[31]

The constitutional mandate making cities responsible for managing the affairs of their resident populations, their role in the cultural realm, and their tradition as socially responsible actors places cities at the center of immigrant integration. Indeed, in the early 1970s, when federal policymakers clung to the illusion that the guest workers would eventually return to their countries of origin, cities were among the first German institutions (along with unions and churches) to take the then-unpopular position that Germany had become an immigration country and needed to adapt its policies accordingly. Taking the lead, in the early 1970s, many cities undertook initiatives to promote a better cultural understanding and greater cooperation between newcomers and native populations. This marked the beginning of a variety of local-level initiatives known as local *Ausländerpolitik* ("foreigners' policy").[32]

In the context of Germany's sluggish economy and federal and state fiscal problems, the legal and fiscal constraints imposed on cities have become increasingly burdensome beginning in the 1980s, when cuts in federal and state expenditures started to have devastating effects on local authority budgets.[33] At the same time, unemployment and in particular long-term unemployment and increasing numbers of asylum seekers have placed new and rising demands for a range of traditional city services. Foremost among them has been the increasing demand for social assistance.[34]

These economic and fiscal conditions have made it increasingly difficult for cities to live up to the tradition and image of the "social city." Thus, in 1993, the Commission for the Future of the City (Kommission Zukunft Stadt) concluded that "increased migration and rapid structural change" were posing a serious threat to traditional German city life.[35]

Immigrant Settlement: Challenges for Cities

Since its beginning in the mid-1950s and early 1960s, migration to Germany has been gradually transformed from a temporary guest worker system to the permanent settlement of newcomers and their families beginning in the early 1970s.[36] Although the guest worker population grew rapidly in the 1960s and early 1970s, the majority were single men (and a few women) who expected to return to their countries of origin after a few years. Guest workers were recruited for specific jobs, primarily as unskilled and semi-skilled workers in the booming industrial sector. Employers were obliged to provide housing in barracks and other communal-style arrangements, and immigrants had little contact with formal German institutions beyond the workplace.[37] The German government provided some social assistance to these newcomers through the three major welfare organizations (Caritas,

Diakonie, and Arbeiterwohlfahrt), whose local offices were staffed by social workers from the countries of origin.[38]

This situation changed significantly following the oil crisis of 1973, when the German government unilaterally put a halt to further recruitment. Though encouraging guest workers to return to their countries of origin, the government also allowed those unwilling or unable to return to remain and bring their families. Thus the end of guest worker recruitment also marked the beginning of substantial and sustained family migration and increasing settlement, placing new and rapidly rising demands on local institutions, foremost among them those providing housing, education, and health services.[39]

The transformation from guest workers to settlers also coincided with the processes of deindustrialization, in particular the decline of industrial manufacturing jobs. Given that they had been recruited specifically to fill unskilled and semiskilled jobs in the industrial sector, the guest worker population was disproportionately affected by industrial restructuring and the loss of industrial jobs. Guest worker unemployment rates, which had been close to zero until the early 1970s, rose steeply in the early 1980s and have remained consistently higher, often close to double, the rate for native workers.[40]

Although the German government had ended the recruitment of guest workers, allowing only for family migration, the arrival of large numbers of asylum seekers and ethnic Germans in the 1980s contributed to increasing the heterogeneity of Germany's immigrant population and placed additional demands on local authority services. Despite the new heterogeneity, the former guest workers, their families, and descendents make up the large majority of Germany's immigrant population today. Yet this population itself is far from homogeneous, because it includes citizens of the European Union (Italians, Spaniards, Greeks, and Portuguese), who benefit from full freedom of movement and can vote in local elections, and also non-EU citizens, primarily Turks and citizens of the successor states of the former Yugoslavia.

The fall of the Berlin Wall in 1989 and the unification of Germany imposed added financial burdens on the German federal state. Given the principle of subsidiarity, these economic and fiscal problems have reverberated at the local level, where cities have had to confront new budgetary restrictions at a time when the demands for their services have increased. As German cities have struggled to fulfill their obligatory and discretionary tasks, they have also struggled to carve out new policies aimed at managing and integrating an increasingly diverse immigrant population.

German Cities' Responses to Immigration

German city policy initiatives aimed at their foreign populations have addressed three broad issues—political representation and rights, social equality, and cultural recognition and equal access—and they have evolved from their beginnings in the *Ausländerpolitik* (foreigners' policy) of the 1970s and 1980s to the "intercultural city policies" (*interkulturelle Stadtpolitk*) of the present.

Given their constitutional mandate "to manage the affairs of the resident population," local authorities raised concerns about migrants' lack of political rights and representation in the early 1970s, at a time when the federal government steadfastly denied that Germany had become an immigration country and when German citizenship and naturalization laws made guest workers' access to citizenship very difficult. Seeking to provide immigrants with some (albeit limited) local voice, cities began to establish foreigners' advisory councils (*Ausländerbeiräte*) in the early to middle 1970s.[41] Although, initially, such councils were hardly representative of the immigrant population, because council members were German citizens appointed by the mayor's office, council memberships soon evolved to become more representative. Today's council members are primarily immigrants (and their descendents), and members are now elected by the resident immigrant population. Though councils have no formal decisionmaking power, they have acted as liaisons between the immigrant population and elected officials and administrators. More important, they were a first, if clearly limited, response to recognizing that the temporary guest workers were becoming permanent residents and immigrants.

Recognizing that immigrants often confront bureaucratic and cultural barriers when seeking city services, beginning in the 1990s, cities have developed new policies and activities aimed at equalizing their foreign residents' access to communal functions and services. These are known as "the policies of intercultural opening" (*Politiken der interkulturellen Öffnung*).[42]

City concerns about social inequality have centered on housing and education. Though earlier concerns about housing tended to focus on efforts to prevent the spatial concentrations of immigrant populations in particular city neighborhoods, more recently cities have recognized that some degree of spatial concentration is "normal" and have turned to managing and improving amenities and services in districts and neighborhoods where immigrants have concentrated.[43]

Beginning in the 1980s, the unequal educational experience of immigrant children has moved to the forefront. Although the last ten years indicate some progress toward greater equality, the children of immigrants have continued to lag behind their German cohorts. Within Germany's stratified system of education, immigrant children have been disproportionately concentrated in the lowest and least selective school track (*Hauptschule*). They also have been more likely to drop out of school before graduating, and even when they graduate they have been less likely to enter into apprenticeship programs, a prerequisite for skilled blue-collar jobs (e.g., auto mechanics, plumbers, electricians) and many service jobs (e.g., hairdressers, restaurant and hotel management).

Although German cities have traditionally had some control over the allocation of social housing and have tried to use this control to prevent the spatial concentration of immigrant populations whenever possible, the social housing sector has been shrinking rapidly since the 1980s. In their 2001 expert report to the Independent Commission on Immigration, Häussermann and Siebel attribute the comparatively low degree of ethnic spatial concentration and segregation found in German cities (especially when compared with the United States, the United Kingdom, France, and the Netherlands) to past city housing policies aimed at lessening segregation based on class, income, education, and occupation.[44]

German cities' abilities to directly influence educational outcomes have been very limited. Though local authorities are responsible for maintaining the school infrastructure (e.g., buildings and playgrounds), educational policies are made by the states and teachers are state employees. Local authorities are responsible for preschool education (kindergarten) and youth programs, including after-school programs. These programs are not part of the German system of compulsory education, and participation in them is voluntary.

Although kindergarten education is not compulsory in Germany, federal law (the law to help children and youths, Kinder und Jugendhilfegesetz, 2000) mandates that all children above the age of three are entitled to a place in kindergarten.[45] Given German language and educational disadvantages among the children of immigrants, cities have devoted considerable efforts to ensuring that immigrant children have access to kindergartens and after-school youth programs. Frequently working with voluntary associations and parents' groups, cities support a variety of programs for young people and for immigrant women with children. In many of these programs, German language instruction takes center place.

Charged by the Constitution to maintain cultural and leisure institutions and programs, cities have actively supported immigrants' cultural activities and expressions. They have encouraged and supported the creation of immigrant voluntary associations with a variety of goals, providing financial support and making available places for meetings and activities. They routinely sponsor festivals and other cultural expressions and representations, such as exhibitions in local museums, libraries, and street fairs.

Stuttgart and Munich:
Liberal Cities in Conservative States?

Although they differ in population size, Munich and Stuttgart share many economic, political, social, and cultural characteristics. In a recent study of the fifty largest German cities, which examined 100 economic and social indicators (e.g., unemployment rates, crime rates, income, housing), Munich and Stuttgart ranked first and third respectively (Frankfurt was ranked second) in their "economic attractiveness and quality of life." Though Frankfurt did well in income (high) and unemployment (low), the city also had the highest crime rate in Germany. In contrast, Munich's crime rate was below that of other major German cities (e.g., Hamburg, Düsseldorf, Bremen, Berlin, Cologne, and Dortmund), and Stuttgart displayed the lowest crime rate among large cities.[46]

Although both cities are the capitals of conservative states (and as such they are also the location of state government), their city councils and mayors have tended to be liberal. Immigrants make up almost one-quarter of the residents of both cities. Though they hail from a large variety of countries and include ethnic Germans and refugees, the former guest workers and their descendants make up the vast majority of the immigrant populations in both cities and, as noted above, include citizens of the European Union (e.g., Italians, Spaniards, Portuguese, Greeks) and non-EU citizens, primarily from the former Yugoslavia (Croatia, Slovenia, Albania, Serbia, and Macedonia) and Turkey. In both cities, one-third of immigrants are citizens of the European Union. Among non-EU immigrants, citizens of the former Yugoslavia when added together slightly outnumber Turks. In other words, the Turkish population, while sizable, is less dominant than in the industrial cities in Northern Germany such as Cologne or Duisburg.[47]

Stuttgart: Germany's Most Boring City
or a New Multicultural Mecca?

With a population of close to 600,000, the city of Stuttgart is Germany's sixth-largest city.[48] With its location at the center of one of Germany's most dynamic industrial regions, Stuttgart has seen its foreign population grow rapidly, from a low of 1.6 percent in 1955, to 12.6 percent in 1970, to 16.8 percent in 1980, passing the 20 percent mark in 1991, and standing at 22.3 percent in 1994. Though today's foreign population of Stuttgart (the city administration prefers to use the term "residents without a German passport") hails from some 170 countries, former guest workers, their families, and descendents constitute by far the largest contingent. Among them, citizens of Turkey represent the largest group (23,473), followed by Greeks (15,566) and Italians (14,930), Croatians (13,753), and citizens of Serbia-Montenegro (12,513). Together, citizens of the former Yugoslavia outnumber the Turkish population in Stuttgart.[49]

Although the immigrant population in Stuttgart is not evenly distributed throughout the twenty-three city districts because they tend to be more concentrated in industrial and inner-city districts with less expensive and less attractive housing, in terms of the spatial concentration of its foreign population, Stuttgart compares favorably with other German cities with large percentages of immigrants. The proportion of immigrants exceeds 30 percent in only two districts (Wangen, 34.5; and Mitte, 30.2), with the proportions in other districts ranging between 11.4 and 29.3 percent.[50]

The unemployment rate for foreigners in Stuttgart is lower than in Germany as a whole, but it is considerably higher than the unemployment rate for the native German population. In December 2003, when the overall unemployment rate in the city was 7.8 percent, the unemployment rate for foreign residents stood at 19.9 percent. Similarly, the social assistance rate for immigrants is more than double that of the native population (of 1,000 foreigners, 64 received social assistance in 2003, compared with 32 of 1,000 Germans).[51]

In 1999–2000 (before the new immigration law went into effect), 24 percent of students in Stuttgart public schools were non-German. Though the data since 2000 show a decline in that number (19.6 percent for 2003–4), this reflects the fact that students of foreign parents born in Germany receive dual citizenship and are counted as German. In the stratified German system, students generally enter into different-track schools after the fourth grade. At the beginning of the 2003 school year, 53.7 percent of foreign students entered the lowest track (*Hauptschule*). This represents a slight improvement over 2001, when 57.7 percent of the foreign students entered this track (comparison figures for native Germans are 29.5 and 20.8 percent, respectively). Entrance into the middle track (*Realschule*) was more equally distributed between foreign and native students (25.1 percent foreign and

26.7 percent German students for 2003). For those entering the highest track (*Gymnasium*), the numbers are the mirror images of the data for the lowest track. In 2003, 21.2 percent of foreigners and 52.8 percent of Germans entered into this track. These data, too, show a slight improvement over 2001, when only 19.3 percent of foreigners and 51.9 percent of Germans entered into this track.

Foreign students are also more likely to drop out of school before graduation. Thus, at the end of the 2002–3 school year, 7.8 percent of German and 8.9 percent of non-German students left the *Hauptschule* without graduating. Dropout rates for the other school types are also higher among foreign students.[52]

In 2004, the city of Stuttgart received UNESCO's "Cities of Peace" prize for the European region, awarded every two years to a city in each region of the world.[53] The competition had placed particular emphasis on the integration of disadvantaged populations (most notably immigrants and refugees) and the promotion of cultural heterogeneity. In awarding the prize to Stuttgart, the jury was particularly impressed by its "Bündnis für Integration" (Pact for Integration, a program for action developed by the "integration staff" at the lord mayor's office in 2001) and lauded "the great engagement of the city administration and the citizens of Stuttgart in promoting intercultural dialogue and in putting in place a variety of integration measures." In accepting the award, the lord mayor expressed his hope that other cities would emulate the successful work and excellent experiences made by his city to date, and he committed himself to continue to work to furthering integration efforts into the future.[54]

The award represents a crowning achievement in the city's longstanding efforts to improve the living conditions of its foreign populations. Though the city administration's approach and policies have evolved over time, Stuttgart was among the leaders of a progressive policy. In the early 1970s, the then–lord mayor, Manfred Rommel (the son of Erwin Rommel), went against both the federal government's and his state's official policy, declaring that Germany had become an immigration country and that cities had the responsibility to engage their foreign populations.[55]

Stuttgart was among the first German cities to establish an Ausländerbeirat (Foreigners' Council) in 1971. As was the case then, council members were appointed, and membership consisted primarily of Germans who were local representatives of welfare organizations, churches, and unions, with a sprinkling of foreign social workers employed by these institutions. By creating several subcommittees, the council tried to identify and address a variety of emerging issues, in particular the need for better language instruction and better access to information, the problems associated with education and schools, and the lack of sufficient kindergarten spaces for the children of immigrants.[56]

To facilitate greater political participation and the integration of its foreign population into the political process, in 1983, the city replaced the Ausländerbeirat with the Advisory Committee to the Municipal Council (Ausländerausschuss). The new body included sixteen representatives of the Municipal Council, fifteen foreign members who were elected by foreign residents and appointed to the office by the Municipal Council, and four members representing unions and welfare organizations who did not have voting rights. By bringing together members of the Municipal Council and elected representatives of the immigrant population, the new body's goal was to integrate foreigners' issues more closely into the local policymaking process.[57]

The Advisory Committee was replaced by the International Committee (Internationaler Ausschuss) in 1998, and members of the committee were renamed from "commissioners for foreigners" to "integration commissioners." Beyond the symbolic value of this terminology, the changes also included some restructuring. The Advisory Committee is part of the top city administration, headed by the lord mayor himself. Its membership includes thirteen members of the municipal council and twelve non-German members (four are citizens of the EU and eight are noncitizens) who are directly elected by non-EU residents.[58]

Voting participation in elections to the Ausschuss and its predecessor the Ausländerbeirat has been declining from a high of 26 percent in the early 1990s to 13.2 percent in 1995 and a mere 6.4 percent in 2000. In the context of the low voter participation, the city government has recently decided to abolish direct elections to the International Committee. Though one-third of Stuttgart's foreign residents who are citizens of the European Union can participate in local elections, for non-EU citizens, the committee continues to represent an important avenue for participation in local politics.[59]

In terms of its function, the International Committee is considered less a body of communal political representative for foreigners and more as an advisory council for integration issues. As such, the committee focuses less on "social work with foreigners" (*Ausländerarbeit*) but more on developing measures aimed at equalizing the life chances of "residents with a migration background" (independent of their formal citizenship) and at promoting the peaceful coexistence of all Stuttgarters. Thus, the committee addresses itself to broad themes concerning education and schools, work and the economy, housing and neighborhood work, culture and sport, and health and social work, and it provides advice and support to the municipal council, taking positions and making recommendations and suggestions on all questions of interest to the foreign population to ensure that these interests are recognized and taken seriously, and that foreign residents can participate as much as possible in the decisionmaking process.

Also located in the lord mayor's office is the Department for Integration Policy (Stabsabteilung für Integrationspolitik). The department, which has five staff members, specifically aims at promoting equality and reducing structural and individual discrimination, and it supports measures aimed at intercultural dialogue and societal cooperation among various city districts.

The Pact for Integration was a brainchild of the Department of Integration. It sets the direction and outlines the city's new approach to immigrant integration, considered to be a central task for the city as a whole. Toward this end, it outlines an ambitious program aimed at the integration of all residents and the peaceful coexistence of all Stuttgarters, whatever their citizenship. First, it dispenses with the distinctions between guest workers, ethnic Germans (*Aussiedler*), and refugees. Instead of offering targeted programs for each of these groups, the goal is to provide integrative measures for all Stuttgarters "with a migration background" (this includes ethnic Germans who are citizens as well as naturalized former guest workers). Second, aiming to promote legal rights and social equality of opportunity for all, it breaks with previous approaches that dealt with immigrants in terms "of social work with disadvantaged minorities" (*Ausländerpolitik*). Toward this end, the pact outlines several policy areas and goals—in particular the promotion of language proficiency and equality of education, neighborhood integration projects, support for pluralism and diversity, and the strengthening of intercultural self-perception.

Language proficiency and equal access to education are considered key to successful participation in society. Proficiency in German is seen as a major condition for integration in the labor market and for social and political participation. To improve the language proficiency of its foreign population, the city of Stuttgart supports a large network of eighty organizations that provide language instructions for all who do not have sufficient knowledge of German. Most course offerings are decentralized (offered in neighborhoods), with many targeting particular groups such as women and young people. Those aimed at women also offer free child care. Courses are financed by the city with some support from welfare organizations, churches, and voluntary organizations as well as grants from the state. The fees charged are relatively modest.

The city also offers "integration courses" for newcomers. These provide basic knowledge about the city district, the city, the State of Baden-Württemberg, and Germany. The city's Web site currently lists fifteen such courses, with most offering free child care for participants.[60] These have proven to be particularly popular, as 80 percent of graduates have wanted to enroll in additional courses.

Given that cities do not directly control the compulsory German educational system, and given that early childhood education is considered key to language acquisition, city educational programs have focused on kindergartens in particular. In accordance with federal law, the city of Stuttgart guarantees a kindergarten slot for all children above the age of three. Because they are not part of the compulsory education system, kindergartens may be run by voluntary organizations, in particular churches and welfare organizations, or by the city itself (*städtische Kindergarten*).[61] The city encourages foreign parents to send their children to kindergartens, and an increasing number of kindergartens offer an intercultural and multilingual setting staffed with teachers trained in intercultural and multilingual education.

The stratified German educational system represents a major barrier to all children of working-class background, a barrier that is only reinforced for children with immigrant backgrounds.[62] It is in this area that the city has few options, given that education remains in the domain of states and that the State of Baden-Württemberg pursues a traditional education policy structured by the stratified school system, consisting of three tracks, each leading to different occupational opportunities. Like Bavaria and unlike all other German states, the state does not offer the option of a comprehensive school (*Gesamtschule*) that combines the three tracks, similar to the American high school.[63] At the heart of the city's activities for school-age children are a variety of youth programs that provide after-school help with homework, language support and advice to foreign youths in the transition from school to work, and help in finding apprenticeship programs. In addition, the city offers programs to support parents and teachers in the goal of increasing the diversity in secondary schools (university preparatory schools, *Gymnasium*), where the children of immigrants continue to be underrepresented.

Neighborhood integration programs have included local district offices and voluntary associations that organize cultural activities and engage in intercultural dialogues among various ethnic groups. As pointed out above, the overall ethnic spatial concentration in Stuttgart is low, and even the three districts with relatively high concentrations are ethnically diverse, because no ethnic group dominates in any district.[64]

To promote its intercultural agenda, the city engages a variety of cultural institutions. It has always been the center of many cultural institutions and organizations, and these have been complemented by new migrant cultural organizations. In 1996, the lord mayor, Wolfgang Schuster (who was then mayor for culture), founded the Forum for Culture (Forum der Kulturen), a peak association that brings together some 200 non-German and intercultural organizations active in the city. Since 2001, it has published a magazine, *Interkultur Stuttgart*. The Deutsch Türkisches Forum (German Turkish Forum) was founded by a group of German and Turkish citizens in 1999. The goal of the forum is to bring Turks and Germans together to promote better cultural understanding. Both are financially supported by the city. In addition, the city's Culture Department has stepped up its activities by supporting a variety of cultural projects initiated by immigrant groups. The public library system stocks a wealth of books, magazines, and newspapers in different languages, and over a third of its users are foreign nationals.

The city of Stuttgart is clearly serious about integrating its foreign population. Though its efforts go back to the early 1970s, and though the Pact for Integration represents an innovative approach, the issues addressed in the pact have not changed appreciably since the early 1970s. What has changed is the realization that these issues are not limited to immigrants but affect the entire population of the city, whatever their citizenship or migration background. If Stuttgart wants to remain a livable city, it must integrate its foreign population.

It is difficult to assess the effects of past and present city policies. Many favorable outcomes can be partially attributed to the city's (and larger regions') favorable economic and industrial climate, reflecting comparatively low unemployment rates in general and by extension for immigrants, low social assistance rates, and low levels of immigrant concentration in neighborhoods.

Overall, Stuttgart compares favorably with many other German cities, especially relative to cities with equally high percentages of foreign populations. In 2003, the Department of Integration added several questions concerning the current situation of "foreign co-citizens" and their degree of integration to the annual citizen survey conducted by the city.[65] Although immigrants were less satisfied with their immediate environment and their apartments than Germans, 80 percent of the foreign population replied that they liked living in Stuttgart. When asked about the city's programs to support integration, foreign respondents' responses were overwhelmingly positive. Despite low voting participation in the last election for the International Committee, 86 percent of foreigners viewed the committee as an agent for integration (89.3 percent of non-EU citizens, 80 percent EU), and 94 percent (86 percent of Germans) strongly supported language instruction programs and other measures of integration.

Munich: World City with Heart (Weltstadt mit Herz) and "Southern Comfort"

In the minds of most Americans, Munich is equated with beer, Oktoberfest, and lederhosen.[66] This rather skewed popular image notwithstanding, Munich has been consistently identified as the most attractive city in Germany.[67]

With a population of 1.3 million, Munich is Germany's third-largest city, and one of three with a population above 1 million (after Berlin and Hamburg). In terms of the proportion of its foreign residents (23 percent), the city is equal to Stuttgart and only slightly lower than Frankfurt. Unlike Stuttgart (with the exception of the Nazi period), Munich has always been home to a sizable foreign population,[68] and it has long considered itself the cultural center of Southern Germany. In addition to its prominence in culture and education (especially its well-known and respected universities), it is also home to major industries. As was the case for Stuttgart, the first Italian guest workers arrived in the mid-1950s, soon to be joined by guest workers from other Southern European countries, from the former Yugoslavia, and somewhat later from Turkey.

Although today's foreign residents come from 180 nations, almost 32 percent are citizens of the European Union. Among non-EU citizens, Turks represent the largest contingent, followed by citizens of Yugoslavia (Serbia-Herzogovina and Croatia). As is the case for Stuttgart, together citizens of the former Yugoslavia make up the largest group.

The spatial distribution of the foreign population in Munich's twenty-five districts is similar to that of Stuttgart. The proportion of foreigners in one district (Schwanenthalerhöhe) reaches the 40 percent mark, and the proportions in two additional districts are in the low 30s (Milbertshofen-Am Hart, 33.7; Ludwigvorstadt-Isarvorstadt, 31.1), with most districts around 20 percent. The smallest proportion is found in the district of Passing (16.6).[69]

Bavaria is universally considered Germany's most conservative state (since World War II, it has been governed by the Christian Social Union, the more conservative sister party of the Christian Democratic Union). Though the city of Munich has been governed by liberal coalitions, in the field of education, the state's conservative policies have added additional challenges for urban policy makers. Thus, resisting the federal mandate that guarantees kindergarten places for all children above the age of three, the Bavarian government moved kindergarten education—normally in the domain of the youth and child services that are allocated to local authorities— to the domain of education, which is controlled by the state government. As a consequence, Munich does not get support from the state in its efforts to provide a place for each child above the age of three; and despite massive efforts by the city, not every child has been able to get a space in kindergarten.

In 1998 the city supported 473 kindergartens, offering 26,726 spaces. Of these, more than half were in city-run institutions (14,750). Since the 1980s, the proportion of city kindergartens in the overall number of kindergartens has increased dramatically as the city has almost doubled the spaces available. In contrast, noncity kindergarten spaces have increased only moderately. Foreign children occupied 27.5 percent of all available kindergarten spaces in 1998. In districts with high percentages of immigrants (e.g., Schwanenthalerhöhe, Ludwigvorstadt-Isarvorstadt, and Milbertshofen), the proportion of foreign children in neighborhood kindergartens ranges from 41.8 to 44.3 to percent.[70]

As is the case throughout Germany, foreign children continue to be over-represented in the lowest track, the *Hauptschule,* and underrepresented in the highest track, the *Gymnasium.* Indeed, during the 2000–1 school year, only 10 percent of *Gymnasium* students were immigrants, whereas the proportion in the *Hauptschule* stood at 48 percent. As was the case in Stuttgart, the proportion of foreign students attending the *Realschulen* was similar to that of German students (about 20 percent). Most alarming is the fact that every fourth foreign student in Munich leaves the *Hauptschule* without graduating.[71]

Munich was somewhat slower than Stuttgart to respond to the growing presence of its foreign populations. It was not until 1972, when its foreign population stood at 15 percent, that the city commissioned its first study to investigate the "local political aspects of the growing proportion of foreigners in the population."[72] The study identified the lack of access to political participation as one of the main barriers to the integration of newcomers. Following the recommendation of a subsequent commission established to study this issue, the municipal council (with the support of all political parties) created a Foreigners' Commission (Ausländerbeirat) in 1974.

As was the case in Stuttgart, all thirty-nine members (twenty-six foreign nationals and thirteen Germans) of the newly created council were appointed. The thirteen German members included four from the city council and eight individuals representing groups involved in "foreigners' issues." Its main duties were to advise the council and the administration concerning all questions related to foreigners; to promote connections between the native and foreign populations; and to promote cultural, sports, and social activities among the foreign populations.[73]

The council's membership composition and recruitment procedures changed in 1979, when Germans were eliminated from the council and all members were proposed by groups working in "foreigners work" (*Ausländerarbeit*) and appointed by the city council. Since 1989, members of the council (they can be naturalized citizens or noncitizens) have been directly elected by the foreign-born population for a period of six years. At the same time, the council's domain of activities was broadened beyond the narrow confines of communal municipal administration to include all areas of life under state policy. In 1991 the Ausländerbeirat became the official representative organ of the foreign population in Munich, with representatives from eight different countries, elected in direct elections by the foreign population.

Today, the forty non-German or naturalized citizen members of the council are elected for a period of six years. The council's main functions are to influence the communal policymaking process and public cultural functions, and to keep intensive contact with voluntary organizations and clubs active in the area of immigration, and they have not changed significantly over time.

The work of the council is divided into five subcommissions (youth, family, and education; women, work, and health; culture, religion, sports, and leisure; legal issues, including discrimination; and the allocation of subsidies). Each subcommission is responsible for preparing and developing issues and recommendations that are then voted on in the commission as a whole. The Ausländerbeirat has direct access to the municipal council, the lord mayor, and individual mayors and the city administration. The commission sends positions on issues, recommendations, and requests to all

three, while the municipal council sends requests for positions to the commission and various offices of the municipal administration offices (office
for culture, social issues, schools, work and science, district administration,
and the "post" for intercultural cooperation, Stelle für Interkulturelle
Zusammenarbeit.

The Munich Ausländerbeirat has addressed a wide variety of topics and
issues. In the past six years, it has passed numerous agreements and recommendations in all five areas—legal; education and language; housing,
work, and the economy; and culture, sports, and leisure. In 2004, the city
gave €130,000 to enable some one hundred foreign organizations to provide information, organize culture and sports festivals, offer German
courses, and help with homework. At the end of its last election period in
April 2004, the lord mayor gave special thanks for the integrative work done
by the commission and the fact that it has become an important partner in
the political work of the city council.[74]

As has been the case in Stuttgart and throughout Germany, participation
in elections to Munich's foreigners' council has been declining in the past
decade.[75] In view of the 6 percent participation rate in the 2004 election,
and the considerable cost associated with the organization of elections, the
city has decided to discontinue direct elections to the council.[76] The council will continue its work of representing those foreigners who have no other
voice, in particular non-EU citizens.

The Stelle für interkulturelle Zusammenarbeit (Office for Intercultural
Cooperation), located in the Sozialreferat (Department of Social Affairs), is
charged with promoting cultural diversity and tolerance, developing integration measures, and encouraging measures aimed at reducing the occupational, educational, ethnic, and cultural disadvantages of the immigrant
population. The Stelle, which has a staff of six, is engaged in antidiscrimi-
nation work, provides advice and support for migrant organizations, promotes public information, publishes material and studies on intercultural
understanding, and dialogues and organizes exhibits and conferences for
social workers and people engaged in the field of integration.

In the 1970s, the city's culture department first organized the "day of the
foreigner." Today the city supports a wide variety of cultural activities for
immigrants, including citywide events, activities, events in city districts,
such as "district culture days" and street festivals and fairs. The Department
of Culture also includes a specialized office for "intercultural art and immigrant art," with the specific mission to create an equal opportunity context for culture groups of foreign origin.[77] The Multi-Kulti Festival Ander

Art (roughly translated as Multicultural Festival of a Different Kind) is in its eighth year and draws large numbers of people each year. A recent project is the Eine-Welt Haus (literally, One-World House) in the Schwanenthalerhöhe neighborhood.

The Munich city administration has been at the forefront of the movement of intercultural opening. The Perspektive München (Perspective Munich), a long-term planning perspective developed by the Department of City Planning and Construction, aims at changing the "communal social policy" of the past into a new "social communal policy."[78] The specific goal is to empower all foreigners living in Munich for a longer period to participate in the city's social life, labor market, culture, and educational activities while maintaining their cultural identity.[79]

A 1997 study by the Department of City Planning and Building Order (Stadtplanung and Bauordnung) investigating the living conditions of foreign citizens in Munich found that although the homes of foreigners were equipped with fewer amenities, they expressed greater satisfaction overall with their homes. As is the case throughout Germany, the study also found that foreigners pay higher rents than Germans for similar housing and, not surprisingly, that foreigners were most dissatisfied with the high cost of rents in the city. Foreigners were also somewhat more likely to rent than own their homes or apartments (79.9 percent of foreigners rent, compared with 74 percent of Germans) and more likely to live in social housing (20 percent are in social housing, as compared with 14 percent of Germans). Turkish households are more likely to live in such housing than any other nationality (31.3 percent). Participants in a city program subsidizing homeownership include 20 percent foreigners.[80]

As a city called "a left-of-centre island within Germany's most conservative state,"[81] Munich has developed numerous policies and actions aimed at overcoming some of the disadvantages and inequalities faced by its foreign population. As was the case for Stuttgart, the overall position of immigrants in the city compares favorably with many other German cities. And also as with Stuttgart, much of this is due to the city's robust labor market, its low unemployment rate, and its low social assistance rate. Though housing, in particular its high cost, is a concern, the major concern is education, a policy area over which local authorities have little control. In the case of kindergartens, Munich has faced the additional disadvantage associated with its location in Germany's most conservative state, but it has been working hard and has made considerable strides toward guaranteeing kindergarten places for all entitled children.

Conclusion: For German Cities and Immigrants, the Future Remains Open

As indicated above, in 2001 the Independent Commission on Immigration concluded that local authorities had contributed significantly to the integration of immigrants, while bearing most of the cost at a time when they were confronting difficult financial problems.[82] Although Germany is often perceived as unwelcoming to immigrants, and the federal state has taken a long time to officially recognize that Germany had become a country of immigration, with the exception of isolated incidents Germany has thus far been able to avoid the serious clashes between ethnic groups witnessed in neighboring European countries, including those that have long recognized their status as immigration countries and has pursued specific integration programs (e.g., multiculturalism in the Netherlands and race relations projects in the United Kingdom).[83]

On January 1, 2005, two laws that have a direct impact on Germany's foreign population and the relationship between the federal government and cities came into effect: the immigration law and the welfare reform law. After years of parliamentary debates, the German Bundestag passed the immigration law (Zuwanderungsgesetz) in July 2004. Although many of its aspects remain controversial, this historic law gives legal recognition to the fact that Germany is a country of immigration. In replacing a patchwork of previous laws, the new law regulates all aspects of immigration (temporary as well as permanent). The new law also includes federal integration policies, such as a mandate for German language courses for all new immigrants who cannot express themselves in simple German. Though cities have welcomed the language instruction provisions, making language instruction for new immigrants a federal domain, they have disagreed with the restrictions limiting language instruction to new arrivals, excluding those who have been in the country for some time. Thus, they argue that the integration program in the new law is not sufficient to support the long-term better integration of immigrants.[84]

Although the new welfare law, known as Hartz IV, affects all legal residents (both German citizens and immigrants), given their higher unemployment and social assistance rates, immigrants are disproportionately affected by the new law, which streamlines and simplifies the old system and imposes restrictions and lower benefits on the long-term unemployed. It abolishes previous differences between *Arbeitslosenhilfe* (the second tier of unemployment benefits for the long-term unemployed who had exhausted the higher benefits from the first tier, *Arbeitslosengeld*) and *Sozialhilfe* (social assistance, a benefit available to all legal residents independent of whether they had worked), providing only one benefit for the long-term unemployed and requiring that they must accept a job offered them by the authorities. Though cities have supported the spirit of the law, they have raised concern about new administrative costs and have urged that these should be borne by the federal government, which is in charge of labor market policy.

The effects of these laws on the division of labor between city, state, and federal government and the long-term integration of immigrants cannot be assessed at this point. Unfortunately, these laws do not address one of the major issues concerning immigrant integration: the German school system. Because up to 40 percent of fifteen-year-old students in most cities now "have a migration background,"[85] the education of the second and third generations looms as one of the most significant challenges confronting German society as a whole. Though the overall mediocre performance of fifteen-year-old German students (tested in mathematics, reading competence, and natural sciences)[86] has produced considerable reflections and soul searching on the part of many sectors of German society, despite some tinkering with the current system, including the push for more all-day schools, the types of school reforms necessary to rigorously address these issues remain beyond the horizon.[87]

Notes

1. Gary Freeman, "Immigrant Incorporation in Western Democracies," *International Migration Review* 38 (2004): 945–69; Christian Joppke and Ewa Morawska, "Integrating Immigrants in Liberal Nation-States: Policies and Practices," in *Toward Assimilation and Citizenship: Immigrants in Liberal Nation States,* ed. Christian Joppke and Ewa Morawska (New York: Palgrave, 2003), 1–36.

2. Robert Park, "Human Migration and the Marginal Man," *American Journal of Sociology* 33 (1928): 881–93; the quotation here is on 881.

3. Cf. Saskia Sassen, *The Global City: New York, London, Tokyo* (Princeton, N.J.: Princeton University Press, 1991); John Friedmann, *The Prospects of Cities* (Minneapolis: University of Minnesota Press, 2002).

4. Audrey Singer, *The Rise of New Immigrant Gateways* (Washington, D.C.: Center on Urban and Metropolitan Policy, Brookings Institution, 2004).

5. Victoria Waltz, "Migration und Urbanität," in *Integration in Städten und Gemeinden,* ed. Beauftragte der Bundesregierung für Ausländerfragen (Berlin: Beauftragte der Bundesregierung fur Ausländerfragen, 2000), 7–22.

6. Deutscher Städtetag, *Statistiksches Jahrbuch deutscher Gemeinden* (Berlin: Deutscher Städtetag, 2002).

7. This chapter focuses only on the former West Germany, which is home to over 90 percent of the foreign population.

8. Immigration policy generally refers to policies directly aimed at controlling the flow and composition of immigrants admitted. Immigrant policy refers to policies that structure the rights and privileges and obligations and responsibilities of those admitted. In short, immigration policy focuses on gate keeping, while immigrant policy is concerned with integration.

9. At the end of 2003, about 7.3 million legal aliens lived in Germany, representing 9 percent of the population. Of these, 2 million were Turkish citizens. Including about 3 million ethnic Germans and approximately 2 million naturalized Germans and illegal immigrants, the total number of people of immigrant origin is roughly 13 million, about 16 percent of the population. Cf. Schrader Stiftung et al., *Immigrants in the City: Recommendations for Urban Integration Policy* (Darmstadt: Schrader Stiftung, 2005), http://www.zunwanderer-in-der-stadt.de, 11.

10. It is important to note that the German welfare state has acted as an agent of integration, as immigrants have been included in all aspects of the welfare state. See Andrew Geddes, *The Politics of Migration and Immigration in Europe* (London: Sage, 2003); Michael Bommes and Andrew Geddes, eds., *Immigration and Welfare: Challenging the Borders of the Welfare State* (London: Routledge, 2000); Barbara Schmitter Heisler, "Institutional Dimension of Social Exclusion in the Welfare State: An Assessment of Trends in the Netherlands and Germany, 1985–1992, *Journal of European Public Policy* 3 (1996): 168–91.

11. This is the title of his 1995 article detailing postwar immigration and policy responses: Dietrich Thränhardt, "Germany: An Undeclared Immigration Country," *New Community* 1 (1995): 19–35.

12. Jutta Helm, "Introduction: German Cities between Globalization and Unification," *German Politics and Society* 16 (1998): 7; Jürgen Bremm and Peter Asche, "International Changes and the Single European Market: Impacts on the Spatial Structure of Germany," *Urban Studies* 30 (1993): 991–1007.

13. Dietrich Thränhardt, "Zuwanderung und lokale Politik in Deutschland," *Neue Praxis* 29 (1999): 360.

14. German local government is divided into independent cities (*kreisfreie Städte*) with populations over 100,000 and above and districts (*Kreise*), which are administrative units consisting of several small towns and rural areas.

15. The principle of subsidiarity (*Subsidiarität*) originates in the Catholic and Social Democratic traditions. It is based on the active participation of churches and the joint responsibility and cooperation of church and state for ensuring a life worthy of human dignity. In the realm of organizations engaged in providing benefits toward this goal, the idea is that organizations closest to the people should be in charge of benefits of the last order, e.g., social assistance.

16. Grundgesetz für die Bundesrepublik Deutschland, http://www.datenschutz-berlin.de/recht/de/gg/gg1_de.htm#art28.

17. Walter Hanesch, "Konzeption, Krise und Optionen der sozialen Stadt," in *Überlebt die Soziale Stadt?* ed. Walter Hanesch (Opladen, Germany: Leske + Budrich 1997), 21–56; the quotation here is on 25.

18. Though the idea of the social city can be traced to Imperial Germany and its basic principles were developed in the Weimar Republic, these principles found some expression in the booming 1960s when cities were able to expand their social services. See

Adelheid von Saldern, *Vom Einwohner zum Bürger: Zur Emanzipation der städtischen Unterschicht Göttingens 1890–1920* (Berlin: Von Duncker & Humbolt GmbH, 1973); and Hartmut Häusserman and Walter Siebel, "Multikulturelle Statdpolitik: Segregation und Integration," in *Jahrbuch StadtRegion,* ed. Institut für Soziologie, University of Oldenburg (Oldenburg: Institut für Soziologie, University of Oldenburg, 2001), 133–36 (*Jahrbuch StadtRegion* is an annual; the special topic for 2001 was Einwanderungsstadt).

19. The Independent Commission to Study Immigration (Zuwanderungskommission) was appointed by Interior Minister Otto Schily in the fall of 2000. In July 2001, the commission, under the chairpersonship of Rita Süssmuth, the former president of the German Bundestag, published a comprehensive final report. The report provides a good overview of post–World War II immigration to Germany and makes a variety of recommendations concerning a new immigration policy and the need for more aggressive future integration policies. See Unabhängige Kommission Zuwanderung, *Zuwanderung Gestalten, Integation Fördern* (Berlin: Bundesministerium des Inneren, 2001), available at http://www.bmi.bmd.de.

20. A publication by the office of the Beauftragte der Bundesregierung für Ausländerfragen provides examples of specific activities (e.g., education, health, and intercultural communal administration) in specific cities. See Beauftragte der Bundesregierung fur Ausländerfragen, *Integration in Städten und Gemeinden.*

21. Good examples are Sophie Body-Gendrot and Marco Martinelli, eds., *Minorities in European Cities: The Dynamics of Social Integration and Social Exclusion at the Neighborhood Level* (New York: St. Martin's Press, 2000); and Rinus Pennix et al., eds., *Citizenship in European Cities: Immigrants, Local Politics and Integration Policies* (Aldershot, U.K.: Ashgate, 2004). The latter book presents findings from a UNESCO-funded comparative research project. Although the city of Cologne was included in the research project, this book does not include a chapter on that city.

22. For Berlin, see Steven Vertovec, "Berlin Multikulti: Germany, 'Foreigners'" and 'World-Openness,'" *New Community* 22 (1996): 381–99; Hartmut Häussermann, "The Integration of Immigrant Populations in Berlin," in *Immigrants, Integration and Cities: Exploring the Links,* ed. Organization for Economic Cooperation and Development (Paris: Organization for Economic Cooperation and Development, 1998), 137–60; and Franz-Josef Kemper, "Restructuring Housing and Ethnic Segregation: Recent Developments in Berlin," *Urban Studies* 35 (1998): 1765–789. For Frankfurt, see John Friedman and Angelika Lehrer, "Urban Responses to Foreign In-Migration: The Case of Frankfurt-am-Main," *Journal of the American Planning Association* 63 (2002): 61–78; Brett Klopp, "Integration and Political Representation in a Multicultural City: The Case of Frankfurt am Main," *German Politics and Society* 49 (1998): 42–67; and Frank-Olaf Radtke, "Multiculturalism in Germany: Local Management of Immigrants' Social Inclusion," *International Journal on Multicultural Societies* 5 (2003): 55–76. The attention focused on Frankfurt is also due to the fact that Frankfurt is a self-proclaimed multicultural city with a special Office of Multicultural Affairs founded by the former student leader Daniel Cohn-Bendit. In the case of Berlin, much of the visibility of that city, in addition to the fact that it is the capital of united Germany, can be attributed to the high visibility of the city's former commissioner for foreigners, Barbara John.

23. Ruud Koopmans, "Migrant Mobilization and Political Opportunities: Variation among German Cities and a Comparison with the United Kingdom and the Netherlands," *Journal of Ethnic and Migration Studies* 30 (2004): 449–70; the quotation here is on 450.

24. Koopmans's research focuses on differences in migrant "claims making" in the context of different political opportunity structures at the local level, and he finds significant differences in immigrant claims making between more liberal cities such as Frankfurt and Berlin, and cities deemed more conservative, such as Munich and Stuttgart. Finding that immigrants make more claims in Frankfurt and Berlin, he attributes the differences to differences in local political opportunity structures. His methodology, however, equates the political opportunity structures of cities like Munich and Stuttgart with their respective states, and he does not include any analysis of local policy in "conservative" cities, assuming that they reflect state policy. Though cities in conservative states may also be conservative, this need not be the case. As we shall see below, some cities have directly opposed the policies of their state with regard to immigrants.

25. Patrick Ireland, *Becoming Europe: Immigration, Integration and the Welfare State* (Pittsburgh: University of Pittsburgh Press, 2004).

26. Ireland attributes this to a variety of local policy factors, including the very fact that the state government, Bavaria, was less hospitable and more tight-fisted, forcing Nünberg to engage in greater policy innovation.

27. On the basis of my past research and the following analysis of two cities, Stuttgart and Munich, both located in conservative states, I argue that all large German cities have pursued liberal policies aimed at improving the life chances of their immigrant populations. See Barbara Schmitter, "Immigration and Citizenship in Germany and Switzerland," PhD dissertation, University of Chicago, 1979; and Barbara Schmitter Heisler, "Immigration and German Cities: Exploring National Policies and Local Outcomes," *German Politics and Society* 49 (1996): 18–41. This does not mean that there are no differences between cities or differences in outcomes. Some of the differences may be due to the exceptional personal engagement of individuals, such as the former commissioner for foreigners in Berlin, Barbara John. It also does not mean that conservative states' policies have no effect on city policies, but as Patrick Ireland has shown in the case of Nünberg, cities may well engage in greater innovation to overcome the negative effects of their location in a conservative state. As we shall see below, the city of Munich, has had to innovate to overcome the conservative school policies of the State of Bavaria to fulfill a federal promise that all children have the right to attend kindergarten, a right the city considers particularly crucial for the children of immigrants.

28. Although cities do not have formal representation at the EU level, many EU economic, social, and cultural decisions and policies also have increasing repercussions at the local level. See Dietrich Thränhardt, "Die Kommunen und die Europäische Gemeinschaft," in *Kommunalpolitik: Politisches Handeln in den Gemeinden,* ed. Roland Roth and Hellmut Wollmann (Opladen, Germany: Leske+Budrich, 1994), 361–77; and Thränhardt, "Zuwanderung und Lokale Politik."

29. In addition to the municipal services in the fields of public order, energy, water supply, housing, garbage removal, and cemetery administration, the core activities of the local welfare state include kindergarten and day care, youth work, health care, social aid, and services for the elderly.

30. Hartmut Häussermann, "The Relationship between Local and Federal Government Policy in the Federal Republic of Germany," in *State Restructuring and Local Power: A Comparative Perspective,* ed. Chris Pickvance and Edmond Preteceille (London: Printer Publishers, 1991), 89–121.

31. The system of revenue funding in Germany has been an ongoing political issue,

and cities have long lobbied for constitutional change. For more detail on the current system, see Wolfgang Jaedicke et al., *Lokale Politik im Wohlfahrtsstaat: Zur Sozialpolitik der Gemeinden und ihrer Verbände in der Beschäftigungskriese* (Opladen, Germany: Westdeutscher Verlag, 1991); Arthur Gunlicks, *Local Government in the German Federal System* (Durham, N.C.: Duke University Press, 1986); and Häussermann, "Relationship between Local and Federal Government Policy."

32. This term is no longer used.

33. The German Institute for Urban Studies (Deutsches Institut für Urbanistik) does an annual survey concerning problems of city development and communal policy that has found that cities consider "communal financing and household consolidation" the most pressing problems. Deutsches Institut für Urbanistik, "Kommunalfinanzen und Haushaltskonsolidierung sind die Hauptprobleme," http://www.difu.de/publikationen/difu-berichte/1_03/artikel109.shtml.

34. The new Welfare Reform law (Hartz IV) has been supported by cities. Under the old system, the unemployed who had exhausted their unemployment benefits *(Arbeitslosengeld)* financed and administered by a federal agency were entitled to a second-tier unemployment benefit *(Arbeitslosenhilfe)* financed and administered by local authorities. In addition, citizens and noncitizens who had never worked, the elderly, and women with children were entitled to social assistance *(Sozialhilfe)*, also administered and financed by local authorities. Given the increasing rate of long-term unemployment and reliance on social assistance, social assistance had become the largest item in city budgets in the 1990s. See Hans Karrenberg and Engelbert Münstermann, "Gemeindefinanzbericht 1997," *Der Deutsche Städtetag,* March 1997, 129–59; Hans Karrenberg and Engelbert Münstermann, "Kommunale Finanzen," in *Kommunalpolitik,* ed. Roth and Wollman, 195–221. See also "City Mayors: German Local Taxation," http://www.citymayors.com/news/german_tax1.html. For a discussion of how local authorities have tried to move the long-term unemployed from their rolls and onto the rolls of the federal government, see Barbara Schmitter Heisler, "Institutional Dimensions of Social Exclusion in the Welfare State: An Assessment of Trends in the Netherlands and Germany, 1985–1992," *Journal of European Public Policy* 3 (1996): 168–91.

35. Kommission Zufkunft Stadt 2000, *Bundesministerium für Raumwesen und Städtebau* (Bonn: Kommission Zufkunft Stadt 2000, 1993), 10.

36. In this chapter, I use the terms "guest workers," "former guest workers," "guest workers and their descendants," "immigrants," and "foreigners" interchangeably. The term "guest worker" was first used by the German government in the late 1950s and early 1960s, and the term is still used in a variety of sources. The term "foreigner" is used in the official literature referring to long-term residents who are not German citizens (which until recently have included most of the second generation). Another, more politically correct, term, "foreign co-citizens" *(Ausländische Mitbürger)*, is frequently used by pro-immigrant groups and organizations, including in many city publications. The term "immigrant" is not commonly used in official German discourse but is increasingly used by immigration scholars.

37. They did have contact with trade unions. See Barbara Schmitter, "Trade Unions and Immigration Politics in West Germany and Switzerland," *Politics and Society* 10 (1981): 251–68.

38. The recruitment of guest workers was controlled by the Bundesanstalt für Arbeit, the federal labor office. The German government concluded bilateral recruitment

264 BARBARA SCHMITTER HEISLER

agreements with Italy (1955), Spain and Greece (1960), Turkey (1961), Morocco (1963), Portugal (1964), Tunisia (1965), and the former Yugoslavia (1968). For more detail, see Schmitter, "Immigration and Citizenship," 10–113.

39. See the articles in *From Foreign Workers to Settlers? Transnational Migration and the Emergence of New Minorities—The Annals of the American Academy of Political and Social Science* 485 (May 1986), ed. Martin O. Heisler and Barbara Schmitter Heisler.

40. Although it is higher than the unemployment rate for Germans, the unemployment rate for immigrants varies with nationality, with Turks exhibiting the largest rate. See Stefan Bender and Wolfgang Seifert, "Zur beruflichen und sozialen Integration der in Deutschland lebenden Ausländer," in *Deutsche und Ausländer: Freunde, Fremde oder Feinde,* ed. Richard Alba, Peter Schmidt, and Martina Wasmer (Wiesbaden: Westdeutscher Verlag, 2000), 55–91.

41. See an early study by Paul Kevenhörster, *Ausländische Arbeitnehmer im politischen System der BRD* (Opladen, Germany: Westdeutscher Verlag, 1974). For a more recent account, see Lutz Hoffmann, *Vom Gastarbeiterparlament zur Intteressenvertretung ethnischer Minderheiten: Die Entwicklung der kommunalen Ausländerbeiräte im Kontext der bundesdeutschen Migrationsgeschichte,* ed. Arbeitsgemeinschaft der Ausländerbeiräte Hessen und der Arbeitsgemeinschaft kommunaler Ausländervertretungen Niedersachsen (Wiesbaden: Osnabrück, 1997).

42. The concept of intercultural opening has been interpreted differently. Narrower interpretations focus on offering foreign languages in local government administrations and seeking to promote the employment of immigrants. Broader interpretations see it as a larger effort to develop personnel with intercultural competences. Filsinger identified two ideal type strategies, one focusing primarily on social/spatial issues, and the other on institutional issues; the former is concerned primarily with social disadvantage and social problems, and the latter with citizenship, viewing migrants as normal users of the infrastructure. These strategies are often combined, but local authorities' emphases may differ. Dieter Filsinger, "Entwicklung der kommunalen Integrationspolitik und Integrationspraxis der neunziger Jahre," *IZA-Zeitschrift für Migration und Soziale Arbeit* 2 (2002): 13–19.

43. Though German cities have not been able to escape the spatial concentration of immigrants, compared with other European countries and the United States, spatial concentration and segregation tend to be relatively low. Cf. Sako Musterd and Marielle De Winter, "Conditions of Spatial Segregation: Some European Perspectives," *International Journal of Urban and Regional Research* 22 (1998): 665–73; and Kemper, "Restructuring of Housing and Ethnic Segregation." This can be attributed to several characteristics of the German housing market, especially its relative heterogeneity. See J. O'Loughlin, "Chicago an der Ruhr or What? Explaining the Location of Immigrants in European Cities," in *Foreign Minorities in Continental European Cities,* ed. G. Glebe and J. O'Loughlin (Wiesbaden: Steiner Verlag, 1987), 52–69; Herbert Babel, "The City of Stuttgart and Immigration: Policies and Experiences," in *Immigrants, Integration and Cities,* ed. Organization for Economic Cooperation and Development, 161–72; Barbara Schmitter Heisler, "Housing Policy and the Underclass: The United Kingdom, Germany and the Netherlands," *Journal of Urban Affairs* 16 (1994): 203–20; Schmitter Heisler, "Immigration and German Cities"; and Schmitter Heisler, "Institutional Dimensions of Social Exclusion."

44. Hartmut Häussermann and Walter Siebel, "Soziale Integration und ethnische Schichtung: Zusammenhange zwischen räumlicher und sozialer Integration," Gutachten

im Auftrag der Unabhängingen Kommission 'Zuwanderung,' " Berlin/Oldenburg, March 2001, http://www.schrader-stiftung.de/docs/haeussermann_siebel_gutachten.pdf.

45. For more detail on the law and German preschool education, see Gerdi Jonen and Thomas Eckhart, *The Education System in the Federal Republic of Germany 2004* (Bonn: Secretariat of the Standing Conference of the Ministers of Education and Cultural Affairs of the Federal Republic of Germany, 2006).

46. Institut der Deutschen Wirtschaft, *Deutsche Grossstädte im Vergleich* (Cologne: Institut der Deutschen Wirtschaft, 2004).

47. These differences can be partially attributed to the timing of guest worker recruitment. The Southern German region began recruiting guest workers in the mid-1950s when Italy was the first recruitment country. Recruitments from Turkey did not start until the 1960s.

48. Landeshauptstadt Stuttgart, Statistisches Amt, "Aktuelle Zahl—Einwohnerzahl und Wirtschaftsdynamik in Stuttgart," http://www.stuttgart.de/sde/item/gen/145664.htm.

49. Landeshauptstadt Stuttgart, Stabsabteilung fur Integrationspolitik, *Bündnis für Integration,* August 2004, 9.

50. Ibid., 13.

51. Ibid., 12.

52. Landeshauptstadt Stuttgart, "Referat für Kultur, Bildung und Sport," *Schulbericht 2003,* May 2004.

53. In 2005 the city also received one of the four prizes awarded by the Ministry of Interior and the Bertelsmann Foundation for its entry into a competition titled "Successful Integration Is No Accident: Strategies for Communal Integration Policy" (my translation). Among the four communities receiving the award, Stuttgart was the only large city; see http://www.stuttgart.de/4/sixcms/detail.php?id=23474.

54. See http://www.stuttgart.de/sde/item/gen/14357.htm.

55. A 1973 document from the Ministry of Health and Social Welfare and Work of the State of Baden-Württemberg, *Denkschrif: über Ausländische Arbeitnehmer in Baden-Württemberg* (Ministerium fur Arbeit, Gesundheit und Sozialordnung), notes that the integration of foreign workers will create "serious conditions in the labor market" and that foreigners should be encouraged to return. See Schmitter, "Immigration and Citizenship," 232. Manfred Rommel, who was lord mayor from 1974 to 1996, has been credited as the father of Stuttgart's liberal foreigners' policy, a policy that continues under the new lord mayor, Wolfgang Schuster.

56. Ibid.

57. Babel, "City of Stuttgart and Immigration"; personal communication, Yvonne Hapke, Stabsabteilung für Integration, Landeshauptstadt Stuttgart, December 26, 2004.

58. The committee also includes several nonvoting members who are selected by the municipal council.

59. Political parties and civic organizations are open to anyone interested in participating. The *Vokshochschule* (literally "peoples' high school," i.e., adult education) organizes lectures about the historical, political, and legal themes.

60. For a list of language and integration courses offered in Stuttgart, see http://www.stuttgart.de/sde/item/gen/134435.htm.

61. According to the lord mayor, Stuttgart wants to become the most "child-friendly" large city in Germany. In the last several years, the city invested more than €20 million toward better child care services for children between the ages of three and six years.

The city created 1,525 kindergarten slots in 2001–3 and planned to create 1,000 more in 2004 (http://www.stuttgart.de/kits).

62. The Organization for Economic Cooperation and Development's Program for International Student Assessment (PISA; http://www.pisa.oecd.org) study showed the German system to be the most class based among the thirty-two countries in the study. The relationship between socioeconomic background and school performance was greatest in Germany. Isabel de Pommerau, "Germany: Schools That Divide," *Christian Science Monitor,* October 22, 2002.

63. Though the proportion of students attending the comprehensive school is only around 2 percent in most states, the city-state of Berlin stands out with a 20 percent enrollment in such schools. This has been an important factor influencing the success rate of foreign students.

64. Landeshauptstadt Stuttgart, "Stabsabteilung für Integrationspolitik der Landeshauptstadt Stuttgart," *Ein Bündnis für Integration: Grundlagen einer Integrationspolitk in der Landeshauptstadt Stuttgart,* August 2004, graphic, 13.

65. Respondents were divided into German and non-German (the latter not allowing for differences between nationalities and legal statuses). Though the overall response rate was 35 percent, foreign residents' response rate was only 16 percent (German was 40 percent). Petra Reichle, "Integration ausländischer Mitbürger in Stuttgart—Ergebnisse der Bürgerumfrage," *Statistik und Informationsmanagement Monatshefte* 5 (2004): 135–44.

66. The title of this section was the headline of an article about Munich in *Time Europe,* July 26, 2004.

67. Ibid.

68. Landeshauptstadt München, Amt fur Statistik und Datenanalyse, "Entwicklung des Augländeranteils in München seit 1925," *Münchener Statistik,* no. 4, 1974.

69. Landeshauptstadt München, Statistisches Amt, *Statistiches Jahrbuch,* 2002, 52–53 (the data are for 2001).

70. Landeshauptstadt München, Statistisches Amt, "Die Entwicklung der Kindergarten in den vergangenen 15 Jahren," *Münchner Statistik,* no. 6, 1999, 87–90.

71. Landeshauptstadt München, Sozialreferat, "Bildung und berufliche Ausbildung," http://www.muenchen.de/print?depl=prod&oid+49287. In a position paper responding to the PISA study findings that children whose parents were born abroad did poorly in school, the Ausänderbeirat München lists a variety of problems that need to be addressed if the situation is to improve, including the guarantee that all children above the age of three can get a place in kindergarten, better language instruction in kindergartens, better transition from kindergarten to school, and more all-day schools. See "Chancengleichheit von Migrantenkindern im bayrischen Schulsystem nach PISA," http://www.auslaenderbeirat-muenchen.de/aktu/chancen.htm.

72. See Landeshauptstadt München, Stadtentwicklungsreferat, "Kommunalpolitische Aspekte des wachseneden ausländischen Bevölkerungsanteils in München," *Arbeitsberichte zur Fortschreibung des Statentwicklungsplans,* no. 4, April 1972.

73. See http://www.auslaenderbeirat-muenchen.de/hist.

74. Landeshaupstadt München, *Ausländerbeirat,* 2004.

75. Lutz Hoffmann, "Krise und Perspektive der Ausländerbeirate" Referat im Ausländerbeirat München, May 26, 2003, http://www.auslaederbeirat-muenchen.de/aktu.htm.

76. See http://www.aulaenderbeirat-munechen.de/aktu/presse/04-05-10.htm.

77. Landeshauptstadt München, Kulturreferat, http://www.muenchen.de/Rathaus/kult/ansprechpartner/interkult/48940/wir.html.

78. Department of Urban Planning, City of Munich, *The Munich Perspective: A Summary of the 1998 Urban Development Strategy* (Munich: Department of Urban Planning, City of Munich, 1999).

79. Hubertus Schröer, "Interkulturelle Orientierung und Öffnung des Sozialreferates—Erfahrungen mit einem strategischen Ansatz," in *Landeshauptstadt München, Sozialreferat, Stelle für Interkulturelle Arbeit. Fachtagung—Vielfalt gestalten—Dokumentation,* ed. Landeshauptstadt München (Munich: Landeshauptstadt München, 2003).

80. Landeshauptstadt München, "Referat für Stadtplanung und Bauordnung," in *Lebenssituation ausländischer Bürgerinnen und Bürger in München,* Perspektive München (Munich: Landeshauptstadt München, 1997).

81. See http://www.citymayors.com.

82. Unabhängigen Kommission Zuwanderung, *Zuwanderung.*

83. Schrader Stiftung et al., *Immigrants in the City,* 14.

84. Deutscher Städtetag, Zuwanderungsgesetz 2004, http://www.staedtetag.de/10/presse/dst_beschluesse/artikel/2004/0608/00065.

85. For a brief summary of the results, see PISA–Konsortium Deutschland, PISA 2003, Kurzfassung der Ergebnisse, http://www.pisa.ipn.uni-kiel.de/Kurzfassung_PISA 2003.pdf.

86. As noted above, PISA included forty-one countries; see http://www.pisa.oecd.org.

87. In 1999 the Ministry for Traffic, Building, and Housing, together with the federal states, initiated a program titled City Districts with Special Needs for Development: The Socially Integrated City to improve the quality of life in districts with an accumulation of social, economic, and housing problems. The program provides federal funds for city neighborhoods that meet these characteristics (see *Soziale Stadt. Info,* July 2000). The program also reports on "best practice" research on selected topics. Schools have been one of those topics. See *Soziale Stadt, Info 16,* February 2005 (http://www.sozialestadt.de/veroeffentlichungen/newsletter). Though there are a variety of programs trying to address the schooling of socially disadvantaged children, including the children of immigrants, and case studies that have evaluated these programs, these have not produced the political will to reform the stratified German system.

10

Urban Migrants and the Claims of Citizenship in Postcolonial Africa

Dickson Eyoh

By specifying conditions for admitting immigrants and other policies, states profoundly affect the manner of integration of migrants into host economies and societies. Legal definitions of who is a citizen and the extent to which immigrants are included or denied the rights, obligations, and privileges of national citizenship are perhaps the most important juridical premises by which states shape the experiences of migrants. Citizenship remains a unresolved and highly contested issue in contemporary Africa. The classification and attendant differentiation of the rights of citizens and migrants have been major factors in recent and ongoing civil and interstate wars on the continent.

The roots of the 1994 Rwandan genocide, for example, lie in the transformation of intergroup relations during colonialism, which resulted in the creation of an ethnic hierarchy of colonial subjects. The genocide was fueled by Hutu irredentists' categorization of their Tutsi compatriots, who were privileged in the colonial ethnic hierarchy, as descendants of foreign invaders and thus undeserving of full citizenship in Rwandan society. A major trigger of the civil war, which culminated in the genocide, was the frustration of the citizenship claims of descendants of generations of Rwandans who had migrated to Uganda mostly as agricultural laborers during the colonial era and postindependence streams of predominantly Tutsi refugees. In the early 1980s, the Ugandan government, continuing the reluctance of previous postindependence governments, prohibited or severely restricted extending citizenship to members of long-resident Rwandan communities. Many would join, with several, such as Rwanda's current president, Paul Kagame, occupying leadership positions in Yoweri Musevini's armed insurgency, with the expectation that citizenship would be extended to their community in "postliberation" Uganda. Once in power, opposition from wide sections of Uganda's elite and ordinary citizens compelled President Musevini to renege on this promise. Faced with the prospect of the continued marginalization in Ugandan society, they elected to return "home" by military means.[1]

The rival rights' claims of "migrants" and "citizens" are a salient ingredient in the conflicts that have convulsed the Great Lakes Region over the three decades. In the eastern region of the Democratic Republic of the Congo (formerly Zaire), for example, much of the conflict and the changing constellation of armed factions engaged in it are rooted in the opportunistic manipulation of the citizenship status of Banyamulenge communities. A reformulation of citizenship laws in 1985 by the government of Mobutu Sese Seko restricted natural citizenship to persons belonging to groups that had been residing in the country before 1885, that is, before its very existence. The law was tantamount to a denationalization of the Banyamulenge, whose migration into the region predated the colonial demarcation of the country's borders but accelerated during the colonial era.[2]

This trend toward exclusionary conceptions of citizenship and the resistance to it by affected communities is a leading cause of the ongoing civil war in Ivory Coast. The growth of the Ivorian economy, based on smallholder and plantation agriculture during colonialism and its impressive expansion in the postcolonial era, depended on migrant labor from Burkina Faso and other landlocked Sahelian states. The postindependence regime of Felix Houphouet-Boigny maintained a liberal migration regime that easily extended citizenship to migrants and their descendants who were well integrated in rural and urban economies and societies. As the economy contracted in the 1980s and struggle to succeed Houphouet-Boigny remained unresolved, factions of the elite, who felt their hold on power threatened, resorted to propagation of an ideology of *ivorité* ("Ivorianness" or "being Ivorian") to mobilize communal political support. This nativist ideology of citizenship insisted on differentiating members of autochthonous communities who were considered to be natural citizens of the nation and descendants of migrants increasingly seen as not entitled to equal citizenship.[3]

The economic hardships that have confronted African states since the 1980s and have more recently been compounded by neoliberal adjustment policies, along with tentative processes of political liberalization, have engendered complex struggles over economic rights and resources at local, national, and regional levels.[4] The reconfiguration of political and economic relations has spurred new patterns of migration flows within and across countries and heightened conflicts between migrants and citizens. The tensions generated by the competing claims of citizens and migrants over livelihoods are most acute in cities, were the migrant presence has always been most visible. It is in Africa's burgeoning and decaying cities, which bear the deep scars of economic stagnation, that the "increasing streams of internal and foreign migrants and established residence confront each other in a struggle for material survival" through ever more inventive strategies.[5] In these struggles, citizens invoke claims of their superior rights to economic resources and opportunities over migrants. These struggles appear to be prompting states into ever more arbitrary measures to curb the inflow of foreigners and to disregard the basic human rights of the overwhelming majority of mostly unskilled and poor migrants who are without legal protection.

For example, Botswana, which had maintained a relatively open immigration regime and had actively recruited foreign professionals to sustain its impressive diamond-propelled economic expansion from the late 1960s, began to tighten its immigration controls in the late 1990s. It has reduced the employment benefits extended to foreign professionals, built a 5,000-kilometer electrified fence partly to curb the dramatic increase of Zimbabweans fleeing their country's devastated economy and political repression, introduced steep fines for migrants without proper documentation and citizens who harbor them, and so on. A recent law prescribes the public flogging of undocumented immigrants who for long were not of much concern to the state and its citizens, who profited from the cheap labor they provided.[6] The comparative dynamism of the postapartheid South African economy has positioned that country as the choice destination of documented and undocumented migrants from Southern Africa and beyond. Mind-boggling inequalities and the destitution of its numerically preponderant black urban populations have stoked a virulent anti-immigrant xenophobia directed mainly at black African immigrants. The postapartheid state appears to have responded to public anxiety over immigration by retreating to the "fortress South Africa" mentality of the apartheid state that was determined to exclude entry of black Africans. Urban encounters between the vast majority of black African migrants who are located at the bottom of socioeconomic hierarchies, agents of the state security apparatus, and ordinary citizens are marked by casual violence.[7]

Rising anti-immigrant xenophobia in postapartheid South Africa and Botswana has received extensive commentary, undoubtedly because both are among the few relatively "strong states" in Africa with capacities to design and implement public policies. But anecdotal evidence suggests that the growing unwelcomeness of immigrants, even if less repugnant in expression, is not limited to these two states. This trend attests to the increasing vulnerability of old and new immigrant communities in Africa's cities within ongoing processes of economic and political reconfiguration.

This chapter is a tentative exploration of the ways shifting political and economic circumstances, which underpin the complex dynamics of cross-border migrations, shape the attitudes of Sub-Saharan African states toward immigration and the legal protections or lack thereof that they extend to different categories of immigrants. The chapter begins from the unexceptional premise that states do have a sovereign right to manage the flow of immigrants into their societies. In a world of increasing transnational migration and the challenges this poses for absorbing culturally different and socioeconomically heterogeneous groups, states also have a moral and practical responsibility to facilitate the settlement and integration of immigrants in their societies. The elaboration of rights for migrants that do not condone discrimination against them because of their lack of citizenship—in others words, rights that protect their human dignity—is imperative to the discharge of these responsibilities.

The chapter explores these issues with a broad brush, and its aims are both modest and ambitious. They are modest in the sense that it does not pretend to offer a systematic audit of migrant rights, the historical conditions in which these rights have been determined and transformed, or the level of protection they have afforded immigrants. It is ambitious in that it seeks to unravel how continuities and shifts in official attitudes toward immigrants have been conditioned by the changing dynamics and patterns of cross-border migrations for states whose histories are quite diverse. African nation-states, practically all of which are artificial constructions of European colonialism at the turn of the twentieth century, have never been effective containers of their fundamental economic and social processes.

These have been and continue to be shaped by overlapping regional contexts. Thus, teasing out patterns of continuities and changes in the dynamics of migration can help to clarify the sources and nature of challenges to be confronted in the struggle to elaborate rights for migrants that enhance their prospects for building meaningful lives in Africa's turbulent urban environments. The chapter is organized around a threefold periodization of the modern African trajectory: the colonial era, roughly from 1900 to the 1950s; the postindependence era of state-directed nation building and development from the late 1950s to 1980s; and the post-1980s period characterized by a crisis of postcolonial state legitimacy, economic stagnation, experimentation with neoliberal reforms, and an uneven, tentative process of political liberalization.

Making "Foreign" Migrants and Citizens: Colonial Antecedents

Contemporary notions of citizens and immigrants who do not enjoy legal membership in a national political community have their origins in European colonization and the establishment of territorially delimited state administrations. Africa has historically been a continent on the move, a continent of frontier societies as low populations densities facilitated the intermittent movement of peoples across short and long distances. Precolonial migrations were prompted by demographic-resource pressures and political protests by groups escaping unacceptable political authority. These movements commonly led to the permanent relocation and integration of migrants into host communities.[8] The establishment of states and the development of colonial economies set into motion new patterns of movement, which involved the enlargement and spatial upscaling of migration flows. Under colonialism, migration became predominantly a movement of labor, most of it brutally exploited cheap labor that was confined to the bottom of colonial socioeconomic hierarchies. A critical determinant of the shifts in the patterns and logics of migration was the spatially uneven character of colonial economic development, which rested on a combination of resource endowments and the needs of metropolitan economies. The dynamic agricultural and mineral-rich regions acted as magnets of labor from more poorly endowed areas within and across colonial territories.[9]

Although Africa has a rich history of urbanization that predated colonialism by centuries, the urbanization of the continent is primarily a phenomenon of the twentieth century that was driven by the enclave character of colonial economies.[10] Colonial cities, some of which were built on or replaced preexisting towns and others of which were created from scratch, functioned as commercial and administrative centers of colonial extractive economies. Their growth, slowly in the first two decades of the twentieth century and then rapidly after World War II, was propelled by immigration, initially from their immediate hinterlands and then increasingly from more remote locations and internationally.[11]

Colonial states—though fabled for their authoritarian and militaristic tendencies and their outer vestments as Leviathans bent on the total domination of subject populations—lacked the capacity to regulate immigration. Colonial borders remained porous, and movement across them was unhindered. In fact, economic necessity disinclined colonial regimes from any rigorous control of immigration. Labor scarcity, owing to the fact that the majority of Africans were free peasants with secure access to land, was the main constraint on economic expansion. Consequently, colonial regimes were preoccupied with generating and facilitating the movement of labor to areas of most need and tended to adopt a transterritorial approach to the labor question. The manner and intensity of the coordination of labor and economic policies between administrations varied and depended on large measure on the contiguity of territories within and between imperial zones. It thus was more pronounced in the case of French West Africa and French Central Africa, imperial zones with high territorial contiguity; British East Africa, which comprised the contiguous territories of Kenya, Uganda, and Tanzania; and Britain's Southern African colonies.[12] In French West Africa, for example, landlocked Burkina Faso was officially treated as a labor reserve for the coastal plantation economy of Ivory Coast, while it and other landlocked Sahelian states supplied labor for Senegal's groundnut economy. The Southern African British colonies, together with the Portuguese colony of Mozambique, were part of a highly regulated migrant labor system feeding the labor needs of South African mines.[13] This transterritorial approach to the labor question extended to the minuscule group of African skilled workers and middle-class professionals. For example, Sierra Leoneans were employed in colonial administrations, commercial firms, and missionary societies across British West Africa, whereas Senegalese and Dahomeans were similarly engaged in French Western and Central African colonies.[14] In a word, with or without official guidance, labor moved freely within and across imperial zones. Where there existed official concerns about migration, as was especially the case for French colonial administrations, these concerns were mainly about emigration. The imposition of compulsory labor through the infamous *code indignant* by French administrations, which was only abolished in the 1940s, provoked protest migrations as Africans seeking to escape its multiple exactions often elected to move to neighboring British-governed territories.[15]

Migrations, Economic Diasporas, and Hierarchies of Colonial Subjects

Despite the lack of official impediments to the mobility of Africans within and across imperial zones, the establishment of territorially bounded administrations with overarching political authority signaled a wholly new conception of the "migrant" as the eternal "other." The formation of economic diasporas, distributed in varying configurations across colonies, embedded this new "Othering" of migrants. The formation of economic diasporas was a natural outgrowth of migration dynamics. For much of the colonial period, internal and cross-territorial migration was circulatory as labor moved back and forth between spaces of labor and commerce and place of origin. Over time, for many migrants, the periods spent in spaces of labor became increasingly longer, transforming them into permanent residents even as they maintained ties of varying strength with their home communities. The importance of colonialism's economic diasporas to the new "Othering" of migrants lay in the complex articulations of multiple hierarchies of colonial subjects and the socioeconomic and cultural relations and networks deployed by migrants in their struggle to fashion lives in foreign spaces.

As already intimated, citizenship, specifically the exclusion of Africans from citizenship, was at the heart of colonial governance. In powerful analysis of the technologies of colonial rule, which is echoed in the magisterial account of the African colonial state by Crawford Young, Mamdani argues that colonial domination was secured through a double—institutional and spatial—segregation of state and society.[16] In this double segregation, Europeans and the handful of Westernized middle-class urban Africans were treated as citizens and governed by European-derived civil law. The rest of the population were treated as subjects and governed through customary law and tradition. As variously conceived and operationalized by imperial authorities, the practice of indirect rule—whereby local populations were assumed to belong to distinct and unchanging tribes and were thus best managed through their traditional authorities—was the institutional linch-pin of native subjugation.

This representation of the essence of colonial rule, whose nuances it is not possible to capture in the available space, highlights the reality of the absence of citizen rights for African colonial subjects. France and Portugal professed assimilationist doctrines—whereby their African subjects could ascend to citizenship upon acquisition of the requisite European cultural values and behaviors—extended this status to an infinitesimal number of Africans. A notable example of the "success" of the assimilationist doctrine was the granting of citizenship status to members of four communes (Saint Louis, Dakar, Rufisque, and Goree) in colonial Senegal. Even in this case, the citizenship status of the *originaires* of the four Senegalese communes (and of *evolues* across Portuguese and French colonies) remained ambiguous and contested because it was never obvious that it made them coequals of their European compatriots.[17]

The architecture of colonial rule and the circumstances that compelled colonial regimes to adopt "liberal" migration regimes made the designation of "indigenous" and "foreign-born" subjects largely irrelevant to the ways in which Africans constructed urban lives and relationships. Colonial societies were structured as racial-caste systems, and racial divisions informed the spatial design of colonial cities. They were divided into "white towns," which were adequately serviced by urban amenities, and "native towns" for the servants of colonialism, which were deprived of the most basic amenities. In the native peripheral zones of colonial cities, housing and other amenities were obtained through informal arrangements. Ethnic and other communal ties structured the networks through which native and foreign-born African subjects organized access to resources and opportunities in urban spaces.[18]

But often missing or not adequately captured in analyses of the technologies of colonial rule, which accent the shared subject status of Africans, is an exploration of the multiple and hierarchical layering of subjects that incubated contemporary notions of migrants and citizens with different rights and obligations to the state. First, colonial administrations treated Africans as subjects of a single imperial authority (French, British, Portuguese, etc.) with rights of mobility and residence within imperial zones. Out of this practice emerged a distinction of subjects of the same imperial authority and foreign subjects from areas governed by different imperial authorities. Second, and more consequential, with the imposition of territorially delimited administrations, Africans were classed as subjects of particular territories from which they originated, that is, as "foreigners" from different territories even when these were administered by the same imperial authority. Thanks, in part, to colonial insistence on the primacy of ethnic identities for Africans, the sense of national belonging or citizenship remained meaningless for the vast majority of Africans for much of the colonial era. Cross-border migrations by Africans during the colonial era entailed movement to specific cities or locales as spaces of economic opportunity, rather than relocation to new countries with the prospect of acquiring new nationalities.[19] Yet these distinctions encouraged the marking of external migrants as "foreign nationals." That is, although foreign, like internal, migrants tended to self-identify primarily by ethnicity, members of their host territories were inclined to attach "national" labels to them. Instead of, or along with, ethnic labels, foreign migrants were Nigerians, Dahomeans, Cameroonians, Senegalese, Kenyans, Ugandans, and so on.

Colonial cities were veritable laboratories for the fashioning of new identities and creation of hyphenated subjects. They were polyglot cultural spaces in which internal and foreign migrants had to assume new roles and construct new modes of social interaction. Their residents, permanent and temporary, were simultaneously imbricated in multiple overlapping communities: urban laboring communities, middle-class society, different commercial circuits, diasporic communities, and ethnic networks within these broader diasporic communities.[20] They produced and were simultaneously engaged in lifestyles that, in Ferguson's terminology, were cosmopolitan (the result of the ongoing blending of foreign and indigenous cultural elements) and localist (rooted in particular communal traditions and idioms) in orientation.[21] However, networks that were predicated on constantly elaborated and redefined ethnic and other kin-based affinities were most significant to the socialization of internal and external migrants in cities.[22] The improvement of transportation and communications permitted urban migrants to remain in continuous contact with their ethnic "homelands" through more or less regular visits, the acquisition of partners, the arrival of new migrants from these homelands, and the like.[23] The centrality of ethnic and other kin-based networks to the migration experience added to the "Othering" of foreign migrants. Besides enabling the creation and reproduction of urban ethnicities, they led to the concentration of migrants in particular occupational sectors. For example, in the Gold Coast (contemporary Ghana), Yorubas, the largest group of Nigerian migrants, were the dominant African group in the local diamond and timber industries. Fishermen from the Gold Coast were conspicuous in fishing economies along the entire West African Coast; Ibos from the eastern region of Nigeria controlled the commerce in manufactured goods in British-ruled Southern Cameroons; Rwandan immigrants in Uganda were predominantly agricultural laborers; and Ghanaians were the most visible of African skilled workers and professionals in Liberia.[24]

Last, the imposition of an overarching political authority in the form of colonial administrations altered the dynamic of political relations between migrants and their host communities. Though precolonial urban migrants were often spatially segregated, their stay depended on the continued welcome of local political authorities and they were therefore motivated to nurture political links with host rulers.[25] Colonial migrant communities of necessity had to interact with traditional authorities for a range of reasons (access to land, mediation of disputes between migrants and their native hosts, etc.). They were also involved in the overlapping ethnic-based patronage networks that defined colonial urban politics.[26] But in confining the reach of traditional authority to preexisting cultural groups within demarcated territories, indirect rule dampened pressures on migrants to nurture close relations with indigenous political rulers. Its core principle allowed for much ambiguity and tensions in political relations between urban migrants and local traditional rulership and communities. It placed urban migrants simultaneously within and outside the structures of local native politics as it left open the option of their seeking political redress directly from colonial authorities. Moreover, with the enlarged scale of migration, urban migrants constructed parallel political structures for the management of their internal affairs and mediation of relations between them and their hosts. In many instances, indigenous traditional rulers in towns and cities who were more intensely supervised than their rural counterparts were content to leave responsibility for migrants to colonial administrators. In sum, the socioeconomic, cultural, and political factors that underpinned the positioning of migrants as eternal "others" would make them vulnerable in the future contests of rights between citizen and migrant.

Postcolonial Moment One:
Nation Building, Citizenship, and Migrant Rights

The end of colonial rule in Sub-Saharan Africa, which began with the independence of Ghana in 1957, marked a significant moment in the differentiation of citizens and foreign migrants and their respective rights and obligations to states. Nation building and economic development were the defining projects of elites who inherited colonial states. The nation-building project called for the transformation of spaces inherited from colonialism into viable national political communities. It presupposed the fortification of international boundaries as the referent of state sovereignty, the definition of who legally belonged to emergent national political communities, and the nurturing of symbiotic relations between their subjects and rulers.

In one of the few analyses of citizenship laws in postcolonial Africa, Jeffrey Herbst maintains that postcolonial states hardly modified citizenship laws inherited from colonialism.[27] Herbst's argument is influenced by a "bellicist perspective" on state formation, associated with Charles Tilly and others, which regards war as the main driver of modern state formation in Europe.[28] In this argument, postcolonial African states were born in an international environment in which war had ceased to be an accepted means of expanding and defending the territorial boundaries of states. This, together with the acceptance of colonial boundaries and the doctrine of non-interference in the internal affairs of other states that anchored the postcolonial African international system, relieved ruling elites of the need to invest in the hardening of state boundaries and effective broadcast of state power across the territories over which they claimed sovereign authority.[29] Though citizenship remained one of the few rights postcolonial states could provide to their subjects, clarifying and drawing hard boundaries between citizens and foreigners has thus not been a pressing obligation for postcolonial ruling elites. Jennifer Seally, in a preliminary analysis of mostly Francophone states that builds on Herbst's, suggests that though colonial legacies have been important, there have been significant revisions of citizenship laws. These revisions reveal no clear trends toward more restrictive or liberal citizenship laws, and postcolonial citizenship regimes exhibit mixtures of the three principles of jus soli (citizenship based on birth in a sovereign's territory), jus sanguinis (citizenship based on descent according to blood kinship), and naturalization through established legal procedures. The acquisition of citizenship through naturalization has been exceedingly rare and typically involves foreign spouses.[30]

The status of Africans as subjects, rather than citizens, combined with the legal right to mobility of subjects of territories within imperial zones, made for a lack of clarity as to who was entitled to citizenship in emerging states. This was quickly resolved through the hardening of notions of the native born and foreigner that had been incubated by the hierarchal positioning of African subjects in colonial states. The foundational, if often un-written, principle for defining citizenship in the new states was membership in ancestral kin-based communities existing in territories when colonial boundaries were demarcated. Independence thus brought with it the legal exclusion from national citizenship of those were regarded as non-native-born migrants, regardless of length of residence in colonial territories, or at best made their claims or expectations of citizenship a highly contested issue.

The vulnerability of foreign migrants arising from this "nativist" conception of the basis for citizenship or national belonging became apparent in the growth of "antiforeigner" protests and expulsions of migrants as anticolonial struggles, in which they were also deeply involved, intensified. In the terminal decade of colonial rule, Ghanaian fishermen who plied their trade across the West African Coast were expelled from Nigeria, Ivory Coast, and other colonies. In 1954, the first African-led preindependence government in Ghana ordered the repatriation of large numbers of Nigerians, apparently as punishment for their support for rival political parties. Members of Nigerian and other migrant communities who assumed their long residence qualified them as citizens with political rights in the emerging sovereign state were thus pitted against an African-led government and an indigenous population generally insistent on their exclusion from citizenship. In 1958, educated unemployed young men rioted in Abidjan, Ivory Coast, to demand the expulsion of foreigners whom they held responsible for their lack of employment. They succeeded in compelling the government to repatriate at short notice large numbers of Nigerians, Dahomeyans, and Togolese.[31] The sudden mass expulsion of "foreigners" would turn out to be one of the favorite means of managing immigration in postcolonial Africa.

The core premise of citizenship in the new states resolved for the most part who was entitled to political rights as it excluded migrants from participation in formal political arenas. With the exception of a handful of states, such as Senegal, Botswana, and Gambia, which retained more or less competitive multiparty political systems, the widespread trend toward authoritarian rule in the postcolonial era attenuated the significance of the distribution of political rights between citizens and migrants to the ways in which the majority of foreign migrants constructed, reproduced, and transformed urban lives. The political rights of migrants reemerged as a contentious issue in the 1980s as the crisis of legitimacy of postcolonial states became pronounced and regimes were increasingly confronted by popular demands for political liberalization. As noted in the aforementioned cases of the Democratic Republic of the Congo and Ivory Coast, the "denationalization" of entire communities because of their migrant origins would become a tactic for asserting control over such communities.

For citizens, participation in formal political arenas—through elections, local party organizations, trade unions, and other functional interest groups that typically were incorporated as organs of official one parties—became a mere ritual of support for incumbent regimes rather than an ideologically driven contestation over public policy. The elaboration of neopatrimonial networks as the institutional bedrock of political power and the preeminence of informal over formal arrangements meant that personal ties to those who controlled power became the primary channels of access to public goods.[32] Migrants, especially the well-heeled, were incorporated into networks of patronage and could easily exploit personal ties to those in power to secure favors from governments. In not a few instances, they exercised considerable influence in national politics through patronage connections to rulers and political elites.[33] African authoritarian regimes, like most others, are notorious for their aversion to the rule of law and penchant for the arbitrary exercise of power. In these political environments, self-preservation recommended that migrants, even more so than national citizens, be very cautious about engaging in politics, including organized demands for rights.

It was in the competition over economic rights and resources in urban society that the differentiation of citizens and migrants and their respective rights mattered the most. The lack of citizenship status exposed migrants to aggressive citizen-rights-based claims to economic resources and opportunities. Postcolonial regimes entered into elaborate bilateral and regional agreements on labor mobility and the protection of foreign workers. But these legal protocols have remained just that, formal agreements without much import for state practices.[34] Significantly, the reception extended to foreign migrants and their vulnerability to citizens' claims to economic resources was and continues to be premised on social class differences. The small group of highly skilled and professional African migrants, whose services were deemed essential for development, enjoyed legal protection and their integration in host economies and societies was fairly uneventful. The most vulnerable, without legal protection, remained the preponderant majority of poor, unskilled, and semiskilled laborers engaged in low-wage employment and in informal commercial sectors where the struggle over livelihoods would be unrelenting. The salience of competition over economic rights and the class-dependent vulnerabilities of migrant groups were conditioned by the interrelationship among the favored development strategies of postcolonial regimes, urbanization trends, and the dynamics of cross-border migration flows.

Urbanization rates across Sub-Saharan Africa, which began to rise significantly at the end of World War II, accelerated after independence. During the 1960s and 1980s, urban populations grew by an annual average of 5 to 6 percent, ahead of the national population growth rates of 3 to 4 percent. In the same period, principal national cities grew faster, at an annual average of 9 to 11 percent. The pace of urbanization varied across regions and states, with the least urbanized registering the fastest growth rates.[35] However, any randomly selected set of examples would confirm the magnitude of the pace of urbanization on a continent that was simultaneously the least urbanized and fastest urbanizing in the world after World War II. The population of Lagos in Nigeria increased from 288,000 in 1950 to 469,000 in 762,000 in 1960, over 1.4 million in 1970, and just below 2.6 million in 1980. Douala in Cameroon grew from 101,000 in 1950 to 172,000 in 1960, 292,000 in 1970, and 522,000 in 1980. The population of Abidjan in Ivory Coast increased from 59,000 in 1950 to 180,000 in 1960, 553,000 in 1970, and nearly 1.3 million in 1980. That of Accra grew from 250,000 in 1950 to 395, 000 in 1960, 746, 000 in 1970, and to over 1 million in 1980; and Bamako in Mali grew from 34,000 in 1960 to 61,000 in 1960, 126,000 in 1970, and 260,000 in 1980.[36] The rapid space of urbanization was fueled by rural migration, especially by youth. This pattern of growth continued through the 1980s, after which it appeared to slow down moderately in favor of small and midsized cities and with some evidence of increased urban-rural migration.[37]

Statist Development, the Permanent Crisis
of Urban Reproduction, and Migrant Rights

In keeping with the prevailing Keynesian-inspired theories of economic growth and African nationalist ideology, the postindependence development model positioned states as the main agents of economic transformation. States expanded their control over economies, invested in physical infrastructure, and fostered the development of industry through public enterprises or in partnership with multinational corporations, as well as sponsoring programs to improve education, health care, and other social services. Bureaucracies mushroomed to cater for these development ambitions, and states became the primary employers of labor in the formal sector. Urban centers, especially principal cities, received the lion's share of public- and private-sector corporate investments. The urban bias of state-directed development accentuated the preeminence of cities as locations of all sorts of possibilities, even when the realization of these possibilities would remain illusory for most of the young migrants swelling their populations.

On gaining independence, states imposed new legal controls on immigration, including work and residence permits for foreigners. Despite the battery of legal controls, most lacked regulatory mechanisms and the capacity to manage migration. The paucity of basic demographic data on African states makes reliable estimates of the scale and pattern of international migration flows impossible; nonetheless, its generally agreed that cross-border movements continued relatively unhindered. The bulk of international migration involved the movement of semiskilled and unskilled labor to neighboring countries. Ecologically distressed states and those experiencing economic stress due to mismanagement and political instability contributed most of the migrant flows. Examples include resource-poor Upper Volta, Niger, and Mali, which continued their colonial-era roles as labor reserves for Ivory Coast; Ghana, whose economy experienced severe decline through the late 1960s and 1970s, with significant numbers of its citizens forced to migrate to Nigeria, Ivory Coast, and other West African states; and Uganda, where the collapse of the economy and political violence under Idi Amin's maniacal rule forced many to seek refuge in Kenya and other Eastern African states.[38]

On the eve and early years of independence, skilled and professional foreigners employed in colonial administrations and commercial enterprises returned to their home countries. Their decision to depart was on occasion involuntary because they were under pressure to make way for nationals; but for the most part, it was voluntary because independence also meant equal or greater opportunities in their home countries. African states had to rely on foreign sources to compensate for domestic deficits in skilled professional workers to sustain their development goals. High-performing economies—such as Ivory Coast, whose growth was premised on agro-industry; oil-rich Nigeria and Gabon, which used windfall revenues from the spikes in oil prices in the mid-1970s induced by the Organization of the Petroleum Exporting Countries to embark on ambitious public investment programs; and diamond-rich Botswana—all actively recruited skilled workers and professionals from other African countries through the 1970s and 1980s. This need for skilled professionals and the lack of regulatory

mechanisms and capacity to manage migration produced two broad categories of foreign migrants: a small proportion of professionals and skilled
workers who enjoyed legal protection; and the vast majority of mostly undocumented migrants without such protection.

For all the preoccupation of postcolonial states and international development institutions with large-scale corporate enterprises, the main sources
of livelihood for expanding urban populations remained artisan production,
small-scale manufacturing, and commerce. By the 1950s, the more prosperous colonial economies like Ghana, Ivory Coast, Senegal, and Nigeria
in West Africa were already experiencing what colonial administrators
dubbed a "school leavers" problem, that is, the growth of unskilled and
semiskilled urban youth with some formal education who could not be gain-
fully employed in urban economies.[39] Some of the early preindependence
expulsions of foreigners from West African territories noted above were in
part responses to the crisis of reproduction of urban youth. The development strategies of postcolonial regimes exacerbated the structural basis for
the material insecurity of urban youth. Befitting an ideological orientation
that positioned youth as the primary agents and beneficiaries of modern-
ization, African governments undertook substantial investments in education, often at levels higher than the average of other developing regions.
Between 1965 and 1985, for example, primary and secondary school en-
rollments across Sub-Saharan African states increased from 41 to 68 percent of the eligible population while tertiary enrollment increased at a much
lower but steady rate.[40] However, the technology-intensive modes of im-
port-substitution industrialization to which regimes were drawn offered few
employment opportunities for the growing ranks of urban youth with some
formal education.

States provided few services to which their citizens were universally
entitled. The limited social services they offered (housing, health care, education, etc.) were typically made available as benefits for middle-class
professionals in their employ and for political elites. The rapid pace of urbanization outstripped their capacities to expand or maintain basic urban
services. The distribution of urban services became even more skewed in
favor of the planned neighborhoods of elites, while the chaotically expanding shantytowns and slums to which internal and foreign migrants fluxed
received little. In these zones of informal settlement and economic activity,
individual and communal initiative supplied housing and other basic urban
services. Thus, development strategies and the dynamic of urbanization but-

tressed the structural foundations of what can be accurately represented as a permanent crisis of reproduction of the urban poor.

In this regard, the "liberal" migration regimes of the postindependence era, which were predicated on their lack of capacity to manage immigration rather than outcomes of deliberate policy choices, were a double-edged sword for foreign migrants. On the one hand, they permitted easy cross-border movement, which, combined with the lack of social entitlements for citizens, meant that states did not meaningfully affect the choices available to and strategies used by poor, unskilled, and semiskilled foreign urban migrants. In other words, social class, rather than citizenship, determined the possibilities and challenges of constructing meaningful lives for migrants to foreign cities. On the other hand, the lack of legal protection for the less privileged migrants exposed them to harsh and arbitrary treatment. In times of national economic distress, many states continued to resort to the sudden expulsion of foreigners as a solution for their economic problems. Antiforeigner hostility became, in effect, a palliative for the crisis of urban reproduction. As Gray has written with reference to Gabon, antiforeigner protests served as the main premise on which citizens sought to establish their entitlement to economic rights and privileges through the exclusion of foreigners. For states that offered their citizens few social services, antiforeigner hostility was the key ingredient used by political elites to nurture a sense of national identity.[41]

The wave of mass expulsions of foreigners from the 1960s through mid-1980s often targeted specific country nationals either because of their high visibility among urban migrant populations or their perceived dominance of particular commercial sectors or labor market segments. For example, in 1967, Nigerians who were prominent in retail trade were expelled from Cameroon. In 1969, the Ghanaian government ordered the expulsion within a two-week period of over a quarter million foreigners from Nigeria, Niger, and Upper Volta without work and trade permits. In the late 1960s and 1970s, Ivory Coast repeatedly carried out mass deportations of Nigerians, Dahomeyans and Beninoise, and Nigerians were expelled in large numbers from the Democratic Republic of the Congo and Equatorial Guinea in the mid-1970s and 1980s. Gabon, which had a number of bilateral arrangements granting entry for semiskilled and skilled labor, periodically expelled large numbers in reaction to popular urban protests in this period.[42]

The most dramatic instance in the wave of mass deportations occurred in Nigeria in 1983. After the cessation of its civil war and with the rapid

growth of oil revenues in the mid-1970s, the country embarked on an unprecedented expansion of its industrial economy and mass investments in
infrastructure development and social sectors. The economic boom made it
the preeminent destination of migrant labor from neighboring countries.
Private firms and public institutions actively recruited professionals and
skilled labor from African countries and other regions. The boom also attracted huge numbers of undocumented unskilled and semiskilled migrants.
These were mainly engaged in informal-sector commercial activities and in
menial jobs (household servants, guards, cleaners, drivers, et al.), with
wages below what Nigerians were prepared to accept.

When oil prices dropped in the late 1970s and the economy went into recession, foreigners were blamed for rising unemployment and growing urban social problems (crime, prostitution, housing shortages, degradation of
urban physical infrastructure, etc.) and agitation for their removal intensified. Responding to xenophobic citizenship-based claims to economic opportunity, the Nigerian government, in January 1983, decreed that all illegal foreigners depart or be forcefully expelled from the country within two
weeks. An estimated 2 million foreigners, mainly from neighboring countries and approximately half of whom were Ghanaians, were affected by the
order. The order was exemplary of the class bias in the treatment of foreign
migrants by postcolonial regimes. It expressly excluded professional and
technical workers and extended the time for the regularization of the status
of other valued skilled workers.[43] Another expulsion order, this time affecting over 150,000 migrants, was carried out in 1985. Though unprecedented and since unrivalled in scope, the violence to the human rights and
dignity of the most vulnerable group of foreigners represented by such expulsions is by any measure extreme. In short notice, the most vulnerable are
forced to abandon painfully accumulated meager assets and social relations
and networks nurtured over varying periods of residency. For many, forced
repatriation meant return to places and communities where they may no
longer have significant social ties.

Postcolonial Moment Two: Migration Flows and Migrants'
Rights in the Age of Globalization and Neoliberal Adjustment

African states have been beset by unrelenting economic adversity over the
past four decades. Most economies, which had experienced unspectacular
but steady rates of growth since independence, began to stagnate in the mid-

1970s. They steadily declined during what has been dubbed the lost decades of the 1980s and 1990s.[44] Only a limited number of states, such as Botswana, Mauritius, and Lesotho, escaped the trend. As Stren and Halfani put it, "The most prominent institutional casualty of the crisis situation was the state and its agencies."[45] By the early 1980s, most were unable to meet recurrent expenditures for basic services, pay salaries regularly, and finance any form of public investment. For populations across the rural-urban divide, economic adversity translated into growing mass poverty and destitution.

Neoliberal structural adjustment programs, which were designed and managed by the Bretton Woods institutions (International Monetary Fund, World Bank, etc.), failed to arrest the decline. Policies intended to promote market-friendly reforms and to open up economies to trade and foreign investment bore little fruit, and the marginality of African economies in the expanding global economy increased. The continent was virtually bypassed in the dramatically increased flows of capital and goods during 1980s and 1990s as the value and competitiveness of its primary commodity exports diminished. Underpinned by an ideologically driven determination to "roll back the state," whose profligacy and excessive intervention in economies were blamed for the crisis, neoliberal policies to bring discipline to public expenditures compounded the negative social ramifications of the crisis. These policies typically required steep reductions in social spending (the elimination of subsidies for basic wage goods, the imposition of user fees for health, education, and other services, etc.) and the retrenchment of public-sector employment. Demands for the privatization and the restructuring of state-owned enterprises led to further joblessness.

Experimentations with neoliberal reforms advanced the complex rearrangements of economic relations between states and their citizens brought about by the exhaustion of statist models of development and nation formation. This impasse in development fed destructive forms political conflict, which further corroded the feeble legitimacy of postcolonial states and their limited capacities for social regulation. It weakened the ability of regimes to nourish the patronage networks on which their power was predicated, giving lease to ruthless competition among elite groups and communities over shrinking resource pools. In some instances, elite competition transformed states into instruments of predation and led to civil wars and the collapse or near collapse of states (Zaire, Somalia, Liberia, Sierra Leone, etc.). More positively, albeit with contradictory effects for foreign migrants, neoliberal economic reforms increased popular disaffection with authoritarian rule and prompted the rise of prodemocracy movements that succeeded in returning multiparty electoral competition to most countries in the early 1990s.

The economic, social, and political turbulence of the past four decades has resulted in mass displacements of populations that have made the continent home to the largest number of internal and external refugees in the world. This turbulence has also led to an upsurge in transnational migration flows, in ways that often make it difficult to distinguish between migrations motivated by political and economic considerations. Though there is much continuity in dynamics and patterns of cross-border movements, there is growing evidence of novel features in recent transnational migration flows.[46]

Prominent among these is, first, the spatial upscaling and diversification of migration destinations. In contrast to the past, when cross-border migrations mostly entailed movement to contiguous states, recent transnational flows have increasingly involved movement, both spontaneous and long-term, across longer distances. In other words, as opportunities for work have contracted in regional magnets of migration, people are compelled to journey to regions with fewer or nonexistent historical, cultural, and economic ties. This reconfiguration of regional complexes of emigration and immigration is most noticeable in the upsurge of migration from Western, Central, and Eastern Africa states to South Africa after the end of apartheid in 1994 led to the relaxation of severe controls on black African immigration. It is also evident, albeit on a much smaller scale, in the novel movements from Western Africa to Northern African countries, which often serve as staging posts for further journeys to Europe and North America.

The second novel feature of recent transnational migration flows is the increase in female migration when previously the migration experience was male dominated.[47] The increase in female migration is partly for familial reasons, as females, who typically remained at home, are forced to join their partners or other family members whose absences have became more extended and remittances less regular. For a significant proportion, migration is an independent decision to search for more promising livelihood opportunities. Though a small portion of female migrants are professionals, the majority have to survive through informal commercial activities (as petty traders, hairstylists, dressmakers, et al.) and exploitative domestic services, including prostitution.

Third, and related, is the shift from labor to predominantly commercial migration. Faced with a paucity of remunerative employment in their temporary or permanent destinations, the new streams of migrants have little choice but to become "self-employed entrepreneurs in the informal commercial sector."[48] As in the past, commercial migrations are embedded in both long-established and newly constituted and constantly redeployed transnational mercantile networks operating across wide geographies. For example, the economic lives of the new wave of commercial migrants to South Africa from outside Southern Africa often involve the importation of unique goods from their countries of origin or elsewhere and the use of the proceeds to export South African goods to their home countries. In this hardly unique context, recent transnational commercial migrations re-inscribe the complexity of migration as a simultaneously temporary or more or less long-term or permanent condition. What appears as a place of primary residence is likely to be just one of several national nodes in a complex web of networks and relations through which migrants organize their livelihoods. In these times of generalized economic, social, and political insecurity, the possibility of further movement to alternative frontiers of imaged opportunities is perpetually open and networks of migration and urban reproduction are subject to constant renegotiation.

Finally, professional and skilled workers facing a decline in their living standards caused by economic stagnation and neoliberal reforms are increasingly forced to elect migration as a survival strategy. The pressures to resort to migration as a survival strategy are heightened in the case of the swelling ranks of young graduates of tertiary institutions. The contraction of bureaucracies, which were the main employers of young graduates, has removed prospects for meaningful employment in their societies. Highly skilled professionals are able to secure remunerative employment and to enjoy legal protection in place of migration. The situation is less auspicious for more recent graduates, most of whom are likely to be undocumented and have to survive through informal-sector commercial activities and poorly paid work that they would have been unwilling to perform in their home countries.

Conclusion

This chapter has sought to sketch the dynamics of continuity and change in patterns of cross-border migrations in Sub-Saharan Africa since the colonial era. The main purpose of the analysis has been to deepen appreciation of the ways in which shifting political and economic conditions shape patterns of cross-border migrations and the attitudes of states toward immigration and their willingness to protect the human rights of migrants.

Colonialism gave birth to new patterns of migration, with the movement of labor being the defining characteristic of colonial-era migration. By implying membership in kin-based communities within their geographical borders as the basis for "national belonging," colonial states hatched novel conceptions of the "nonnative" or "foreign" migrant as the eternal other. The advent of independence led to a hardening of distinctions between "citizens" and "migrants." The core of this process has been the common, if rarely acknowledged, use of membership in ancestral communities existing in territories when colonial boundaries were demarcated as the foundational premise of natural citizenship in postcolonial states. The exclusionary conceptions of citizenship, which are fostered by this "nativist" view of the basis for national belonging, have left migrants, often regardless of their duration of residence, vulnerable to citizen-based rights claims to economic resources and political participation.

The paucity of institutional mechanisms and capacity to regulate migration, combined with the dearth of social services they provide to the overwhelming majority of their citizens, has meant that postcolonial states generally have had little influence on the abilities and strategies deployed by immigrants to construct lives, however precarious, in foreign cities. Yet, as highlighted in this analysis, these same factors have facilitated the creation and reproduction of two broad categories of migrants and their differential treatment based on social class distinctions: the privileged minority of professional and skilled workers who are afforded legal protection; and the vast majority of unskilled and semiskilled migrants without legal protection. It is the latter category of migrants who have been most susceptible to harsh and arbitrary treatment by states. Disproportionately young, it is they who must confront steady flows of internal migrants and established residents in ever more dire struggles for material reproduction in the informal economies of Africa's burgeoning cities. The historical-structural roots of their vulnerability lie in what has been dubbed the crisis of urban reproduction, engendered by the interrelationship among the strategies of development and the dynamic of urbanization. The crisis of urban reproduction became manifest in the terminal phase of colonial rule, has only intensified in the postcolonial era, and is unlikely to abet in the foreseeable future.

Transnational migration flows, spurred by the economic and political turbulence in which they have been enveloped over the last four decades, reaffirm the reality that postcolonial African states, as much as their colonial predecessors, have never been effective containers of their fundamental economic and social processes. These have always and will continue to be shaped within overlapping regional contexts. This reality intimates that preference for immigration policies that are unduly restrictive is bound to be counterproductive to national and regional economic and political well-being. The reality makes imperative legal and institutional frameworks that protect the essential human rights of migrants and facilitate their integration into host societies and economies. The apparent increase in conflicts between so-called migrants and citizens over rights to economic resources and political participation intimate that this is no easy task in societies where the determination of who is and is not a member of the national political community still awaits resolution. But these conflicts exacerbate the economic and political problems that are their cause and therefore affirm the urgent need to especially protect the basic human rights, including the right to livelihood, of the most vulnerable class of migrants.

Notes

1. Mahmood Mamdani, *When Victims Become Killers: Colonialism, Nativism and Genocide in Rwanda* (Princeton, N.J.: Princeton University Press, 2001).

2. P.-L. Pabanel, "La question de nationalite au Kivu," *Politique Africaine* 41 (1991): 32–40; Bogumil Jewsiewicki and Leonard N'sanda Buleli, "Ethnicities as 'First Nations' of the Congolese State: Some Preliminary Observations," in *Ethnicity and Democracy in Africa,* ed. Bruce Berman, Dickson Eyoh, and Will Kymlicka (Oxford and Athens: James Currey and Ohio University Press, 2004), 240–56.

3. See Siddartha Mitter, "Ebony and Ivorite: War and Peace in Ivory Coast," *Transition* 13, no. 4 (2003): 30–55; F. Akindes, "Racines des crises politiques et sens de l'histoire en Côte d'Ivoire," paper presented at CODESRIA–Nordic Africa Institute Conference on Identity, Security and the Renegotiation of National Belonging in West Africa: Reflections on the Ivorian Crisis, Dakar, May 15–16, 2003; and S. Bredeloup, "La construction de l'étranger en Côte d'Ivoire: Les stratégies identitaires des ressortissants de l'Afrique subsaharienne implantés en Côte d'Ivoire," paper presented at CODESRIA–Nordic Africa Institute Conference on Identity, Security and the Renegotiation of National Belonging in West Africa: Reflections on the Ivorian Crisis, Dakar, May 15–16, 2003; and Ebrima Sall, "Social Movements in the Renegotiation of the Basis of Citizenship in West Africa," *Current Sociology* 52, no. 4 (2004): 595–614. For a broader discussion of the link between citizenship and conflict, see Said Adejumodi, "Citizenship, Rights and the Problem of Conflicts and Wars in Africa," *Human Rights Quarterly* 23, no. 1 (2001): 148–70.

4. See chapter 5 in this volume by Simone.

5. Loren Landau, *Democracy and Discrimination: Black African Migrants in South Africa,* Global Migration Perspectives 5 (Geneva: Global Commission on International Migration, 2004), 5.

6. Eugene Campbell and John Oucho, *Changing Attitudes to Immigration and Refugee Policy in Botswana,* Southern African Migration Project Migration Policy Se-

ries 28 (Cape Town and Kingston: IDASA and Queens University, 2002); Eugene Campbell, "Attitudes of Botswana Citizens toward Immigrants: Signs of Xenophobia?" *International Migration* 44, no. 4 (2003): 72–110; and Francis Nyamnjoh, "Local Attitudes towards Citizenship and Foreigners in Botswana: An Appraisal of Recent Press Stories," *Journal of Southern African Studies* 28, no. 4 (2002): 757–76.

7. Jonathan Crush, "Fortress South Africa and the Deconstruction of Apartheid's Migration Regime," *Geoforum* 30, no. 1 (1999): 1–11; Jonathan Crush and Clarence Tshitereke, "Contesting Migrancy: The Foreign Labor Debate in Post-1994 South Africa," *Africa Today* 48, no. 3 (2001): 50–70; Ransford Danso and David McDonald, "Writing Xenophobia: Immigration and the Print Media in Post-Apartheid South Africa," *Africa Today* 48, no. 3 (2001): 115–37; Alan Morris, " 'Our Fellow Africans Make Our lives Hell': The Lives of Congolese and Nigerians in Johannesburg," *Ethnic and Racial Studies* 21, no. 6 (1998): 1116–36; and Marion Sinclair, " 'I Know a Place That Is Softer Than This . . .'—Emerging Migrant Communities in South Africa," *International Migration* 37, no. 2 (1999): 465–81.

8. See Igor Kopykoff, "The Internal African Frontier: The Making of African Political Culture," in *The African Frontier: The Reproduction of Traditional African Societies,* ed. Igor Kopykoff (Bloomington: Indiana University Press, 1987); and A. I. Asiwaju, "Migrations as Revolt: The Example of Ivory Coast and Benin before 1945," *Journal of African History* 17, no. 4 (1976): 113–27.

9. See Samir Amin, "Migrations in Contemporary Africa: A Retrospective View," in *The Migration Experience in Africa,* ed. J. Baker and Tade Aina (Uppsala: Nordic Africa Institute, 1995); and Samir Amin, "Introduction" in *Modern Migrations in West Africa,* ed. Samir Amin (Oxford: Oxford University Press for the International African Institute, 1972).

10. On precolonial urbanism, see William Bascom, "Urbanism as a Traditional African Pattern," *Sociological Review* 7, no. 1 (1959): 29–43; and the rich collection of essays in *Africa's Urban Past,* ed. David Anderson and Richard Rathbone (Oxford: James Currey, 2000).

11. For informative surveys, see Catherine Coquery-Vidrovitch, "The Process of Urbanization in Africa (from the Origins to the Beginning of Independence)," *African Studies Review* 34, no. 1 (1991): 1–98; and Hilda Kuper, ed., *Urbanization and Migration in West Africa* (Berkeley: University of California Press, 1965).

12. On migration in colonial British Africa, see William Gould and R. Mansell Prothero, "Migration between Commonwealth Countries of Africa," in *Commonwealth Migration: Flows and Policies,* ed. T. E. Smith (London: Macmillan, 1981), 170–200.

13. Jonathan Crush, Allen Jeeves, and David Yudelman, *South Africa's Labor Empire: A History of Black Migrancy to the Gold Mines* (Cape Town: David Philips, 1991).

14. See the interesting case of a Sierra Leonean diaspora in Nigeria by Mac Dixon-Fyle, *A Saro Community in the Niger Delta, 1912–1984: The Potts-Johnson Family of Port Harcourt and Their Heirs* (Rochester: University of Rochester Press, 1999).

15. See Asiwaju, "Migrations as Revolt."

16. See Mahmood Mamdani, *Citizens and Subjects: Contemporary Africa and the Legacies of Late Colonialism* (Princeton, N.J.: Princeton University Press, 1996); and Crawford Young, *The African Colonial State in Comparative Perspective* (New Haven, Conn.: Yale University Press, 1994).

17. See Mamadou Diouf, "The French Colonial Policy of Assimilation and the Civility of the Originaires of the Four Communes (Senegal): A Nineteenth-Century Glob-

alization Project," in *Globalization and Identity: Dialectics of Flows and Closure,* ed. Brigit Meyer and Peter Geschiere (London: Blackwell, 1996); and Catherine Coquery-Vidrovitch, "Nationalité et citoyenneté en Afrique Occidentale Française: Originaires et citoyens dans le Sénégal Colonial," *Journal of African History* 42, no. 2 (2001): 285–305.

18. See Catherine Coquery-Vidrovitch, *Histoire des villes d'Afrique noire: Des origines à la colonisation* (Paris: Albin Michel, 1993); Lynn Schler, "Ambiguous Spaces: The Struggle over African Identities and Communities in Douala, 1914–45," *Journal of African History* 44, no. 1 (2003): 51–72; and Richard Stren and Mohamed Halfani, "The Cities of Sub-Saharan Africa: From Dependency to Marginality," in *Handbook of Urban Studies,* ed. Ronald Raddison (London: Sage, 2001), 466–85.

19. Elliot Skinner, "Strangers in West African Cities," *Africa* 33, no. 4 (1963): 311–15.

20. Carole Rakodi, "Global Forces, Urban Change and Urban Management in Africa," in *The Urban Challenge in Africa: Growth and Management of Its Large Cities,* ed. Carole Rakodi (Tokyo: United Nations University Press, 1997), 32–34.

21. James Ferguson, *Expectations of Modernity: Myths and Meaning of Urban Life on the Zambian Copperbelt* (Berkeley: University of California Press, 1999).

22. For classic case studies, see Michael Banton, *West African City: A Study of Tribal Life in Freetown* (Oxford: Oxford University Press, 1957); and Abner Cohen, *Custom and Politics in Africa: A Study of Hausa Migrants in Yoruba Towns* (Berkeley: University of California Press, 1969).

23. The ability of "foreign" migrants to reconstitute and reproduce their cultural identities varied, depending, in large measure, on the cultural proximity or distance between them and host communities. E.g., in South Africa, the mainly unskilled and poor immigrants to that country from Swaziland, Mozambique, Zimbabwe, and Lesotho who shared cultural and dress styles with local black populations spoke one or more of local African languages and intermarried with "locals" with time easily blended into local communities or became indistinguishable; see Morris, " 'Our Fellow Africans Make Our Lives Hell.' "

24. See Margaret Piel, "The Expulsion of West African Aliens," *Journal of Modern African Studies* 9, no. 2 (1971): 205–29; Margaret Piel, "Ghanaian Aliens," *International Migration* 8, no. 3 (1974): 367–81; Thomas Lothan Weiss, *Migrants Nigérians: La diaspora dans le Sud-Ouest du Cameroun* (Montreal: Éditions l'Harmattan, 1998); and Niara Surdakas, "The Economic Status of the Yoruba in Ghana before 1970," *Nigerian Journal of Economic and Social Studies* 17, no. 1 (1975): 11–27.

25. See Skinner, "Strangers," 312–15.

26. See, e.g., Sandra Barnes, *Patrons and Power: Creating a Political Community in Metropolitan Lagos* (Bloomington: Indiana University Press, 1986).

27. J. Herbst, "The Role of Citizenship Laws in Multiethnic Societies: Evidence from Africa," in *State, Conflict and Democracy in Africa,* ed. Richard Joseph (Boulder, Colo.: Lynne Rienner, 1999), 267–84.

28. Cf. Charles Tilly, "War Making and State Making as Organized Crime," in *Bringing the State Back In,* ed. Peter Evans et al. (Cambridge: Cambridge University Press, 1985), 169–98; the term "bellicist perspective" is burrowed from Miguel Centeno, *Blood and Debt: War and the Nation-State in Latin America* (University Park: Pennsylvania State University Press, 2002).

29. This argument is elaborated in Jeffrey Hersbt, *States and Power in Africa: Com-*

parative Lessons in Authority and Control (Princeton, N.J.: Princeton University Press, 2000).

30. Jennifer Seally, "The Roots of African Citizenship: An Analysis of Francophone States," paper prepared for the annual convention of the International Studies Association, Portland, February 25–March 1, 2004. The rarity of citizenship through naturalization owes to most immigrants being unaware of this possibility or disinterested because, often contrary to reality, they regard their stay as temporary and acquisition of new citizenship immaterial to their survival.

31. On these and other cases of expulsion of aliens during the terminal years of colonialism and early postindependence years, see Skinner, "Strangers," 311–15; and Peil, "Expulsion of West African Aliens."

32. For analyses of postcolonial politics that accent the ubiquity of patrimonial arrangements of power, see Jean-Francoise Bayart, *The State in Africa: The Politics of the Belly* (London: Longman, 1999); Richard Joseph, *Democracy and Prebendal Politics in Nigeria: The Rise and Fall of the Second Republic* (Cambridge: Cambridge University Press, 1987); and Michael Bratton and Nicholas van de Walle, "Neopatrimonial Regimes and Political Transitions in Africa," *World Politics* 46, no. 4 (1994): 453–89.

33. Cf. William Reno, *Corruption and State Politics in Sierra Leone* (Cambridge: Cambridge University Press, 1995), which highlights the political and economic clout of the Lebanese diaspora in that country.

34. Aderanti Adepoju, "Regional Migration in Sub-Saharan Africa: Challenges and Prospects," *International Migration* 39, no. 6 (2001): 43–57.

35. See David Simon, "Urbanization, Globalization, and Economic Crisis in Africa," in *Urban Challenge in Africa,* ed. Rakodi.

36. These figures are culled from *World Urbanization Prospects: The 2001 Revisions: Table and Highlights,* http://www.un.org/esa/population/wup2002/wop201dh.pdf.

37. Cecilia Tacoli, "Urbanisation and Migration in Sub-Saharan Africa: Changing Patterns and Trends," in *Mobile Africans: Changing Patterns of Movement in Africa and Beyond,* ed. M. de Bruijn, R. van Dijk, and D. Foeken (Leiden: Brill, 2001), 141–52; and Deborah Potts, "Shall We Go Home? Increasing Urban Poverty in African Cities and Migration Processes," *Geographical Journal* 161, no. 3 (1995): 245–62.

38. For surveys of international migration through the 1980s, see John Arthur, "International Labor Migration Patterns in West Africa," *African Studies Review* 34, no. 3 (1991): 65–87; John Oucho, "Regional Integration and Labor Mobility in Eastern and Southern Africa," in *Emigration Dynamics in Developing Countries: Volume 1, Sub-Saharan Africa,* ed. Reginald Appleyard (Aldershot, U.K.: Ashgate, 1998); Adepoju, "Regional Migration in Sub-Saharan Africa"; and Hania Zolnick, "Migrants' Rights, Forced Migration and Migration Policy in Africa," paper prepared for Conference on African Migration in Comparative Perspective, Johannesburg, June 4–7, 2003.

39. See A. Callaway, "Unemployment amongst African School-Leavers," *Journal of Modern African Studies* 1, no. 3 (1963): 351–71, Richard Rhoda, "Migration and Employment of Educated Youth in Ghana," *International Migration Review* 14, no. 1 (1980): 53–76; and Philip Forster, "Educated Youth in Ghana: Myth and Reality," *Harvard Educational Review* 34, no. 4 (1964): 537–58.

40. Thandika Mkandawire and Charles Soludo, *Our Continent, Our Future: African Perspectives on Structural Adjustment* (Trenton, N.J.: Africa World Press, 1999), 16–17.

41. Christopher Gray, "Cultivating Citizenship through Xenophobia in Gabon, 1960–1995," *Africa Today* 45, nos. 3–4 (1998): 389–410.

42. On postcolonial expulsions, see note 31 and J. 'Bayo Adekanye, "Conflict, Loss of State Capacities and Migration in Contemporary Africa," in *Emigration Dynamics in Developing Countries, Volume 2: Sub-Saharan Africa World,* ed. Reginald Appleyard (Ashgate, U.K.: Ashgate, 1998), 190–92; and Gray, "Cultivating Citizenship."

43. See Akin Adebayo, "Brain Drain within the ECOWAS Region," *Issue: A Journal of Opinion* 14, no. 2 (1985): 37–38; and A. A. Afolayan, "Immigration and Expulsion of ECOWAS Alien in Nigeria," *International Migration Review* 22, no. 1 (1988): 4–27.

44. For an overview, see Dickson Eyoh and Richard Sandbrook, "Pragmatic Neo-Liberalism and Just Development in Africa," in *States, Markets and Just Growth: Development in the Twenty-First Century,* ed. Atul Kohli, Chung-in Moon, and Goerg Sorensen (Tokyo: United Nations University Press, 2003), 227–57; and on the impact on cities of economic crisis and Africa's progressive marginalization in the global economy, see Simon, "Urbanization."

45. Stren and Halfani, "Cities of Sub-Saharan Africa," 471.

46. This summary of recent transnational migration flows draws from chapter 5 in this volume by Simone; Aderanti Adepoju, "Trends in International Migration in and from Africa," in *International Migration Prospects and Policies in a Global Market,* ed. D. S. Massey and J. Taylor (Oxford: Oxford University Press, 2004); Aderanti Adepoju, "Continuity and Changes in the Configuration of Migration to and from South Africa," *International Migration* 42, no. 2 (2003): 3–28; and Zolnick, "Migrant Rights."

47. See Naira Sadarkasa, "Women and Migration in Contemporary West Africa," *Signs* 3, no. 1 (1977): 178–89; S. Finley, "Migration and Family Interactions in Africa," in *Family, Population and Development in Africa,* ed. Aderanti Adepoju (London: Zed Books, 1997); and Christiana Oppong, "African Family Systems in the Context of Economic Crisis," in *Family, Population and Development in Africa,* ed. Adepoju.

48. Aderanti Adepoju, "Changing Configurations of Migration in Africa, Migration Policy Institute, 2004, available at http://www.migrationinformation.org/Africa.cfm.

Contributors

Caroline B. Brettell joined the faculty of Southern Methodist University in 1988. In 2003, she was named Dedman Family Distinguished Professor. At Southern Methodist University, she has served as director of women's studies (1989–94), as chair of anthropology (1994–2004), and as president of the Faculty Senate and a member of the Board of Trustees in 2001 and 2002. She was born and raised in Montreal and received her BA in Latin American studies from Yale University and her MA and PhD in anthropology from Brown University. In 2000–1 she served as president of the Social Science History Association, and between 1996 and 1998 she was president of the Society for the Anthropology of Europe. Her main research interests are migration and immigration, the cross-cultural study of gender, the intersections of anthropology and history, and European ethnography.

Dickson Eyoh, who was born in Cameroon, is currently associate professor of political science and African studies at the at the University of Toronto, where he formerly was director of the African Studies Program. He previously taught at the University of Jos in Nigeria and at York University. He received his undergraduate degree from Rhodes College, Memphis, his MA from the University of Toronto, and his PhD from York University in Toronto. His main research interests are the political economy of African development and culture, identity, and politics in Africa. His recent publications include *Encyclopedia of Twentieth Century African History* (coedited with Paul Zeleza; Routledge–Taylor & Francis, 2003) and *Ethnicity and Democracy in Africa* (coedited with Bruce Berman and Will Kymlicka; James Currey Publishers and Ohio University Press, 2004).

Allison M. Garland is the program associate with the Comparative Urban Studies Project at the Woodrow Wilson International Center for Scholars. She served previously as senior program associate in the Wilson Center's Latin American Program, where she worked from 1993 to 2000. Before joining the Woodrow Wilson Center, she worked for the American Jewish World Service, an international development organization, and for the National Commission for the Promotion and Protection of Human Rights in Managua. She has conducted research and prepared publications for the U.S. Department of State Office of Research, the U.S. Agency for International Development, and the United Nations Research Institute for Social Development. Her research interests focus on urban poverty, social policy reform, and citizen security in Latin America. She received a BA in political science from Wellesley College and an MA in international relations from the Paul H. Nitze School of Advanced International Studies of Johns Hopkins University.

Lisa M. Hanley is a PhD candidate in city and regional planning at Cornell University. She was formerly the program associate with the Comparative Urban Studies Project at the Woodrow Wilson International Center for Scholars. She holds an MA from the University of Texas at Austin and a BA from George Washington University. Her research interests include the Andes, urban revitalization, migration, identity, and culture. She has conducted fieldwork in Ecuador and was a recipient of a Fulbright grant, a Ford Foundation Area Studies grant, and a Tinker Foundation grant. Before joining the Woodrow Wilson Center, she served as a Peace Corps volunteer in Guatemala working on municipal development and as assistant director of the Bretton Woods Committee in Washington.

Barbara Schmitter Heisler is professor emerita of sociology at Gettysburg College. Beginning with her dissertation ("Immigration and Citizenship in

Germany and Switzerland"), she has worked in the area of international migration and immigrant integration in advanced industrial societies. She has received fellowships from the Social Science Research Council and the German Marshall Fund of the United States, has won the Berlin Prize awarded by the American Academy in Berlin, and has published numerous articles in the field of comparative immigration, focusing primarily on Europe. Her current research focuses on the experiences of World War II German prisoners of war in the United States.

Serin D. Houston (Dartmouth College, AB; University of Washington, Seattle, MA) is a National Science Foundation Graduate Research Fellow and PhD student in the departments of geography and women's studies at Syracuse University. Her current research focuses on two primary themes: (1) immigrant settlement and displacement within North America; and (2) the linkages between racial mixing in households and economic change within cities. She has also conducted research on women's entrepreneurship in the Czech Republic, identity performances within the Tibetan diaspora, changing gender identities within indigenous communities in Nepal and Madagascar, and the racial discourses and experiences of mixed-race households in Tacoma, Washington. This research has been funded by a combination of local and national grants and fellowships from the United States and Canada. Houston has presented her research at conferences throughout the country and has published co-authored articles in leading geography journals.

Michael Jones-Correa is professor of government at Cornell University. He taught at Harvard University as an assistant and associate professor of government from 1994 to 2001, and he has been a visiting scholar at the Russell Sage Foundation (1998–99) and at the Woodrow Wilson International Center for Scholars (2003–4). His research interests include immigrant politics and immigration policy, minority politics and interethnic relations in the United States, and urban and suburban politics. He is the author of *Between Two Nations: The Political Predicament of Latinos in New York City* (Cornell University Press, 1998) and the editor of *Governing American Cities: Inter-Ethnic Coalitions, Competition and Conflict* (Russell Sage Foundation, 2001).

David Ley is Canada Research Chair in Geography at the University of British Columbia in Vancouver. From 1996 to 2003, he was the University of British Columbia's director of the Vancouver Centre, which is part of the International Metropolis Project immigration research and policy network. He has written or edited a number of books on the social geography of the contemporary Western city. His recent research has primarily focused on migration from the Chinese diaspora into Canadian cities since the mid-1980s. His projects have examined housing market effects, immigrant entrepreneurialism, churches as settlement agencies, citizenship issues, and transnational relations, including collaborative and comparative work in Australia. His forthcoming book, *Millionaire Migrants,* examines the transnational migration of wealthy Hong Kong and Taiwanese business families to (and from) Vancouver and Toronto.

Rhacel Salazar Parreñas is professor of Asian American studies at the University of California, Davis. She is the author of *Servants of Globalization: Women, Migration and Domestic Work* (Stanford University Press, 2001) and *Children of Global Migration: Transnational Families and Gendered Woes* (Stanford University Press, 2005).

Jason Pribilsky is assistant professor of anthropology at Whitman College, Walla Walla, Washington. He received his MA from Reed College and a PhD in cultural anthropology from Syracuse University. His research interests are in the areas of medical anthropology, Latin American studies, and migration. Since 1995, he has been conducting ethnographic research in the south-central Ecuadorian Andes looking at the varied effects of transnational migration between this region and the United States. He is the author of *La Chulla Vida: Gender, Migration, and the Family in Andean Ecuador and New York City* (Syracuse University Press, 2007).

Blair A. Ruble is currently director of the Kennan Institute of the Woodrow Wilson International Center for Scholars, where he also serves as chair of the Comparative Urban Studies Project. He received his MA and PhD, both in political science, from the University of Toronto, and an AB degree with highest honors in political science from the University of North Carolina at Chapel Hill. He has edited a dozen volumes and is the author of five monographic studies. His book-length works include a trilogy examining the fate of Russian provincial cities during the twentieth century: *Leningrad: Shaping a Soviet City* (University of California Press, 1990); *Money Sings! The Changing Politics of Urban Space in Post-Soviet Yaroslavl* (Woodrow Wilson Center Press and Cambridge University Press, 1995); and *Second Me-*

tropolis: Pragmatic Pluralism in Gilded Age Chicago, Silver Age Moscow, and Meiji Osaka (Woodrow Wilson Center Press and Johns Hopkins University Press, 2001). His latest monograph—*Creating Diversity Capital: Transnational Migrants in Montreal, Washington, and Kyiv* (Woodrow Wilson Center Press and Johns Hopkins University Press, 2005)—examines the changes in such cities as Montreal, Washington, and Kyiv brought about by the recent arrival of large transnational communities.

Chantal Saint-Blancat is associate professor of sociology at the Faculty of Political Science of the University of Padova. Since 2000, she has been vice director of Intercultural Processes and Communication in the Public Space, the university's PhD program in sociology. She has degrees from the University of Paris (Institut d'Études Politiques and Institut d'Urbanisme) and Padova (Facoltà di Scienze Politiche). She received her PhD in sociology and social research from the University of Trento. Her research focuses on the sociocultural changes among minority groups and their social strategies. Since 1990, she has specialized in the study of Muslim communities in Europe, including socioreligious and juridical aspects, cultural conflicts, models of integration, changes in gender identity and family structures, and the building of a Muslim diaspora. She is the author of *L'islam de la diaspora* (Bayard Editions, 1997) and the editor of *L'islam in Italia* (Edizioni Lavoro, 1999).

AbdouMaliq Simone is visiting professor at the Wits Institute of Social and Economic Research, University of Witwatersrand and professor of sociology, Goldsmiths College, University of London. He was trained in social psychology and sociology. He has carried on research in many African countries and has published widely on subjects ranging from urban policy and culture to international relations and critical theory. He is the author of *In Whose Image: Political Islam and Urban Practices in the Sudan* (University of Chicago Press, 1994), and *For the City Yet to Come: Changing Urban Life in Four African Cities* (Duke University Press, 2004), as well as editor of the collection *Urban Africa: Changing Contours of Survival in the City* (Codesria and Zed Press, 2005).

Richard Wright holds the Orvil E. Dryfoos Chair in Public Affairs and is a professor of geography at Dartmouth College. With grant support from the Guggenheim Foundation, National Science Foundation, the Social Science Research Council, and the Russell Sage Foundation, he has authored more than fifty scholarly papers. His research primarily concerns the mutual constitution of space and race. His work on immigration analyzes labor and housing market ooperations, nativism, the racialization of immigrants (and the native born), and transnationalism. His other current research concerns the neighborhood location of mixed-race partners and the racial identities of their children. With Mark Ellis, he is writing a book— *Patterns on the Land*—on nativism and immigrant geographies in the United States.

Index

A *t* following page numbers indicates tables.

acculturation, 228–29
adaptation, 5
Africa: "antiforeigner" protests and
    expulsions, 280, 285–86; colonial era,
    273–78, 290; colonial exclusions, 13;
    migration to Johannesburg
    summarized, 11; nation building,
    278–82, 287; official attitudes
    summarized, 12–13; postcolonial (first
    era), 278–82; postcolonial (second
    era), 286–89; postcolonial state, 13;
    statist development, 282–84, 287;
    threefold periodization, 273
African Americans: Dallas, 146–47,
    147–48, 148t, 149, 151t; Fairfax
    County, VA, 30t; 30; Fort Worth,
    172–73n15; Montgomery County,
    MD, 29t, 29; one view of immigrants,
    92; residential sorting compared, 20;
    in suburbs, 21, 22t, 24, 155; Washing-
    ton, DC, area spatial sorting, 31, 41
African immigrants, in Washington, DC,
    area, 31, 32f
Albanian refugees, 64
allocative issues, 27
Amazing Glory Covenant Church
    International Partakers Chapel, 137
Anand Bazaar, 168, 169–70

apartments, 65–67
appearances, "normalcy" of, 98
Asia, TB rates, 197
Asian population: Canada, 183–89;
    Dallas and suburbs, 157, 158t, 165–66,
    166; Fairfax County, VA, 29–30, 30t;
    inner-city Filipinos, 56; mixed-race
    gay couple, 87–91; models followed,
    25; Montgomery County, MD, 29t, 29;
    in U.S. suburbs, 24, 155; in Washing-
    ton, DC, area, 31, 35f, 36. *See also*
    Chinese immigrants; Filipina domestic
    migrants; Filipino migrants; Indian
    immigrants; Japan; Sikh temples;
    South Korean immigrants; Taiwanese
    immigrants; Vietnamese immigrants
assimilation policy: in African colonies,
    276; cultural vs. economic, 190;
    European crisis, 97; France, 190;
    trends, 1, 2; U.S. discourse, 183
asylum seekers, 182, 243
Atlanta, GA: Dallas and Phoenix
    compared, 174n28; immigrant
    populations, 153t, 155, 157
Australia: ethnic advantage, 179;
    Muslims, 194n26; views of
    multiculturalism, 178–79, 182
authoritarian regimes, 280, 281

303

Bavaria, 253–54, 262n26
Belgium, 103, 240
belonging: citizenship status, 90; colonial
    Africa, 290; dislocation after 9/11, 84;
    at household level, 77–78; language
    choices, 85–86; linguistic choices,
    76–77; mixed households, 92; naming
    children, 86–87; nonbelonging, 51, 59;
    personal history of migration, 81–82;
    residential location, 85
Beninoise immigrants, 285
Berlin, Germany, 240
Beurs in France, 97
Bissoondath, Neil, 181
Botswana, 271, 272, 280, 283, 287
boundaries of new states, 279
brokers, 5
Bryan, John Neely, 146
Burgess, Ernest, 22
Burkina Faso, 274
Business Immigration Program, 184

Cameroon, 282; immigrants, 130
Canada: Asian immigrants, 183–89;
    erosion of multiculturalism, 183;
    integration process, 195–96n48;
    Ontario and *shariah* family law, 190,
    196n54; prescription drugs, 203;
    Quebec diversity debates, 190; views
    of multiculturalism, 178, 179. *See also*
    multiculturalism; Vancouver, Canada
Canadian Jewish Congress, 191
Cañari people, 206–7
case studies, utility of, 8
Catholic Church, mosque construction,
    103
census categories, 89
Central American immigrants in New
    York, 171
central cities: immigrant mobilization,
    25–26; inner-city Filipinos, 56; social
    class, 22; suburbs versus, 19
Charter of Rights and Freedoms
    (Canada), 183
check fraud, 134
Chicago School, urban studies, 97

Chinese Canadian redress, 180
Chinese immigrants: in Canada, 180,
    184, 185–89, 191; in Dallas, 160t, 161,
    166; in Washington, DC, area, 36–38
chulqueros (money lenders), 208
churches: Congolese congregations,
    135–38; evangelical, 138;
    Johannesburg, 124, 128, 135–38;
    smuggling activities, 138
cities: African, 123, 271, 274, 276; as
    central municipalities, 3; colonial
    African, 274, 276, 277; comparative
    framework, 144–45; confrontation
    with otherness, 98; cultural ethos of,
    145, 209; European, with strong
    Muslim presence, 100; German,
    described, 238–39; German federal
    system and, 239, 241–42; as historical
    layers, 9; as locations for immigrants,
    237; migrant magnet cities, 3–4; as
    multicultural sites, 97; for new
    immigrants, 73; role as venue of
    exchange, 5–6; social context of, 144;
    symbolic control, 97; temporal and
    spatial dimensions, 144; as units of
    analysis, 11–12; urban/immigrant
    labor markets, 144; use of concept, 2;
    U.S. second-tier metro areas, 143–44
"Cities of Peace" prize, 248
citizenship: as African issue, 269, 281,
    294n30; belonging, 90; claims and
    commercial gain, 180; colonial
    exclusions in Africa, 13, 273–78;
    concept of, 7; cultural, 169–70;
    European origins of concept, 273;
    evolutionary concepts, 270; flexible
    citizenship, 16n24; law changes in
    Germany, 238; post-9/11 concerns, 84;
    postcolonial laws, 279–81; Rwandan
    conflict, 270; significance, 269;
    Vietnamese refugees, 84–85; young
    European Muslims, 110, 112
citizenship rights: Canada, 179–80;
    Marshall framework, 7; monster house
    conflict, 185–86, 188
"city as context" concept, 5–6, 145, 209

civic engagement, 170
civic identity, inclusive, 6
civil society, global trend, 9
class identity conflicts, 61
colonialism: ethnic "homelands," 277; immigration, 274; impact in Africa, 272; imperial subjects, 276; indigenous political rulers, 278; indirect rule, 275–76; nature of economic development, 273; political authority, 278; racial-caste systems, 276; territorial subjects, 276–77; young European Muslims, 110
commercial migration, 288–89
Commission for the Future of the City, 242
communautarism, 108, 109
communities of origin, 3
community: aspects listed, 171; compact, 25; creating, 169; definitions, 164; levels of participation, 171; public health services, 201; Rockland County, NY, 215; in suburbia, 33–34
community health: initiatives, 229–30; use of term, 201
community of mind, 217
Congolese immigrants in Johannesburg, 124; check fraud, 134; described, 126–27; from Kinshasa, 127, 129, 133, 137; from Lubumbashi, 127, 129, 132–33, 134, 135; hairdressers, 130, 131; night clubs, 134–35; strategies summarized, 138; taxi drivers, 130
Constitution Act (Canada, 1982), 179
contexts of reception, 209
cosmopolitan lifestyles, 277
county governments, budgetary crises, 39
crime rates, German, 246
cultural celebrations/events, 169–70; Germany, 252, 256–57; limits of, 179
cultural citizenship, 169
cultural competence practices in public health, 200–201, 217, 221–25; concept of, 222; influence, 227–28; role viewed, 228, 229–30
cultural ethos of cities, 145, 209

cultural identity: colonial Africa, 277, 293n23; traditional healers/approaches, 229
cultural pluralism, Europe, 106–8
cultural proximity, 293n23

Dahl, Robert, 25
Dahomeyans, 274, 277, 280, 285
Dallas, TX: population growth, 146, 147, 148t, 150, 151t; white ethnic immigration, 148–49
Dallas–Fort Worth metroplex: economic conditions, 150–51, 152–53; foreign-born population, 156t, 157; as gateway city, 11–12; historical overview, 145, 146–50; immigrant populations, 153t, 153, 153–54, 154t; immigration patterns, 145, 148t, 150–63; mainstream media interest, 170; as technology center, 152; use of term, 145, 150. *See also* Fort Worth, TX
Dallas International festival, 170
day laborers, 213–15, 216
decentralization, 9
democracy, how hierarchies function, 16n24
democratic citizenship, 7
Democratic Republic of the Congo (DRC), 126, 130–31, 270, 281, 285
demographic multiculturalism, 189
Department of Canadian Heritage, 181
Department for Integration, Stuttgart, 250, 252
deterritorialized immigrants, 165–66
DFW Hindu Temple, 167
difference, concept of, 97, 98
displacement, odd couple, 80–83
distributive issues, 27
diversification, Washington, DC, area, 31
diversity: of cities, 6; Europe, 106; of neighborhoods, 78
domestic workers: backgrounds of, 56–59; exploitative in Africa, 288; median age, 58–59; social isolation, 60; spatial deference, 51
Dominican immigrants, 199

dual housing markets, 24
Dynamique de la Foi, 136

Eastern European immigrants, 238
economic development, postcolonial
    Africa, 282–83, 286–87
economic motives, 5
economic transnationalism, 208–9
Ecuador, 206–7, 219
Ecuadorian immigrants: Cañari people,
    206–7; census figures, 233n22; debt
    burden, 207–9, 221; gendered aspects,
    220; indigenous concentration, 205–6;
    reasons for immigration, 232n20; TB
    rates, 199–200, 219; transmigration,
    203; trip north, 197–98, 219
education: Chinese-language, 36–38;
    Congolese immigrants, 130; Germany,
    244–45, 247–48, 250–51, 254, 257,
    259, 266nn62, 70, 267n87; "school
    leavers" in Africa, 284
Ek Nazar Web site, 168–69
elderly care workers, 60, 67–68
electoral politics, 281
employment: apprenticeship programs,
    245; Dallas, 149, 151–52; Filipino
    profile in Los Angeles, 55; German
    guest workers, 243, 244–45, 257,
    264n40; Stuttgart, Germany, 247
English as a second language teaching,
    165
Equatorial Guinea, 285
equity issues, 7, 49
esquineros (corner guys), 213–14, 216
ethnic advantage, 179
ethnic communities: ethnic organization
    in suburbs, 26; Los Angeles Filipino,
    61; two-way relationships, 5
ethnic enclaves: businesses, 63–64;
    mixing, 75; as place-based strategy,
    52; where they occur, 164
ethnicity, used to renegotiate urban
    citizenship, 12
ethnic neighborhoods, 8
ethnic networks and organization, 20, 26;
    European Muslim, 104; as standard

lens, 75; suburban and central city, 41;
    Washington, DC, area, 33–38, 41
ethnic niches, 73
Europe: anxieties over migration, 98–99;
    barriers to immigration, 189;
    multiculturalism opposed, 181–82;
    Muslims in public spaces, 98;
    reterritorialization of Muslim
    identities, 108–16. *See also* mosques
    issue
European Union (EU), 241, 243, 246,
    249, 253, 262n28
exit option, 22–23

Fairfax County, VA: budget crisis, 39;
    demography, 29–30, 30t; zoning
    inspectors, 39–40
family, defined, 77
family reunification programs, 54, 58,
    100
Federation for American Immigration
    Reform (FAIR), 234n42
female migration, trends, 288
Ferrari, Aurelio, 103
festivals. *See* cultural celebrations/events
Filipina domestic migrants:
    characteristics of sample, 57–59;
    methodology, 56–57; race, class, and
    space, 59–69; summarized, 10; trends,
    50. *See also* domestic workers; Los
    Angeles, CA; Rome, Italy
Filipino migrants: destinations, 71n4;
    mixed-race couple, 87–91
flexible citizenship, 16n24
food vending, 63–64
foreign co-citizens, 263n36
foreigner, use of term in Germany,
    263n36
foreigners' advisory councils, 244,
    248–49, 255
"foreigners' policy," 240, 242, 244
foreigners' work organizations, 255
foreign-language library holdings, 39
formal economy, Congolese in
    Johannesburg, 131–32
Fort Worth, TX, 146, 147, 172–73n15

Fort Worth–Arlington, immigrant populations, 153t, 153
Forum for Culture, Stuttgart, 252
Foundation for Pluralism, 171
France, 102–3, 105; African colonies, 274–75, 276; assimilationist model, 190; multiculturalism opposed, 181; religious pluralism, 107–8; suburban riots (2005), 190; UOIF, 114, 121n53; veil issue, 105, 108, 109; young Beurs, 97
Frankfurt, Germany, 240, 241
FunAsia community center, 166

Gabon, 285
Gambia, 280
gateway cities: cultural diversity, 178; Ecuadorian immigration, 206; emerging, 153t, 153; emphasis on, 238; German, 240; migrant interactions summarized, 10; migrants in suburbs, 10; Rockland County, NY, 206, 209, 211–17, 227; types of, 144; Westchester County, NY, 227
gathering places in Dallas, 165–66
generational differences among mosques, 100–101
gentrification, 50
German reunification, 243
Germany: characteristics, 238–39; child-friendly policies, 265–66n61; education, 244–45, 247–48, 250–51, 254, 259, 266n62, 70, 267n87; foreign-born described, 238; guest worker history, 242–43; immigrant claims-making, 262n24; immigration figures, 260n9; integration efforts, 239–40, 242, 250, 251–52, 258; kindergarten, 245, 254, 257, 265–66nn61, 70; responses to immigration, 244–46; stereotypes challenged, 12. *See also* guest workers; Munich; Stuttgart
Ghana, 278, 280, 283, 284
Ghanaian immigrants, 130, 278, 286
global capitalism, 49

globalization, 8, 9, 164
Gold Coast, 277–78
Greater Dallas Asian American Chamber of Commerce, 166
Great Lakes region, 130–31, 270
Guatemalan immigrants, 199, 216
guest workers in Germany: early views, 242; first official response, 244; history, 242–43; Italian, 253; recruitment, 263–64n38, 265n47; Stuttgart, 247; use of term, 263; Yugoslavian, 253

Haitian immigrants to Rockland County, NY, 199, 211, 215
halal consumption: 114–15, 117, 121n56; fast food restaurants, 114; meat, 115, 117, 122n59
haram concept, 113, 114
Hartz IV welfare law, 258–59, 263n34
health care for immigrants. *See* public health
health industry, Filipino migrants in, 60
health insurance, for immigrants, 214
heterogeneity in suburbs, 27
heterolocalism, 154
Hindu temples, 167
Hispanic population: Dallas, 149–50, 151t; Dallas and suburbs, 157, 158t, 172n12; Fairfax County, VA, 29–30, 30t; Fort Worth, 173n15; models followed, 25; Montgomery County, MD, 29t, 29; in suburbs, 24, 155
history of immigration, U.S., 73
homogamous relationships, 73, 77
homogeneity, cocoon of, 13
homosexual couples, 87–91
Hong Kong Chinese immigrants, 36, 38; in Canada, 184
host cities, 3
host societies: changing conditions, 2; two-way relationships, 5
Houphouet-Boigny, Felix, 270
household: Andean concepts of, 224; expansive definition, 74–75; joint interviews, 83; as unit of analysis, 74

household scales, 74, 77, 78; dynamic concept, 93; methodology, 79; opportunities offered, 78–79; race and ethnicity, 93
housing: colonial Africa, 276; Ecuadorian immigrants, 222–25; Germany, 244, 245, 257; inner-city Johannesburg, 127–30; official regulations for renters, 130
hybrid identity, 170
hybridity, space of, 9
hybridity rhetoric, 188

Immigrant Coalition, Rockland County, NY, 228
immigrant enclaves, 73
immigrant isolation: assumptions, 74; research on, 75
immigrant neighborhoods: lacking in Rockland County, 215, 232n20; mixing, 75; Washington, DC, area, 31
immigrants: as agents, 165; black in Washington, DC, area, 31, 32f; mobilization research, 25–26; in suburbs, 21, 22t
immigration: transformational power, 91; use of term, 231n9; U.S. growth in 1990s, 153
Immigration Act (U.S., 1965), 76
Immigration and Refugee Protection Act (Canada, 2002), 195–96n48
immigration-fear-security concerns, 98
immigration policy: Germany, 238; use of term, 260n8
income disparities, 8
income levels, 24
Independent Commission on Immigration (Germany), 239, 245, 258, 261n19
index of dissimilarity, 150
India Association of North Texas, 167
Indian immigrants: to Canada, 184; to Dallas, 160t, 161, 165, 166, 167–70; to Rockland County, NY, 199
Indian Independence Day, 169

indigenous peoples: Ecuador, 200, 205–6; Los Angeles, 171
individual preference revelation attributes, 23, 25
informal networks: Johannesburg, 127; Washington, DC, area, 38
informal sector: commercial migration, 288–89; Filipino retail, 54; food vending, 63–64; inner-city Johannesburg, 125–26, 132–34; residential buildings, 128
information levels and class/racial sorting, 23
intercultural city policies, 244, 256
intercultural opening, concept of, 264n42
International Committee, Stuttgart, 249–50
International Metropolis Project, 171n1
international migrants, figures, 4
Internet neighborhoods, 167–68
Islam: public Islam, 113; radical, 110; young people in Europe, 111, 112–16
Italian immigration to Germany, 253
Italy: exclusion strategy, 104, 105–6; *halal* meat, 115, 117; mosque construction, 102, 103, 105; presence of religion in public space, 107; Sikh temple, 107; UCOII, 114, 121n53. *See also* Rome, Italy
Ivory Coast, 270–71, 274, 280, 281, 282, 283, 284, 285

Japan, immigration restrictions, 190
Japanese Canadian redress, 180
Jewish communities: in Britain and Canada, 191; Rockland County, NY, 210, 215
Johannesburg, South Africa: demographic shifts, 138–39. *See also* Congolese immigrants in Johannesburg
joint scripts, 91
Jordan, 203
jus sanguinis principle, 238

Kagame, Paul, 270
kebab shops, 115, 117

Kerala Association, 157
kindergarten in Germany, 245, 254, 257, 265–66nn61, 70

labor market peripheralization, 53
labor markets: of cities, 144; migration in colonial Africa, 273; scarcity in colonial Africa, 274
labor segmentation, 49
language choices: belonging, 76–77, 85–86; citizenship concerns, 83–85; English instruction, 165; instruction in Germany, 245, 250–51, 258; naming children, 86–87; non-native language slips, 87–88; pronoun switching, 88
language education: Chinese, 36–38; Fairfax County, VA, libraries, 39
language of recourse, 126
lateral mobility, 138
Latina domestic workers, 57, 60, 69
Latin America: immigrants in Washington, DC, area, 31, 34f; TB rates, 198
"Latino" model of TB, 200
legal requirements for immigrants: economic rights and, 281–82; Germany, 238, 258; Italy, 53–54, 58, 67; naturalization rates, 192, 294n30; postcolonial Africa, 279–80, 281–82, 283–84, 285, 290–91; South Africa, 125, 127; sovereign states' rights, 272; TPS in United States, 161
Lega political party (Italy), 62, 104, 105, 106, 118n3
Le Pen movement (France), 181
Lesotho, 287
Liberia, 278, 287
libraries, 39
local governments: adaptive change, 27; advocacy, 41; anticipatory responses, 41–42; bureaucratic missions, 27–28, 39, 42; client-serving vs. administrative, 28, 42; Dallas, 150, 165; Germany, 239, 241–42, 245–59, 260n14; inner-city Johannesburg, 125, 138; Metropolitan Washington Council

of Governments, 30; monster house conflict, 187; mosque construction, 102–3; negative feedback, 41; Rockland County, NY, 216–17; Washington, DC, area, 38–40, 41; as where diversity occurs, 237
localism, 164
localist lifestyles, 277
locality research, 164
Lodi mosque construction conflict, 102, 103
Los Angeles, CA: class stratification among Filipinos, 52, 61, 68; Filipino migrants described, 54–56; Native Americans in, 171; placelessness, 52, 67–69; residential patterns, 75
Loving v. Virginia (1967), 76
lower-income groups: exit option, 23; residential sorting, 22

Mali, 282, 283
Mancini enclave, Rome, 64–65, 72n40
marriage, interracial, 76
marriage networks, 130
Martelli Law (1989–90), 54
Maryland, 29t, 29, 39
Mauritius, 287
medical doctors, Congolese, 126–27
melting pot, 97
metroplex, term coined, 151
Metropolis project (Dallas), 165
Metropolitan Washington Council of Governments, 30
Mexican Americans, in Dallas, 147, 149
Mexican domestic workers, 69
Mexican immigrants: to Dallas, 159, 160t; health care strategies, 203; to Rockland County, NY, 199
migrant communities: barriers, 8; transnational migration view, 4
migrant-community affirming events, 157
migrant magnet cities, 3–4
migrants: as actors, 2; changing conditions, 2; demands process, 7–8; recasting historical divisions, 13; ties to home communities, 3

migration: approaches to, 4–5; directional analysis, 15n13; disciplinary approaches, 5; as dynamic global process, 5; stability and coherence related, 11; use of term, 231n9

Migration Information Source (Web site), 1, 2

Migration Policy Institute, 1

migration studies, 15n13

military, mixed households, 94n10

minorities: debates and assumptions, 21–22; in suburbs, 21, 22t

mixed households: common themes, 91–92; defined, 74; hypervisibility, 76; in Seattle, 79; stigmatization, 76; summarized, 10–11. *See also* households; household scales; Seattle, WA

mixed-race partnerships, 79

mobilization, research on, 25

monster house issue, 12, 185–89

Montgomery County, MD, demography, 29t, 29

moral regions, 97

mosque, in Richardson, TX, 170

mosques issue: building as symbolic, 101; communication issues, 103–5; differences among mosques, 100; European public space, 99; generational differences, 100–101, 108–16; increasing number of mosques, 100; invasion and pollution fears, 105–6; local construction, 102–3; "open mosque days," 117; resistance to pluralism, 106–8; significance, 116; summarized, 11, 108; symbolic dimension of urban space, 105–6; symbolism, 11. *See also* Hindu temples; Sikh temples

multicultural diversity management, 177–78, 188, 189

multiculturalism: Canadian critique, 181; cities as sites of, 97; as defining Canadian value, 179, 191; demographic, 189; as ethnic advantage, 179, 180; as ghettoization, 181; place making and residential dispersal, 175n37; public attacks on, 181–83, 189; trends, 1; value summarized, 177

Multiculturalism Act (Canada, 1988), 179, 183

multicultural policy: research, 178–81; Vancouver, Canada, 183–89

Munich, Germany, 246, 253–57; emphasis on, 240–41

Musevini, Yoweri, 270

music, 212, 234n34

Muslim immigration to Australia, 194n26

Muslim immigration to Europe, 99–100; cultural discontinuity, 110; differentiated visibility, 98, 116; multiculturalism retreating, 182; new young elites, 104–5, 108–16; shared experience, 109–10; silent Islam, 111; social discrimination measured, 119n5; violence in recent past, 110; visibility strategies, 112–16, 116–17

naming children, 86–87

national origins, essentialization of, 181

Native Americans, in Los Angeles, 171

nativity: aspects of migration, 81–82; within households, 79; and race overlapping, 77

naturalization rates, 192, 294n30

neofundamentalism, 113

neoliberalism, 179, 271, 287–88

Netherlands, 181–82, 240

New York City, TB rates, 199

Niger, 283

Nigeria, 277–78, 280, 282, 283, 284; mass deportations, 285–86

Nigerian immigrants, 125, 130, 285

Niger immigrants, 285

nonbelonging, dislocation of, 51, 69. *See also* belonging

nurses, recruitment of, 60

oil economy, 283, 286

One Nation Party, Australia, 182

Organization of Petroleum Exporting Countries (OPEC), 283
Other: colonial Africa, 275, 277; granting communal land to, 105; migrants as, 13; new modes of interaction, 99; urban confrontations with, 98

Pact for Integration, Stuttgart, 248, 250, 252
Padania region, 118n3
partition of space, 50
patronage systems, 278, 281, 287
performativity as lens, 10
peripheralization, 49, 50; spatial deference related, 53
personal identity: Canadian identity, 181, 192–93, 194n19; colonial cities, 277; hybrid identity, 170; Muslim youth, 111–12, 117, 121n46
personal services, 49
Perspective Munich program, 257
Peruvian immigrants, 64
Phillips, Trevor, 182, 191
Phoenix–Mesa, AZ, immigrant populations, 153t, 157, 174n28
Picard, Paul, 102–3
piracy, urban economies of, 125–26
place, renegotiations of, 7
placelessness: features of, 59; Los Angeles, 52, 67–69; return migration, 69–70; Rockland County, NY, 212–13; Rome, 61, 62; temporary status and, 69; use of term, 52
place making, 164, 166, 170, 175n37
places of encounter, 146
place-stratification theory, 24–25, 26
plan of book, 9–13
pluralism, inclusive, 6
pockets of gathering, 59, 62, 64, 67–68; in Dallas, 165–66; places of encounter, 146
Polish domestic workers, 64
political activism, 89–90
political economy of health, 202, 218–21
political participation, Germany, 254–55, 256

political posts held by immigrants, 180
political rights: of immigrants, 244; postcolonial Africa, 280–81
population decline, 189
Portugal's colonial empire, 276
Portuguese immigrants, 192
power relationships, 13, 16n24
praying rooms, 100
private spaces: apartments, 65–67; church centers, 65–66; concept of privacy, 66–67; Filipina domestic workers, 52, 60; lack of privacy, 60
professional African migrants, 126–27, 281, 283–84, 289, 290
pronoun switching, 88
Proyecto Humanitario para Jornaleros/Jornaleros Project, 205
public goods: levels of information, 23; suburbs, 23
public health: assumptions of acculturation summarized, 12; fieldwork with immigrants, 202, 204–6; immigrant programs, 200–201; migrant lives, 221–25; role of, 227
public policy: suburban, 20; towards immigrants, 237
public space: de Certeau's notion of space, 71n8; Filipina domestic workers, 50–51, 54, 62–63, 68–69; French definitions, 108; mosque issue, 101; Muslim visibility in Europe, 98, 108–9, 112–16; parks, 68–69; race and class solidarity, 68–69; religious tolerance and, 11; renegotiating boundaries, 6–7; self-imposed restrictions, 54; surveillance, 60

Queens, New York City: Rockland County compared, 212–13; undocumented migrant health, 205
Quichua (Quechua) speakers, 198, 207, 212, 216, 218, 228, 229

racial/ethnic identity: mixed households, 83, 92; and mobilization in suburbia, 25–27

racial/ethnic minorities: mixed households, 75; Washington, DC, area, 28–29, 29t
racial/ethnic sorting: central cities vs. suburbs, 19; colonial Africa, 276; research, 20; suburban variance in, 26
racial incidents, 62–63
racial mixing: household sampling, 79–80; Seattle rates, 79
racial prejudice, Italy, 52, 62
racial sorting: across suburbs, 25; variance, 41; Washington, DC, area, 41
racism: monster house conflict, 187; multiculturalism and, 179
radical Islam, 110
real estate prices, 50, 184–85
receiving institutions: in Dallas area, 165; Filipinos in Rome, 53–54; in suburbs, 27–28; Washington, DC, area, 38–40
Redress Settlement (Canada, 1988), 180
reframing, 104
refugee status, 125, 127, 288
religious affiliation, 119n17
religious identity, 101
religious institutions, Dallas area, 166–67
religious observance, 112–16, 118, rates compared, 119n11
religious pluralism: assimilation, 190; backlash, 191; Europe, 11, 101, 106–8, 117; European exception, 99, 106
religious resocialization, 111
religious tolerance, 117
remittances, 217, 221, 220, 230
renegotiation, 6; of citizenship, 7; of landscapes, 6–7; of place, 7
residential clustering, Filipinos in Los Angeles, 55
residential dispersal: community and, 33–34; Filipinos in Rome, 53, 62–63; place making and multicultural expression, 175n37; in suburbs, 20, 42; in Washington, DC, area, 31–32, 33f

residential patterns, Los Angeles, 75
residential sorting: Germany, 264n43; networks and organizations, 20; public policy, 20; Seattle choices, 85; suburbs, 10, 20; upper-income groups, 22; Washington, DC, area, 31–32
retirement villages, 57–58
return migration, 69–70
Rockland County, NY: anti-immigrant views, 216, 234nn42, 43; fieldwork, 204–6; foreign-born population, 234n42; history, 209–11; as immigrant gateway, 199, 211–17; immigrant history, 215–16; Latino immigrants, 210; reasons for immigration, 232n20; as urban mosaic in suburbs, 229
Rockland County Department of Health, NY (RCDOH), 200; TB patients studied, 204
Rome, Italy: Filipino migration described, 53–54; Mancini enclave, 64–65, 72n40; placelessness, 62; racial prejudice, 52, 62
Rommel, Manfred, 248
rural to urban migration in Africa, 123
Rwanda, 131, 278
Rwandan genocide (1994), 269–70

salafi groups, 112–13
Salvadoran immigrants: to Dallas, 160t, 161, 171; to Rockland County, NY, 199
Sanctuary Movement, 232–33n20
Sandercock, Leonie, 183
Seattle, WA, mixed households in, 74, 78–79
secularization in Europe, 106, 109, 116–18
segregation in space: African Americans in Dallas, 149, 150; African Americans in Fort Worth, 172–73n15; Filipina domestic workers, 50; Germany, 245; mixed households summarized, 10–11; mosques, 101
Seko, Mobutu Sese, 270
self-medication, 225–27

Senegal, 274, 276, 280, 284
Senegalese immigrants, 125
September 11, 2001: citizenship concerns after, 84; Dallas hate crimes, 175n45; elusive behavior of immigrants, 223–24; immigration/insecurity themes after, 107; Muslim immigration concerns, 98; non-Western religions after, 191
service bureaucracies, 28, 40, 42
settlement experiences: Filipina domestic workers, 51, 56, 70; issues raised, 163; mixed households, 92; race and class, 51, 70
sexuality, belonging, 90–91
shariah family law, 190, 196n54
Sierra Leone, 287
Sikh temples, 107
Singapore: domestic workers in, 51, 70; immigration restrictions, 190
skilled workers, 289, 290
slavery, 146
smuggling activities: churches, 138; getting people across borders, 133, 207–9, 219
social action, defined, 16n28
social assistance in Germany: 242, 247, 257, 258, 260n10, 263n34. *See also* social services in Africa; welfare state, Germany
social blending goal, 239
social city concept, 239, 260–61n18, 267n87
social class: among Filipino migrants, 54–55, 56; Congolese immigrants, 130; middle class and domestics, 61; race/ethnicity and spatial location, 22; widening disparities, 49
social context of cities, 144
social exclusion: Islamic youth, 111; Italy, 104; sources of, 51–52; systems of grouping, 89
social isolation: assumptions about, 74; of domestic workers, 60
social mobility, 123, 138
social movements, 16n28

social networks, Washington, DC, area, 38
social segregation: assumptions about, 74; double African, 275–76; of Filipinos in Italy, 54, 67; mixed households, 92
social services, in Africa, 284, 287. *See also* social assistance
societies, mutable nature of, 2
Somalia, 287; immigrants, 125
South Africa: anti-immigrant xenophobia, 271–72; apartheid-era labor migration, 217; commercial migrants, 289; cultural proximity, 293n23; economic opportunities, 124–25; "fortress South Africa," 272; migration upsurge, 288. *See also* Johannesburg, South Africa
South Korean immigrants: in Canada, 184; in Dallas, 160t, 161, 166; in New York City, 164
South Shaughnessy Property Owners' Rights Committee, 185–86
Soviet Union, former: immigration to Germany, 238; immigration to Rockland County, NY, 199; TB rates, 198
space: de Certeau's notion, 71n8; meanings changing, 99; mixed households, 77–78
Spanish-language library holdings, 39
spatial assimilation theories, 24–25, 26
spatial deference: of domestic workers, 51, 59; labor market peripheralization, 53; racial incidents, 62–63
spatial peripheralization: defined, 50; by race and class, 50
spatial sorting: in suburbs, 22–25; Washington, DC, area, 31–32, 41
state, neutrality in Europe, 107
Stuttgart, Germany: 246–53, 265–66n61; emphasis on, 240–41
subsidiarity principle, 239, 243, 260n15
suburban homogeneity, arguments for, 24, 27
suburbs: African Americans and immigrants in, 21, 22t; central cities

suburbs (*continued*)
versus, 19; changes summarized, 19–20; community in, 33–34; in Dallas–Fort Worth area, 163; Dallas–Fort Worth immigrant, 150, 154–55, 155f, 156t, 157t, 166; exclusionary middle- and upper-income whites, 24; exit options, 22–23; immigrant mobilization research, 25–26; Mexican immigration, 159; minority growth, 155; as new immigrant gateways, 229; physical characteristics, 27; racial/ethnic incorporation, 19–20; relationship to cities, 3; Rockland County, NY, 211–17; stereotypes, 21

Tabernacle des Vainqueurs, 137
Taiwanese immigrants, 36, 37–38; in Canada, 184
Tappan Zee Bridge, 210–11
taxi drivers, 130, 192
TB. *See* tuberculosis (TB)
Temporary Protective Status, 161
Termini station (Rome), 62, 63
Texas, immigration trends, 174n27
Tiebout hypothesis, 22–23
Togolese, 280
town planning, 102, 103
trade, unofficial, 125–26
traditional healers/approaches, 203, 206, 217, 225–27; cultural identity, 229; *yachaks*, 226
transmigration, 202–3
transnational competence, 228
transnational hierarchy of resort, 203–4
transnational migration: concept of, 202–3; economic transnationalism, 208–9; novel features of African, 288–89; as survival strategy, 230
tuberculosis (TB): Andean-specific beliefs, 225–26; background, 197–98; biomedical perspective, 218; Direct Observation Therapy (DOT), 221–22; migrant outbreaks in Rockland County, NY, 217, 218–21;

noncompliance, 228; role of cultural barriers, 200; severity and delayed care, 226–27; trends, 230n2
Turkish immigrants in Germany, 243, 246, 247, 252, 257

UCOII (Italy), 114, 121n53
Uganda, 131, 270, 278, 283
undocumented immigration: 194n26; elusive behavior, 223–34; fieldwork research, 204–5; Mexican compared to South African, 217; Queens, NY, 205; use of term, 231n9
unemployment benefits, 258–59
UN Habitat, 4
United Chinese Community Enrichment Services Society (SUCCESS), 191
United Kingdom: African colonies, 274; comparative research, 240; views of multiculturalism, 178, 179, 182
United States: assimilation discourse, 183; immigration opposed, 182–83; views of multiculturalism, 178, 182–83
University of Chicago researchers, 22
UOIF (France), 114, 121n53
upper-income groups: explicit bias, 23; residential sorting, 22
Upper Volta, 283; immigrants, 285
urban citizenship, meanings of, 6–8
urbanization: African rates, 282; demands on state, 9; enclave nature in Africa, 273–74; migration in Africa, 124
urban reproduction crisis, 284–85, 290
urban space: Islamic youth, 114; symbolic control, 97; use of, 50
urban sustainability, 77
urban youth: African, 284–85, 290; Muslims in Europe, 112–16

values, urban ethos and, 209
Vancouver, Canada: managing cultural diversity, 177–78, 188; monster house issue, 12, 185–89; multiculturalism policy, 183–89
van Gogh, Theo, 181–82

veil issue, 105, 108, 109
Victory Gospel Ministry, 136–37
Vietnamese immigrants: in Canada, 192;
    in Dallas, 159, 160t, 160, 170; refugees,
    84; in Washington, DC, area, 166
Virginia, 29–30, 30t, 39
virtual spaces, 167–68
visibility strategies, Muslim youth,
    112–16
volunteering, 191
voting practices, 89–90

Washington DC metropolitan area: case
    study, 28–40; demographic shifts, 28;
    diversification, 28–29, 29t; ethnic
    networks and organization, 33–38
Web sites, 168–69
welfare state, Germany, 242–43, 258–59;
    core activities, 262n29. *See also* social
    assistance in Germany
White Australia Policy, 182
whiteness, assumptions of shared, 82–83
Who Governs? (Dahl), 25
women and girls, 111, 288
Word of Faith Mission, 137
workplace diversity programs, 170–71
World Life Assembly, 136–37

Yemen, 203
Yoruba peoples, 277–78
Yugoslavian immigrants in Germany,
    246, 247, 253

Zaire, 287
zoning, exclusionary, 23
zoning inspectors, 39–40